Toppling Foreign Governments

TOPPLING FOREIGN GOVERNMENTS

The Logic of Regime Change

Melissa Willard-Foster

PENN

UNIVERSITY OF PENNSYLVANIA PRESS

PHILADELPHIA

Published by
University of Pennsylvania Press
Philadelphia, Pennsylvania 19104-4112
www.upenn.edu/pennpress

Printed in the United States of America on acid-free paper
1 3 5 7 9 10 8 6 4 2

A Cataloging-in-Publication record is available from the Library of Congress
ISBN 978-0-8122-5104-3

For Amelia, Evan, and Maggie

CONTENTS

Introduction

On March 19, 2011, eight years to the day after the start of the Iraq War, the North Atlantic Treaty Organization (NATO) began launching airstrikes at Libya in the third American-led attempt in a decade to topple a foreign leader. After two costly wars in Iraq and Afghanistan, few would have predicted President Barack Obama would lead the United States into another attempt at regime change. As a senator, he had opposed doing so in Iraq, insisting Saddam Hussein posed no imminent threat and could be contained given the weakened Iraqi economy and military.[1] Like Saddam, Libya's Muammar Qaddafi posed no threat to the United States. He had weakened his own military in order to coup-proof his regime. He also no longer had the allies or the chemical weapons he had once possessed to protect himself. Qaddafi's military vulnerability should have given him the incentive to seek a settlement and avoid a war that he could not win. But if Qaddafi, like Saddam, could have been coerced and contained, why was the United States pursuing regime change again?

The failure to establish stable, friendly regimes in Afghanistan, Iraq, and Libya has led scholars and politicians alike to question the wisdom of foreign-imposed regime change (FIRC), and perhaps for good reason. Studies show FIRC (or simply "regime change," as I will also refer to it) increases the risk of civil war in the target state and rarely creates democratic regimes. In addition, studies examining whether FIRC improves relations with the target state show mixed results.[2] But despite FIRC's dubious record, regime change has been a persistent feature of the international system for centuries. It has taken many forms throughout this history—from foreign-instigated coups to large-scale military invasions, but whatever the form, the goal has been the same: to change the policies of other states by changing their policymakers.

Regime change, however, is but one arrow in the quiver from which states can draw to achieve their foreign-policy objectives. And, as recent American experience suggests, it can be a costly one. Rather than replacing the opposing side's leaders, states could bargain with them instead. The state seeking change could use coercion and/or inducement to obtain a favorable deal, formal or otherwise. It could also soften some of its demands to attain its most central policy aims. It could even give up on those aims altogether and accept the status quo—in essence, accepting a deal on the target's terms. Conflicts between states can be resolved in a variety of ways. Why do states take on the costs and risks associated with regime change to resolve their conflicts, instead of pursuing these other options?

Standard accounts in the historical and intervention literature suggest a seemingly straightforward answer to this question. States depose foreign leaders because they expect they can install like-minded ones with whom they will not have to bargain. Accordingly, much of this scholarship focuses on the policy objectives underlying FIRC, rather than on why states use it to obtain their objectives.[3] What remains unclear is why a state would risk blood and treasure to install a more pliant leader when it could use presumably less costly means, such as coercion and/or inducement, to change the preferences of the current leader. Even when a state must apply limited military force to coerce a foreign leader into a settlement, it could still avoid the potentially heftier costs of installing a new leader by bargaining instead.

The question of why states forsake bargaining for regime change becomes all the more puzzling when we consider that leaders typically targeted with regime change should be relatively easy to coerce into settlements.[4] The history of FIRC is replete with militarily weak and friendless heads of state, like Saddam and Qaddafi, toppled after wars they could not win.[5] I define FIRC as the decision by one state to abandon bargaining with another and to remove that state's leaders or political institutions with the intention of restoring the target state's sovereignty. Of the 133 cases in this study, 75 percent (see the lightly shaded regions in Figure 1) involve major powers attacking minor ones.[6] Regional powers also frequently undertake regime change as well, but they too target weak states. In fact, on average, regimes targeted for change have a mere 11 percent of the imposing state's military capabilities.[7] Although states also target the equally powerful, that parity disappears by the time they achieve the military victory necessary to impose regime change. Hence, unequal power is a near-universal feature of FIRC. Though this asymmetry of power makes an imposed change feasible, it should also make that change unnecessary. To avoid being overthrown, militarily weak leaders who are bereft of allies should back down when

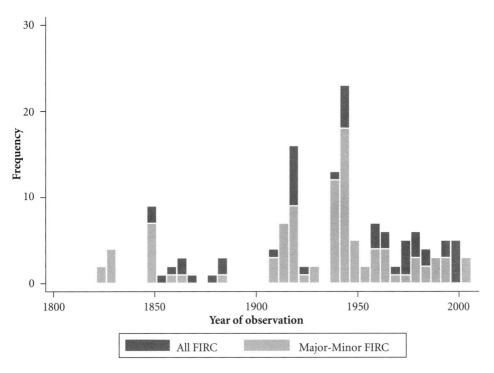

Figure 1. Foreign-Imposed Regime Change Attempts, 1816–2007

confronted by stronger states. Instead, FIRC targets sometimes appear to invite their fate by defying stronger states. To fully understand FIRC, we must, therefore, explain why it occurs when it should be least necessary.

The Logic of Foreign-Imposed Regime Change

This book explains why states choose to overthrow foreign leaders or regimes rather than bargain with them. In so doing, it addresses three related questions: (1) Why do the weak resist the strong? (2) Why do the strong respond by imposing regime change? And, (3) when is FIRC aimed at deposing a leader versus at upending or transforming political institutions? The answers to all three questions, I argue, hinge on the strength of the targeted leader's domestic political opposition. When a conflict of interest arises between a strong and weak state, the stronger state may pressure the weaker one to accept a settlement. Targeted leaders, however, have an incentive to resist or renege on these settlements whenever compliance will weaken them at home. If leaders accept terms that compromise their already tenuous political positions, their domestic opponents may challenge them. These opponents could be rivals within the regime or insurgents seeking to overthrow it. Opposition can also be latent, ready to erupt if the leader's concessions provoke widespread anger. No matter its form, the stronger this opposition already is, the more successful its domestic challenge will likely be and, thus, the more resolved the targeted leader will be to reject the foreign power's demands. Even when defeated in war and forced to accept imposed terms, leaders may later renege to shore up their domestic political power.

Two conditions must be met for a foreign power to achieve its aims at the bargaining table and reject attempting regime change. First, the foreign power must give the target reason to concede by proving that the foreign threat the target faces is greater than its domestic one. Although the foreign power may have a greater military capacity, the targeted leader may not believe the more powerful state will use its full capabilities. To make its threats credible, the stronger state can use "costly signals," actions so costly that less resolved actors would avoid them. By mobilizing troops or acquiring arms and allies in preparation for war, a foreign power could convince others of its determination to fight. To be sure, costly signals may not always convince the target to back down. When targeted leaders face particularly intense domestic threats, they may risk war, hoping to hold out in a protracted conflict. Yet, even in these cases, foreign powers often can convince militarily weak leaders to concede by applying coercive force or, in extreme cases, defeating the target militarily. Once the foreign power achieves a military victory, it should be able to force the targeted leader to accept its terms.

Second, once the targeted leader submits to a settlement, the foreign power must give that leader reason to abide by it. If the agreement requires the weaker nation to implement politically risky policy changes, its leader might try to avoid doing so once the stronger state's initial threat diminishes. A variety of enforcement mechanisms can be used to monitor the targeted leader's adherence to the agreement and punish violations of it. The foreign power, for example, could call on a third party to ensure the agreement is carried out. Or, it could keep its own troops mobilized or stationed on the target state's soil to maintain a credible threat to renew hostilities if cheating occurs.

When these two conditions are met, a lasting settlement with the targeted leader should be feasible and regime change should be unnecessary. The problem, however, is that the measures necessary to achieve these conditions can be costly for the foreign power. These expenses entail a variety of costs—not just financial ones, but also political, military, diplomatic, reputational, humanitarian, and opportunity costs. For example, mobilizing troops can impose diplomatic and domestic political costs on the stronger state if its allies or domestic public oppose war. Even when the foreign power's public and allies support belligerencies at the outset, the long-term stationing of troops might later become unpopular, making enforcement measures politically and diplomatically costly over time. Non-military coercion, such as economic sanctions, can also entail costs beyond financial ones. If sanctions take a humanitarian toll on the target state's people or hurt an ally's commercial interests, they might alienate allies and/or damage the foreign power's international reputation. The foreign power could soften its demands to let the targeted leader save face. However, even these dispensations could cost the foreign power by upsetting its public, angering its allies, damaging its reputation, and/or generating humanitarian costs.

The size of the costs the foreign power incurs to achieve a sustainable bargain depends on the strength of the targeted leader's domestic opposition. The stronger this opposition, the more extensive the measures the foreign power must take to convince the target to accept a politically risky settlement: the larger the army it must mobilize, the bigger the coalition it must build, the harsher the sanctions it must employ, and/or the more bombs it must drop to force compliance. This means that it can be especially costly to coerce leaders facing strong opposition at home into lasting settlements, because their incentive to resist or renege forces the foreign power to spend more to obtain their compliance.

The strong must, therefore, choose. They can either invest in the measures necessary to obtain and enforce a settlement, or they can attempt regime change. Given that their targets are typically militarily weak, the strong are often inclined to exploit their power advantage and forcibly impose the leaders they want. But there is something else that also tempts policymakers to pursue regime change—the target's domestic opposition; that is, the force also driving the target's resistance. Politically weak leaders can appear not only costly to coerce into lasting settlements but also comparatively cheap to overthrow. The stronger the domestic opposition, the greater the burden it can carry in helping the foreign power impose regime change. This presumes, of course, that the opposition is willing to collaborate with the foreign power. Yet, even when their interests are imperfectly aligned, the opposition is often willing to trade policy concessions for foreign assistance in attaining power. When the opposition causing the leader to resist also opposes the foreign power, other opposition groups are often willing to collaborate. Thus, domestically weak leaders should be especially prone to FIRC. Their domestic vulnerability increases the stronger power's expected costs of obtaining a settlement with them, while simultaneously decreasing its expected costs of overthrowing them.

Leaders without opposition will not necessarily concede to a foreign power's demands. Their decision to make concessions (or not) depends on other factors as well. If they have the means to defend themselves from military or economic coercion, for example, they may resist, even though they face no domestic threats. Leaders may also resist for fear that concessions will create domestic opposition. However, all else being equal, politically strong leaders can be expected to make greater concessions than leaders facing stiff opposition, because compliance costs them less. Foreign powers are also more likely to negotiate with these leaders because there is no alternative to them. In contrast, when faced with politically weak leaders, not only is the foreign power less likely to exact concessions, but also it can install the opposition as an alternative bargaining partner.

I do not contend that FIRC is cheaper than negotiating an enforceable settlement. Rather, I offer a rational choice argument that explains why a foreign power's expected costs of negotiating might be less than its expected costs of FIRC.[8] Such expectations can turn out to be wrong, and, indeed, in some instances but not all, they are wildly off the mark.[9] Yet, as I show in this book, neither miscalculation nor misperception—on either side—is necessary for FIRC to occur. Contrary to conventional wisdom, even rational policymakers with complete information may pursue regime change, based on the expectation that a bargain will be too costly to achieve.

Skeptics might note that rational choice arguments rest on the heroic assumption that human beings are utility maximizers who choose among competing strategies based solely on their relative costs and benefits. This criticism is understandable but misplaced. By starting with idealized assumptions, rational actor theories can show what would happen in a world populated by decision makers unhindered by misperception, emotion, or psychological bias. These theories show that even in this perfect world, rational actors might still choose to fight. This means that even if we could reduce our leaders' misperceptions, emotions, or psychological biases, they might still attempt to overthrow foreign leaders rather than negotiate with them.

In this book, I bracket discussion of why states' interests diverge to focus on the question of why they use FIRC when their interests diverge. States may enter into disputes for any number of reasons, but the causes of those disputes do not necessarily dictate the means used to resolve them. Policymakers, for example, may prefer to replace the opposing side's leader in an ideological dispute, but they may be forced to bargain if they cannot defeat that leader militarily. Similarly, policymakers may be inclined to negotiate when a dispute arises with a longtime ally, but they may find themselves pursuing regime change if that ally suddenly refuses to cooperate. Although my argument indicates that domestic forces play a pivotal role in determining the strategies states use to resolve their disputes, it does not reject the possibility that other forces could explain why those disputes occur. Psychological bias, ideological competition, credibility problems, bureaucratic pressures, and miscalculation could each generate a dispute, but how that dispute gets resolved, I argue, depends on the target's domestic opposition. The argument in this book is meant to complement theories on the causes of interstate disputes by helping us better understand when those disputes will end in FIRC.

In addition to explaining why states choose FIRC, this book also addresses how states impose it. I argue that whether they remove the leader or change political institutions depends on the type of opposition the targeted leader faces. All else being equal, strong states prefer to effect what I call *full regime change*, the installation of an entirely new set of political institutions. To do so, they work with those I call *external opposition groups*. These groups are composed of domestic opponents who live either in the target state or in exile, and who are disadvantaged by the current regime and, therefore, have an incentive to overthrow it. External opposition groups are often motivated to collaborate with the foreign power. However, they can be costly to install, because they cannot seize power from within. Full regime change, therefore, often requires the foreign power to launch an invasion or assist rebels in obtaining a military victory over the government.

When the external opposition lacks sufficient strength to overturn the government, the greater power might instead turn to the leader's *internal*

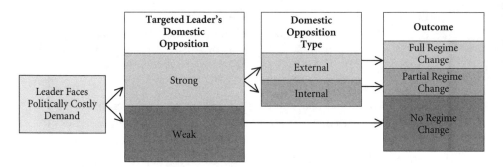

Figure 2. The Logic of Foreign-Imposed Regime Change

opposition to bring about *partial regime change.* This involves removing the target state's leader or top policymakers, whether by convincing regime insiders to launch a coup or by pressuring the leader to resign. Partial regime change also involves risk for the foreign power. Internal rivals are often less willing to accommodate the stronger power's policy aims because they are vulnerable to some of the same domestic political costs as the targeted leader. As a result, even when a leader's internal rivals are willing to launch a coup, the foreign power may have to maintain incentives to ensure their cooperation over time. When a coup is not feasible, the foreign power may attempt to coax the leader into stepping down. Successful attempts to coerce the leader's resignation, however, are surprisingly rare. Not only is it difficult to convince leaders whose supporters remain loyal to sacrifice power, but this approach is also less likely to leave behind a stable, friendly regime. I address the benefits and costs associated with both approaches to regime change—full and partial—in Chapter 2. Figure 2 diagrams my argument.

Why Study Foreign-Imposed Regime Change?

In the years since President George W. Bush's administration ordered the invasion of Iraq, a rich literature has blossomed attempting to explain the causes of that war. Yet only a handful of studies, most of which predate the Iraq War, examine the causes of FIRC writ large. Although these studies offer valuable insight, they tend to focus on only one specific type of FIRC, such as that which occurs after a major war, entails covert methods, or involves just the removal of the target's institutions rather than its leaders.[10] Few studies examine the causes underlying the full spectrum of FIRC. This is surprising, given the frequency with which states, particularly strong ones, have sought to use regime change to attain their foreign policy aims. Since becoming a major power in 1898, the United States has been involved in a total of thirty-eight regime-change attempts. Since 1816, the United Kingdom has undertaken nineteen regime change attempts; the Soviet Union/Russia, seventeen; Germany, fifteen; and France, thirteen (see Appendix 1).

The vast majority of studies on FIRC examine its consequences rather than its causes. These are of undeniable importance, but the causes of FIRC could very well determine the nature of the consequences we observe. If FIRC is more likely to occur in states already experiencing domestic insta-bility, then we might expect that domestic instability commonly follows FIRC. If so, it would be wrong to infer that FIRC causes domestic instabil-ity, though we could conclude that FIRC does little to correct for it. We might also find that FIRC seldom creates democratic regimes because the domestic instability that plagues the target state hampers efforts to democ-ratize the target. The methods states use to impose FIRC may also affect the outcomes we observe. Partial regime change, for example, may enable a foreign power to obtain its short-term objectives relatively cheaply but may fail to produce lasting change. It may also be less likely to resolve the underlying domestic struggle for power that led to regime change, and so leaves the target susceptible to additional FIRC attempts. In short, we must study the causes of FIRC in the many forms it can take to fully understand its consequences.

The study of FIRC is also important for understanding whether and when it can be avoided. Critics of the decision to impose regime change in Iraq, and later, in Libya, argued that these were wars of choice, not neces-sity.[11] The dominant rationalist explanations for war, however, imply that there is no such thing as a war of choice, because if an enforceable bargain were attainable, policymakers would choose it. War, according to these the-ories, occurs because information or credibility problems impede a bar-gaining agreement. War, therefore, results because a peaceful bargain is impossible, which makes war unavoidable and, hence, not a choice. This book challenges the conventional view that states would prefer a bargain if one were possible. Instead, I show that while bargaining agreements often are feasible between states of asymmetric power, the costs of obtaining and enforcing them can make these agreements undesirable. This may prompt policymakers to choose war, even though a peaceful settlement is possible.

Studying FIRC also paves the way for new insights into international relations theory. Neorealism, which typically sees international conflict as stemming from structural forces, such as a change in the balance of power, has difficulty explaining why nations would expend resources to replace foreign leaders and regimes.[12] If security threats are mainly determined by growth in another state's military power or alliances, then replacing its leadership should do little to diminish the threat that it poses. By explaining why policymakers care about who rules in a target state, this book expands our understanding of why states fight.

Although my argument has implications for the study of all conflict, I focus on FIRC because it represents a unique and particularly puzzling type. Wars can be fought for many reasons and in many different ways, but FIRC is unique in that it excludes a settlement with the enemy. In this sense, FIRC is akin to what Thomas Schelling calls "brute force," which differs from coercive force not so much in degree as in intent.[13] Brute force involves taking what you want.[14] In contrast, coercion entails the use of negative incentives to ensure an opponent prefers to give you what you want. Although both can involve military hostilities, coercion is aimed at achieving an agreement with the opposing side's policymakers, while brute force is aimed at eliminating those policymakers altogether. Even when coercive methods are used to obtain agreements that require regime change, the goal is still to remove the leader rather than continue dealing with the leader. Schelling argues that the advent of nuclear weapons made war more of a "bargaining process" in which coercive force dominates.[15] And yet the persistence of FIRC shows that some conflicts still very much involve brute force. The strong still sometimes take what they want by imposing the leaders they want. This book explains why.

Alternative Arguments

I test my argument against two sets of alternative explanations: those that suggest policymakers, at least on one side, are too deluded to avoid FIRC and those that suggest that actors cannot avoid FIRC even when rational. These explanations are common in the conflict literature and historical accounts of individual cases but only sometimes appear in studies on the causes of FIRC. I focus on them because they can explain why states would use FIRC, despite its costs, rather than negotiate with the targeted state's existing leaders.

More typically, scholarly work focuses on the policy aims states seek to attain when pursuing FIRC. These can include ideological goals, humanitarian aims, security interests, economic incentives, or domestic political gains.[16] Although these arguments can tell us why states enter into disputes, they do not tell us why those disputes end in FIRC. If regime change is too costly to impose, states may be forced to set aside their ideological convictions, normative values, or interests, however defined, and negotiate with the target. Even when it would seem their goals can only be attained through FIRC, they could still reduce those goals, if necessary, to negotiate deals that satisfy less ambitious aims. Targeted leaders have incentive to negotiate as well. If they could anticipate their fate, surely they would rather preempt it by negotiating. Why conflicts of interest arise between states is an undeniably important question, but only arguments that can explain why states overthrow leaders to resolve their conflicts, when they should neither need nor want to, can fully explain FIRC.

The first alternative approach suggests that policymakers are too blind to the true costs of FIRC to know they should avoid it. Two arguments commonly used to explain why policymakers enter into conflicts they later come to regret assert that either psychological bias or pressure from bureaucrats and/or lobbyists can cause leaders to err in their judgments. These theories imply that policymakers, whether misled by their own biases or by self-serving domestic actors, choose regime change because they lack the ability to make judgments in the state's best interest.[17] Psychological-bias arguments and arguments focusing on bureaucratic and/or interest-group pressure are often used to explain the targeted leader's behavior as well.[18] Leaders like Saddam and Qaddafi are said to resist because they are too delusional or too deceived by domestic actors to know when to back down.

Arguments that emphasize misperception may be helpful in explaining the origins of conflict, but the logic of these arguments is limited when it comes to explaining FIRC. Biased policymakers may be prone to disputes, but not all disputes end in regime change, which suggests that even biased policymakers sometimes choose to settle. Biases may also cause actors to underestimate the costs of FIRC, but this does not necessarily mean that actors with better judgment would have chosen differently. They might merely pursue FIRC differently. Although the many high-profile cases of failed regime change might suggest that the choice to pursue FIRC is the product of flawed judgment, such thinking rests on a "fallacy of the converse" in which the converse of an argument is erroneously assumed to be true.[19] Just as we cannot assume that a cancer victim is a smoker simply because smoking causes cancer, neither can we assume that regime change stems from poor judgment because poor judgment can lead to failed regime change. FIRC can fail for a variety of reasons, even when the decision-making that led to it was based on strategic logic.

A second problem with arguments attributing FIRC to errors in judgment is that they cannot explain regime-change cases that end successfully. Regime change may have a poor reputation, but successful cases are more than mere outliers. American policymakers, for example, generally achieved their aims by imposing regime change on Germany (1945), Japan (1945), Grenada (1983), and Panama (1989).[20] And although the Soviet Union's attempt at regime change in Afghanistan failed disastrously, its attempts in Mongolia (1921, 1984), Hungary (1956), and Czechoslovakia (1968) were more successful. Likewise, France successfully used regime change to protect its interests in Spain (1823) and, much later, in Gabon (1964), as did the United Kingdom in Iran (1941) and Iraq (1941). Success, of course, can have many meanings, but if defined to mean that the imposing state achieves its central policy aims, then not all regime change ends in failure. As such, there is little reason to infer that poor judgment causes it.

Just as not all policymakers pursuing FIRC do so because their judgment is poor, not all targeted leaders suffer regime change because they foolishly challenge a more powerful state. Although some defy the foreign power's demands until deposed, others offer concessions but are overthrown anyway. Czechoslovakia's Alexander Dubček, for example, indicated he was planning to resign in a phone call with Soviet leader Leonid Brezhnev on August 13, 1968. Yet just one week later, Brezhnev ordered a massive military invasion to overthrow him.[21] Similarly, in 1909, Nicaraguan President José Santos Zelaya made concessions, including his own resignation, to prevent a conflict with the United States. Instead, the United States persisted in backing Nicaraguan rebels until they seized power.[22] These cases suggest that even if defiant leaders were to make concessions, they might still get deposed.

In this book, I show that psychological-bias models and bureaucratic and/or interest-group models, although potentially helpful in explaining why conflict occurs or why a chosen policy fails, fall short when it comes to explaining why states pursue regime change. Neither the quantitative nor the qualitative evidence I review in this book supports the argument that biased decision-making leads policymakers to pursue FIRC. Indeed, in the case studies, I show that the very same policymakers, faced with two similar cases at roughly the same time, might choose to negotiate in one instance but impose regime change in the other. So even when we would expect little variation in policymakers' biases or bureaucratic/lobbyist pressures, different outcomes may result. I also show that the experience of a failed FIRC does not necessarily deter policymakers from trying it again. Rather than inferring that FIRC fails, policymakers may simply conclude that it should be carried out in a different way. Psychological-bias arguments and bureaucratic and/or interest-group theories may still inform our understanding of various other aspects of FIRC, but to understand the choice to pursue it, we need to look elsewhere.

The second set of alternative arguments I address stems from the rationalist literature on war. The two dominant rational actor approaches tell us that conflict arises either because there are problems of incomplete information (one side doubts the other's threats)[23] or problems of credible commitment (one side doubts the other's promises) that make an enforceable bargain impossible to achieve.[24] Several arguments employ the problem of credible commitment to explain FIRC. In separate studies on wartime termination, Dan Reiter and Alex Weisiger contend that states seek regime change when they doubt the defeated leader will uphold a settlement.[25] Similarly, Bruce Bueno de Mesquita and his coauthors argue that popular leaders will depose other popular leaders because the latter cannot be trusted to stick to a politically unpopular settlement.[26] Other arguments focus on the role of incomplete information in driving asymmetric conflict, which commonly characterizes FIRC. According to these arguments, the weaker side's doubts about the stronger side's threats cause the weak to resist, which causes the strong to choose war.[27]

I do not argue that the standard rationalist arguments are wrong, only that they are incomplete. Credible-commitment and incomplete-information problems help us understand why bargaining is difficult and thus why conflicts arise between states. But these theories on their own do not explain why states continue fighting when they have the means to overcome the problems that impede a settlement. I show that if the weaker party doubts the stronger side's resolve, as occurs in cases marked by the incomplete-information problem, the more powerful state can demonstrate its resolve by using costly signals or applying limited force to make its threats more credible and convince the target to concede.[28] When the victor doubts that the vanquished will uphold a settlement, as occurs when the credible-commitment problem is present, the victor can employ enforcement mechanisms to obtain the target's compliance. It can use third-party inspectors or its own troops to force the target to carry out the settlement terms.[29] In fact, the unequal power relations that characterize the conditions under which regime change occurs should make resolving problems of information and commitment easier. The strong have the military capacity to make their threats credible and also to enforce the terms they impose on weak states. The question thus remains, why do the strong sometimes fail to use this capacity to obtain enforceable agreements that would spare them the costs of regime change?

My argument builds on the standard rationalist arguments by showing why states fail to use costly signals, limited force, and enforcement mechanisms when they could. I draw from a small and often overlooked set of rationalist models that illuminate the paradox that threatening to use force can be more costly than using it. These "costly peace" models show that coercion can be expensive when states confront rivals who are either highly resolved to resist[30] or must be coerced indefinitely to comply.[31] The costs of peace can cause policymakers to prefer war.

What these models do not clarify, however, is *when* the strong will see coercing the weak as more costly than war. Weak leaders may be relatively cheap to defeat, but because of this weakness, they should also be relatively cheap to coerce, even indefinitely. At the same time, leaders who are highly resolved to fight may be costly to coerce, but they should also be costly to defeat because their resolve makes them willing to fight longer and harder.[32] What we lack is a theory that can explain why a leader would be committed to resist (and thus costly to coerce) but, at the same time, comparatively cheap to defeat. In this book, I show that a leader's domestic opposition can make the difference, making the leader at once more resolved to resist and more vulnerable to regime change.

Defining Regime Change

FIRC can take a variety of forms. Some cases involve large-scale military invasions, such as those undertaken by the Allies in Germany and Japan during World War II and by the Soviet Union in Afghanistan in 1979. Others entail support for insurgents, much like the 1909 American intervention in Nicaragua, American support for the Nicaraguan Contras during President Ronald Reagan's administration, or NATO's overthrow of Qaddafi in 2011. FIRC can also include foreign-orchestrated coups such as the Soviet-sponsored communist takeovers in Czechoslovakia and Poland or US covert operations in Albania in 1949, Iran in 1953, and Chile in 1973. Paradoxically, FIRC can also occur through a negotiated agreement. In 1994, for example, President Bill Clinton threatened an invasion to convince Haiti's military junta to step down.

These cases may not appear on the surface to be alike, but they share at least three important traits. I use these traits as conditions to identify cases of FIRC for this study. First, policymakers in the imposing state have explicitly abandoned negotiations that would allow the target state's leader(s) to remain in power. Second, policymakers in the imposing state have implemented a specific plan to replace the target state's leaders and/or political institutions. Third, policymakers target a sovereign state and intend to restore sovereignty to that state. I explain each of these conditions below.

First, to qualify as an instance of FIRC, policymakers in the imposing state must reject any bargaining agreement with the targeted head of state that would leave that leader in power. This distinction makes it possible to distinguish between cases in which the stronger power's primary aim is to change the opposing side's policies and those in which the goal is to change its policymakers. This is an important distinction because countries can threaten regime change when it is not their primary goal. In the 1980s, for example, the Central Intelligence Agency (CIA) made plans to topple Qaddafi, but President Reagan made clear that if Qaddafi abandoned his support for terrorism, the United States would abandon regime change.[33] Reagan's main goal was a change in Libya's policies, not necessarily in its top policymaker. States may also sponsor rebels to coerce policy change. The United States and Iran backed a Kurdish rebellion in Iraq to pressure Saddam Hussein into signing the 1975 Algiers Agreement. To identify sincere threats to impose regime change, I look for evidence that the imposing state refused to abandon regime change in exchange for policy change.

States may also demand regime change as part of a negotiated settlement, as the Clinton administration did in Haiti. Although states employ coercive bargaining tactics to attain these settlements, these cases qualify as FIRC. The foreign power is determined to oust the leader rather than accept an agreement that would let the leader remain in power. To exclude these cases would be to eliminate from the data instances in which the foreign power shares the same goal as other states seeking regime change but adopts different methods. I distinguish instances of coerced regime change by looking for evidence that the imposing state explicitly demanded that the targeted leader step down. The settlement ending the Franco-Prussian War, for example, obligated France to hold new elections. In contrast, Germany's 1940 invasion of France, which coincided with a change in French leadership, is not included because France's Vichy regime assumed power before seeking an armistice.[34]

In addition to the methods used to impose regime change, the extent of political change can vary as well. States may either remove the target state's top leaders, or they may transform its political institutions. Some studies exclude leadership change from the definition of regime change because the target state's institutions are left intact and, therefore, its regime, traditionally defined as a set of political institutions, does not change. However, this distinction conflates how regime change ends with how it is pursued. Foreign powers sometimes depose leaders to produce institutional change. The United States, for example, helped facilitate Iran's transition from a constitutional monarchy to an authoritarian state through leadership change in 1953. By removing that country's popular prime minister, Mohammad Mosaddeq, and supporting the Shah, the United States obtained institutional change, but it did not impose institutions. In Chapter 2, I discuss the various ways in which states effect regime change, including what level of force they use and whether they transform the target state's institutions or simply depose its leaders. The data used in Chapter 3 include both types of FIRC.

The second criterion for regime change requires that policymakers implement a plan explicitly aimed at replacing the target state's leaders or political institutions. By requiring that the initiator implements a plan of action, I can exclude cases in which policymakers call for regime change largely for symbolic or domestic political reasons. After the 1979 revolution in Iran, Ayatollah Ruhollah Khomeini called for regime change in Iraq and encouraged Iraqi Shi'a to revolt, but the Iranian government did not pursue a direct course of action aimed at removing Saddam Hussein from power. After Iraq invaded Iran in 1980, however, Iran counterinvaded and actively pursued regime change in Iraq.[35] As this case also shows, attempts to pursue regime change need not be successful. In my data, I include cases in which states eschewed bargaining and pursued regime change but ultimately abandoned that aim. These cases are important to include because the conditions that cause states to pursue regime change should apply regardless of whether their attempts succeed or fail.

Finally, for a case to qualify as an instance of FIRC, there must be evidence that the attempt to overthrow the leader or regime was driven at least as much by foreign actors as by domestic ones. To make this distinction, I use evidence that the foreign power sent its own personnel to the target state, provided military aid that the opposition needed in order to act, or assumed a controlling stake in the operation.[36] For example, the United States' effort to assist the White movement in Russia following the communist revolution involved thousands of American troops and thus is included as a regime-change attempt.[37]

The third and final condition requires that the initiator intends to restore sovereignty to the target state. In contrast to annexation or colonization, in which the target state or territory remains under the direct control of the intervening state, regime change involves the installation of a new or restored sovereign government. I identify cases of regime change by looking for evidence that the foreign power was not planning to exercise permanent control over the target state. The foreign power may rule its target temporarily, but it must at least plan to restore sovereignty. Nazi Germany, for example, ruled the Netherlands, Belgium, and Denmark (after 1943) through military governors but did not plan to annex or dissolve these states, as it did Czechoslovakia, Austria, and Poland.[38] The former qualify as regime-change events, the latter do not. In some instances, a third state may help an ally annex another. The United States, for example, attempted to overthrow the North Korean government to bring it under the jurisdiction of the South. In these cases, I code the third state as engaged in regime change because it seeks to replace one government with another. I do not, however, code the state annexing the other as engaged in regime change because it does not intend to restore the target's sovereignty. In cases with multiple initiators, I include only those primarily responsible for the regime-change attempt.

FIRC is also distinct from state creation. Newly liberated states or states created by secession do not qualify as instances of regime change because there is no sovereign regime to depose. I also exclude attempts to eliminate nonstate actors, such as the so-called Islamic State, because these are not sovereign states ruled by internationally recognized governments. In sum, whether it succeeds or fails, regime change constitutes an attempt by a state to replace the leadership of a sovereign state to which it intends to restore sovereignty. Though the foreign power's aim may be to produce policy change, its purpose is to install leaders more willing to embrace that change.

Method and Case Selection

I use several methods to establish the logic of my argument and test its empirical validity. The argument itself is based on a game theoretic model. To keep the argument accessible to readers unfamiliar with game theory, I lay out the informal version of the argument in Chapter 1 and present the model in Appendix 2. I also derive hypotheses from my argument, which I test with both quantitative and qualitative evidence alongside alternative arguments. For the statistical analysis, I test my main hypothesis—that domestic opposition in a target state increases the likelihood of FIRC—on a data set that includes 133 cases of attempted FIRC (see Appendix 1). These tests help establish the generalizability of my argument, showing its ability to explain a large number of cases, even when controlling for alternative explanations.

Statistical tests, however, are less effective in testing an argument's causal logic. For this, I rely on a series of case studies. If my argument is correct, I should find evidence that when leaders faced significant domestic opposition, they resisted complying with foreign demands that could put their political power at risk. I should also find that, as long as the opposition was not more opposed to the foreign power than the leader, the foreign power attempted to use the opposition to overthrow the leader. When the leader did not face significant domestic opposition, I should find that the foreign power agreed to some form of settlement. This settlement may have taken a variety of forms, ranging from one that involved concessions from the targeted leader to one that resembled the status quo or even entailed concessions from the foreign power. Findings that would challenge my theory include evidence that leaders facing strong domestic opposition acquiesced to politically costly demands without an equally strong incentive from the foreign power to do so. Evidence that the foreign power rejected regime change and pursued negotiations in such instances would also challenge my theory. Additionally, the theory would also be falsified if a foreign power attempted to overthrow a targeted leader without the existence of a strong, friendly domestic opposition.

I use a most-similar case design in which I analyze similar events that share a number of features but differ in their outcome—one ending in a settlement, the other in regime change.[39] First, I compare the response of President Dwight Eisenhower's administration to liberal governments in Guatemala and Bolivia in 1954. I next look at the Soviet Union's response to nationalist governments in Poland and Hungary in 1956. Finally, I examine the US decisions to impose regime change on Iraq in 2003 but negotiate with Libya, only to pursue regime change in Libya eight years later.

By choosing cases that share numerous traits, I can test my argument's causal logic while controlling for alternative hypotheses. For example, in each case study, the targeted leaders' regime types and ideologies are similar, which suggests that neither factor can explain the decision to pursue FIRC in these cases.[40] The target state's geostrategic location (i.e., within or outside the imposing state's sphere of influence) is also similar in each case, which suggests that stronger powers might be just as likely to negotiate as to overthrow leaders within (or outside) these regions. Finally, the same individual(s) made policy in the stronger state during roughly the same time period. Because it is unlikely that policymakers' personalities, views, biases, or domestic pressures varied much during the time frames involved, it is also unlikely that these influenced the divergent outcomes.

Variation across the cases also allows me to introduce additional controls. I have paired states with different regime types to control for arguments suggesting that certain combinations are more likely to lead to FIRC. In the studies of American involvement in Bolivia and Guatemala, a democracy squared off against two democratically elected leaders. In the cases of the Soviet responses to Poland and Hungary, the more powerful state was a nondemocracy, whereas its targets were popularly supported communist leaders. In the study of US responses to Libya and Iraq, the stronger nation was democratic and its targets were not. The cases also vary in terms of the structure of the international system. The first two cases occurred during the Cold War, a period of bipolarity, whereas the last took place in the post–Cold War era, a period of unipolarity in which the United States faced no peer competitors. The cases vary as to the timing of the decision to pursue regime change too. In the first and last cases, the decision to pursue FIRC in one instance preceded the decision to negotiate in the other. In the second case, the decision to pursue negotiations preceded the decision to pursue FIRC. Finally, to maximize the range of cases, I have chosen ones that varied in the amount of force used and the type of regime change pursued. The first case involves a covert operation aimed at partial regime change. The second involves a military invasion aimed at partial regime change, and the third set includes two cases aimed at full regime change, one involving a military invasion and the other a foreign-backed insurgency. Table 1 shows the three case studies and the control variables.

Another element dictating case selection is the availability of primary source materials. Access to meeting minutes, memos, and various other governmental documents allows for better insight into the policies as they were conceived at the time. The CIA and State Department have released a wide variety of materials related to the deliberations of the most central players in Guatemala and Bolivia.[41] The minutes of the Central Committee of the Communist Party of the Soviet Union (CPSU CC) Presidium are available for the discussions about Poland and Hungary.[42] They shed light on how Soviet decision makers weighed their policy options during the two uprisings. Finally, in the aftermath of the US invasion of Iraq, researchers acquired access to translated and transcribed recordings of high-level meetings between Saddam Hussein and his top advisers.[43] Access to all these materials enhances our ability to interpret the behaviors observed.

Outline of the Book

Chapter 1 presents my argument. I explain why strong states opt to remove foreign leaders or regimes in weak states rather than negotiate settlements that would allow them to retain power. I also explain how targeted leaders respond when they know another nation seeks to depose them. I end with a discussion of alternative arguments, from which I derive testable hypotheses. In Chapter 2, I expand my argument to explain how stronger powers choose between overthrowing the target state's leaders and overhauling its domestic institutions. I also address the costs and risks associated with these different forms of regime change and why decision makers sometimes anticipate regime change to be cheaper than it actually is.

In the chapters that follow, I subject my argument to a series of empirical tests. Chapter 3 presents the statistical tests of my hypothesis that the probability of FIRC increases with the strength of the target's domestic opposition. I also discuss the quantitative measures that I use as proxies for the opposition's strength and the variables for alternative arguments.

Table 1. Foreign-Imposed Regime Change Case Studies: Within-Case and Cross-Case Controls

	Chapter 4		Chapter 5		Chapter 6		
	Guatemala 1954	Bolivia 1954	Poland 1956	Hungary 1956	Iraq 2003	Libya 2003	Libya 2011
Target's Characteristics							
Regime Type	Popularly Elected President	Popularly Elected President	One-party rule	One-party rule	Personalist dictator	Personalist dictator	Personalist dictator
Regime Ideology	State-controlled capitalism	State-controlled capitalism	Communism	Communism	Arab nationalism	Arab nationalism	Arab nationalism
Proximity to Major Power	Within region	Within region	Within region	Within region	Outside region	Outside region	Outside region
Region	Latin America	Latin America	Eastern Europe	Eastern Europe	Middle East	North Africa	North Africa
Foreign Power's Characteristics							
Regime Type	Democracy	Democracy	Democracy	Democracy	Democracy	Democracy	Democracy
Decision Maker	Eisenhower	Eisenhower	Khrushchev	Khrushchev	Bush	Bush	Obama
Timing of Decision	June–August 1953	June–August 1953	October 1956	October 1956	Summer 2002–January 2003	Summer 2002–March 2003	March 2011
Polarity	Bipolarity	Bipolarity	Bipolarity	Bipolarity	Unipolarity	Unipolarity	Unipolarity
Interest at Stake	Security/economic	Security/economic	Security	Security	Security	Security	Humanitarian
Outcome	Partial FIRC: Covert	Settlement	Settlement	Partial FIRC: Invasion	Full FIRC: Invasion	Settlement	Full FIRC: Air Campaign

Chapters 4, 5, and 6 present the case studies. In Chapter 4, I compare the Eisenhower administration's policies toward the revolutionary governments of Guatemala and Bolivia, the latter having seized power in 1952, just as the first covert plot to overthrow the former was materializing. Both governments depended on the support of Marxist and communist factions, passed major agrarian and political reforms, and implemented policies that threatened the economic interests of American investors. Though the Eisenhower administration overthrew Guatemala's Jacobo Árbenz in 1954, it chose to support the Bolivian government, offering it what would become the largest per capita aid package in the world at that time.[44]

In Chapter 5, I compare the Soviet Union's 1956 decision to negotiate with Poland's Wladyslaw Gomulka with its choice a few weeks later to overthrow Prime Minister Imre Nagy of Hungary. Both Poland and Hungary experienced anti-Soviet protests, and both leaders responded with reforms to placate protestors and quell unrest. Nikita Khrushchev initially reacted to the Polish uprisings with threats of force and an attempt to push aside Gomulka. Yet ultimately, he conceded to Gomulka's reforms. In Hungary, Khrushchev did the opposite. He initially accepted Nagy's reforms, including multiparty elections. Overnight, however, Khrushchev changed his mind and launched an invasion to depose the Hungarian leader.

Finally, in Chapter 6, I examine the differing American approaches to former Iraqi president Saddam Hussein and Libyan leader Muammar Qaddafi. In the first two cases, I focus on the Bush administration's decision in 2003 to impose regime change on Iraq but to renounce it in Libya, which had also supported terrorism, maintained programs for weapons of mass destruction (WMD), and used chemical weapons. I then compare these cases with the Obama administration's decision in 2011 to support an international coalition to topple Qaddafi. In addition, I examine previous US attempts to negotiate with and overthrow each leader.

In the Conclusion, I summarize my argument and explain how it expands our understanding of both regime change and war. I then discuss my theory's major foreign policy implications. The first implication is that when the foreign power's threat to impose regime change lacks credibility, the targeted leader can become more difficult to overthrow and to coerce. If the targeted leader anticipates the foreign power will use covert and/or indirect methods, or that it may be bluffing, the leader may take defensive measures to make regime change more costly to impose. By aligning with the foreign power's rivals, conducting domestic purges to wipe out potential political rivals, or acquiring WMD, targeted leaders may be able to safeguard their regimes. States making idle threats or using covert and indirect methods to impose regime change can, therefore, exacerbate a "rogue" state's roguish behavior.

My theory also has implications for the coercive-bargaining literature. Conventional wisdom holds that politically weak leaders are more vulnerable to coercion than those with strong domestic support. My argument, however, indicates just the opposite. Politically weak leaders require additional incentive to comply when the opposing side's demands could undermine their already fragile power. Politically secure leaders, in contrast, can make those concessions without jeopardizing their political survival. Although they may have other reasons to resist, all else being equal, their domestic strength should make them easier to coerce. My theory also suggests that what is commonly defined as a failure of coercion is often not a true failure of coercion. Rather, coercion may appear to fail because states tend only to use it when it is least likely to work—that is, when they lack a credible threat to use force. Once their threats become credible, however, they are often no longer interested in negotiating but prefer, instead, to impose regime change.

Lastly, although my theory is not designed to explain the success or failure of regime change, it suggests a number of reasons why FIRC may fail to deliver the substantial benefits and low costs policymakers often expect. In particular, the stability of an imposed regime depends on whether the former regime and its supporters can still pose a threat to it. When faced with domestic opposition, a new leader may prove just as unwilling or unable to cooperate as the former one. As a result, whether regime change pays off will depend on whether the foreign power invests the resources necessary to eliminate the domestic instability in the target state that led it to seek regime change in the first place.

One implication of this result is that regime change may appear more successful when preceded by a major war. A decisive military defeat makes it harder for the regime's members and supporters to organize a challenge to the new one. In contrast, when regime change is imposed rapidly and with little fighting, as often occurs when great powers target weak states, instability may be more likely. In these instances, if the former regime and its supporters escape and are offered little incentive to recognize the new regime, they may launch an insurgency to challenge it. The foreign power may then find itself stuck in a quagmire as it supports its protégé. If it fails to provide this support, the new regime may be forced to concede to the opposition, potentially putting it at odds with the foreign power.

Nevertheless, even when the costs of regime change turn out to be higher than anticipated, this does not necessarily mean that states would have chosen to negotiate if better informed of those costs. Negotiated agreements can be costly to attain and maintain too. If policymakers are also reluctant to pay those costs, then their attempts to negotiate a sustainable agreement will fail also. Indeed, neither regime change nor coercive bargaining has a strong track record of success, in part because states seldom want to pay the variety of costs often required to make them work. States, therefore, will not necessarily abandon regime change when they experience failure, because they may have already concluded that coercion does not work either. Instead, their past experiences may simply convince them to adopt different regime-change policies. The fact remains that the conditions that lead policymakers to believe coercion is more costly than regime change are ever present. The world is full of militarily weak and politically vulnerable leaders. Regime change, as such, is a constant temptation. For this reason, FIRC has been an enduring feature of the international system and, for better or worse, will likely remain so.

CHAPTER 1

Why the Strong Impose Regime
Change on the Weak

On August 25, 1941, British and Soviet forces launched an invasion of Iran that would end with the overthrow of the Iranian monarch, Reza Shah Pahlavi. The invasion, however, was not initially aimed at regime change. After the Nazi invasion of the Soviet Union in June, the British and Soviet governments looked to secure their interests in Iran. Although they initially focused on forcing Reza Shah to expel German residents, the British were mainly concerned with safeguarding Iran's oil fields, while the Soviets wanted to secure a land route for military aid from the West.[1] Neither of these goals required regime change. Yet, Reza Shah's lack of cooperation with Anglo-Soviet demands appeared to invite it. Although he had little hope of repelling the invasion, the shah delayed when pressed to expel the German residents. Even after the invasion, he still held out, attempting to negotiate the terms of the cease-fire. He insisted on safe passage for the German residents, the withdrawal of British and Soviet troops from specified locations, the return of captured arms and ammunition, and the payment of an indemnity.[2] With the odds stacked so heavily against him, why did Reza Shah not bow to British and Soviet demands to save his regime?

The problem for Reza Shah was that he could ill afford the domestic political costs of conceding to the Allies' demands. He had subjected Iranians to heavy taxes and conscription to build a modern army capable of fending off a foreign invasion. But when faced with an invasion, he had ordered his troops to cease resistance after only a few days of fighting.[3] The decision angered the population. The Iranian foreign minister confessed to the British minister that, without some concessions from the Allies, Reza Shah's government could not survive.[4] When Reza Shah was informed that the Allies planned to expel the German residents themselves, he exclaimed, "We will lose face."[5]

The British were well aware of Reza Shah's unpopularity. Frustrated by his stalling and eager to distance themselves from him, they forced him to abdicate by waging a propaganda campaign.[6] Radio London conveyed reports that the reason for the ongoing food shortage was that Reza Shah had sold all provisions to the Germans.[7] British Persian-language broadcasts accused him of seizing the crown jewels and criticized his "tyrannical rule."[8] The broadcasts enraged the public even more. Having intentionally stoked unrest, the Allies insisted on occupying Tehran to stabilize the situation.[9] The shah, on learning of the impending occupation, passed power to his son Mohammad Reza Shah Pahlavi, counseling him to learn from his father's experience and, "Bow your head till the storm passes."[10]

This chapter explains why strong states pursue FIRC in militarily weak states whose leaders should be relatively easy to coerce into settlements. I argue that the targeted leader's domestic opposition not only gives that leader cause to resist the stronger state but also gives the stronger state reason to believe regime change will be relatively cheap. Much like Reza Shah, targeted leaders often resist making concessions that will jeopardize their political power. In many instances, strong states can increase their threats to compel these leaders to accept some form of settlement, but strong states must make their threats credible to do so. They may have to mobilize an army or apply limited force to convince the leader to concede, or they may have to soften their terms to let leaders like Reza Shah save face. To ensure the leader upholds the terms of the deal, the stronger state may also have to maintain a credible threat to renew hostilities if the leader reneges. These measures can entail a variety of costs for the stronger state that range from military and economic expenses to diplomatic and domestic political costs. But rather than bear the costs of these measures, policymakers may see it as less costly to exploit the targeted leader's domestic vulnerability and oust that leader from power. Targeted leaders may resist a foreign power's demands for reasons other than domestic political pressure. A lack of domestic opposition in the target state will, therefore, not necessarily ensure a deal on the foreign power's terms. But when targeted leaders face domestic opposition, the foreign power has both a motive and opportunity for regime change. The opposition causes the targeted leader to resist or renege on the settlement, thus giving the foreign power reason to oust the leader, while simultaneously providing the foreign power a means to replace that leader.

In this chapter's first section, I explain more fully why domestic opposition would cause a militarily weak leader to resist or renege on an agreement with a stronger state. I then explain how the strength of the targeted leader's domestic opposition affects the stronger side's costs of obtaining and enforcing a settlement with that leader. Finally, I explain why policymakers in the stronger state are more likely to estimate low regime-change costs when the targeted leader faces domestic political opposition. I also address how leaders respond to the threat of regime change and explain when such threats might exacerbate so-called rogue-state behavior. I end by examining alternative arguments for FIRC and derive from them hypotheses that I later test against my argument. A formal model of my argument can be found in Appendix 2.

The Logic of Foreign-Imposed Regime Change

The Leader's Incentive to Resist

When a more powerful state demands a settlement that will strengthen the hand of the domestic opposition, the targeted leader will have a strong incentive to resist. The settlement terms could strengthen one or both types of domestic opposition that leaders face. The first, the internal opposition, consists of the leader's political rivals who operate within the existing political system. These rivals compete for some of the same supporters as the leader does.[11] In dictatorships, internal opponents may include rivals within the ruling party or junta seeking to supplant the leader. In democratic systems, internal opponents may head opposition parties that compete for power in elections or may be members of the ruling coalition vying to lead it.

The internal opposition is most likely to gain political advantage when the stronger power demands policy change that could hurt the targeted leader's supporters. The leader's rivals can then point to those concessions as a sign of the leader's weakness. If the rivals' claims that they can avoid making the same concessions appear credible, the rivals might be able to lure the leader's supporters away and assume power.[12] For this reason, targeted leaders may resist or violate international agreements that could give their internal rivals opportunity to garner supporters.[13] For example, although the Serbian government had conceded to Austria-Hungary's annexation of Bosnia-Herzegovina in 1909, it did little to uphold that pledge in the years that followed. One reason was the political power of ultranationalists, whose role in the 1903 coup earned them influence in the Serbian government. By stoking pan-Serbian sentiments, the ultranationalists made it politically costly for Serbian government officials to comply with Austria-Hungary's demands. The activities of the ultranationalists would eventually lead to the assassination of the heir to the Austro-Hungarian throne and, subsequently, to World War I.[14]

The second type of domestic opposition that leaders face is external opposition. This type of opposition includes domestic groups excluded or disadvantaged by the existing political system. External opposition groups may or may not be living in exile. In autocratic systems, the external opposition might include members of a majority group that would benefit from majority rule, or a minority group looking to supplant another. In contrast, under democratic systems, external opponents might be elites who prefer an authoritarian leader to protect their interests.[15] The state's political institutions help the leader manage threats from the external opposition. Leaders may rely principally upon coercive agencies, such as secret police and domestic spy bureaus, to repress external opposition groups, or they may use politically inclusive measures, such as holding elections or offering bureaucratic appointments, to buy off their external opponents.[16] In either event, the stronger these institutions, the better able the leader is to keep external domestic threats at bay.

Because the regime's domestic institutions help the leader manage the external opposition, when foreign powers make demands that will weaken those institutions, the external opposition stands to benefit. Dictators that comply with demands to limit repression or implement reforms could risk losing power. Panama's Manuel Noriega, for example, could not comply with the Reagan administration's demands for free and fair elections without giving up his power and influence.[17] Likewise, leaders who are forced by a foreign power to grant influential bureaucratic appointments or legislative seats to the opposition could increase their risk of a coup. Once the external opposition holds influence within the system, it can use its proximity to the leader or new-found political power to mount an internal challenge.[18] Communists, for example, were able to seize power in Poland after World War II with the help of Moscow, which pushed for the creation of a communist-dominated government. Despite the communists' initial lack of popular support, once they attained political influence, they were able to rig elections and persecute their enemies to consolidate power and assure communist rule.[19]

How resolved a targeted leader will be in resisting a foreign power's demands depends on the strength of the opposition the leader already faces. The stronger the opposition is, the better it can exploit the opportunity provided by the leader's concessions to challenge the leader. Autocratic leaders might be able to comply with foreign demands to hold elections when their external opposition is too weak to win, but when the opposition is strong, such concessions could imperil the leader's survival. Similarly, leaders who already have broad popular support might be able to trade on their popularity and concede to unpopular policy changes. Leaders without such support, however, could face a coup or rebellion when making similar concessions. The stronger the opposition is relative to the leader, the greater the risk to the leader of accepting demands that will further strengthen the opposition; as a result, the more determined the leader will be to resist the stronger state's demands.

Targeted leaders often have good reason to prioritize their domestic enemies over their foreign ones, despite the foreign power's greater military capabilities.[20] First, a foreign enemy might put only a moderate value on the issue at hand, whereas domestic enemies are often highly resolved to attain power, especially if their survival depends on it. Second, when domestic opposition groups seize power, they are more likely to kill or imprison the deposed leader to prevent that leader from returning to power.[21] Third, domestic opponents are closer in proximity than foreign ones. If they operate within the government, they may be able to overthrow the leader without having to wage war. But even when they operate outside the government, they can seize resources, cities, and infrastructure, without having to launch a foreign invasion first. Finally, foreign enemies eventually leave, while domestic ones can be an indefinite menace. Because domestic opponents can pose more severe and longer-lasting threats, leaders may be willing to risk war with a foreign power to protect themselves from home-grown perils. When the United Kingdom's Lord Lytton pressured Afghanistan to accept the stationing of British officers there in 1878, the emir's representative, fearing a domestic rebellion, pleaded, "You must not impose upon us a burden which we cannot bear."[22] The emir subsequently refused Lytton's demands. After invading and installing a new Afghan ruler, the British found themselves facing the rebellion the emir's representative had predicted.

Leaders facing little opposition will not necessarily yield to all of the foreign power's demands. Their willingness to concede depends not only on their political vulnerability but also on their military and economic weakness. Leaders with the resources to resist a foreign power's pressure may refuse concessions even though the political costs of conceding are low. Politically strong leaders may also avoid concessions they fear could create opposition. These leaders can often afford to take a firmer bargaining position because they know that the foreign power has no credible threat to replace them. Nevertheless, when compared to leaders who have similar resources, but face staunch domestic threats, leaders without domestic opposition should be more willing to make concessions. The threat to their political survival is much lower. Domestically weak leaders, in contrast, will require greater incentive to accept settlement terms that increase their political vulnerability. For scholars, then, the issue becomes determining the conditions under which the foreign power will give a politically weak leader sufficient incentive to accept an agreement.

The Foreign Power's Costs of a Settlement

To attain a favorable settlement, first the stronger state must convince the targeted leader to accept its terms; second, it must convince the leader to uphold them. The first task requires the stronger state to incur coercion costs, while the second entails enforcement costs. In this section, I detail both sets of costs, showing how each is influenced by the domestic threat the targeted leader faces.

THE COSTS OF COERCION

To convince a targeted leader facing domestic opposition to accept a settlement that could be politically costly, the foreign power must first demonstrate that it poses a greater threat than the leader's domestic threat.[23] Simply possessing greater military capabilities is not enough. The foreign power must also convince the target it will follow through on its threats. This could be difficult to do, especially if the foreign power has interests that span the globe. If the issue at stake is outside its core security interests, its target might well doubt the foreign power's willingness to sacrifice significant resources in a less important arena.[24] In the rationalist literature on war, such doubts drive what is known as the incomplete-information problem.[25] When actors cannot judge their opponents' capabilities or resolve, they often resist at the bargaining table, believing they can do so with impunity. Although each side could theoretically communicate its resolve and capabilities, neither has reason to trust the other since each has incentive to bluff. Targeted leaders that believe their domestic enemies are more resolved to challenge them than their foreign ones may, therefore, resist a foreign power's demands to protect their political positions.

One way to overcome an incomplete-information problem is with a *costly signal*, which entails actions a less committed actor would avoid.[26] Whereas a bluffer might make a verbal threat to go to war, only truly resolved ones will bear the costs of actually preparing for it. Costly signals can also include verbal threats for which policymakers would incur political costs if they failed to follow through. But preparing for war has an additional benefit that verbal threats do not: war preparation measures increase the chances of military victory.[27] A state that mobilizes a large invasion force, for example, is far more likely to achieve a military victory than one that does not. Likewise, states that form military alliances or attempt to weaken their targets with military or economic pressure are more likely to prove victorious than ones that simply threaten war. Thus, the size and scope of the foreign power's war-preparation measures, more so than mere verbal threats, can convince a targeted leader of the foreign power's resolve to fight. Consequently, they can also influence which enemy—the foreign or domestic one—the targeted leader sees as more dangerous.

Mobilizing for war may not be enough to convince some leaders to concede. They might be facing such deadly domestic threats that they would rather risk a fight with the foreign power. They may hope to hold out in a protracted conflict or, like Reza Shah discussed earlier, settle for terms that allow them to save face. Though such targets may be difficult to intimidate, agreements are often still possible. The state demanding concessions can use limited force to weaken the target's defenses, resolve, or both. Bombing or economic blockades can be used to deny the target the means to hold out or to weaken its resolve.[28] The foreign power can also target the leader's supporters, imperiling their interests to ensure they see compliance as necessary.[29] The stronger state can also use positive incentives, such as offers of aid or security guarantees, to make compliance more appealing, or it can soften its terms to attain its core aims. It can also use scorched-earth tactics to make resistance very costly for the target or defeat the target militarily, leaving it no choice but to accept a settlement.[30] Of course, some targets may possess such powerful military capabilities or resolve that they cannot be defeated. But if the foreign power can defeat the target and impose regime change, then it should be able to convince the target to accept a settlement as long as that settlement offers the leader the chance to remain in power.

The problem with obtaining a bargaining agreement, however, is that policymakers may not want to bear the costs necessary to secure them. Whether the stronger state uses a costly signal to convince the target to concede, uses force to wear down the adversary's will or ability to resist, or uses positive incentives to induce concessions, agreements can be costly for the side seeking change. Costly signals, for example, must be costly to the state making the threat to be effective.[31] Targeted leaders understand that a less resolved adversary will tolerate moderately costly signals to achieve its aims at the bargaining table. Thus, in order to convince the target to back down, the state making the threat must mobilize a large army or take some other costly action to prove its determination to win *at all costs*.[32] The same holds for the use of limited force and the offer of positive inducements. The more resolved the target is to remain in power, the more is required to obtain the target's concessions.

The expense of an agreement typically goes beyond monetary costs. These expenses can also include political, diplomatic, opportunity, humanitarian, reputational, and military costs. Mobilizing an army, for example, could generate diplomatic costs by alienating the stronger state's allies. For example, Vietnam's relations with China deteriorated after Vietnam responded militarily to Cambodia's border incursions in 1977.[33] War-preparation measures could also prove unpopular at home.[34] The fear of incurring domestic political costs kept both the Reagan and George H. W. Bush administrations from publicly threatening to use military force in Panama to oust Noriega.[35] Maintaining foreign bases, allies, and weapons systems to ensure a credible military threat against a foreign leader can create opportunity costs by drawing resources away from domestic priorities or from deterring other foreign threats. Bombing campaigns or sanctions can also entail costs. The 1998 NATO bombing campaign in Kosovo, for example, created diplomatic costs by aggravating US-Russia relations at a time when the two countries were reconciling.[36] Sanctions and bombing campaigns that generate high civilian casualties can also create reputational costs, as the foreign power comes to be seen as the aggressor. States may attempt to avoid these costs by restricting the kinds of sanctions they use or the types of targets they bomb. But these efforts usually undermine the coercive threat by convincing the opponent that the foreign power's resolve to win is indeed limited. Even inducements can carry costs. Offering rewards to a leader widely regarded as oppressive, for instance, could create domestic political, reputational, and/or humanitarian costs for the foreign power.

The size of the costs the coercer incurs depends on the strength of the target's domestic opposition. The more severe the targeted leader's domestic threat, the more resolved the leader will be to resist, and the larger the threat the coercer must make to convince the leader to back down. This means that the greater the leader's domestic threat, the greater the foreign power's mobilization must be, the larger the international coalition it must build, and/or the more bombs it must drop to overwhelm the target's incentive to resist.[37] In extreme cases, the foreign power may even have to achieve a military victory before a leader with a strong domestic incentive to resist agrees to a settlement.[38] To be sure, foreign powers may encounter some of the same costs when carrying out regime change. However, as I will explain later, the key difference between expected coercion and regime change costs is that, as the opposition's strength grows, the former will rise, while the latter will fall. All told, foreign powers may have to incur a variety of high costs to convince targeted leaders to accept politically risky settlements, and these costs could exceed the expected costs of regime change.

THE COSTS OF ENFORCEMENT

The long-term costs of enforcing a settlement can also inflate the cost of a bargaining agreement. As long as targeted leaders face domestic opposition that makes their compliance with a deal politically costly, they will be tempted to renege on their commitments as soon as the foreign power's pressure diminishes. In the rationalist literature, actors who have an incentive to cheat on a settlement face what is known as a commitment problem. The stronger state anticipates the targeted leader will cheat once the opportunity arises and so rejects the possibility of bargaining and resorts to war. In some cases, the threat of renewed hostilities may deter the target from reneging. But if the target state doubts the stronger side's willingness to enforce the settlement or if it acquires greater military capacity, it may attempt to renege. After World War I, for example, Germany challenged the Treaty of Versailles once it became apparent the victors were reluctant to enforce it. Similarly, Joseph Stalin authorized North Korea's invasion of

South Korea in 1950, believing that the Truman administration would not interfere.[39]

To assure compliance, the stronger state must convince the lesser power's leaders that cheating would be detected and punished. To do this, it can use international observers to monitor compliance or it can take more invasive (and potentially more effective) measures, such as demanding partial policy control or stationing troops on the target state's soil. France and Belgium, for example, occupied the German Ruhr region from 1923 to 1925 to enforce the reparation terms imposed on Germany after World War I. Less than two decades later, Nazi Germany enforced its armistice with Vichy France by occupying northern France. Other enforcement measures include peacekeeping missions, which are frequently deployed to monitor cease-fire agreements.

Much like coercion, enforcement measures can entail a variety of costs, ranging from monetary and military ones to domestic political and reputational costs. For example, the French and Belgian troops in the Ruhr encountered a campaign of passive resistance, which forced the French to increase their occupation force from 80,000 to 140,000.[40] Fears of casualties and their attendant domestic political costs led US policymakers to push for the downsizing of the small United Nations (UN) peacekeeping mission in Rwanda during the 1994 genocide in that country.[41] Enforcement measures must also be maintained as long as the target retains an incentive to renege. Over time, these costs add up. Peacekeeping missions in such places as Cyprus (1964), the Sinai (1981), and Kosovo (1999) are still in operation today, though the conflicts that generated them have long since ended.

The potentially high cost of indefinitely enforcing a settlement explains why the stronger state sometimes refuses the resignations of targeted leaders. If complying with a settlement will be just as politically costly for the targeted leader's chosen successor as it was for the leader, then that successor will have the same incentive to renege. Unless the more powerful state installs a new leader who is reliant on a different set of supporters and/or political institutions, then it may find itself stuck paying high enforcement costs. This is why Soviet leader Brezhnev ignored Dubček's offers to resign as first secretary of the Communist Party of Czechoslovakia in their phone call one week before the Warsaw Pact invasion. Letting Dubček resign would have left reformers in charge. Brezhnev hoped that an invasion would instead prompt Czechs aligned with Moscow to seize power and overturn the reforms of the Prague Spring.[42]

The costs of forcing a leader to accept and to abide by a settlement may tempt the more powerful state to pursue FIRC as a cheaper alternative, especially when domestic opposition drives the targeted leader's refusal to concede. As I will explain, while the target's domestic opposition can make a settlement appear costly to attain, that opposition can also make the leader appear cheaper to depose. As long as the opposition is marginally more willing to make concessions than the leader, then the stronger power may conclude that it can attain its policy aims at a lower cost by partnering with the opposition to overthrow the leader.

The Costs of Imposing Regime Change

Some of the costs of coercing a target to accept and abide by an agreement are the same as those associated with regime change. The financial, political, and diplomatic costs of launching an invasion to coerce the leader will also be borne if an invasion is required to depose the leader. The long-term costs of enforcing an agreement could also be matched by the long-term costs of propping up a puppet. But there is an important difference between the costs of bargaining with a leader and the costs of overthrowing a leader. Whereas strong domestic opposition increases a foreign power's costs of obtaining an enforceable agreement, strong domestic opposition will decrease the expected costs of regime change. This is because politically weak leaders are not just more resolved to resist; they are also often easier to overthrow. As long as the stronger state can find an opposition group willing to collaborate, the more powerful that group, the more it can assist the foreign power in toppling the leader, thereby reducing the costs of regime change to the foreign power. This opposition need not be the same as the one causing the leader's resistance. A leader, for example, might refuse the foreign power's demands in order to defend against an internal rival, while the foreign power uses external opposition to impose regime change.

In what follows, I first address how domestic opposition, whether internal or external, affects the foreign power's estimates of regime-change costs and why foreign powers can often find opposition groups willing to collaborate. I end with a discussion of how major events or crises can serve as catalysts for regime change by prompting policymakers to reassess the costs of using military force.

THE STRENGTH OF THE DOMESTIC OPPOSITION

A domestic opposition's power depends primarily on two attributes—the extent of its military capabilities and the size and unity of its political following. Opposition groups with military capabilities can lower the costs of removing their nation's leader in a variety of ways. First, they can conduct military operations and absorb casualties, thus reducing the number of troops that the foreign power must contribute to a military invasion. In 1852, Brazil looked to partner with local actors to overthrow Argentinean dictator Juan Manuel de Rosas. Knowing it could not overthrow Rosas on its own, Brazil instead aligned with the politically ambitious Argentinean governor of Entre Ríos, Justo José de Urquiza. It was Urquiza's army of twenty thousand, assisted by a much smaller number of Brazilians and Uruguayans, that ultimately defeated Rosas.[43] Even when relatively small in number, opposition fighters can still contribute militarily to a foreign power's invasion by conducting sabotage operations, providing intelligence, harassing enemy troops, and generating propaganda to hasten a military victory. Both Nazi Germany and the Soviet Union built their informal empires by relying on pro-Nazi and pro-Soviet domestic opposition groups that served as a fifth column.[44]

Opposition groups that represent a former ruling faction often have a ready-made group of supporters willing to fight for them. During the nineteenth and early twentieth centuries, liberal and conservative regimes in Central America intervened repeatedly in neighboring states to restore their ideological allies to power.[45] Between 1855 and 1907, Honduras experienced regime change seven times as liberal and conservative leaders in both Guatemala and Nicaragua assisted Honduran liberals and conservatives in seizing power.

Opposition to the leader can also be latent. In these instances, widespread opposition may exist, but the majority of the population is too intimidated to organize and fight. Foreign powers may have to contribute greater military aid to mobilize latent opposition, but they may still judge the costs of regime change as low because the population is unlikely to rally to the leader's defense. Foreign powers may also anticipate (rightly or wrongly) that their invasions will inspire the latent opposition to fight. Uganda's Idi Amin faced latent opposition as a result of his regime's brutality. When Tanzanian troops invaded in 1978 to topple Amin, liberated civilians, encouraged by the arrival of foreign forces, joined the fight.[46]

Unpopular leaders may also attempt to ward off coups by conducting purges that strip the military of its talent and resources. This may leave the military unable to fend off a foreign invader and thereby lower the foreign power's anticipated costs of an invasion. Amin's purges and abuses had led to such low morale among Ugandan troops that many were reportedly more interested in looting or fleeing than fighting off the Tanzanian invasion.[47]

The stronger state can also use dissident groups to reassure the target population that it does not have imperial designs. When Vietnam invaded Cambodia in 1978, it sought to assuage long-standing Cambodian fears of Vietnamese domination by cobbling together the Kampuchean United Front for National Salvation (KUFNS) from pro-Hanoi Communists and Khmer Rouge defectors. Although the KUFNS's military contribution was small, Vietnamese leaders saw the group as a way to win broad Cambodian support.[48] The foreign power may also reduce its diplomatic and reputational costs by using domestic opposition groups to legitimize its regime-change operation to an international audience. Tanzanian president Julius Nyerere, for example, looked to dodge international criticism of Tanzania's invasion of Uganda by using exiles to take control of Kampala.[49]

Foreign powers may also use indirect or covert force to avoid the military and political costs of direct military force. They may, for example, use economic pressure or covert propaganda campaigns to weaken the leader politically and encourage a coup; or, they may supply rebels with military aid, assistance, and training. In 1949, President Harry Truman's administration attempted to overthrow the Communist government of Albania by covertly training, funding, and transporting Albanian exiles and Albanian Americans to that country's shores.[50] In 1957, the Eisenhower administration began covertly funding Indonesian rebels to take down President Sukarno, whose government it feared would fall prey to communist influence.[51]

Foreign powers can also avoid using direct military force by encouraging the internal opposition, which operates within the government, to undertake a coup. The internal opposition has access to military and political power, which it can use to oust the leader. The United States, for example, overthrew the Iranian prime minister, Mohammad Mosaddeq, in 1953 without the use of military force. Foreign economic pressure and domestic political violence had sapped Mosaddeq's once strong domestic support. With his political position weakened, the CIA was able to orchestrate a coup by organizing protests, bribing high-ranking army officials, and pressuring Mohammad Reza Shah to collaborate.[52] External opposition groups that manage to gain influence may also be able to launch coups. The Communist Party of Czechoslovakia, for example, acquired control over the army, police, and key ministries after performing well in the 1946 elections. When it began losing support in 1948, Moscow urged the party to orchestrate a takeover by purging noncommunists from the security forces and ministries under its control. When noncommunist government ministers resigned in protest, the party staged demonstrations. Fearing the Soviets would use the unrest as a pretext for intervention, the noncommunist president, Edvard Beneš, ceded to the communists' demands, allowing for their complete takeover.[53]

In some instances, foreign powers may accomplish regime change simply by convincing the target state's military not to fight. In 1909, for example, the United States supported Nicaraguan rebels in their attempt to overthrow the populist president José Santos Zelaya. When the rebels proved unable to defeat the Nicaraguan army, the United States stationed marines between the two sides, supposedly as a neutral force to protect Americans. The US commander then forbade the Nicaraguan army from firing in the direction of the rebels. The Nicaraguan army stood by, helpless, as the United States continued supplying the rebels with weapons and funds.[54] Once Zelaya realized a military victory was impossible, he offered to step down.

Over the long term, opposition groups with either popular support or military capabilities may also require less foreign aid to survive if they do attain power. When the opposition has a large following, the population is less likely to question its right to rule, which may spare the foreign power from having to help prop it up. This is often the case when foreign powers reinstall popularly supported governments, much as the Allies did in Nazi-occupied countries following World War II. Alternatively, when opposition groups lack a large following but possess significant military capabilities, they often use those capabilities to eliminate their opponents. In Chile, for example, the United States helped facilitate a military coup in 1973, after which the military used its monopoly on the use of force to violently suppress dissent.[55]

In choosing regime change, the foreign power must also consider whether the opposition shares its policy preferences. This requirement, however, is often easily met, as opposition groups may willingly compromise their policy positions to attain foreign assistance in securing power. As long as the opposition is at least marginally closer than the leader to the foreign power's policy preferences, the foreign power will expend fewer resources coaxing the opposition to cooperate than it would the leader. In many instances, the external opposition already shares some of the foreign power's policy preferences. But even when the external opposition is more opposed to the foreign power than the leader, or too weak to fight, the foreign power can often coerce or induce the leader's internal rivals into trading policy concessions for help in attaining power. In the next chapter, I explain in more detail when the foreign power is likely to find willing collaborators among the external and/or internal opposition. I also explain how the relative strength of these two groups affects the type of regime change the foreign power imposes.

In all, as long as a foreign power can locate strong and marginally sympathetic opposition groups, it is more likely to estimate the costs of regime change as low. That the very element causing a leader to appear susceptible to overthrow—domestic opposition—is also the very element causing the leader to resist is what tempts foreign powers to use regime change to resolve disputes with recalcitrant foreign leaders. Domestic opposition makes the leader appear more costly to coerce but also cheaper to overthrow. Leaders without opposition will not necessarily be more conciliatory. Though their domestic compliance costs are lower, their concessions will still depend on how vulnerable they are to military and economic pressure. But when compared to leaders with similar resources, domestically strong leaders will make greater concessions than their domestically vulnerable counterparts.[56] Among leaders facing domestic opposition, greater military vulnerability should also increase the likelihood of FIRC. Although states have been known to attempt regime change in their peer competitors, large disparities of military power should lower the expected costs of FIRC, making its use more likely. All told, my argument suggests the following three hypotheses:

H1a$_1$: When states' interests diverge, the stronger one side's internal or external opposition is, the greater the probability that the opposing side will pursue FIRC.

H1a$_2$: The greater the military vulnerability of one state in a dispute, the more likely it is that the stronger state will attempt regime change when the weaker state's leader faces domestic opposition.

H1b$_1$: All else equal, targeted leaders without domestic opposition will make more concessions than those with opposition.

The Effect of Major Events and Crises

Major events and crises can serve as catalysts for regime change. They can affect the timing of the foreign power's policy decision to impose regime change by prompting policymakers to reassess their policy options and change course. They can also influence how policymakers estimate the costs of using military force. A crisis involving a military confrontation with the target's forces, for example, could lower the domestic political costs of using one's own military by increasing popular or elite support for the use of force against the target. If the target appears to be the aggressor, a crisis might also lower the reputational and diplomatic costs of using force. Nevertheless, though the foreign power's expected costs of using military force may drop, this will not necessarily lead to a decision to impose regime change. In the absence of domestic opposition, a major event or crisis might prompt policymakers to use greater military force, but that force will be in pursuit of a settlement, not regime change.

The death of a US service member in Panama, which precipitated the 1989 US invasion there, illustrates the role crises can play in the decision to pursue regime change. Prior to the invasion, the Bush administration had steadily increased pressure on Noriega to democratize but had stopped short of threatening direct military force to remove him. The Defense Department and the Joint Chiefs of Staff (JCS) warned that a military confrontation might lead to another Vietnam-style quagmire.[57] The Bush administration's policy abruptly changed, however, when a US service member died after a run-in with Panamanian soldiers on December 16, 1989. The service member's death not only offered a *casus belli* but also helped convince the Defense Department and the JCS that the military costs of removing Noriega would be low compared to the cost of leaving him in power. As Colin Powell, chairman of the JCS at the time, explained to the president, "There will be a few dozen casualties if we go. . . . If we don't go, there will be a few dozen casualties over the next few weeks, and we'll still have Noriega."[58] Yet, though the service member's death influenced the timing of regime change and the manner in which it was imposed, it was not the primary cause. Had Noriega enjoyed strong domestic support, he would have been far more costly to remove and also possibly less combative. Under these circumstances, the service member's death would have been far less likely to trigger an invasion aimed at regime change.

The events and crises that give rise to regime change are often a consequence of the targeted leader's domestic political weakness. Targeted leaders, in the course of resisting the foreign power's demands, may adopt confrontational behavior that sets the stage for a crisis. Noriega, for example, had responded to US pressure by delivering fiery speeches, increasing harassment of US citizens, and declaring war on the United States.[59] His nationalist rhetoric and attempts to play upon anti-US sentiments were measures designed to boost his popularity and weaken his domestic opposition. But his posturing also heightened tensions with the United States and ultimately led to the crisis that prompted the Bush administration to invade.

Not all events or crises stem from the target's domestic political vulnerability. In some instances, exogenous events or crises elsewhere in the world can prompt policymakers to undertake regime change in the target state. For example, the failure of the US congress to ratify the second Strategic Arms Limitation Talks treaty (SALT II) in 1979 influenced the Soviet decision to invade Afghanistan by convincing Soviet leaders that détente was crumbling. The Soviet leadership concluded that there was no need to worry about how an invasion would affect relations with the United States since those relations were already deteriorating.[60] Regime change can also occur without a previous crisis or confrontation with the targeted leader. A foreign power may decide to remove a seemingly conciliatory leader because the foreign power anticipates this leader will renege on cooperation. France, for example, overturned the 1964 coup that ousted Gabonese leader Léon M'ba, despite the new government's assurances that it would maintain a pro-French policy. French President Charles de Gaulle anticipated this new government would be less accommodating than M'ba had been in satisfying French demand for uranium.[61]

In sum, when a foreign power confronts a domestically weak target, a major event or crisis can play a role in the ultimate decision to impose regime change. The event or crisis not only prompts policymakers to reassess their policy options, but it can also lower the expected costs of using military force. Events or crises may arise from the target's defiant behavior or they may be unrelated to it. Either way, although crises and events may hasten a regime-change decision, they do not cause it. That decision still depends on the targeted leader's domestic opposition and the effect that opposition has on the foreign power's expected costs of bargaining and regime change. This suggests the following hypothesis:

> $H1a_3$: When a foreign power confronts a domestically weak leader, a major event or crisis can serve as a catalyst for the decision to impose regime change.

Responses to the Threat of Regime Change

Targeted leaders may be able to anticipate when their resistance to a stronger power's demands will lead that state to use their domestic enemies against them. How they respond in these instances depends on the immediacy of the foreign power's threat to impose regime change. When the foreign power plans to use direct military force and mobilizes for an invasion, the threat of regime change is more immediate and thus more credible. A targeted leader might then offer partial or temporary compliance to defuse a crisis and forestall an attack. The target's cooperation can also increase the diplomatic and domestics costs of regime change for the more powerful state by making the target appear conciliatory and the aggression against it unwarranted.

When the stronger power plans to use indirect or covert force, however, its threats to impose regime change are more remote. The foreign power's regime-change operations may not only take longer to succeed, but they may also be less likely to succeed, because of the foreign power's reluctance to use direct force. Given this longer time horizon and lower odds of success, the targeted leader (if he or she suspects the foreign power has plans for regime change) is likely to adopt defensive measures to increase the costs of regime change and force the foreign power to negotiate. Targeted leaders, for example, may crack down on their domestic opposition to eliminate any alternative to their own rule. Other defensive measures include attempts to align with an adversary of the foreign power, as Cuba did during the Cold War, or to acquire nuclear weapons, as North Korea ultimately did.[62] These measures will not only shore up the target's defenses against

FIRC, they may also enhance its ability to resist the foreign power's coercive pressure.

The defensive policies of Albanian chief of state Enver Hoxha demonstrate how indirect or covert threats of regime change can end up exacerbating a targeted leader's defiance. Yugoslavia attempted to topple Hoxha after he refused to join a Yugoslav-dominated union in 1946. Hoxha responded by exploiting the rivalry between Stalin and Yugoslavia's Josip Broz Tito to secure Soviet protection.[63] Stalin ordered the construction of a military base in Albania and also sanctioned Hoxha's elimination of his internal rivals.[64] After Stalin's death, Hoxha came under pressure from Moscow to mend relations with Belgrade. He managed to survive subsequent Yugoslav and Soviet covert attempts to oust him by preemptively purging his opponents. By the 1960s, he was able to exploit another rivalry—this time between the Soviet Union and China—to gain Chinese assistance.[65] In all, Hoxha succeeded in making regime change infeasible for his foreign enemies. By threatening it, Belgrade and Moscow had inadvertently made Hoxha more difficult to control. Indeed, he was the only leader of a Warsaw Pact state to successfully withdraw from the treaty during the Cold War.

In short, threats to impose regime change can be self-defeating when they lack immediacy or credibility. Insincere regime-change threats, whether made to please a domestic audience or to coax the target to the bargaining table, may only encourage that target to take defensive action. Even when committed to the target's overthrow, if the foreign power relies on covert or indirect military action, the target is likely to respond by acquiring arms, aligning with a rival power, or cracking down on domestic opponents. These measures can make the targeted leader more difficult not only to overthrow, but also to coerce if they reduce the target's vulnerability to foreign military and economic pressure. In sum, my argument implies the following hypothesis:

> $H1b_2$: *A targeted leader is more likely to adopt defensive actions when the foreign power threatens regime change but does not signal the intention to use direct force.*

Additional Explanations

The theories that offer the most complete explanation for FIRC can explain not only why states would want to remove a foreign government but also

why they would bear the costs of doing so. Not all theories do. Many arguments in the literature on regime change and foreign intervention focus on
the policy objectives states seek to attain when they intervene in the domestic politics of other states. These objectives can include ideological and normative goals, security and economic interests, or domestic political gains.[66]
Such objectives may very well motivate states to take action, but they do
not explain why that action takes the form of regime change. Presumably,
states could achieve these objectives by using coercion and/or inducement
to pressure the targeted leader into making concessions. This would allow
them to avoid the costs of installing a new regime. Moreover, targeted leaders should also have reason to make concessions to deny the foreign power
reason for regime change. Actors who are ideologically committed to their
positions might set aside their beliefs and negotiate to avoid the costs of
either suffering or imposing regime change. Arguments focusing on ideological, normative, security, economic, or domestic political motivations
may tell us why states enter into disputes, but they cannot necessarily tell
us why states use regime change to resolve those disputes.

Two theoretical approaches stand out for their ability to explain why
states would eschew bargaining and pursue regime change, despite its
potentially high costs. The first suggests that actors either ignore or underestimate the costs of replacing foreign regimes. Theories along these lines
suggest that either psychological biases or bureaucratic actors and lobbyists
mislead policymakers, causing them to underestimate the costs of regime
change. The second comes from the rational choice literature, which
assumes states are rational unitary actors but face conditions that make
bargains impossible to attain. The dominant arguments in this vein stress
the problems of credible commitment and incomplete information.

PSYCHOLOGICAL-BIAS ARGUMENTS AND BUREAUCRATIC-POLITICS OR INTEREST-GROUP ARGUMENTS

Scholars in the field of international relations have developed a rich body
of research aimed at explaining why states end up in costly wars they come
to regret. Very few of these arguments focus on regime change per se, but
they can be used to explain why FIRC occurs despite its costs to both sides.
One prominent strain focuses on the psychological biases that can influence
actors' decision-making. These biases can help us understand why actors
might refuse to set aside their beliefs to negotiate with a foreign leader. In
his influential writings on misperception, Robert Jervis explains that the

desire for "cognitive consistency" can lead actors to disregard information incompatible with their preexisting beliefs.[67] Once convinced a target is hostile, policymakers may overlook evidence to the contrary and consider that nation's concessions to be insincere or unacceptable. They then pursue policies that antagonize the target and make cooperation impossible. Decision makers are especially likely to cling to their beliefs when they are already highly confident in them and face ambiguous situations in which their beliefs cannot be easily refuted.[68] Cognitive consistency can also lead actors to hold firm to policies once they have made a decision. After deciding to pursue regime change, for example, policymakers may ignore new evidence that challenges their reasoning or initial cost estimates.[69]

Psychological bias may also lead policymakers to see regime change as the only effective way to deal with an adversary. When interpreting the source of another person's actions, human beings have an inherent tendency to attribute any resistance or hostility to the personality, beliefs, or character of that person. In doing so, they tend to overlook the external conditions that could be causing that person's resistance or hostility, including their own provocations.[70] As a result, policymakers may be quick to conclude that the opposing side in a conflict is inherently problematic and that installing a friendly regime is the only effective way to neutralize the threat.[71] In short, psychological bias can cloud actors' judgments, causing those actors to dismiss other policy options and conclude that regime change is the only feasible course of action.

Another alternative explanation for why states end up in costly wars aimed at regime change focuses on the role of influential domestic political actors. Theories of international relations commonly assume that states function as rational unitary actors whose policy is set by a single decision maker. But leaders rely on the counsel of others to arrive at decisions—others who may attempt to steer policy along a course that benefits them personally. In his work on bureaucratic politics, Graham Allison notes that the advice presidents receive may reflect the bureaucratic incentives of their cabinet officials.[72] Whether attempting to justify their budgets or enhance their own influence, bureaucrats may be inclined toward solutions that give the departments they represent an advantage. The professional training of these advisers, as well as the culture of their professional organizations, can also shape how they perceive the world and the policies they recommend.[73] Military and defense officials, for example, may be more apt to see military force as effective and, thus, advocate regime change, whereas officials schooled in diplomacy may push for negotiations.

Interest groups might also convince leaders to pursue regime change. Lobbyists representing large and politically influential groups can use the threat of political punishment to pressure policymakers into pursuing regime change. When they have close personal or business ties to government officials, lobbyists may also be able to persuade policymakers to serve the lobby's interests by removing a foreign leader. Jack Snyder, for example, contends that the expansionist policies of many great powers were the result of influential interest groups looking to satisfy their own economic and political interests.[74]

Arguments based on psychological bias and arguments based on bureaucratic and/or interest-group pressure suggest the following hypotheses with respect to FIRC:

> H2: FIRC is more likely to occur between two states engaged in a dispute when psychological bias causes policymakers to view the opposing side's leader as the source of that dispute.

> H3: FIRC is more likely to occur between two states engaged in a dispute when bureaucrats or interest groups push for the removal of the opposing side's leader.

RATIONAL ACTOR ARGUMENTS

In contrast to arguments that stress misperception as a central cause of conflict, rationalist theories focus on the conditions that engender conflict by causing bargaining to fail. Because my argument incorporates the problems of incomplete information and credible commitment, I do not argue that these explanations are wrong. Rather, I argue that they are insufficient. Actors should be able to resolve information and commitment problems by using signals, coercive force, and enforcement mechanisms. What is critical to determine is when policymakers will employ these measures to attain sustainable bargains.

Arguments relying on the logic of a commitment problem are common in the literature on FIRC. These arguments assert that policymakers pursue regime change because they do not trust the target to cooperate. Reiter, for example, contends that states are more likely to pursue total war, aimed at deposing the target state's regime, when they anticipate that the current regime will renege on the wartime settlement. By replacing the target regime, the victor can ensure that the vanquished uphold the settlement.[75] Similarly, Bueno de Mesquita and coauthors argue that leaders who depend on large coalitions for political support (e.g., democratic leaders) are more likely to replace other popularly supported leaders with pliant dictators.[76] The authors explain that leaders dependent on public support are obliged to provide their supporters with public goods, such as national security. Such leaders are more likely to depose other popularly elected leaders, because these leaders are equally beholden to their domestic public, and so more likely to renege on settlements that will prove unpopular domestically. Dictators, in contrast, can be bribed into doing a foreign power's bidding. A commitment problem can also undermine the credibility of the foreign power's promises. Todd Sechser argues that targeted leaders often resist making concessions because they fear that once they give in, the foreign power will demand more.[77]

Commitment-problem arguments show that fears of cheating can make sustainable bargains difficult to achieve. However, the question of why states do not use enforcement mechanisms to resolve such fears remains unexplained. Even when targets fear their concessions will be exploited, if the stronger state's threats are sufficiently credible and punitive, the target should make those concessions to avoid a far worse outcome. My argument holds that states forego enforcement measures because they find them to be more costly than regime change. Another possibility, however, is that under certain conditions, enforcement measures are impossible. Kenneth Schultz, for example, suggests that the possibility of covert action may undermine the credibility of a commitment. He argues that when rebel groups contesting the government of one state reside in a neighboring one, the state harboring the rebels cannot credibly pledge to withdraw its support, because it can assist them covertly.[78] Buffer states wedged between two great powers may encounter a similar problem. Although the government of the buffer state could pledge neutrality to avoid antagonizing either power, the ability of each to aid the government (or its opposition) covertly undermines that pledge. As a result, each great power has incentive to intervene in the buffer state before its rival does.[79] Thus, states may abandon bargaining in favor of regime change, not because enforcement is costly, but because conditions make it impossible.

Scholars have also used the role of incomplete information to explain conflict between strong and weak states, which often ends in FIRC.

Research on asymmetric war, for example, suggests that weak states may doubt the resolve of their stronger adversaries, which prompts them to resist, leading the stronger state to resort to war. Like problems of credible commitment, problems of incomplete information do not explain why the stronger side fails to signal its resolve or increase its coercive pressure to convince the target that resistance is futile. My argument posits that states may give up on using signals and coercive force because of the relatively high costs. However, as with commitment problems, it may be that certain conditions make it impossible for states to signal their resolve. States with a history of backing down in a crisis, for example, may face greater difficulty convincing their targets to back down. Alternatively, certain regime types may be more or less effective at communicating threats. Democracies, for example, may be more likely to encounter resistance because their targets believe they are too casualty sensitive to risk war. Alternatively, dictators' threats may be less credible because they can back down on them without suffering domestic political punishment. All told, certain conditions could make regime change the only option by undermining states' abilities to make credible threats and/or promises.

In sum, rationalist explanations for FIRC suggest the following testable hypotheses:

> H4: FIRC is more likely to occur when conditions undercut the ability of one or both sides in a dispute to prove their commitment to an agreement.

> H5: FIRC is more likely to occur when conditions undercut a foreign power's ability to credibly threaten a target state in a dispute.

In Chapters 3 through 6, I test the hypotheses associated with the alternative arguments, alongside my own, with both quantitative and qualitative data.

Conclusion

In this chapter, I have argued that a targeted leader's domestic opposition can increase a foreign power's estimated costs of bargaining while decreasing its estimated costs of regime change. Targeted leaders have a strong incentive to resist or renege on settlement terms that threaten their domestic political power. The stronger the targeted leader's domestic opposition —whether composed of rivals within the regime or external groups looking to overthrow it—the more resolved the leader will be to resist or renege on the settlement. To convince these targeted leaders to acquiesce, stronger powers can signal their resolve, apply coercive pressure, and use enforcement mechanisms. The foreign power could also offer positive inducements or settle for the status quo. However, all these actions entail costs for the stronger power. Further, the more reluctant the targeted leader is to comply, the greater the costs to the stronger state of attaining a settlement will be. While the target's domestic opposition causes the foreign power's estimated costs of bargaining to rise, it can simultaneously cause the foreign power's estimated costs of regime change to fall. By partnering with the opposition, the foreign power may be able to reduce its military costs of ousting the leader. It may also lower its political and diplomatic costs by using the opposition either to legitimize the operation or to carry out a covert one. For these reasons, the costs of overthrowing domestically weak leaders can appear less than the costs of negotiating with them.

I have also argued that even when targeted leaders can anticipate the foreign power's attempts to impose regime change, they will not necessarily back down. In fact, when leaders believe the foreign power's threats are not likely to be pursued in the near future or lack credibility, they are more likely to take defensive measures to safeguard their regimes. In this context, threats to topple a regime can exacerbate the target's resistance. In the next chapter, I detail the ways in which foreign powers impose regime change. Specifically, I explain when states are likely to transform the target state's political institutions and when they will settle for merely deposing its top leaders. I also explain the consequences of these approaches and why the costs of regime change are sometimes greater than what policymakers expect.

CHAPTER 2

How States Impose Regime Change

States can pursue regime change in a variety of ways, each with its own set of costs and risks. Some strategies, aimed at remaking the target state's institutions, require considerable investment up front but may give the foreign power greater control over the long term. Other strategies, aimed at replacing the leadership, can be cheaper to effect in the short term but can leave former regime members with the power to influence policy in the target state. As a result, the foreign power might spend more to ensure the new regime's cooperation over the long term.

Understanding the various ways in which foreign powers impose regime change is important, because the strategy chosen can affect whether—and in what way—regime change succeeds. Yet almost no research addresses how states pursue regime change. Some studies focus on certain types of regime-change operations, such as covert missions or wartime campaigns.[1] These may explain why policymakers adopt particular methods, but they cannot explain the full range of methods. Others adopt a narrow definition of regime change, limiting it only to cases in which the target's political institutions, rather than just its leaders, change.[2] This approach mistakenly presumes that only institutional transformation produces policy change. Many attempts at policy change, however, rest on changing only the leader. In fact, the leader's ouster can lead to institutional change if the newly installed leader dismantles the state's political institutions. The United States, for example, helped to transform political institutions in Guatemala (1954) and Chile (1973) by facilitating coups that brought to power new heads of state willing to undo each country's democratic institutions. Rather than limit the definition of regime change, a more useful approach is to explain the conditions under which states either oust leaders or transform political institutions to obtain their policy objectives.

In this chapter, I explain how strong states choose between what I refer to as full regime change—the transformation of the target state's political institutions—and partial regime change—the removal of the target state's leader and/or top policymakers. I use the terms *partial regime change* and *full regime change* rather than more commonly used terms, such as *leader FIRC* and *institutional FIRC*, to avoid conflating how regime change is carried out with the end results. Partial regime change may lead to institutional change, either immediately or over time, or it could preserve the state's institutional structure altogether.

I argue that the choice between full and partial regime change depends on the relative strength of the external and internal opposition in the target state. When the external opposition is strong, foreign powers prefer to partner with it to effect full regime change, which tends to produce more reliable allies. When such opposition is lacking, however, the foreign power may pursue partial regime change, either by conspiring with the internal opposition to oust the leader in a coup or by directly pressuring the leader to relinquish power. I also explain why foreign powers generally prefer orchestrating coups to forcing leaders to resign and under what conditions they will seek a leader's resignation as an option of last resort.

The only instance in which a foreign power might attempt full regime change, despite the absence of a strong external opposition group, is when the target state is expected to gain or regain military power rapidly. Under these circumstances, the internal opposition is more likely to prove an unreliable ally over time. Because the leader's internal rivals often share some of the leader's policy preferences, they may revert to the former leader's policies once equipped with the military means to resist the foreign power. Rather than incur the long-term costs of ensuring compliance from such leaders, the foreign power may prefer to bear the greater short-term costs of installing the weak, but more reliable, external opposition.

Although policymakers sometimes achieve their objectives through regime change at relatively low cost, they also at times find themselves caught in quagmires with little hope of reward. In this chapter, I also address how policymakers estimate costs, why their estimates are sometimes off, and how their goals can influence their odds of success. I also explain why failed missions sometimes convince policymakers to choose a different approach to regime change rather than abandon the task altogether.

Partnering with the Opposition

For states to see regime change as worth their while, they must have some assurance that the opposition in the target state will help them achieve their foreign policy objectives. This is likely to be the case whenever the opposition—internal or external—has preferences that are at least marginally closer than the leader's preferences to those of the foreign power. Although the foreign power may still have to incentivize the opposition's compliance, the costs of doing so will be less than the costs associated with coercing the leader. Of the two types of opposition, the external opposition's preferences are typically closer to those of the foreign power. For this reason, the stronger the external opposition is militarily, the more likely the foreign power will be to use it to carry out full regime change. In the sections that follow, I detail why the external opposition tends to share the foreign power's preferences and explain why leaders cannot simply change their policies to convince the foreign power to abandon regime change.

Full Regime Change

When a foreign power pursues full regime change, its priority is to transform the target state's domestic political institutions. By structuring those institutions such that only certain actors can attain political power, the foreign power can ensure that only actors who share its preferences determine policy. At the same time, the foreign power can also ensure that those opposed to its preferences are denied political power, which means that only by overthrowing the political system could they reverse the foreign power's policies. Full regime change thus increases the likelihood of longer-lasting policy change.

The stronger the external opposition, the more likely it is that the foreign power will collaborate with it to bring about full regime change. External opposition groups are more likely than internal opposition groups to accommodate the foreign power's policy preferences. Unlike the internal opposition, the external opposition appeals to a different set of supporters from that on which the current leader relies for power. Because the interests of these supporters rarely overlap with those of the leader's supporters, it is unlikely the foreign power's demands would harm the interests of this group. Indeed, in some instances, the external opposition's interests may overlap entirely with those of the foreign power. The external opposition may share an ideology, ethnicity, or religion with the foreign power or adhere to similar political values. Yet, even when neither side shares an identity, the external opposition may view the foreign power as a natural ally due to its shared antipathy for the targeted leader. Because the external opposition is disadvantaged by the existing political system, it may also be able to convince its followers to compromise their policy preferences to attain the foreign power's help in overthrowing the system. Thus, the same policy changes that the current leader's supporters would reject might be embraced by the external opposition and its supporters in order to attain power.

The external opposition not only relies on different supporters from the current leader, it also often prefers very different political institutions. External opponents of an authoritarian leader, for example, often prefer more representative institutions that will ensure their power. Opponents vying with a democratic regime, in contrast, often favor more autocratic forms of government to protect their personal interests. In either case, the external opposition's desire to transform institutions enables it to accommodate the foreign power's demands in ways neither the current leader nor internal opposition can. Whereas authoritarian leaders might jeopardize their power by relenting to foreign demands for elections, an external opposition group that favors popular rule would face fewer costs when complying with such demands. Indeed, instituting these reforms may be their goal. Though Panamanian dictator Manuel Noriega could not hold free and fair elections without risking his political power, his popularly supported opposition was seeking to institute democratic rule and, therefore, could embrace such elections.

Just as it is more costly for dictators to comply with demands to liberalize than it is for their popularly supported opponents, so too is it more costly for popular rulers to accommodate foreign demands for unpopular policies.[3] King Charles Albert of Piedmont-Sardinia, who attempted to fashion himself as a popular monarch by instituting representative government, discovered the difficulty of trying to maintain domestic popularity while placating the regional hegemon. In 1848, he went to war against Austria-Hungary to win independence, but after suffering defeat on the battlefield, he accepted an armistice. In the months following the defeat, Charles Albert found himself under domestic political pressure from leftist revolutionaries agitating for a return to war. He relented to their pressure and reneged on the armistice, only to be defeated again by the Austrians. This time, he was forced to abdicate. Learning from his father's experience, his son suppressed the leftists and restored the monarchy's power.[4]

Targeted leaders cannot prevent regime change simply by persuading their supporters that placating the foreign power is an unfortunate necessity. Although the leader could submit to the foreign power's demands once assured domestic political support, the leader's supporters will only accept the need for concessions when convinced that resistance is pointless. To convince them of this, the foreign power must threaten to make resistance more costly than compliance. Threats of an invasion accompanied by war preparation measures, for example, might persuade the leader's supporters that concessions are necessary. But if the foreign power wants to avoid the various costs of those actions, it may never undertake them. Instead, it may avoid the costs of using direct force altogether by using covert or indirect measures to oust the leader. Without a visible or even verbal threat from the foreign power, the leader's supporters will continue to see capitulation as unnecessary and will punish the leader for conceding. Hence, unlike the external opposition, the leader cannot accommodate the foreign power and dissuade it from pursuing regime change without incurring political costs.

Though partnering with a targeted leader's external opposition can have its advantages, a foreign power may at times be forced to look elsewhere for help in overthrowing a leader. First, in some instances, the external opposition's policy preferences may be more opposed to those of the foreign power than to those of the current leader. Such groups may still threaten the leader, prompting the leader to resist the foreign power, but they will be of little help to the foreign power in overthrowing the leader. Second, the external opposition can also be costly to install in power. Even when external opposition groups share the foreign power's preferences, as political outsiders, they cannot engineer coups from within the political system. The only exceptions are when the leader has already tried to co-opt them by bringing them into the government or when they partner with the internal opposition, which leads the coup. More typically, the external opposition must rely on military force to overthrow the standing regime. This means that outside powers may have to fund an insurgency, support a popular rebellion, or conduct a military invasion to effect full regime change. Due to these potentially high costs, the foreign power's preference for full regime change depends on the external opposition's strength. The stronger it is, the more likely the foreign power will pursue full regime change, as long as the external opposition remains marginally more willing than the leader to comply. Otherwise, foreign powers may look for less costly ways to overthrow the targeted leader.

My argument thus far suggests the following testable hypothesis:

$H1a_4$: *When a state seeks to effect regime change in another state, it is more likely to pursue full regime change when the external opposition to the targeted leader is strong relative to the targeted leader.*

Partial Regime Change

When external opposition to the targeted leader is too weak to make full regime change feasible, the foreign power may instead settle for partial regime change—the removal of the targeted leader. Partial regime change can be carried out in one of two ways. Foreign powers can either conspire with the leader's internal opposition to remove the leader or pressure the leader directly to step down from power. I address each in turn in the next sections.

COUPS

States can pursue partial regime change by urging internal rivals of the targeted leader to undertake a coup. The leader's internal opposition is composed of political rivals who compete for power based on the established rules governing the existing political system.[5] They may work directly alongside the leader as members of a ruling coalition, party, or junta, or they may head opposition parties that compete for power in accordance with the established rules. To carry out a coup, a rival must convince both the military and at least some of the leader's supporters to abandon the leader.

Orchestrating a coup can be a relatively cheap way for a foreign power to bring about regime change. Because the internal opposition can use its power and influence within the existing political system, it may not need outside military aid to spearhead a popular revolt or insurgency, as the external opposition would.[6] The leader's internal rivals could, for example, seize power by using their bureaucratic privileges to conduct purges and

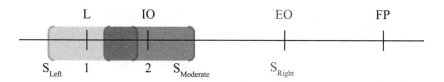

Figure 3. Policy Positions of the External Opposition, Internal Opposition,
Leader, and Foreign Power

isolate the leader. Or, they could use their proximity to the leader to kill or imprison him or her. If members of the military, they could also use their weapons to forcibly take control. All told, the internal opposition's ability to seize power from within means the foreign power can use less costly covert or indirect force to facilitate regime change.

The disadvantage to installing the leader's internal rivals in power is that they may share some of the deposed leader's policy preferences. The leader's internal rivals compete with the leader for the same set of supporters and so will tend to promote policies that will satisfy those supporters. For partial regime change to be worthwhile for the foreign power, the foreign power must convince the leader's rivals not only to overthrow the leader but also to abandon some of their traditional supporters and move closer to the foreign power's policy position. Figure 3 shows the conditions under which the foreign power may see advantage in partnering with the internal opposition. In this scenario, the external opposition (EO) is too weak to help the foreign power (FP) impose full regime change. The leader (L) maintains power by appealing to a critical number of supporters (S) whose policy preferences lie between S_{Left} and $S_{Moderate}$ (e.g., within range 1).[7] Members of the leader's internal opposition (IO) compete with the leader for power by attempting to lure some of the leader's supporters into a new coalition, for example, within range 2. Because this coalition also includes new supporters with preferences closer to the foreign power, the rival can make concessions to the foreign power that the leader would refuse (i.e., policies lying within the portion of range 2 that does not overlap with range 1).

The foreign power can often convince the leader's rivals to undertake a coup by exploiting their desire for power. Much like the external opposition, the rivals may only need the promise of material support to move against the leader. In some cases, rivals from within might already be willing to oust the leader, and they seek only the foreign power's tacit support. Generals in South Vietnam, for example, had attempted to oust President Ngo Dinh Diem several times before seeking American support in August 1963. President John F. Kennedy and his administration needed only to consent to the plot and withdraw US support for Diem to facilitate the coup against him.[8] Although a targeted leader can attempt to buy off his or her rivals by offering them greater political power or perquisites, the leader cannot compete with offers from a foreign power to help the rivals take power for themselves. As a result, the leader cannot easily preempt his or her internal rivals from conspiring with the foreign power to stage a coup.

To orchestrate a successful coup, the foreign power and the leader's rivals require the cooperation of two pivotal players. First, the target state's military must be convinced either to acquiesce to or lead the coup. Otherwise, the targeted leader could simply use the military to preempt or overturn the coup. Second, the foreign power must also convince at least some of the leader's supporters to abandon the leader. Without their support, the rival may not be able to acquire a sufficiently strong political base to seize power.

To obtain the cooperation of these two groups, the foreign power often attempts to drive a wedge between them and the leader. Although the primary interest of most leaders is to retain power, the supporters and military are more interested in retaining the goods the leader provides them.[9] The state seeking regime change can often weaken the leader's ability to provide these goods by using economic sanctions, covert political action, propaganda, and displays of force.[10] Though the military and supporters of the targeted leader might remain loyal under the status quo, if these measures damage their interests sufficiently, both parties may conclude that they are better off abandoning the leader. In some cases, the leader's supporters may not even be aware their defection will facilitate a foreign-backed coup. In Chile, for example, US President Richard Nixon tried to undermine popular support for the democratically elected president, Salvador Allende, by using sanctions to "make the economy scream."[11] Although these measures failed to secure Nixon's immediate goal—to prevent Allende's inauguration—the administration continued its economic pressure, combining it with covert political action to divide Allende's supporters and organize his opposition.[12] These efforts helped generate resentment toward his regime, which encouraged his opponents in the military to move against him.[13]

Once a critical number of the leader's supporters become willing to accept the foreign power's demands, hypothetically, the leader could reshape his or her coalition, abandoning supporters that oppose the foreign power and picking up ones who do not. The leader might then be able to appease the foreign power without suffering domestic political punishment. However, the foreign power may not accept the leader's concessions, because once it withdraws its threat, the leader could cease cooperation, reverting back to the status quo ante or, at the very least, offering incomplete compliance. The Soviet Union encountered this problem during its 1968 invasion of Czechoslovakia. Moscow had launched the invasion anticipating that it would prompt pro-Moscow Czechs to oust the reform-minded Czech leader Alexander Dubček. But when it became apparent that hardliners lacked the following to do this, the Soviets arrested Dubček and his fellow reformers, brought them to Moscow, and pressured them to accept Soviet demands for "normalization."[14] Although Dubček was returned to power and gradually began overturning the reforms, his pace was too slow for Moscow. When an anti-Soviet riot erupted six months later, Moscow insisted on regime change. It used the threat of another invasion to demand Gustav Husák be installed. Husák had been among the reformers brought to Moscow and had since adopted the view that conceding to Moscow's demands was an unfortunate necessity. Once in power, he became a loyal ally to Moscow, purging the party of its reformers and completing the process of "normalization."[15]

Convincing a member of the internal opposition to construct a new coalition closer to the foreign power's policy position, however, may not be enough to make regime change worthwhile for the foreign power. Just like the former leader, these new leaders could also face political pressure to abandon their new coalition and revert to the status quo ante. They are less likely to reverse course, however, when they transform the state's political institutions. By rewriting the rules governing access to power, new leaders can diminish the political influence of the former regime's supporters and guarantee that of their new coalition. Accordingly, they become more likely to comply with the foreign power's policy preferences over the long term because their ability to maintain power now depends on satisfying constituents who support those policies. As a result, foreign powers that use partial regime change typically choose internal rivals who can and will implement institutional change. Husák, for example, completely abandoned his reformist ideas and reinstituted authoritarian rule in Czechoslovakia. In Chile, General Augusto Pinochet established a dictatorship, brutally cracking down on Allende supporters. In Iran, Mohammad Reza Shah Pahlavi transformed Iran's political system twice. He first agreed to rule as a constitutional monarch following his father's ouster in 1941; twelve years later, he consolidated authoritarian control after the CIA coup against Prime Minister Mohammad Mosaddeq.

In some instances, internal opponents, once in power, cannot transform the political system without undermining their own political interests. When this is the case, regime change may ultimately do little to alter the target state's policies. In Panama, for example, George H. W. Bush had initially considered orchestrating a military coup against Noriega, but Colin Powell, chair of the JCS, advised against it, noting that a new military leader would likely rule much as Noriega had.[16] President Bush agreed that an invasion would be necessary to overhaul the current regime and democratize Panama. Whether the foreign power encounters a leader who is willing to transform the target state's institutions, or whose interests lie in preserving them, depends on several variables. These can include the nature of the foreign power's demands, its offer of assistance to the new leader, and the domestic political strength of groups hostile to the foreign power. These contingencies can affect the likelihood of producing a stable, reliable regime when working with the external opposition too. However, the difference remains that the leader's external opposition has a much stronger incentive to overhaul the existing political order. As a result, though the internal opposition may be easier to install, the foreign power prefers to partner with the external opposition when possible as it is more likely to accommodate the foreign power's interests.

LEADER RESIGNATIONS

Internal coups are not always feasible. Ethnic, religious, racial, or class loyalties may prevent supporters from abandoning the head of state, who can deliberately play upon societal divisions to ensure supporters and the military remain loyal.[17] Leaders may also be able to shield supporters and the military from foreign pressure.[18] Under such circumstances, foreign powers may still attempt partial regime change, but instead they may directly pressure the leader into stepping down. By coercing or inducing the head of state to resign, regime change can occur without a military confrontation.

The leader's resignation, however, can be a costly and risky option for at least three reasons. First, such deals are often unappealing to the leader. Once the leader resigns, the domestic opposition could seek retribution or the foreign power could renege on its promises of amnesty. In fact, even if domestic amnesties could be made credible, the International Criminal Court (ICC) does not guarantee they will be respected.[19] Further, resignation deals tend to be pursued when the foreign power is reluctant and the external opposition, though popularly supported, lacks sufficient military force. The leader is, therefore, in a relatively strong position and knows that the costs for resisting the deal will be low. Given the risks of conceding power, leaders have little incentive to accept such deals unless the foreign power can demonstrate that forced removal is the leader's only other option. In Haiti, for example, the George H. W. Bush and Clinton administrations tried but failed to convince the military junta to step down by using sanctions. It was not until President Clinton mobilized forces for an invasion that the junta agreed to return power to deposed president Jean-Bertrand Aristide.[20] States may, therefore, have to bear the costs of signaling their willingness to depose a targeted leader militarily before they can succeed in convincing that leader to step down.

A second reason resignation is often the foreign power's option of last resort is that it leaves the leader's coalition of supporters intact but with little incentive to accept the new regime. In contrast to an internal coup, in which at least some of the leader's supporters are first induced or coerced to accept it, the leader's resignation does not require their consent. Although the foreign power can pressure a new leader to co-opt the former one's supporters, both sides may resist cooperation. Haiti's President Aristide, for example, reneged on his promise to offer amnesty to opposition members once back in power.[21] Former leaders can also capitalize on their supporters' grievances to return to power or use them to meddle in politics back home. Liberia's Charles Taylor continued to interfere in Liberian politics after his exile to Nigeria. His meddling later led the United States to demand his extradition for trial at the ICC.[22] Finally, due to the lack of a credible foreign threat, leaders may only step down when offered a deal that effectively preserves their power. The deal the Reagan administration offered Panama's Noriega was, according to Marlin Fitzwater, Reagan's acting press secretary, like "getting the fox out of the henhouse, then giving him quarters next door." Even with these inducements, Noriega refused to step down.[23]

Finally, the leader's resignation is more likely to leave behind a new regime that is either unstable or uncooperative. Because states only tend to pursue the leader's resignation when reluctant to forcibly install the external opposition, their preference for a low-cost approach may incline them to skimp on aid that the new leader needs to consolidate power. This aid can involve more than just money; foreign troops may be necessary too. For example, the United States tried to reduce its costs of using American troops to stabilize Haiti by working with the Haitian army to maintain order, even though the army had been complicit in the coup against Aristide.[24] Without sufficient support from the foreign power, political instability may persist. Aristide's efforts to reconsolidate power divided his supporters, some of whom later joined with former members of the Haitian army to oust him in 2004.[25] Ultimately, the leader's resignation often fails to address the sources of instability in the target state that precipitated regime change in the first place.

Because leader resignation is typically an option of last resort, rarely do foreign powers successfully coax leaders to step down without a fight. When leaders do step aside, their supporters have usually already defected or rebels are poised to seize power. In these cases, regime change is primarily undertaken by domestic actors. Though the foreign power may play a supporting role in negotiating the leader's departure, these are not true instances of FIRC, because the leader would be removed regardless of the foreign power's actions. For example, although Aristide claimed the United States ousted him in 2004, armed rebels were already on the verge of removing him from power.[26]

When foreign powers are primarily responsible for the leader's resignation, their efforts tend to be aimed at helping a popular but militarily weak external-opposition group attain power. In these cases, the foreign power is often under domestic or international pressure to act but has only nonvital interests at stake and so is unwilling to bear the high military costs of directly installing the external opposition. As such, the foreign power often seeks the leader's resignation as a quick-fix, low-cost solution to the crisis. The ouster of Haiti's military junta in 1994 and Liberia's Taylor in 2003 exemplify this approach. Both were largely humanitarian efforts to remove leaders accused of human rights violations. Unfortunately, as both cases also illustrate, a leader's removal may not ensure lasting political stability.

In sum, when the external opposition lacks sufficient strength, foreign powers can pursue one of two types of partial FIRC, coups or leader resignations. Coups are more effective because some of the leader's supporters are convinced to abandon the leader and support the new regime. When the leader resigns, in contrast, those supporters may not only lack incentive to support the new regime, but they may also retain the ability to challenge it. Accordingly, instances of successful foreign-coerced leader resignation are rare. Finally, as I explain in the next section, foreign powers pursue partial regime change only when the targeted state is not expected to rapidly gain or regain military power. Otherwise, they may persist in seeking full regime change. All told, my argument suggests the following hypotheses on partial regime change:

> $H1a_5$: *When the external opposition to a targeted leader is weak and the internal opposition is strong, states seeking regime change are more likely to pursue coups in target states that are not expected to rapidly gain or regain military power.*

> $H1a_6$: *When the internal opposition to a targeted leader is weak and the popularly supported external opposition requires military assistance, states seeking regime change are more likely to pursue the leader's resignation if they lack a strategic motive to use military force.*

The Exception of Rival Powers

Foreign powers generally prefer to install the external opposition, when feasible, because it is the most effective way to minimize the influence of those who prefer the policies of the former regime. The high military costs of installing the external opposition, however, can be a deterrent. But there is an important exception. When foreign powers anticipate that the target could rapidly gain or regain power, they may prefer the high cost of installing a weak external opposition to the higher long-term costs of installing the potentially unreliable internal opposition. This is most likely to occur when the target state is either a defeated rival power or is expected to acquire nuclear weapons.

Foreign powers know that internal opposition members could revert to the previous leader's policies to win greater domestic support once in power. Although the foreign power can use positive and negative incentives to ensure their compliance, this strategy presumes the target state is weak enough that the leader might respond to such incentives. Should the target state rapidly gain or regain military power, however, the costs of incentivizing the new leader's cooperation could rise. No longer vulnerable to military pressure or in need of aid, the newly installed leader could refuse to comply and revert to the former regime's policies. In effect, internal rivals face a commitment problem. Although they may accept the foreign power's terms when their state is militarily weak, they may later renege on those promises once their state acquires greater military capabilities.

In theory, this commitment problem could be resolved. The foreign power could demand and enforce settlement terms that keep the target state weak in perpetuity. The disarmament clauses of the Treaty of Versailles, for example, were intended to incapacitate Germany militarily to ensure it would never again pose a threat.[27] Such punitive settlements, however, will be deeply unpopular in the target state. The new leadership, therefore, has an especially strong incentive to renege on them. Consequently, the foreign power may have to take active enforcement measures, such as using its own troops to carry out the terms or to monitor the target's compliance with them. France and Belgium, for example, occupied the German Ruhr region to force Germany's compliance with the reparation terms following the Treaty of Versailles.[28] In addition, as the memory of war recedes and concerns over new postwar threats arise, the foreign power's own domestic public and allies may question the need for such strict enforcement measures. This was the case in the United Kingdom after World War I, where the Labour Party championed the notion that the Treaty of Versailles was too harsh, particularly its reparation terms. Forcing Germany to pay them, critics of the treaty argued, could bring about the collapse of the German economy, endanger international trade, and imperil the United Kingdom's economic recovery.[29] Foreign powers may also encounter international criticism for punishing a weak adversary that can no longer pose a threat. Confronted with these political, diplomatic, and reputational costs, future policymakers may acquiesce to the target's attempts to alter the postwar settlement. Once they do, the target state can regain its power, as Germany ultimately did after World War I, at which point the target may become too costly to coerce.

To avoid this outcome, policymakers may choose to bear the greater expense of effecting full regime change at the outset. By installing the more reliable external opposition, they can save themselves the high costs of enforcing a punitive settlement indefinitely. Indeed, the Allies' decision to impose full regime change on Nazi Germany reflected the lessons of the post–World War I era, particularly the difficulty of enforcement. It was widely believed that failure to enforce the postwar settlement had led to Germany's revival. President Franklin D. Roosevelt was an especially firm believer that no German leader could credibly commit to upholding a settlement that kept Germany weak.[30] Thus, the only way to secure lasting peace was to transform Germany by imposing full regime change.

What made partial regime change especially unattractive to Roosevelt was that the only opposition to Adolf Hitler that stood a chance of ousting him came from within his regime. Several high-level German military officials, mainly from the Prussian aristocracy, had tried on various occasions to contact the Allies to discuss the possibility of a coup and a settlement. Roosevelt, however, steadfastly refused to deal with "these East German Junkers."[31] The Prussian elite had played a major part in making the decisions that led to World War I. Some had also initially supported the Nazi Party and advocated noncompliance with the Treaty of Versailles.[32] In that context, Roosevelt saw the anti-Nazi Germans as no better than the Nazi Party. Accordingly, he refused to recognize them, insisting instead on unconditional surrender, which would allow the Allies to impose a completely reformed regime led primarily by the relatively weak external opposition.[33] In short, when faced with a state expected to gain or regain power, strong states are more likely to pursue full regime change. The internal opposition is a less reliable partner that could become too costly to coerce later on.

My argument suggests the following testable hypothesis:

H1a$_7$: When a state seeks to effect regime change in another state, it is more likely to pursue full regime change if the targeted state is expected to gain or regain military capabilities in the near future.

Estimating the Costs of Regime Change

My argument assumes actors base their choice of strategy on estimates of relative costs. I do not assume that their estimates are correct, only that any other rational actor with complete information would arrive at a similar estimate. Of course, policymakers can, and sometimes do, miscalculate. But this does not mean that miscalculation drives regime change. Indeed, by showing that even rational actors with access to complete information may choose regime change, I argue that miscalculation is not necessary for regime change to occur. More accurate cost estimates might affect the success of an operation, but they will not necessarily prevent it from occurring. Even if leaders could perfectly predict costs, this knowledge might only affect how they bring about regime change. In this section, I discuss how policymakers estimate costs, why their estimates are sometimes wrong, and why, despite a questionable record of success, states continue to pursue regime change.

How Leaders Estimate the Costs of Regime Change

The high costs and seemingly modest benefits of recent regime-change operations in Afghanistan, Iraq, and Libya have rightly raised questions concerning the wisdom of overthrowing foreign leaders. Regime change, however, does not always fail. Although success can be defined in a number of ways, states sometimes do achieve their primary objectives when installing foreign regimes. These objectives may include installing democratic allies, as when the United States pursued regime change in Germany, Japan, and Panama, or installing a puppet that will serve the foreign power's interests, as when the United States toppled leaders in Chile, Guatemala, and Iran. Nevertheless, even when states achieve their central aims through regime change, their success is often qualified, at best. The United States, for example, may have turned Iran into an ally after the 1953 coup, but the CIA's involvement inspired anti-Americanism that came to a head twenty-six years later with the Iranian Revolution. How is it then, that despite a modest record of success, policymakers come to believe regime change is the cheapest way to attain their aims?

When policymakers choose regime change, they do so on the basis of relative costs. They do not necessarily expect that regime change will be cheap but that it will be cheaper than the alternative—namely, coercing the leader into a deal. Policymakers seeking regime change may also have direct experience with that alternative, having tried to coerce or induce their targets first. If their efforts met with resistance, they may have already concluded that coercion is costly. In contrast, because the foreign power has not yet tried overthrowing the regime, its cost estimates for deposing the leader come with a wider margin of error. The long-term costs of a regime-change operation may be especially unclear. These costs can depend on events and developments that arise during the post–regime change phase, and that can be difficult to predict. Rebel leaders, for example, may turn out to be better at fighting than governing. Likewise, tactical errors that let former regime members escape or that antagonize the population could have costly consequences down the line. Even when policymakers anticipate these developments, they may overestimate their ability to manage them.

This may lead policymakers to favor the more uncertain costs of regime change to the "known" high costs of coercion.

Policymakers consider more than just the relative costs when making their decisions; they also consider the relative odds of success. In this respect, policymakers may still be tempted to seek regime change, because coercion has a lackluster track record as well. Although some coercive measures may be more effective than others, the academic literature on coercion suggests its overall success rate is low.[34] The case of Serbian leader Slobodan Milošević illustrates the difficulties associated with coercing foreign leaders. NATO's bombing campaign against Serbia during the Bosnian War (1992–1995) ultimately succeeded in bringing about a settlement in that conflict, but it did not deter Milošević from launching another ethnic cleansing campaign in Kosovo just three years later. Milošević later backed down again, but only after another NATO bombing campaign.[35] Thus, like regime change, coercion is not necessarily doomed to fail, but the expense required to ensure its success can lead policymakers to seek out other options, such as regime change.

States, of course, could give up on both coercion and regime change and do nothing. But the costs of inaction can also convince policymakers that some kind of action is required. When Ugandan dictator Idi Amin ordered an invasion of Tanzania's Kagera Salient region, Tanzanian president Julius Nyerere concluded that inaction would only encourage Amin's aggression.[36] The same was true for Vietnam, whose 1978 invasion of Cambodia was prompted by the massacre of hundreds of Vietnamese civilians during Khmer Rouge border attacks.[37] Policymakers may, therefore, opt for regime change, not because they see it as cheap and effective, but because they have concluded that leaving the leader in power is more costly and ineffective.

Why Policymakers Sometimes Get the Costs Wrong

Although policymakers do not always underestimate regime-change costs, the historical record is full of instances in which policymakers assumed erroneously that they could install a foreign leader at little cost to themselves. Policymakers are especially likely to misjudge the costs of regime change when they rely on the targeted leader's domestic opposition for intelligence. External and internal opposition groups alike may give rosy estimates of what it will take to dislodge the leader in an effort to convince the more powerful nation to aid them. Saddam Hussein, for example, relied on the advice of exiled Iranian politicians and generals in planning Iraq's 1980 invasion of Iran. Eager to recover the livelihoods they had lost, these exiles assured him that the Ayatollah Ruhollah Khomeini's regime lacked popular support.[38] Saddam thus believed his troops would be greeted as liberators, as did the administration of George W. Bush when American troops invaded Iraq twenty-three years later.

When a foreign power bases its estimates on its own intelligence and/or experience, it is less likely to be led astray by opposition groups seeking foreign assistance. In 1861, for example, Mexican conservatives petitioned the United Kingdom, Spain, and France for assistance in establishing a monarchy, but only France took up their cause. The United Kingdom's Lord Palmerston explained that, while he believed a monarchy would be "much more stable than a Republic," he knew that the Mexican conservatives were weak.[39] When they had previously approached the British government, "it came out that they required . . . many millions sterling, and 20,000 European troops to give any chance of success."[40]

Still, policymakers may back the domestic opposition for several reasons, even if its claims of a low-cost mission lack credibility. First, when faced with time pressure, policymakers may act on the information available to them rather than take the time to cultivate reliable intelligence. For Napoleon III, the American Civil War created a unique opportunity to install a friendly government in Mexico at a time when the United States could not afford to counter a French invasion.[41] Second, if relations between the stronger state and its target have been poor for some time, the stronger state may have withdrawn its representatives, inhibiting its ability to gather intelligence. Without a reliable intelligence network, the foreign power may be forced to rely on third parties, such as the opposition, for its information.

Third, even when the foreign power retains its representatives in the target state, these individuals are likely to have close ties to the opposition if their own government has been at odds with that of the target government. As a result, the information they collect may come directly from the opposition, whether or not policymakers back home realize it. The French minister in Mexico, Alphonse Dubois de Saligny, staunchly opposed the government of Benito Juárez. He played an influential role in convincing Napoleon III that the majority, "if not almost all" Mexicans, looked forward to a European intervention.[42] Mexican representatives protested that

Dubois not only had never left the capital, and thus could not comment on opinion in the countryside, but also had hosted reactionaries in his home and was influenced by "an exceptional and eccentric minority."[43]

Another reason policymakers may underestimate the costs of regime change is that they may overestimate their ability to manage the political turmoil that led to regime change in the first place. The stability and cooperation of the new regime, much like the former one, depends on whether it can eliminate or co-opt its opposition. This opposition could come either from remnants of the former regime or from the same group that plagued the former leader. In Vietnam, for example, the Buddhist activists, whose confrontations with Diem had precipitated the 1963 coup against him, continued to agitate against the post-Diem leadership. The attempts by successive governments to deal with this powerful political force helped inspire many of the coup attempts that followed Diem's overthrow.[44]

If the foreign power fails to provide the new leadership sufficient aid to manage these threats, the leader may attempt to survive by buying off the opposition and granting it concessions contrary to the foreign power's interests. In Afghanistan, for example, former President Hamid Karzai refused to sign a long-term security agreement with the United States, released Taliban militants, and accused American forces of war crimes. It was later revealed that Karzai had been negotiating in secret with the Taliban, whose threat NATO forces had been unable to eliminate.[45] Thus, the very domestic instability that inspired the foreign power to pursue regime change in the first place can complicate its attempts to install a stable, cooperative government.[46]

The task of eliminating or co-opting the new leader's opposition may be even more difficult when the foreign power seeks to install a democracy. Not only must the new leader build political coalitions across a society that may already be deeply divided, but also democratic norms may limit the leader's ability to crack down on opposition. Potential opponents to the new regime could take advantage of the greater freedoms a democracy allows, as well as its constraints on the use of force, to organize opposition to it. Even attempts at co-opting the opposition may prove difficult. The opposition may reject these offers if it anticipates it can seize full power simply by waiting for the foreign power to withdraw. In Vietnam, post-Diem rulers avoided cracking down on the Buddhist movement as Diem had done, for fear of suffering the same fate. American policymakers ultimately grew frustrated by the restraint Vietnamese leaders showed and came to favor rulers whose methods were similar to Diem's.[47] Thus, when foreign powers seek to install democracies, their political goals may conflict with their goal for a stable government. The greater the tension between these two aims, the more likely the foreign power is to encounter unexpected costs as it tries to reconcile them.

States may also underestimate costs when imposing democracy because they tend to assume the target population will welcome their efforts. And, indeed, the population may welcome regime change in the wake of a humanitarian crisis or after years of a brutal dictator's rule. But once that dictator is gone or the crisis is over, opposition groups may begin vying for political power. Even in the relatively successful case of Panama, the heads of the new democratic government began fighting among themselves within a year of Noriega's removal.[48] Domestic groups may not be the only ones to cease cooperation once the dictator is gone or the crisis ends. The foreign power may also lose interest in making the kind of long-term investment necessary to build a viable democratic regime once domestic or international pressure to act has abated. In sum, the foreign power's actions during the course of a regime change operation can affect just how much the actual costs and success of the operation diverge from expectations.

How Past Failures Affect Future Endeavors

Although policymakers may err in their cost estimates, this does not necessarily mean that they would have avoided regime change had their estimates been more accurate. Even when the costs of regime change are high, policymakers may still regard the costs of a settlement or inaction as still higher. For this reason, previous failed attempts at regime change may simply prompt policymakers to adopt a different approach to regime change rather than to abandon it altogether. They may, for example, forsake their goal of establishing democracy and settle for a "strongman" capable of providing stability, as the United States did before withdrawing from Vietnam. Or, they may swap their military tactics for new ones. The First Anglo-Afghan War, for example, ended disastrously for the United Kingdom in 1842. But in 1878, British India's viceroy, Lord Lytton, launched another attempt to install a pliant Afghan emir, believing he could avoid the mistakes of his predecessor by using more competent military commanders.[49]

Past failures can also prompt the foreign power to shift from partial to full regime change or to change its level of force. The memory of the Vietnam War, for example, did not prevent American leaders from attempting regime change in the decades that followed. Instead, the experience in Vietnam changed how they pursued it. With the exception of Grenada, the Reagan administration looked to topple foreign governments by funding insurgents indirectly rather than directly.[50] In 1977, Vietnam abandoned its indirect regime change strategy, after failing to generate an internal uprising against Cambodia's Khmer Rouge. Instead, Hanoi adopted a direct strategy focused on an invasion. The Vietnamese foreign minister insisted that there were still at least nine battalions and twenty provincial leaders in Cambodia sympathetic to Hanoi who would assist in the invasion.[51] Simply put, although policymakers' cost estimates are sometimes wrong, more accurate ones would not necessarily cause them to forsake regime change. As long as the targeted leader appears not only resistant, but also susceptible to overthrow, FIRC will remain a constant temptation.

Conclusion

In this chapter, I have argued that whether the foreign power seeking regime change replaces the target state's institutions or leader depends on the relative strength of the external and internal opposition to the targeted leader. States seeking regime change prefer to align with strong external opposition groups because those groups are more willing to accept the foreign power's terms. When the external opposition to the targeted leader is weak, however, the foreign power may instead encourage the leader's internal rivals to launch a coup. Although foreign powers can also pressure the leader to step down, resignation is less likely to resolve the political instability in the target state. For this reason, it tends to be an option of last resort, pursued when the external opposition has popular support but requires direct military aid, which the foreign power is unwilling to provide. The only instance in which the foreign power might pursue full regime change despite a weak external opposition is when the target is expected to rapidly gain or regain military power. Because the internal opposition can be a less reliable ally, the foreign power is often reluctant to install it when the target state may recover the means to resist militarily.

Table 2 presents a summary of the hypotheses proposed by my argument and those of alternative ones. In Chapter 3, I test several of these hypotheses using quantitative data. A statistical approach allows me to test

Table 2. Hypotheses on Foreign-Imposed Regime Change

The Effects of Domestic Opposition

H1a: The Causes of FIRC
1. When states' interests diverge, the stronger one side's internal or external opposition is, the greater the probability that the opposing side will pursue FIRC.
2. The greater the military vulnerability of one state in a dispute, the more likely it is that the stronger state will attempt regime change when the weaker state's leader faces domestic opposition.
3. When a foreign power confronts a domestically weak leader, a major event or crisis can serve as a catalyst for the decision to impose regime change.
4. When a state seeks to effect regime change in another state, it is more likely to pursue full regime change when the external opposition to the targeted leader is strong relative to the targeted leader.
5. When the external opposition to a targeted leader is weak and the internal opposition is strong, states seeking regime change are more likely to pursue coups in target states that are not expected to rapidly gain or regain military power.
6. When the internal opposition to a targeted leader is weak and the popularly supported external opposition requires military assistance, states seeking regime change are more likely to pursue the leader's resignation if they lack a strategic motive to use military force.
7. When a state seeks to effect regime change in another state, it is more likely to pursue full regime change if the targeted state is expected to gain or regain military capabilities in the near future.

H1b: Responses to FIRC
1. All else equal, targeted leaders without domestic opposition will make more concessions than those with opposition.
2. A targeted leader is more likely to adopt defensive actions when the foreign power threatens regime change but does not signal the intention to use direct force.

Alternative Hypotheses

H2: Psychological Bias
FIRC is more likely to occur between two states engaged in a dispute when psychological bias causes policymakers to view the opposing side's leader as the source of that dispute.

H3: Bureaucratic or Interest-Group Pressure
FIRC is more likely to occur between two states engaged in a dispute when bureaucrats or interest groups push for the removal of the opposing side's leader.

H4: Credible-Commitment Problem
FIRC is more likely to occur when conditions undercut the ability of one or both sides in a dispute to prove their commitment to an agreement.

H5: Incomplete-Information Problem
FIRC is more likely to occur when conditions undercut a foreign power's ability to credibly threaten a target state in a dispute.

my argument across a large number and diverse array of cases, while controlling for the effects of alternative arguments. Statistical tests, however, have their limitations. They are less helpful in proving a causal relationship or testing hypotheses that defy quantification. Some of my argument's hypotheses are indeed difficult to test quantitatively. In particular, the hypotheses on the effects of major events or crises ($H1a_3$), the leader's response to regime change ($H1b_1$ and $H1b_2$), and the foreign power's preference for partial versus full regime change ($H1a_4$ through $H1a_7$) require a more nuanced understanding of conditions and events surrounding each case. Accordingly, I test these hypotheses in the case studies that follow Chapter 3. If my argument is valid, we should observe that domestic opposition in the target state increases the risk of FIRC. In particular, we should find that it constrains the leader's ability to make concessions to the foreign power, while at the same time making the leader more vulnerable to overthrow. Leaders without such opposition will not necessarily make concessions, particularly if they have the military means to resist making them. But their stronger base of domestic support should nevertheless cause the foreign power to prefer a settlement by making regime change too costly to pursue.

CHAPTER 3

Testing the Logic
of Foreign-Imposed Regime Change

Scholars since Plato have posited that domestic political turmoil in a state inspires other states to intervene.[1] But despite this broad consensus, the literature has yet to establish a definitive link between domestic opposition in the target state and the foreign overthrow of its government. Many statistical studies, for example, focus on the broader concept of foreign intervention, which includes cases other than regime change. In contrast, studies that focus explicitly on FIRC often exclude a number of cases that arguably qualify. One study, for example, focuses on regime change imposed after war and, therefore, excludes cases of covert and indirect FIRC.[2] Others examine a broader range of FIRC cases but neglect to consider the conditions under which regime change is not pursued.[3] Without testing nonevents, we cannot know whether the conditions argued to cause FIRC are just as likely to occur when states negotiate.

The statistical tests presented in this chapter serve three purposes. First, they help fill a gap in the literature by analyzing whether the long-hypothesized link between domestic opposition in the target state and FIRC does indeed exist. Second, they test my theory's core causal claim while controlling for other possible explanations. If my theory is empirically valid, at a minimum, we should find that variables measuring domestic opposition in the target state are substantively and statistically significant. Failure to find such a relationship would seriously challenge the theory. If the variables associated with alternative arguments have a stronger effect, this would also cast doubt on my theory's explanatory value. Finally, the tests in this chapter can also indicate whether my argument is generalizable across a broad range of cases.

The results show that the target's domestic opposition levels are positively correlated with the probability of FIRC. These results hold throughout a variety of model specifications and robustness checks. In contrast, variables representing arguments based on psychological bias, bureaucratic or interest-group pressure, credible commitment, and incomplete information are either insignificant or lose their significance when subjected to additional tests.

Statistical tests, however, have their limitations. The existence of a correlation between domestic opposition in the target state and FIRC does not imply a causal relationship. Certain types of leaders may be prone to domestic opposition, and it could be attributes of these leaders, and not their opposition, that explain their overthrow. Domestic opposition may also lead to FIRC for reasons other than those proposed by my theory. States plagued by domestic instability, for instance, may be subject to FIRC because other states fear the trajectory of their policies. The proxies I use to measure domestic opposition might also capture other effects that explain FIRC. Lastly, coding decisions can lead to the exclusion or inclusion of certain cases and, therefore, could influence the results.

These limitations can be diminished in some instances. To reduce the potential influence of coding decisions, I test my model on FIRC data compiled by other scholars, in addition to my own. I also test two proxies for domestic opposition to reduce the chance that my variable captures effects other than domestic opposition. I also run a variety of robustness checks to ameliorate such problems as omitted-variable bias and measurement error. Finally, to better test whether a causal relationship exists, I evaluate my theory's causal logic in a series of case studies in Chapters 4, 5, and 6. In all, the statistical results in this chapter constitute an important first step in identifying whether domestically unstable states are prone to FIRC.

In the sections ahead, I explain how I code the 133 cases of FIRC that appear in my data set (see Appendix 1).[4] Then, I describe the structure of the data set and the model I use to test my theory's primary prediction that domestic opposition in the target state leads to FIRC. Next, I discuss the various strengths and shortcomings of the most common approaches to measuring domestic opposition. I then explain how the two proxies I use avoid some of the pitfalls associated with these other approaches. I follow this with a discussion of the covariates in the model, including the controls used to test alternative arguments. The last section of this chapter presents my findings.

The Dependent Variable

I use a dichotomous dependent variable (RC) that is coded 1 for each year that an attempt at regime change occurred. To identify these occurrences, I drew from a variety of existing data sets on foreign intervention, imposed democratization, and FIRC.[5] I also consulted historical sources to identify cases that fit my definition.[6] In assessing the historical record, I looked for evidence that the policymakers of one state (1) chose to abandon negotiations with the leader or regime of a sovereign state, (2) implemented an explicit plan to depose that leader or regime, and (3) did not intend to annex, colonize, or otherwise permanently rule that state.[7] I explain these components of my definition of FIRC more fully in the introduction. In this section, I explain coding decisions that affect how the data appear in the data set.

In contrast to many existing FIRC data sets, my data include instances of attempted FIRC. I include such cases because the circumstances that motivate FIRC should apply whether it succeeds or fails. I code only the first year of an attempt as subsequent years are not independent events. Including them could also bias the statistical results in favor of my argument. When states attempt to overthrow foreign leaders, the aid they provide the opposition typically strengthens it further. Even when their efforts at FIRC ultimately fail, if the intervention empowers the opposition for some period of time, then coding each year of an attempt would increase the chances of finding that higher levels of opposition lead to regime change.

My definition of FIRC also requires that the state seeking regime change implement a plan of action aimed at toppling the targeted leader or regime. When it takes several years for such a plan to come to fruition, I use the first year in which the imposing state takes either covert or overt action toward removing the targeted leader. For example, I code the year in which the Allies initiated their attempt to overthrow the governments of Germany and Japan as 1943. Although hostilities preceded this year, President Roosevelt declared the goal of unconditional surrender in 1943, thereby indicating that the Allies would fight until they achieved the victory necessary to impose regime change. The action undertaken by the imposing state must be more than merely symbolic or ad hoc.[8] States, for example, frequently impose sanctions that they claim are aimed at regime change, though it is well understood that the sanctions are too mild to do more than satisfy a domestic demand for action. In examining such cases, I use evidence that sanctions were part of a larger campaign that included either overt or covert measures to topple the targeted leader.[9] The Nixon administration's sanctions on Chile, for example, were paired with covert operations explicitly designed to foment a coup against President Salvador Allende.

Although my definition excludes cases in which the foreign power annexes the target state or rules it as a colonial possession, I do include cases in which states restore the target's sovereignty but later establish formal control. In 1882, for example, the United Kingdom deposed Ahmad Urabi Pasha al-Misri, commander in chief of the Egyptian army, who had challenged the khedive, Muḥammad Tawfiq Pasha, for power. Although the period following the khedive's restoration is often referred to as a "veiled protectorate," the United Kingdom did not formalize its control until 1914.[10] Nevertheless, some cases fall short of the criteria for statehood as defined by the Correlates of War data set, which I use to construct several of the variables in the model.[11] Because these cases are dropped when running the model, I list them separately in Table 15 of Appendix 1.

Finally, 24 of the 133 cases of FIRC I identify involve more than one intervening state. I include each state that played a major role in the operation if the primary goal of that state was regime change. For example, although I include the US invasion of North Korea, I exclude the South Korean joint invasion, because the South Korean government's goal was to annex the North.[12] I enter these multilateral FIRC events separately into the data, which brings the total number of FIRC events to 148. In the case of Germany following World War II, for example, the Soviet, American, and British decisions to impose regime change are counted as separate observations. Although these events are clearly related, each state's decision to participate (or not) informs our understanding of when states pursue FIRC. To control for the nonindependence between multilateral cases, I use robust standard errors clustered on the target-state year.

The Data Structure and Model

I employ a logit model to test the probability of FIRC. The unit of analysis is the directed-dyad year, which means each observation contains a potential imposing state (Side 1) and target state (Side 2) for every year, starting in 1816.[13] This produces an enormously large data set with many dyads for which the probability of conflict is almost zero. The large number of potentially irrelevant observations poses two problems. First, large data sets can be sensitive to very minor effects, which can overstate the importance of variables that have little explanatory power. Second, because my theory explains how states reconcile conflicts of interests, it assumes a population of dyads with conflicting interests. Testing the model on data that include many dyads with almost no potential for conflict introduces inefficiency and possible bias.

I correct for these problems by limiting the scope of the data in three ways. First, I test the model using politically relevant dyads, commonly used to exclude dyads that have almost no probability of conflict. Politically relevant dyads are dyads in which Side 1 or 2 is a major power or the two states are contiguous.[14] Twelve FIRC events fall short of these criteria. To include these cases, I perform a robustness check using an expanded definition of politically relevant dyads, which includes dyads located in the same region rather than only ones that are contiguous.

Second, I test the model on interstate rivals. Given that rivals engage in repeated disputes, we know that they are likely to have conflicting interests. I use James Klein, Gary Goertz, and Paul Diehl's rivalry data set, which defines rivals as states that have had at least three or more militarized interstate disputes (MIDs) concerning the same issue(s). Rivalries are coded as ending ten to fifteen years after the last dispute.[15] The disadvantage of restricting the population of cases to rivals is that the data exclude dyads that reconcile their differences through negotiation without the use of force. These data also leave out FIRC events that involve nonrivals, such as the United States and Guatemala in 1954.[16] Lastly, to account for these cases, I use a third approach in which I limit the population to dyads that have experienced at least one MID in their shared history. These dyads should have a higher probability of conflict than merely politically relevant ones, though they do not necessarily meet the criteria to be considered interstate rivals.[17]

Measuring Domestic Political Opposition

If my theory is correct, FIRC should become more likely as the targeted leader's external or internal domestic opposition grows in power. Quantitative measures of domestic opposition can be either direct or indirect. Frequently used direct measures include counts of political-unrest events (e.g., riots, insurgencies, coups) or the number of disadvantaged sub-state groups. Direct measures are helpful because they are less likely to pick up effects other than domestic opposition. However, missing data can be a problem. In one of the most commonly used domestic unrest datasets, 75 percent of politically relevant dyads are missing.[18] High levels of "missingness" can introduce bias.[19] Likewise, data on disadvantaged sub-state groups or ethnic-religious heterogeneity is frequently only available for recent time periods. Such figures could produce misleading results if used to proxy for societal divisions further back in time.[20]

Direct measures of opposition also undercount internal and latent opposition. Leaders facing the threat of an internal coup will not necessarily encounter popular protests, insurgencies, or other forms of observable political unrest. Yet the fear of losing supporters to an internal rival could drive a leader to resist a foreign power, while the presence of internal opposition may tempt the foreign power to try regime change. Latent threats from groups that oppose the leader but are unwilling to fight under the status quo can also precipitate FIRC. Leaders may resist a foreign demand for fear of transforming this latent opposition into active opposition. At the same time, the foreign power may attempt to organize, equip, and train members of the latent opposition to carry out FIRC. By ignoring latent or internal opposition, we risk overlooking some of the conditions most likely to lead to FIRC.

Indirect measures of opposition better account for internal and latent opposition. One such approach relies on the assumption that certain regime types are less adept at managing domestic opposition and, therefore, face greater domestic threats. H. E. Goemans, for example, argues that mixed regimes, which are neither fully democratic nor autocratic, are sensitive to domestic challenges because they can rely on neither repression nor democratic institutions to manage opposition.[21] Abel Escribà-Folch and Joseph Wright take a similar approach, arguing, for example, that personalist authoritarian leaders, who exercise personal control over the political system, are more likely to be brought down by sanctions, which undercut their ability to buy off and deter domestic opponents.[22] Indirect measures, however, can be prone to measurement error. For example, one problem with using regime type as a proxy for a leader's domestic vulnerability is that this method overlooks potential differences within regime type. Older, well-established regimes may find ways to compensate for their institutional weaknesses that enable them to fend off foreign meddling. Newer regimes, in contrast, may be more prone to FIRC because they lack the experience, routines, and relationships that can help ensure their power.[23]

Another commonly used indirect measure captures this difference within regime type by using the amount of time that has passed since a major political transition to account for regime stability.[24] Political change, as Edward Mansfield and Jack Snyder argue, can set off struggles between new and old elites, making periods of change and their aftermath prone to political turmoil.[25] Regime transitions, liberal or otherwise, have also been shown to increase the risk of both civil and diversionary wars.[26] Yet, a problem with using regime transitions as a proxy for domestic opposition is that leaders may attempt to counter domestic threats, particularly latent or internal ones, by making minor institutional changes. Though the leader may succeed in the short term, these changes will not necessarily eradicate the domestic threat the leader faces. Indeed, these attempts to alter the political system could backfire and inspire greater opposition that later leads to a major transition. In short, leaders that institute minor political change may be doing so because they face significant domestic political pressure.

The proxies I use for domestic opposition have been designed to mitigate the problems of "missingness" and measurement error associated with existing approaches. The first indicator, which I term IRREG10_L, is a direct measure that counts the number of times irregular activities were used to remove a leader from power in the target state over the ten years prior to the observation. Similarly, IRREG20_L counts the number of times irregular activities were used to remove a leader over the twenty years prior to the observation. Irregular activities can include domestic protests, rebellions, political assassinations, coups, or even instances of FIRC. I use the Archigos data set to construct this variable.[27] Archigos codes instances in which leaders lose power by means other than those proscribed by "the explicit rules or established conventions" for that state.[28] States with higher levels of irregular leader changes should be prone to greater domestic instability, which means their leaders should face higher levels of domestic political opposition.

With only three missing observations, this variable is a more reliable indicator of domestic unrest than other direct measures with high levels of missing data. However, the Archigos data begins in 1875, which means that regime change operations before that year are dropped from the data when using this variable. The IRREG variables can also better account for internal and latent opposition than ones that measure unrest only in a given year. Irregular changes in leadership can create grievances that generate latent or actual opposition over time. They can also establish a precedent for seizing power by nonstandard means and, thus, prompt insiders to attempt additional illegal seizures of power. By using ten- and twenty-year time frames, this variable takes account of the political unrest that can linger after irregular leadership changes.

For my second measure of political instability, I use the Polity IV data set to construct a lagged indicator (POLCHG5_L) that measures the average amount of change in the target state's political system over the five years prior to the observation.[29] Similar to variables that focus on recent regime transition, the assumption underlying this indicator is that political change can both inspire and be inspired by domestic political opposition. Thus, the magnitude of political change, whether positive or negative, over the previous five years should correlate with the level of domestic political threat to a leader. By accounting for change that falls short of a full regime transition, this variable can pick up on more subtle forms of domestic pressure that might come from latent or internal opposition. The Polity IV data on which it is based also extend back to 1816, which means fewer instances of FIRC are dropped than when using the IRREG indicators. To be sure, both the IRREG and POLCHG5_L variables may capture effects other than domestic opposition. A positive and statistically significant correlation between these variables and FIRC, therefore, does not connote a causal relationship. However, to the extent these variables correlate with domestic opposition, they should also correlate with FIRC, if my theory's core causal claim is to be believed; failure to find such a correlation would cast doubt on my argument.

To create POLCHG5_L, I take the absolute value of the change in the state's Polity 2 score for each of the five years prior to the year of the observation and then average the result. The Polity 2 score measures democracy or autocracy on a scale from negative to positive 10, with a score of 10 signifying a full democracy.[30] I use the Polity 2 score rather than the more commonly used Polity score, because the latter codes gradual regime transitions, collapses in central authority, and foreign military occupation as missing. In contrast, the Polity 2 score prorates gradual regime transitions across the span of the transition.[31] The Polity 2 score also codes periods in which central political authority collapses to a neutral score of 0. Only instances of foreign occupation are still coded as missing.

In addition to measures of political change, deteriorating economic conditions may also have an independent effect on the level of domestic opposition in a state. Scholars commonly argue that economic crises lead to major political changes such as democratization or democratic breakdowns, as these crises can generate significant domestic political pressure.[32] If such crises increase the leader's domestic threat level, they should also increase the chance that a foreign power will pursue regime change. To measure economic performance, I use the percent change in the gross domestic product (GDP) per capita for the target state in the five years prior to the observation.[33]

Additional Covariates

My argument also suggests that FIRC should be less costly, and therefore more likely, the more vulnerable the target state is militarily ($H1a_2$). I measure the relative military capabilities of the imposing and target states by using the log of the ratio of the weaker state's military capabilities relative to the dyad's total capabilities ((Ln)MILCAP_L).[34] Nations that are geographically proximate to the foreign power should also be more vulnerable to FIRC, because short distances decrease the costs of projecting military force. I use the logged distance between the dyad's capital cities to measure proximity ((Ln)DISTANCE).[35] Target states lacking allies to protect them should also be more susceptible to regime change. I, therefore, include a variable denoting whether the targeted state has a defense pact with any other state (DEFENSE_L).[36] These variables have been lagged where appropriate to ensure the hypothesized causes precede the effect. Finally, to control for temporal dependence between observations, I include a variable that records the number of years since the targeted state suffered FIRC (Peace Years) and three cubic splines.[37]

PSYCHOLOGICAL BIAS

Arguments that suggest psychological bias causes regime change imply several testable hypotheses. First, if policymakers are inclined to see what they expect, then we might expect to find that states pursue regime change against foreign leaders with whom they have a history of contentious relations. Repeated disputes should, therefore, increase the likelihood of regime change. To test this proposition, I include a lagged indicator (MID10_L) that counts the number of militarized interstate disputes that occurred between the two countries over the previous ten years.[38] I also construct a similar variable that uses the number of hostile disputes (HostileD10_L), which involve the use of force rather than its mere threat.[39]

Second, if psychological bias causes leaders to adhere to their ideological convictions, then FIRC may be more likely between states espousing different ideologies. Policymakers may view the beliefs of a rival political ideology as a threat to the legitimacy of their own.[40] They may also be less inclined to trust foreign leaders who ascribe to a different ideology. Democratic peace theory, for example, implies that FIRC is more likely between democracies and nondemocracies, as the former wage ideological wars against the latter.[41] To test this proposition, I include a lagged indicator for each side's Polity 2 score (POL1_L and POL2_L) and an interaction of the two (POL1xPOL2_L). If democracies are less likely to target other democracies, then the interaction should be significant.

Ideologies may also differ in ways that are not captured by regime type. Authoritarian regimes, for example, could be communist or anticommunist, theocratic or secular. To better account for ideological differences, Suzanne Werner constructs an indicator for a state's "authority structure," using the rules governing the selection of the executive. Although not synonymous with ideology, these rules, she argues, should reflect societal beliefs about how power should be distributed and who can compete for it in society.[42] Werner uses the Polity II dataset, which includes variables on executive recruitment, competitiveness, and openness, and then measures the Euclidean distance between the two states on these three dimensions.[43] I use this method to construct a similar variable (AUTH_DIFF_L) based on the more recent Polity IV dataset to test whether differences in authority structures increase the likelihood of FIRC.[44]

BUREAUCRATIC ACTORS AND INTEREST GROUPS

If regime change occurs because self-interested bureaucrats push for it, then it might well be that military and defense officials are its most vocal advocates. They may view regime-change operations as opportunities to increase or protect their own budgets, prestige, and influence. If true, then we should observe that military governments or civilian ones controlled by the military are more likely to pursue regime change than governments dominated by civilians. To test this proposition, I use an indicator (MILITARY) to denote whether the intervening state's government is controlled by the military.[45]

Finally, if political pressure from interest groups drives policymakers to depose foreign governments, then regime change may be more likely when the two nations have strong economic ties. When a dispute puts those ties at risk, interest groups in the stronger state may push their government to install a more pliant leader in the targeted country, one who will protect their interests. To test this proposition, I use the logged level of trade between the two states in each direction.[46] The variable (Ln)TRADE1_2 measures trade flows from Side 1 to 2, while (Ln)TRADE2_1 measures trade flows from Side 2 to 1.[47]

RATIONAL CHOICE ARGUMENTS

Several studies of FIRC suggest that a commitment problem causes states to seek the overthrow of foreign leaders. For example, Bueno de Mesquita and coauthors argue that leaders who rely on large domestic political coalitions prefer to replace popular leaders with dictators, who are more likely to carry out a foreign power's wishes in exchange for military or economic aid. If true, we would expect to find that FIRC is more likely to be undertaken by states whose government depends on a large coalition of domestic supporters. At the same time, we should also find that such governments are more likely targets of FIRC. I use the W score variable the authors construct to test these hypotheses.[48] The W score is a proxy for the size of the domestic political coalition necessary for a leader to attain political power.[49] The greater the W score in both states, the more likely regime change should be. I include a lagged indicator for both countries' W scores (W1_L and W2_L) and an interaction of the two (W1xW2_L).[50]

Credible-commitment problems might also arise between contiguous states. As Kenneth Schultz notes, contiguous states have the ability to intervene in one another's domestic politics covertly.[51] Because covert action can be difficult to detect, enforcement mechanisms may be insufficient to establish a credible commitment. The inability to use enforcement mechanisms to solve the commitment problem may, therefore, motivate one side to impose regime change on the other. To test whether FIRC is more likely between contiguous states, I include a dichotomous variable denoting that the two states are either contiguous by land or separated by less than twenty-five miles of water (CONTIGUITY).[52]

The problem of credible commitment also suggests that buffer states are more prone to FIRC because the great powers competing over them cannot trust them to remain neutral. If so, then regime change may be more likely when the weaker nation is a neutral buffer state. I use Tanisha Fazal's data on buffer states to assess whether they are more likely to suffer FIRC.[53] Fazal also argues that regime change is a recent phenomenon and that buffer states were more likely to be annexed or dismembered before 1945; therefore, I include an interaction (BUFFERxP45) of Fazal's buffer state variable (BUFFER) and a dichotomous indicator denoting that the observation is post-1945 (POST45).[54] I also test the argument that a simple rivalry between two great powers drives them to impose regime change on states, regardless of whether they are buffers. To do so, I use a lagged indicator to record whether Side 1 is a great power vying with another great power (RIVAL_L).[55] If this hypothesis holds true, the RIVAL_L variable should be both significant and positive.

Finally, the incomplete-information problem suggests that regime change is more likely when the target doubts the credibility of the intervening state's threats. If true, states that are better at making credible threats may be more likely to negotiate because their targets are more likely to believe their threats and offer concessions at the bargaining table. The democratic peace literature suggests that democracies may be better at communicating threats because they are more transparent. Their leaders might also be less likely to bluff because they will be punished at the polls if caught.[56] If so, we might expect to observe that democracies are less likely to impose FIRC, because they can obtain their aims through bargaining more easily than nondemocracies can. Alternatively, democracies may be seen as too sensitive to the political costs of casualties to carry out their threats. If their targets habitually doubt their threats, then democracies may have little choice but to pursue regime change to accomplish their foreign policy objectives. I test these propositions with the lagged indicator measuring the intervening nation's Polity 2 score. Table 3 lists the hypotheses associated with my argument and those for the alternative explanations tested in this chapter. The variables used to operationalize concepts in each hypothesis are listed in Table 3 as well.[57] Table 4 reports the minimum, maximum, mean, and standard deviation for each variable.

Results

Table 5 presents the results.[58] Model 1 uses the POLCHG5_L variable to measure the targeted leader's domestic opposition. Models 2 and 3 use the IRREG10_L and IRREG20_L variables, respectively. These models were

Table 3. Hypotheses on Foreign-Imposed Regime Change and Associated
Independent Variables

Hypothesis	Variables
H1: Domestic Opposition	
a_1. When states' interests diverge, the stronger one side's internal or external opposition is, the greater the probability that the opposing side will pursue FIRC.	IRREG10_L IRREG 20_L POLCHG5_L ECONCHG5_L
a_2. The greater the military vulnerability of one state in a dispute, the more likely it is that the stronger state will attempt regime change when the weaker state's leader faces domestic opposition.	(Ln)MILCAP_L (Ln)DISTANCE DEFENSE_L
H2: Psychological Bias	
a. Repeated disputes increase the likelihood of FIRC.	MID10_L
b. Repeated hostile disputes increase the likelihood of FIRC.	HostileD10_L
c. FIRC is less likely between democracies.	POL1_L, POL2_L, POL1xPOL2_L
d. FIRC is less likely between states with the same authority structure.	AUTH DIFF_L
H3: Bureaucratic or Interest-Group Pressure	
a. Military governments or civilian ones controlled by the military are more likely to pursue FIRC.	MILITARY
b. FIRC is more likely between states with strong economic ties.	(Ln)TRADE1_2 (Ln)TRADE2_1
H4: Credible-Commitment Problem	
a. The pursuit of FIRC is more likely to be undertaken by leaders reliant on large domestic political coalitions and more likely to be aimed at leaders reliant on large domestic political coalitions.	W1_L, W2_L, W1xW2_L
b. The pursuit of FIRC is more likely to be undertaken against neighboring states.	CONTIGUITY
c. The pursuit of FIRC is more likely to be undertaken against buffer states after 1945.	BUFFER, POST45, BUFFERxPOST45
d. The pursuit of FIRC is more likely to be undertaken by states engaged in rivalries.	RIVAL_L
H5: Incomplete-Information Problem	
a. The pursuit of FIRC is less likely to be undertaken by a democracy.	POL1_L
b. The pursuit of FIRC is more likely to be undertaken by a democracy.	POL1_L

Table 4. Summary Statistics for Variables

Variable	Mean	Standard Deviation	Minimum	Maximum
RC	.0007026	.0264983	0	1
POLCHG5_L	.2687483	.6980159	0	8.2
IRREG10_L	.3472057	.808169	0	7
IRREG20_L	.6853809	1.278916	0	10
ECONCHG5_L	8.383069	15.69019	-75.06725	251.8064
(Ln)MILCAP_L	-1.912699	2.352587	-13.56152	.0432975
(Ln)DISTANCE	7.713537	1.17232	1.609438	9.391745
DEFENSE_L	.6578254	.4744389	0	1
MID10_L	.097084	.4502045	0	9
HostileD10_L	.2503255	.9594263	0	10
AUTH_DIFF_L	1.778897	1.601265	0	5.385165
POL1_L	1.18848	7.51851	-10	10
POL2_L	1.188591	7.5185	-10	10
MILITARY	.0658393	.2480016	0	1
CONTIGUITY	.2337108	.4231915	0	1
BUFFER	.2220997	.4156593	0	1
POST45	.6338156	.481762	0	1
RIVAL_L	.6763962	1.120422	0	5
(Ln)TRADE1_2	3.139753	2.924395	-11.56002	13.9966
(Ln)TRADE2_1	3.139748	2.924393	-11.56002	13.9966
W1_L	.5930327	.3178927	0	1
W2_L	.5930327	.3178927	0	1

tested on the politically relevant dyads. The same three models were also run on the rivalry dyads (models 4–6) and the dispute-prone dyads, which I define as dyads that have experienced at least one MID in their shared history (models 7–9). The standard errors, clustered on the target-state year, are reported in parentheses.

I use multiple diagnostics to test each model's fit. First, the log-likelihood Wald chi-square test reports that each model is statistically significant.[59] I also use David Hosmer Jr., Stanley Lemeshow, and Rodney Sturdivant's goodness-of-fit test, which shows whether a model's predicted frequency matches the observed frequency. The larger the p-value, the better the fit.[60] Model 1, which uses POLCHG5_L, has a p-value of .8426, and Model 2, which uses IRREG10_L, has a p-value of .9435; thus, both models appear to fit the data well. Finally, McFadden's R-squared, which approximates the R-squared statistic in ordinary least squares regression, allows us to compare the goodness of fit of two models.[61] A comparison of Model 1 against a similar model, without the indicators for domestic opposition

Table 5. Results of Logistic Regression, Foreign-Imposed Regime Change, Models 1–9

Variables	Politically Relevant Dyads			Rivalry Dyads			Dispute-Prone Dyads		
	Model 1	Model 2	Model 3	Model 4	Model 5	Model 6	Model 7	Model 8	Model 9
POLCHG5_L	0.485***			0.485**			0.483***		
	(0.099)			(0.155)			(0.111)		
IRREG10_L		0.323**			0.357			0.354**	
		(0.112)			(0.225)			(0.129)	
IRREG20_L			0.276**			0.380**			0.285*
			(0.100)			(0.137)			(0.116)
ECONCHG5_L	-0.052**	-0.047***	-0.049***	-0.044**	-0.042***	-0.044***	-0.059***	-0.060***	-0.063***
	(0.011)	(0.010)	(0.011)	(0.014)	(0.012)	(0.013)	(0.016)	(0.014)	(0.015)
(Ln)MILCAP_L	-0.265	-0.341	-0.324	-0.393	-0.397	-0.352	-0.471*	-0.487*	-0.485*
	(0.193)	(0.189)	(0.189)	(0.330)	(0.327)	(0.264)	(0.202)	(0.218)	(0.213)
(Ln)DISTANCE	-0.562**	-0.659**	-0.662**	-0.205	-0.218	-0.198-	0.497**	-0.568**	-0.566**
	(0.207)	(0.201)	(0.206)	(0.183)	(0.161)	(0.163)	(0.191)	(0.198)	(0.201)
DEFENSE_L	-0.290	-0.380	-0.408	0.123	-0.094	0.018	0.560	0.224	0.204
	(0.548)	(0.499)	(0.520)	(0.814)	(0.743)	(0.771)	(0.547)	(0.516)	(0.53 0)
MID10_L	0.521***	0.503***	0.500***	0.148	0.097	0.074	0.297	0.300	0.303
	(0.151)	(0.146)	(0.141)	(0.247)	(0.220)	(0.174)	(0.171)	(0.159)	(0.165)
POL1_L	0.020	0.009	0.008	-0.005	-0.044	-0.042	-0.015	-0.024	-0.024
	(0.043)	(0.041)	(0.041)	(0.058)	(0.065)	(0.061)	(0.059)	(0.059)	(0.058)
POL2_L	-0.022	-0.006	-0.002	-0.080**	-0.070*	-0.064	-0.003	0.023	0.028
	(0.026)	(0.029)	(0.028)	(0.030)	(0.036)	(0.035)	(0.031)	(0.037)	(0.037)
POL1xPOL2_L	-0.007	-0.009	-0.009	-0.007	-0.013	-0.013	-0.006	-0.007	-0.007
	(0.005)	(0.005)	(0.005)	(0.005)	(0.007)	(0.007)	(0.005)	(0.005)	(0.005)
MILITARY	1.134*	0.991	0.941	0.818	0.632	0.599	1.191	1.050	1.024
	(0.540)	(0.528)	(0.513)	(0.935)	(0.793)	(0.754)	(0.783)	(0.733)	(0.735)

Table 5 (Cont.)

Variables	Politically Relevant Dyads			Rivalry Dyads			Dispute-Prone Dyads		
	Model 1	Model 2	Model 3	Model 4	Model 5	Model 6	Model 7	Model 8	Model 9
CONTIGUITY	0.084	-0.040	-0.119	0.070	-0.203	-0.189	-0.891	-1.097	-1.180
	(0.752)	(0.725)	(0.777)	(0.723)	(0.616)	(0.590)	(0.743)	(0.727)	(0.794)
BUFFER	-1.168	-0.855	-0.791	-1.083	-0.763	-0.702	-0.720	-0.535	-0.583
	(1.287)	(1.415)	(1.325)	(1.327)	(1.144)	(1.047)	(1.293)	(1.472)	(1.396)
POST45	0.405	0.475	0.526	-2.065	-1.836	-1.696	-0.276	0.055	0.043
	(1.025)	(1.074)	(1.026)	(1.134)	(1.179)	(1.066)	(0.898)	(0.923)	(0.918)
BUFFERxP45	0.414	0.205	0.169	0.480	0.347	0.192	0.140	0.200	0.325
	(1.751)	(1.807)	(1.752)	(2.010)	(1.735)	(1.656)	(1.795)	(1.836)	(1.805)
RIVAL_L	0.467*	0.338	0.344	0.047	-0.117	-0.047	0.283	0.147	0.128
	(0.219)	(0.245)	(0.246)	(0.392)	(0.439)	(0.391)	(0.253)	(0.308)	(0.300)
Peace Years	0.237	0.112	0.117	0.248	0.115	0.168	0.282*	0.211	0.213
	(0.151)	(0.135)	(0.131)	(0.170)	(0.151)	(0.162)	(0.124)	(0.135)	(0.134)
_spline1	0.001	0.000	0.001	0.001	0.000	0.001	0.001	0.001	0.001
	(0.001)	(0.001)	(0.001)	(0.001)	(0.001)	(0.001)	(0.001)	(0.001)	(0.001)
_spline2	-0.001	-0.000	-0.000	-0.000	-0.000	-0.000	-0.000	-0.000	-0.000
	(0.000)	(0.000)	(0.000)	(0.000)	(0.000)	(0.000)	(0.000)	(0.000)	(0.000)
_spline3	0.000	0.000	0.000	0.000	-0.000	0.000	0.000	0.000	0.000
	(0.000)	(0.000)	(0.000)	(0.000)	(0.000)	(0.000)	(0.000)	(0.000)	(0.000)
Constant	-7.578***	-5.709*	-5.701*	-6.272**	-4.592*	-5.479**	-7.295***	-5.872**	-5.970**
	(2.266)	(2.327)	(2.346)	(2.205)	(1.821)	(1.779)	(2.097)	(2.130)	(1.916)
Observations	79,748	79,105	79,105	6,165	6,007	6,007	20,040	19,726	19,726

Note: Robust standard errors are in parentheses.
*** p < 0.001; ** p < 0.01; * p < 0.05.

(POLCHG5_L and ECONCHG5_L), reports a higher McFadden's R-squared for Model 1, indicating that it provides the better fit. The same holds true when Model 2 is compared against a similar model without IRREG10_L and ECONCHG5_L.

My theory's main prediction is that the probability of FIRC increases with domestic opposition in the target state. We should, therefore, observe that the POLCHG5_L and IRREG measures are significant and positive, while ECONCHG5_L should be significant and negative. The results uphold these expectations. Both the POLCHG5_L and ECONCHG5_L variables are highly significant and in the expected direction across all three populations. The IRREG10_L variable is also significant when tested on data for politically relevant dyads and dyads that have experienced at least one dispute, but not on the smaller population of interstate rivals (Model 5). The exclusion of several FIRC cases from this smaller population may be driving this result. The IRREG20_L variable, however, is significant and in the predicted direction across all three populations. These results also hold when variables measuring hostile MIDs, trade, and W scores are introduced into Model 1, as shown in Table 6. All told, the results strongly support hypothesis $H1a_1$, which indicates that higher levels of domestic opposition increase the probability of FIRC.

To better understand the substantive effects of domestic opposition, I examine how the predicted probability of FIRC changes as domestic opposition increases. Using actual cases to supply the values of the variables enables me to estimate the probability of FIRC occurring in states with similar profiles. For example, the value on the POLCHG5_L variable for Cambodia in 1978 is 2.4. This means that that Polity 2 score for Cambodia changed an average of 2.4 points between 1972 and 1977, the year before Vietnam invaded. This five-year period overlapped with the Khmer Rouge's overthrow of the Khmer Republic and the Cambodian genocide, which led to the deaths of an estimated two to three million people and a flood of refugees.[62] For a state starting off with the mean value for the POLCHG5_L variable (.269), a similar change in its Polity 2 score would increase the predicted probability of FIRC by 188 percent. The case of Cambodia in these years illustrates the effect of latent opposition. Although there was no major internal uprising, the Khmer Rouge's executions, purges, expulsions, and forced labor weakened the population, making popular resistance to Vietnam's invasion unlikely. Dissidents and defectors also fled to Vietnam and later assisted in the invasion of their homeland, primarily by providing

Table 6. Results of Logistic Regression, Foreign-Imposed Regime Change, Models 10–13

Variables	Model 10	Model 11	Model 12	Model 13
POLCHG5_L	0.538***	0.361*	0.508***	0.430***
	(0.114)	(0.151)	(0.123)	(0.084)
ECONCHG5_L	-0.048***	-0.044***	-0.053***	-0.047***
	(0.010)	(0.011)	(0.012)	(0.009)
(Ln)MILCAP_L	-0.335	-0.367	-0.408	-0.331
	(0.195)	(0.280)	(0.215)	(0.189)
(Ln)DISTANCE	-0.519*	-0.927***	-0.828***	-0.404*
	(0.218)	(0.231)	(0.198)	(0.194)
DEFENSE_L	-0.234	-0.124	0.032	-0.240
	(0.526)	(0.730)	(0.570)	(0.502)
MID10_L		0.680***	0.691***	0.522***
		(0.201)	(0.206)	(0.151)
HostileD10_L	0.390***			
	(0.086)			
AUTH_DIFF_L		0.019		
		(0.199)		
POL1_L	0.021	0.038	-0.008	
	(0.042)	(0.071)	(0.045)	
POL2_L	-0.018	-0.031	-0.033	
	(0.025)	(0.031)	(0.027)	
POL1xPOL2_L	-0.007	-0.010	-0.008	
	(0.005)	(0.009)	(0.005)	
MILITARY	1.304*	1.871*	1.688*	1.006
	(0.546)	(0.818)	(0.756)	(0.603)
CONTIGUITY	0.137	-1.683*	-1.243	0.987
	(0.726)	(0.832)	(0.898)	(0.751)
BUFFER	-1.079	-1.134	-1.616	-1.082
	(1.307)	(1.213)	(1.079)	(1.312)
POST45	0.206	-0.192	-0.398	0.270
	(0.969)	(1.121)	(1.269)	(0.933)
BUFFERxP45	-0.353	1.155	1.873	1.710
	(1.983)	(1.769)	(1.548)	(1.475)
RIVAL_L	0.435*	0.344	0.474	0.446*
	(0.218)	(0.255)	(0.271)	(0.199)
(Ln)TRADE1_2			0.189	
			(0.115)	
(Ln)TRADE2_1			-0.075	
			(0.128)	
W1_L				1.518
				(1.289)
W2_L				-0.140
				(1.468)
W1xW2_L				-2.547
				(2.131)

Table 6. (Cont.)

Variables	Model 10	Model 11	Model 12	Model 13
Peace Years	0.241	0.527*	0.416	0.124
	(0.137)	(0.209)	(0.267)	(0.107)
_spline1	0.001	0.003**	0.002	0.001
	(0.001)	(0.001)	(0.001)	(0.001)
_spline2	-0.001	-0.002**	-0.001	-0.000
	(0.000)	(0.001)	(0.001)	(0.000)
_spline3	0.000	0.000**	0.000	0.000
	(0.000)	(0.000)	(0.000)	(0.000)
Constant	-8.310***	-6.220*	-6.850**	-8.482***
	(2.397)	(2.835)	(2.486)	(1.868)
Observations	79,748	75,178	58,962	88,090

Note: Robust standard errors are in parentheses.
*** $p < 0.001$; ** $p < 0.01$; * $p < 0.05$.

a Cambodian face for the operation.[63] The IRREG10_L variable has a similarly strong substantive effect. For example, for a state like Haiti, which experienced five irregular leadership changes in the ten years before the 1994 US intervention there, the probability of FIRC increases by roughly 406 percent compared to the probability in a state experiencing the mean number of irregular leadership changes (.347).[64]

Like the other variables measuring domestic opposition, the ECONCHG5_L variable is statistically and substantively significant across all the models. Countries that experience a decrease in their GDP per capita in comparison to five years earlier are more likely to have their governments overthrown by a foreign power. Panama is emblematic of a country experiencing an economic downturn before experiencing FIRC. Panama's GDP per capita dropped by 13.7 percent in the five years before the United States overthrew Manuel Noriega.[65] For a country starting at the mean of this variable (8.382), a similar economic downturn would increase its probability of FIRC by 170 percent. Table 7 reports the percent change in the predicted probability of FIRC as the variables IRREG10_L, POLCHG5_L, and ECONCHG5_L move from their mean values to those for Haiti (1994), Panama (1989), and Cambodia (1978).[66]

The effects of statistically significant variables can also be seen by graphing the predicted probabilities over a range of values. The first two graphs in Figure 4 display the predicted probabilities, ranging from zero to two standard deviations above the mean, for the variables POLCHG5_L and

Table 7. Percent Change in the Predicted Probability
of Foreign-Imposed Regime Change

	Panama 1989	Cambodia 1978	Haiti 1994
POLCHG5_L: Model 1			
Predicted Probability at Mean (POLCHG5_L = .269)	0.00095	0.00135	0.00085
POLCHG5_L =	.6	2.4	5.6
New Predicted Probability	0.00113	0.00389	0.01417
% Change	18%	188%	1573%
IRREG10_L: Model 2			
Predicted Probability at Mean (IRREG10_L = .347)	0.00207	0.00436	0.00224
IRREG10_L =	1	2	5
New Predicted Probability	0.00271	0.00924	0.01132
% Change	31%	112%	406%
ECONCHG5_L: Model 1			
Predicted Probability at Mean (ECONCHG5_L = 8.382)	0.00042	0.00176	0.00370
ECONCHG5_L =	-13.72335	-7.70855	-22.0807
New Predicted Probability	0.00113	0.00389	0.01417
% Change	170%	121%	283%

IRREG10_L. The bottom graph shows the predicted probability of regime change as ECONCHG5_L moves from two standard deviations below the mean to two standard deviations above the mean.[67] The solid line in each graph represents the predicted probability, and the shaded regions cover the area between the upper and lower bounds of the 95 percent confidence intervals. The graphs show that as the magnitude of political change increases in the five years prior to an observation or the number of irregular leader changes increases in the ten years prior to an observation, the greater the likelihood is that the target state will experience FIRC. Similarly, the

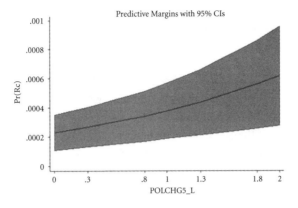

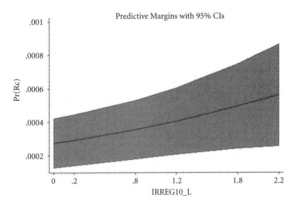

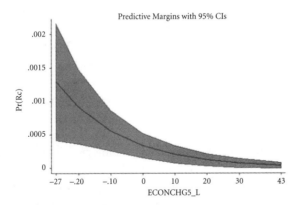

Figure 4. Predicted Probability of Foreign-Imposed Regime Change,
Domestic Opposition Variables (Models 1 and 2)

more a state's GDP per capita has decreased over the previous five years, the more likely FIRC will occur. We also know that the true effect of each of these variables is likely different from zero because the confidence intervals do not cross zero.

The variables measuring the target's vulnerability produce mixed results. Surprisingly, the target's relative military capability ((Ln)MILCAP_L) does not appear to affect the probability of FIRC. This result, however, may be a function of the population of cases on which the models are tested. Major-minor power dyads are overrepresented in the data, which could diminish the effects of the (Ln)MILCAP_L variable.[68] Although major-minor power dyads constitute only 9 percent of all dyads, they make up 81 percent of politically relevant dyads, 38 percent of rivalry dyads, and 50 percent of dyads with one MID. When tested on all dyads, the (Ln)MILCAP_L variable is significant. However, asymmetric military power may also simply be insufficient to generate FIRC on its own. As the case studies in this book show, the strong may opt to use coercion against militarily weak states when the leaders of those states lack domestic opposition.[69] What this suggests is that although targets experiencing FIRC may be militarily weak, their weakness does not make the foreign power any more likely to use FIRC than coercion.

In contrast to the relative military capabilities variable, the variable measuring the distance between the two states in the dyad ((Ln)DISTANCE) is highly significant across all models save one, the population of cases limited to rivals. The negative coefficient on this variable shows that regime change does indeed become less likely as distance grows between two states. Finally, the variable indicating whether the target state has a defense pact with any other state (DEFENSE_L) does not achieve statistical significance in any of the models. This suggests that states with defense pacts are no less likely to suffer regime change than states without them. Indeed, in some instances, the state experiencing regime change had a defense pact with the state imposing it, as Hungary and Czechoslovakia did with the Soviet Union.

Of the hypotheses associated with psychological bias arguments, only one finds qualified support. The variable indicating the number of militarized interstate disputes that the dyad has experienced over the previous ten years (MID10_L) attains statistical significance when the model is tested on politically relevant dyads and those that have experienced at least one dispute in their shared history. This suggests that policymakers may be more likely to resort to regime change when they have a contentious history

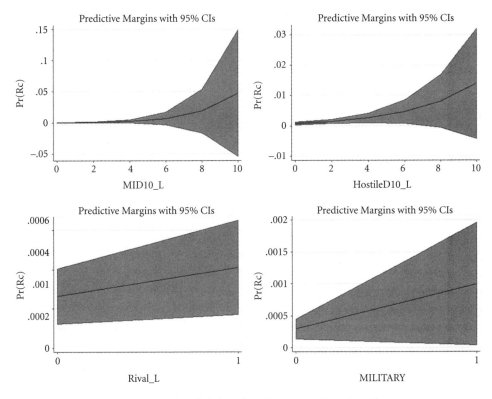

Figure 5. Predicted Probability of Foreign-Imposed Regime Change, Covariates (Models 1 and 10)

with the opposing side. However, a graph of the predicted probabilities for Model 1, as seen in Figure 5, reveals that changes in the number of disputes have little noticeable effect at lower values of the variable. The effect appears to increase after six disputes, but the lower bound of the confidence interval surrounding these higher estimates crosses zero, indicating that the number of disputes might have no effect on the probability of regime change. I also test the marginal effects of hostile disputes (HostileD10_L) in Model 10. The results are the same as those for all disputes.

The only other variables associated with an alternative argument that achieve some support are the MILITARY and RIVAL_L variables. The first of these denotes whether the intervening state is ruled by a military government, which is associated with a bureaucratic politics approach (*H3a* in Table 3). The second, which indicates whether Side 1 is engaged in a great power rivalry, is associated with a credible-commitment problem (*H4d* in Table 3). However, both variables only achieve significance in three of the nine models. Moreover, there is considerable uncertainty surrounding their effects, as the graphs in Figure 5 show. In fact, the lower bound of the confidence interval decreases slightly for the MILITARY variable, suggesting it could have a negative effect on the probability of FIRC. Finally, both variables fail some of the robustness checks discussed next. All told, the evidence for the alternative arguments, as measured by the variables used here, is weak.

Robustness Checks

To test the sensitivity of my results, I subject them to a number of robustness checks. First, the politically relevant data exclude twelve cases of regime change. These twelve cases include instances in which regional powers imposed regime change on neighboring but noncontiguous states. To test whether the results depend on the exclusion of these cases, I expand the definition of a politically relevant dyad to include states within the same region. The results, listed in Table 8, are consistent with earlier results. Another potential source of bias is the small number of FIRC events relative to nonevents. To correct for this, I run Model 1 using a rare-events logit model, which adjusts the standard errors to account for the small number of events. The results are listed under Model 15 in Table 8. They are also consistent with those found earlier.

To further test the robustness of my results, I divide the data and run the model separately on two halves of the data set. This not only tests the data on fewer observations but also allows examination of whether the model's results are driven by recent FIRC. I divide the data at 1968, the median year for politically relevant dyads. The results, displayed under Models 16 and 17 in Table 8, are similar to those for the full range of years. Even when tested on only half the data, the variables measuring the level of domestic opposition in the target state are significant and in the predicted direction. In contrast, the variables denoting the number of previous disputes (MID10_L), rivalry dyads (RIVAL_L), and joint democracies (POL1xPOL2_L) are significant only before 1969.

I also conduct tests to account for possible bias introduced by missing data or selection effects. To correct for missing data, I run Model 1 using multiple imputation. This involves the creation of multiple data sets, each

Table 8. Results of Logistic Regression, Foreign-Imposed Regime Change, Models 14–17, Robustness Checks

Variables	Model 14 Includes Regional Dyads	Model 15 Rare Events	Model 16 1968 and Before	Model 17 After 1968
POLCHG5_L	0.476***	0.491***	0.619***	0.514*
	(0.107)	(0.099)	(0.170)	(0.200)
ECONCHG5_L	-0.059***	-0.051***	-0.050**	-0.063***
	(0.014)	(0.011)	(0.018)	(0.013)
(Ln)MILCAP_L	-0.490**	-0.232	-0.129	-0.506*
	(0.160)	(0.206)	(0.268)	(0.203)
(Ln)DISTANCE	-0.543*	-0.562**	-0.788**	-0.290
	(0.217)	(0.200)	(0.251)	(0.300)
DEFENSE_L	0.229	-0.191	0.189	-0.548
	(0.566)	(0.570)	(1.095)	(0.655)
MID10_L	0.683***	0.567***	0.760***	0.335
	(0.164)	(0.143)	(0.203)	(0.200)
POL1_L	0.034	0.026	0.074	0.017
	(0.044)	(0.047)	(0.080)	(0.039)
POL2_L	-0.014	-0.019	-0.015	-0.032
	(0.024)	(0.026)	(0.051)	(0.041)
POL1xPOL2_L	-0.008	-0.008	-0.017*	-0.001
	(0.005)	(0.006)	(0.009)	(0.004)
MILITARY	1.262**	1.063	1.205	1.002
	(0.430)	(0.542)	(0.656)	(0.760)
CONTIGUITY	1.075	0.146	-0.797	1.704
	(0.747)	(0.700)	(0.784)	(1.038)
BUFFER	-1.363	-0.798	-2.594	-0.020
	(1.286)	(1.277)	(1.453)	(1.172)
POST45	-0.559	0.272		
	(0.920)	(0.998)		
BUFFERxP45	0.740	0.437		
	(1.755)	(1.741)		
RIVAL_L	0.471*	0.481*	0.462*	-0.026
	(0.203)	(0.213)	(0.219)	(0.502)
Peace Years	0.143	0.131	0.375	5.029
	(0.143)	(0.118)	(0.193)	(3.382)
_spline1	0.000	0.001	0.002*	0.014
	(0.001)	(0.001)	(0.001)	(0.010)
_spline2	-0.000	-0.000	-0.001*	-0.007
	(0.000)	(0.000)	(0.001)	(0.005)
_spline3	0.000	0.000	0.000*	0.000
	(0.000)	(0.000)	(0.000)	(0.000)
Constant	-8.427***	-6.007**	-5.289*	-60.918
	(2.157)	(2.196)	(2.415)	(33.469)
Observations	205,314	79,854	39,523	40,331

Note: Robust standard errors are in parentheses.

*** $p < 0.001$; ** $p < 0.01$; * $p < 0.05$.

of which contains imputed values for the missing observations.[70] I run the analysis using five imputed data sets. To control for selection bias, I pre-process the data using coarsened exact matching.[71] Coarsened exact matching uses categorical versions of the covariates to match the data on observable (although not unobservable) confounders and then sorts the data into a control and a treatment group. The only difference between matched pairs is the treatment effect. I define the treatment as any case in which the target state scores above the median value on the POLCHG5_L variable. I then run the model on the matched data using the independent variables from Model 1.

The results for the models using multiple imputation and matching are reported in Table 9. The variables measuring domestic opposition (POLCHG5_L and ECONCHG5_L) remain highly statistically significant across both models, as does the distance variable ((Ln)DISTANCE). The only other variable that achieves statistical significance in both models is the MID10_L variable; however, the effect of this variable remains much as it was in Figure 5, highly uncertain.

To check whether my results are sensitive to coding decisions, I rerun the models using slightly different definitions of FIRC. First, skeptics might argue that attempted regime change is not a true instance of FIRC because the target never actually experiences regime change. To test whether my results are dependent on these cases, I recode the attempted cases as non-events and rerun Model 1. The results, which appear in Table 10, show that the variables measuring domestic opposition in the target state (POLCHG5_L and ECONCHG5_L) remain strongly significant.

Second, I test Model 1 using FIRC data sets constructed by other scholars. Each of these data sets defines FIRC somewhat differently. John Owen, for example, focuses on instances of imposed domestic institutions and thus excludes instances of leadership FIRC.[72] Alexander Downes and Jonathan Monten use a definition of FIRC similar to my own but do not include attempted regime change.[73] Werner's data set focuses on regime change occurring in the aftermath of an interstate war.[74] It thus excludes cases of covert or indirect regime change. Finally, Lo and coauthors use the Archigos data set to construct data on leaders deposed by other countries.[75] Like Werner's data, the Archigos data exclude a number of cases that appear in the data sets of Owen and Downes and Monten.[76]

Table 10 reports the results for Model 1 using data by Owen and by Downes and Monten.[77] The variable POLCHG5_L remains statistically significant in each. The ECONCHG5_L variable is significant when using the

Table 9. Results of Logistic Regression, Foreign-Imposed Regime Change, Models 18–19, Robustness Checks

Variables	Model 18 Multiple Imputation	Model 19 Matching: Politically Relevant Dyads
POLCHG5_L	0.363***	0.514***
	(0.070)	(0.100)
ECONCHG5_L	-0.042***	-0.044***
	(0.006)	(0.011)
(Ln)MILCAP_L	-0.389***	-0.204
	(0.061)	(0.298)
(Ln)DISTANCE	-0.568***	-0.504*
	(0.091)	(0.251)
DEFENSE_L	-0.139	-0.392
	(0.264)	(0.538)
MID10_L	0.700***	0.518**
	(0.080)	(0.149)
POL1_L	0.026	0.050
	(0.018)	(0.048)
POL2_L	-0.063***	-0.004
	(0.018)	(0.029)
POL1xPOL2_L	-0.007**	-0.006
	(0.002)	(0.006)
MILITARY	0.100	1.187*
	(0.511)	(0.515)
CONTIGUITY	0.605*	-0.041
	(0.268)	(0.680)
BUFFER	0.124	-1.225
	(0.348)	(1.183)
POST45	-0.842*	0.364
	(0.373)	(1.581)
BUFFERxP45	0.851	-0.022
	(0.482)	(1.619)
RIVAL_L	0.392***	0.459
	(0.074)	(0.406)
Peace Years	-0.030	0.258
	(0.067)	(0.149)
_spline1	0.000	0.001
	(0.000)	(0.001)
_spline2	0.000	-0.001
	(0.000)	(0.000)
_spline3	0.000	0.000
	(0.000)	(0.000)
Constant	-4.943***	-6.917***
	(0.804)	(1.939)
Observations	345,834	79,845

Note: Robust standard errors are in parentheses.
*** $p < 0.001$; ** $p < 0.01$; * $p < 0.05$.

Table 10. Results of Logistic Regression, Foreign-Imposed Regime Change, Models 20–23, Robustness Checks

Variables	Model 20 Without Attempted FIRC	Model 21 Owen[a]	Model 22 Downes and Monten[b]	Model 23 All Other FIRC Data[c]
POLCHG5_L	0.442***	0.393**	0.523**	0.430***
	(0.133)	(0.128)	(0.161)	(0.096)
ECONCHG5_L	-0.059***	-0.037	-0.050***	-0.035*
	(0.013)	(0.020)	(0.015)	(0.017)
(Ln)MILCAP_L	-0.513*	-0.609***	-0.508*	-0.483**
	(0.224)	(0.165)	(0.256)	(0.153)
(Ln)DISTANCE	-0.686*	-0.648*	-0.379	-0.516**
	(0.288)	(0.276)	(0.279)	(0.184)
DEFENSE_L	-0.367	-0.012	-0.100	0.011
	(0.741)	(0.801)	(0.769)	(0.617)
MID10_L	0.527*	0.652***	0.593*	0.551***
	(0.257)	(0.152)	(0.284)	(0.165)
POL1_L	0.005	-0.018	0.062*	0.014
	(0.043)	(0.044)	(0.030)	(0.030)
POL2_L	0.006	-0.006	-0.016	-0.003
	(0.027)	(0.040)	(0.033)	(0.027)
POL1xPOL2_L	-0.008	-0.010*	0.002	-0.005
	(0.005)	(0.004)	(0.004)	(0.003)
MILITARY	1.229*	1.432	1.032	1.231*
	(0.611)	(0.825)	(0.818)	(0.562)
CONTIGUITY	0.121	-0.211	1.077	0.526
	(1.085)	(0.904)	(1.209)	(0.757)
BUFFER	-1.473	-12.743***	0.052	-1.119
	(1.267)	(2.002)	(1.262)	(1.244)
POST45	-0.671	-0.051	-0.344	-0.168
	(0.888)	(0.766)	(1.260)	(0.790)
BUFFERxP45		14.942***		2.377
		(2.375)		(1.467)
RIVAL_L	0.229	0.246	0.141	0.416
	(0.198)	(0.299)	(0.332)	(0.221)
Peace Years	0.401	0.095	-0.075	0.114
	(0.427)	(0.160)	(0.228)	(0.140)
_spline1	0.001	0.001	0.000	0.001
	(0.002)	(0.001)	(0.001)	(0.001)
_spline2	-0.001	-0.001	0.000	0.000
	(0.001)	(0.000)	(0.001)	(0.000)
_spline3	0.000	0.000	0.000	0.000
	(0.000)	(0.000)	(0.000)	(0.000)

Table 10. (Cont.)

Variables	Model 20 Without Attempted FIRC	Model 21 Owen[a]	Model 22 Downes and Monten[b]	Model 23 All Other FIRC Data[c]
Constant	-8.492*	-6.529*	-7.854***	-7.064***
	(4.155)	(3.253)	(2.301)	(2.101)
Observations	79,854	79,854	72,531	79,748

Note: Robust standard errors are in parentheses.
*** $p < 0.001$; ** $p < 0.01$; * $p < 0.05$.
[a]John M. Owen, "The Foreign Imposition of Domestic Institutions," *International Organization* 56, no. 2 (Spring 2002): 375–409.
[b]Alexander Downes and Jonathan Monten, "Forced to Be Free: Why Foreign-Imposed Regime Change Rarely Leads to Democratization," *International Security* 37 (2013): 90–131.
[c]Downes and Monten, "Forced to Be Free"; Nigel Lo, Barry Hashimoto, and Dan Reiter, "Ensuring Peace: Foreign-Imposed Regime Change and Postwar Peace Duration, 1914–2001," *International Organization* 62 (2008): 717–36; Owen, "The Foreign Imposition of Domestic Institutions"; Suzanne Werner, "Absolute and Limited War: The Possibility of Foreign-Imposed Regime Change," *International Interactions* 22 (1996): 67–88;

Downes and Monten data, but it just misses statistical significance with Owen's data ($p = .065$). The model does not converge when tested on data used by Werner and by Lo and coauthors, which may be a function of the small number of FIRC events in these data. To include cases unique to these two data sets, I combine them with the Owen data and Downes and Monten data.[78] The results show that the effect of the domestic opposition variables on the probability of FIRC is not a function of coding decisions. Rather, the POLCHG5_L and ECONCHG variables remain statistically significant even when using other FIRC data sets. The variables for distance ((Ln)DISTANCE) and Side 2's relative military capabilities ((Ln)MILCAP_L) are also significant in this model, as are the MID10_L and MILITARY variables. However, graphs of the predicted probabilities for these latter two variables resemble those in Figure 5, which indicate that there is still considerable uncertainty surrounding the effects of these variables.

Conclusion

The results presented in this chapter are consistent with my argument's expectation that leaders facing domestic opposition are prone to FIRC. Scholars have long hypothesized that domestic opposition in a state tempts outsiders to impose their preferred ruler, but the literature has yet to show a clear and convincing relationship. Previous work has defined regime change either too broadly or too narrowly, or has neglected nonevents. Testing the effects of domestic opposition is also difficult because latent and internal opposition, though consequential, can be difficult to observe. I use both direct and indirect measures of domestic opposition to test its association with FIRC. Not only are these variables statistically and substantively significant, but their effects hold across a range of model specifications and robustness checks. These measures also outperform variables associated with the main alternative theories used to predict FIRC—psychological bias, bureaucratic or interest-group pressure, commitment problems, and incomplete-information problems. The presence of domestic opposition in the target state does appear to be a powerful predictor of FIRC.

The results discussed in this chapter are just a first step in determining whether domestic opposition to a targeted leader drives FIRC. The next task is to explore further whether the relationship between opposition and FIRC is causal. The case studies in the next three chapters examine the decisions of policymakers to negotiate with one foreign leader and depose another under very similar conditions. In tracing the origins of these decisions, I look at how domestic opposition in the target state influenced the targeted leader's actions as well as the foreign power's estimation of the relative costs of negotiating with and deposing the leader. I also examine the evidence for alternative arguments based on psychological bias, bureaucratic or interest-group pressure, credible commitment, and incomplete information. Finally, I test additional hypotheses drawn from my argument concerning how foreign powers impose regime change and how targeted leaders respond when they learn they are at risk of being deposed.

CHAPTER 4

The Cold War

American Policy Toward Bolivia
and Guatemala, 1952–54

On August 12, 1953, President Dwight Eisenhower authorized the over-throw of the democratically elected president of Guatemala, Jacobo Árbenz.[1] Árbenz's ties to Communist leaders and his agrarian reform bill, Decree 900, had threatened the interests of the Boston-based United Fruit Company and convinced US policymakers that Guatemala was on the verge of becoming a Communist beachhead. As the Eisenhower administration was plotting against Árbenz, however, it was designing what would become the world's largest per capita aid program to prop up Bolivia's government, despite its equally progressive policies and Communist ties.[2] Why would Eisenhower plot to overthrow one communist-supported progressive gov-ernment but offer a large aid package to another?

As I show in this chapter, the key difference between these cases is the degree of domestic political opposition confronting each regime. Árbenz could not comply with US demands without weakening his own position vis-à-vis the Guatemalan elite and the army. He, therefore, maintained his policy course despite the risk of a confrontation with the United States, which ultimately used a band of elite-backed exiles and the army to over-throw him. In contrast, the political costs of conceding to American demands were much lower for Bolivia's ruling party, the Movimiento Naci-onalista Revolucionario (MNR). Bolivia's army and elite had been deci-mated by that nation's 1952 revolution, so President Víctor Paz Estenssoro could make concessions to the United States without undermining his posi-tion. The United States, meanwhile, had greater incentive to negotiate because there was no party with interests more favorable to the United States to install in power.

As a case of partial regime change, the Guatemala case also offers an opportunity to test my hypotheses relating to how major powers impose regime change. I show that when initial attempts to pursue full regime change in Guatemala failed, US officials pursued partial regime change instead, convincing Árbenz's supporters in the army to abandon him and back a coup. I also test my prediction that targeted leaders will take measures to defend themselves, rather than acquiesce, when they anticipate the stronger power will use covert or indirect force to overthrow them. Consistent with my theory, the evidence shows that Árbenz attempted to raise the costs of overthrowing him by exposing evidence of the CIA's plot and appealing to the United Nations for an observer mission, which would have complicated the CIA's efforts.

The divergent outcomes but striking parallels offered by these cases present the opportunity to examine why the same set of policymakers, faced with similar situations, chose different foreign policy tools to deal with them. These parallels allow for controls on at least six potentially confounding variables, which I outline in Table 11. The regime types and ideologies of the Guatemalan and Bolivian governments were similar. Árbenz was the first democratically elected president of Guatemala, whereas Paz Estenssoro had won the last presidential election in Bolivia before the reigning dictator nullified the results. Both the Guatemalan and Bolivian governments were also highly progressive—committed to universal suffrage, land redistribution, and the breakup of foreign-owned monopolies. More significantly, both governments frequently used anti-American rhetoric, cited Karl Marx, and worked with communist factions in enacting their reforms.

The issues at stake and locations of the two targeted states are also similar. The United States had an economic interest in supporting the United Fruit Company, which dominated the Guatemalan economy. In Bolivia, it had both an economic and strategic interest in the country's tin mines, which the MNR planned to nationalize. However, as I show in this chapter, US officials were more concerned that each government might export its reforms throughout the region than they were with protecting American business interests. Finally, in each case, Eisenhower administration officials made the final policy decisions at roughly the same time. Thus, the divergent outcomes in these cases cannot be easily explained by the

Table 11. Controls for Confounding Variables: Guatemala and Bolivia, 1954

	Guatemala	*Bolivia*
Target's Characteristics		
Regime Type	Popularly Elected President	Popularly Elected President[a]
Regime Ideology	Progressive reforms, state-controlled capitalism	Progressive reforms, state-controlled capitalism
Issues at Stake	Nationalist economic reforms, communist influence in government	Nationalist economic reforms, communist influence in government
Region	Central America	South America
Foreign Power's Characteristics		
Decision Maker	Eisenhower administration	Eisenhower administration
Time Period	Cold War, 1953–54	Cold War, 1953–54
Outcome	Partial regime change	Settlement

[a]Bolivian President, Victor Paz Estenssoro, was elected president in 1951, but the results were annulled by the government.

policy preferences of different US presidential administrations or events going on at different times in the region or world.

Despite the numerous similarities in these cases, there remain possible alternative explanations for Eisenhower's different approaches. One involves the effects of psychological bias on US intelligence assessments. Several accounts of the Guatemalan coup suggest that US policymakers grossly overestimated the degree of communist influence in the Guatemalan government. These histories imply that American officials, blinded by their own anticommunist beliefs, failed to appreciate the true nature of Árbenz's reforms. Another approach suggests that the Bolivian government was more diplomatically astute and so successfully reassured US policymakers of Bolivia's desire for cooperation in a way that the Guatemalan government did not.[3]

An argument citing the role of bureaucratic politics and/or interest groups would focus on the pervasive ties between Eisenhower administration officials and the United Fruit Company. United Fruit was heavily invested in Guatemala, but there was no similar concentration of American assets in Bolivia. Americans held less than 30 percent of shares in the largest of Bolivia's tin-mining companies. US reliance on Bolivian tin had also decreased considerably in recent years.[4] In this chapter, I test whether either the psychological biases of the decision makers or their ties to United Fruit explain the decision to pursue regime change only in Guatemala.

I also examine alternative explanations drawn from the two dominant rational choice theories. An incomplete-information problem would suggest that Bolivian officials made concessions because they believed resisting would be costly, whereas the Guatemalan government did not. A credible-commitment approach, in contrast, would indicate that bargaining succeeded in the Bolivia case because US policymakers found the government's promises to cooperate credible. In the Guatemalan case, they did not. I test both arguments in this chapter as well.

My research is based on both secondary and primary source materials, which include memos and dispatches from the US embassies, as well as State Department and CIA reports. For the Guatemalan case, I rely on the CIA's own published account, which includes CIA memos and reports. I also use government documents published by the Department of State as part of its series titled Foreign Relations of the United States (FRUS), 1952–1954—specifically the retrospective volume on Guatemala.[5] For Bolivia, I draw from unpublished State Department reports and embassy dispatches housed at the National Archives and Records Administration (NARA) in College Park, Maryland, and documents in FRUS, 1952–1954, volume four, *The American Republics*.[6]

In each of the case studies, I lay out the demands American officials made of the two nations and how each targeted leader's domestic political position affected his ability to accommodate US pressure. I then show how each leader's domestic costs of compliance influenced the costs to the United States of achieving a settlement. I also explain why the Guatemalan government was viewed as cheaper to overthrow than to coerce, when the Bolivian government was not. Finally, I explore why the United States pursued partial rather than full regime change in Guatemala and discuss how Árbenz responded when informed of the plot against him.

Guatemala, 1954: Partial Regime Change

On June 17, 1952, Guatemala's congress passed Decree 900, a landmark agrarian reform bill developed and promoted by the reformist Guatemalan president, Jacobo Árbenz. The measure was designed to transfer large uncultivated estates, many owned by United Fruit, to peasants and rural laborers. Árbenz viewed land redistribution as vital to the development of a capitalist economy. From the perspective of the United States, however, Decree 900 threatened to increase communist influence in the Guatemalan government and expand executive power, allowing Árbenz to prevent other branches of government from blocking his policies.

American Demands in Guatemala

The US White House knew that Guatemala was desperately in need of land reform. The International Bank for Reconstruction and Development (IBRD), the predecessor to the World Bank, had conducted a study that concluded agrarian reform was necessary for the development of a capitalist economy.[7] As far as US policymakers were concerned, the problem with Decree 900 was not agrarian reform, per se, but how land would be redistributed and what the political consequences would be. In this respect, the United States deemed Decree 900 a security concern. It threatened to upset the traditional balance of economic and political power within Guatemala, giving communists a political advantage. In addition, Decree 900 was designed to liberate the peasants, a majority of the population, who had long suffered under highly repressive land and labor laws that kept them poor, illiterate, and politically inactive. Their political awakening promised to have a dramatic effect in a country where roughly 2.2 percent of the population owned 70 percent of the land.[8]

The land-reform law was explicitly designed to encourage peasant and rural workers to organize politically.[9] The head of the Guatemalan communist party (the Partido Guatemalteco del Trabajo, or PGT), José Manuel Fortuny, had worked closely with Árbenz and other communists in drafting the measure. Fortuny explained later that the PGT had "proposed the creation of peasant committees . . . in order to lay the groundwork for the eventual radicalization of the peasantry."[10] Local agrarian councils would consider expropriation claims that would then be passed to regional-level councils, which were dominated by local peasant unions and workers' syndicates. The law also gave unions and President Árbenz a great deal of influence. Appeals went to the president or a national council in which the national labor unions held considerable sway.[11] A US National Intelligence Estimate concluded in May 1953 that "the net internal political effect of Agrarian Reform will probably be to strengthen the Árbenz administration."[12]

From the view of the White House, the creation of a new peasant-based majority political class would give the PGT greater political influence. The PGT had only five hundred members, and although no known communists held top cabinet positions, several, including Fortuny, did have close ties to the president.[13] A National Intelligence Estimate published in March 1952 noted that communists "already exercise in Guatemala a political influence far out of proportion to their small numerical strength."[14] Árbenz had worked almost exclusively with them in drafting Decree 900. They also played a key role in its realization. As a State Department report warned, "Communists and their sympathizers have infiltrated the National Agrarian Department so extensively that they exert an important voice in both policy making and in the implementation of the law."[15] US policymakers feared it was only a matter of time before the law helped Guatemalan communists cement their political control.

Land reform also had the potential to affect regional stability. Most of Guatemala's neighbors were ruled by authoritarian regimes friendly to the West. They were equally in need of land reform.[16] Successful reform in Guatemala threatened to set off social and political upheaval throughout the region.[17] Moreover, US officials feared that Guatemala could become a haven for communist exiles attempting to undermine neighboring regimes.[18] Finally, the rise of a communist-dominated state in Central America might give the Soviet Union an opportunity to meddle in the region.[19]

In short, both the Truman and Eisenhower administrations saw Guatemala's government as the potential source of a contagion that could infect the entire region. The United States' primary goal was, therefore, to eliminate communist influence in the Guatemalan government and replace Decree 900 with a more limited reform program that was less detrimental to US interests and less advantageous to the communists.[20] As the regional hegemon, the United States had the military capability to coerce Árbenz by making resistance costly for him. Árbenz had no Soviet aid with which to defend himself. Nevertheless, he pushed ahead with his reforms, despite the risk of a confrontation with the United States.

The Costs of Compliance Versus Resistance for Árbenz

Complying with US demands to eliminate communist influence and overturn Decree 900 would have entailed hefty political costs for Árbenz.

Acceptance of either demand would have preserved the economic and political influence of Guatemala's traditional power brokers—the elite and the army. The elite comprised Árbenz's external opposition; they preferred a return to the prerevolutionary era when Guatemalan dictators protected their interests. The army was a potential source of internal opposition. Although mostly loyal to the president, the Guatemalan army was more interested in protecting its monopoly on the use of force than in land reform. The only member of Árbenz's domestic political coalition that shared his agenda was the PGT. For Árbenz, land reform was the only way to preserve the gains of the 1944 revolution, given that it would liberate the peasants, who had a direct interest in preventing a return to authoritarian rule. Had Árbenz cracked down on the communists to appease the United States, he would have alienated the only group willing to help him guarantee that Guatemala's revolution was not overturned.

Guatemala's upper class opposed not only land reform but also the very goals of the 1944 revolution. They favored a return to authoritarian rule and denounced even the more modest reforms of Juan José Arévalo, Árbenz's predecessor. Arévalo had never significantly challenged the elite's economic interests, yet he faced thirty coup attempts during his tenure.[21] The elite-backed opposition, however, lacked a significant following. Though it possessed significant economic power, its military power was weak. Few members of the upper class were actually willing to fight, and those who were willing competed with one another for leadership of the movement.[22] By the time Árbenz assumed the presidency, the elite-backed opposition was losing morale. Although Decree 900 reinvigorated the elite's fears, the opposition lacked the following to pose a major threat to Árbenz.

Árbenz's biggest potential peril came from the army. During Arévalo's administration, Francisco Javier Arana, the chief of the armed forces, had vied with Árbenz, then defense minister, for control of the army. Arana attempted to seize power in 1949 but died in the attempt; his supporters were purged soon after.[23] By the time Árbenz, a former colonel, had come to power, he had won the army's full support. Nevertheless, the Guatemalan army remained staunchly anticommunist. It was also wary of land reform, because Decree 900 threatened to undermine what remained of the military's influence in rural areas. By the time the law had been enacted, the army and labor unions were in full competition for control of the countryside. Military commissioners and police commanders were initiating attacks on peasant activists and blocking land expropriations.[24]

Despite the challenge that Decree 900 posed to the army's interests in the countryside, the military was still willing to support Árbenz, but it was not willing to accept any challenge to its monopoly on the use of force. For example, when it had armed students and workers during the 1944 revolution, and again during a revolt following Arana's death, it pressured civilian leaders to ensure that its arms were returned.[25] Árbenz was fully aware that he required the army's support to retain power. He had warned his supporters that "the army may tire when we least suspect it."[26] So to cultivate its backing, he plied officers with gifts and privileges that included expensive housing and access to easy credit. He also removed generals whose competence and leadership skills made them a threat and replaced them with loyalists.[27] But when rumors later circulated that Árbenz intended to create peasant and worker militias—rumors that turned out to be true—several officers began questioning their support for the president.

Árbenz's supporters within the revolutionary parties also had little interest in land reform. The revolutionary parties were dominated by the Ladino middle class, which had helped lead the 1944 revolution alongside students and young army officers.[28] By the time Árbenz was elected president in 1951, a divide had emerged between political radicals, such as the communists, who favored land and labor reform, and the middle class, which advocated reforms less likely to upset the status quo.[29] The existing land-tenure system ensured the dominance of the Ladino middle class over the indigenous people. Eradicating that system would undermine Ladinos' economic interests while empowering the class they feared most.[30] The Ladinos had a strong racial bias toward the indigenous population, whom they saw as liable to cause mayhem and destruction unless controlled through brute force.[31] Although the students who had helped lead the revolution were less hostile toward the indigenous population, many had since become corrupt officials.[32] Land reform threatened to curtail the power of both these groups by empowering the peasant majority.

The PGT and labor unions were the only political partners Árbenz could rely on to support land reform. The unions considered it vital because the indigenous population made up the bulk of the labor force. Their political liberation, which Decree 900 was designed to facilitate, was necessary for true labor reform. The communists saw the indigenous majority as destined to form the base of a future proletariat. They thought reform a crucial first step in building a communist state. Árbenz also relied on the communists because they were known to be honest and hardworking. As one American embassy official explained, the tragedy was that "the only people who were committed to hard work were those who were, by definition, our worst enemies."[33] Consequently, Árbenz had worked with the communists in drafting Decree 900. On May 10, 1952 he presented the land-reform bill to the legislature, which, pressured by the president and by demonstrations organized by the labor unions, reluctantly approved it five weeks later.[34]

Complying with US demands would have been politically costly for Árbenz by forcing him to cut loose the only segment of his coalition willing to help him accomplish his policy agenda. Had he been less committed to his goals, Árbenz might have preserved his power by implementing modest reforms, as Arévalo had done. Indeed, some of Árbenz's early supporters, as well as many American policymakers, had anticipated he would moderate the revolution's course.[35] It is not clear, however, that the status quo could have been sustained. With the moderates in the revolutionary parties widely regarded as corrupt and inept, Árbenz anticipated the military would tire of civilian rule and install a caudillo through an election or coup. To prevent that, he planned to transform his coalition from one dominated by the army and middle class into one populated by the peasant majority, which had an interest in advancing the revolution.[36]

Though committed to his goals, Árbenz was not an ideologue. The president was highly sympathetic to communism but also pragmatic. He knew the United States would never tolerate a communist regime in Central America.[37] In addition, as an October 1952 CIA report observed, Árbenz understood that Guatemala was dependent on US markets and capital. Still, he intended "to bluff through his defiance of US corporations." The report concluded, "Árbenz will not go that far in bluffing the US. He may, however, bluff too long for the good of his regime."[38] Árbenz did resist the relatively mild pressure applied by the Truman administration to convince him to abandon his policy course. I explain in the next section why this pressure was so mild and why US officials turned to regime change instead of ratcheting up their pressure.

The Costs to the United States of a Settlement with Árbenz

According to my argument, states will incur greater expense when attempting to coerce leaders who have a strong domestic incentive to resist their demands. The more politically costly compliance is for the targeted leader, the greater the threat the stronger power must make to induce compliance.

In this section, I show that American policymakers could not coerce Árbenz to accept the high costs of abandoning the communists without incurring high costs themselves.

The Truman administration initially used relatively mild coercive pressure to convince Árbenz to abandon his political agenda. American ambassador Rudolf Schoenfeld believed Washington simply needed to remind Guatemalans of their dependence on the United States and that, if they desired US assistance, "it behooved them to adjust their actions vis-à-vis the United States accordingly."[39] Toward this end, the Truman administration denied economic aid, pressured the IBRD to reject a much-needed loan, and imposed an arms embargo. It also successfully convinced other countries to ban arm sales to Guatemala.[40] These measures had little effect. The State Department considered imposing more extensive sanctions, but the CIA predicted that economic pressure would push Árbenz closer to the communists.[41] In particular, a coffee embargo—the most feasible of economic sanctions—had the potential to stimulate Guatemalan nationalism. It would also hurt the people most supportive of American interests— the elite owners of the coffee plantations. Due to a worldwide shortage, a coffee embargo would also inflate the price of coffee in the United States. The high price for Guatemalan coffee, meanwhile, ensured that the country could find buyers elsewhere to substitute for US demand simply by lowering its price.[42]

The infeasibility of a coffee embargo, however, did not mean that Árbenz was impervious to economic coercion. As a CIA memo noted, economic pressure might not work, but an economic *crisis* would likely force Árbenz to abandon his agenda.[43] An oil embargo had the greatest potential to precipitate such an emergency. According to Fortuny, as US pressure mounted in the months before the coup, Árbenz became greatly concerned over the potential for an American oil embargo. "The economy could not withstand it," Árbenz warned, "nor would the army."[44] Guatemala depended for its oil on three American oil companies and the British-Dutch-owned Shell. According to the general counsel for the CIA, the oil companies "were very cooperative at the time."[45] An oil embargo was thus likely to trigger the kind of crisis the State Department believed would cause Árbenz to capitulate.

What restrained the Truman, and later Eisenhower, administration from instituting an oil embargo was the diplomatic cost of violating the Good Neighbor policy. Franklin Roosevelt's administration had instituted the policy to reassure Latin American regimes that the United States was a partner rather than an overlord. As Deputy Assistant Secretary of State Robert F. Woodward explained, the policy "was so much the centerpiece of all relations with Latin America that it loomed like Mount Hood or Mount Rainier on the landscape. It was just there. You took it for granted as being something big and immovable."[46] An oil embargo would have made clear that the United States was forsaking the Good Neighbor policy, which in turn would have jeopardized hemispheric relations and stoked nationalism across the region. Although the Eisenhower administration was ready to dispense with the policy in practice, it did not want to be seen as doing so. As one US embassy official put it, there was a critical distinction "between intervention and being caught at it."[47] The United States could afford the former, but not the latter.

Domestic public opinion in the United States also made it costly to induce Árbenz's cooperation with economic aid.[48] The US press had already condemned Árbenz as a communist, making it difficult to justify sending him aid.[49] Moreover, aid might not have been enough to convince Árbenz to change course. It still would have required him to eliminate the one faction supporting his agenda, which would have empowered those opposed to it. Árbenz had little reason to make concessions as long as he believed he could pursue his policies without suffering unbearable costs. Until early fall of 1953, neither Árbenz nor his communist supporters believed the United States would topple the Guatemalan government.[50] What coercive pressure the United States had applied until then was mild. After the fall of 1953, however, US pressure would increase, not to coerce Árbenz, but to depose him.

The Costs of Full and Partial Regime Change in Guatemala

In April 1952, after attempting to coerce Árbenz for roughly a year, the Truman administration stumbled on an opportunity to pursue full regime change using Árbenz's external opposition to oust him from power. At roughly the same time that Árbenz announced Decree 900, President Truman met with Nicaraguan dictator Anastasio Somoza. During the meeting, Somoza boasted that if the United States provided him with the weapons, he could "clean up" Guatemala in no time.[51] Truman did not respond to Somoza's offer but asked the CIA to investigate. Somoza's plan centered on exiles tied to the Guatemalan elite and based in Honduras. Their leader,

Carlos Castillo Armas, was a former Guatemalan army officer, who was also backed by the Dominican Republic's Rafael Trujillo and United Fruit. Castillo Armas was planning to launch an invasion that he claimed would inspire an army uprising and popular rebellion.[52] The chief of the CIA's western hemisphere division, J. C. King, was skeptical. He concluded that without US support, the venture would fail. But he also believed the exiles would attempt an invasion with or without American backing. If the United States failed to support Castillo Armas, King warned, it would miss a window of opportunity to remove Árbenz—a window that would close once the Guatemalan army defeated the exiles, which he believed it would.[53]

Truman authorized the CIA to proceed with planning an operation that would become known as PBFortune. The State Department was initially reluctant to support the CIA's plans to ship contraband weapons to Castillo Armas and warned that if the US role were revealed, it could set back "relations with Latin American countries by fifty years."[54] After meetings with top CIA officials, however, the State Department indicated its support on September 9 and approved a shipment to the rebels.[55] By October, however, the plan had been aborted. The State Department reported that Nicaraguan and Dominican officials were asking when the "machinery" would be delivered. The State Department interpreted this as a sign that the US cover had been blown.[56] Secretary of State Dean Acheson abruptly called off the operation, putting an end to the Truman administration's attempt to remove Árbenz.

PBFortune was likely doomed from the start. The elite-dominated exile opposition had the greatest interest in overthrowing Árbenz and in accommodating US interests. It also had weapons, some training, and the financial support of wealthy Guatemalans, United Fruit, and several regional governments. Yet Castillo Armas's so-called Army of Liberation lacked the numbers to take on the five-thousand-man Guatemalan army. Moreover, the opposition was divided. Castillo Armas faced a number of rivals within the exile opposition. As long as the army was willing to fight for Árbenz, the exile opposition was going to need direct military assistance from outside the country. This, however, would reveal US involvement, making full regime change militarily and politically costly.

As the Eisenhower administration took office, events in Guatemala highlighted Árbenz's growing power, suggesting that the number of options for removing him was shrinking. Decree 900 was already increasing his popularity in the countryside. One month after Eisenhower's November

1952 election, Árbenz legalized the PGT. Then, in February, when Eisenhower was already in office, Árbenz pressured the Guatemalan congress to remove supreme court judges who had ordered an injunction against land seizures. In March, the legislature, whose members frequently used anti-American rhetoric to win popular support, held a moment of silence for Stalin.[57] Finally, after a failed coup attempt in late spring, many opposition leaders residing within Guatemala were imprisoned or forced into exile. Concerned yet again that a window of opportunity was closing, a CIA memo warned of a "deteriorating situation . . . where active opposition and resistance against the present regime is fast disappearing."[58] The situation called for action.

For Eisenhower, covert action offered a way to depose Árbenz at relatively low cost. Like its predecessor, the Eisenhower administration wanted to protect inter-American relations. As a March 1953 National Security Council policy statement warned, "historic anti-U.S. prejudices" had led to a growth in nationalism, which the communists were "exploiting" to weaken hemispheric solidarity. To reverse this trend, the United States would need to work through the Organization of American States (OAS) and "avoid the appearance of unilateral action."[59] At the same time, it could use covert action to take down Árbenz. Eisenhower saw covert operations as a way to protect US security interests without overextending the military or its budget.[60]

Still, covert action would be cheap only if the United States could work with a domestic opposition group both friendly to it and capable of seizing power. In this respect, the weakness of the external opposition posed a problem. Accordingly, the CIA recommended replacing PBFortune with a new plan, PBSuccess, under which the United States would pursue partial regime change by pressuring the army to stage a coup. As a May 1953 National Intelligence Estimate explained, "The Army is the only organized element in Guatemala capable of rapidly and decisively altering the political situation."[61]

To drive a wedge between Árbenz and the army, the officers would have to be convinced that "their personal security and well-being were threatened by Communist infiltration and domination of the Government."[62] Furthermore, they would also have to be convinced that the United States was supporting Castillo Armas and that any confrontation with the rebels would lead to a confrontation with the United States. As Richard Bissell, a CIA officer who participated in PBSuccess, explained years later, there was "a paradox at the heart of PBSuccess," which rested on concealing US involvement to the world while "convincing the Guatemalans that the US was indeed involved."[63] To accomplish this, PBSuccess called for "elaborate covert psywar, political action, sabotage and similar operations" as part of "an overt and covert 'softening-up' effort."[64] Once Árbenz's political support had been sapped, Castillo Armas would invade. The purpose of the invasion was not to precipitate a military confrontation, which Castillo Armas would surely lose, but to force the army to choose between defeating Castillo Armas, and thereby provoking the United States, or toppling Árbenz.[65]

The decision to overthrow Árbenz was made in a National Security Council meeting on August 12, 1953.[66] By October, American efforts to convince the army to abandon him were well under way. The first major move was the appointment of John Peurifoy as the American ambassador. Known for meddling in Greek politics while ambassador there, Peurifoy was deliberately chosen to send the message that the United States was preparing to take action. As the PGT's daily *Tribuna Popular* opined, "It is easy to divine why a man who has been in Greece—more as the mastermind of its struggle against the communists and Greek patriots than as an ambassador—has been sent to our country. The State Department does not need men like Peurifoy in [countries] . . . led by men who are the lap dogs of Yankee monopolies."[67] One Guatemalan colonel remarked that Peurifoy was "an abusive, arrogant ambassador . . . but this was very effective; he scared a lot of officers."[68]

The second major move in pressuring the army was a State Department proposal on a resolution to condemn communist influence in the region at the upcoming OAS Caracas Conference in March 1954. The United States wanted to suggest it was laying the groundwork for multilateral sanctions against Guatemala.[69] American policymakers did not intend to implement them. Rather, they hoped that the mere threat of sanctions would convince the army to forsake Árbenz.[70] By using covert action, while maintaining the pretense that the United States was working toward a multilateral solution, US policymakers hoped to topple Árbenz and overturn Decree 900 without incurring the high diplomatic costs associated with coercion.

Árbenz's Response to the Threat of Regime Change

My argument holds that targeted leaders are more likely to take defensive action when a foreign power employs covert or indirect measures to overthrow them. Events in the Guatemala case are consistent with this pre-diction. By the end of October 1953, Árbenz had evidence that the CIA was planning to overthrow him. A double agent sold the Guatemalan government copies of letters between Castillo Armas and the Nicaraguan government that revealed US support for the exile force. Yet, rather than change policy to appease the United States, Árbenz and PGT leaders concocted a plan to raise the costs to the United States of pursuing regime change. They planned to reveal evidence of the plot just ahead of the Caracas Conference.[71] This would force the Eisenhower administration to abandon its plans by inciting the very nationalism and anti-American sentiment that it wanted to avoid.

In the meantime, Árbenz planned to create peasant and worker militias in case the army failed to defend him. The arms embargo forced Árbenz to turn to the Soviet bloc for the weapons necessary to build these militias. Starting in November 1953, the Guatemalan government began negotiating with the Czechoslovakian government for a covert shipment of roughly two thousand tons of arms.[72] Many within the PGT were also urging that the pace of reform be quickened to assure peasant support to protect the revolution.

Árbenz's efforts failed to deter the United States. When the Guatemalan government revealed evidence of the CIA plot, the American media and US Congress dismissed it as a fabrication.[73] At the Caracas Conference, Secretary of State John Foster Dulles successfully pressured Latin American governments either to vote for the US resolution or to abstain.[74] The United States even succeeded in using Árbenz's attempt to secure Czech arms to turn the army against him. When the *Alfhem*, the ship carrying the weapons, arrived in Guatemala, the United States used its appearance as proof that Árbenz was conspiring with the Soviets. It also used the shipment to justify sending its own arms to Honduras and Nicaragua. This increased the Guatemalan army's concern that the United States was planning to manufacture a border incident to provoke war.

The CIA also used the *Alfhem*'s arrival in Guatemala to exploit the army's long-standing fear that Árbenz was building his own militia. Frank Wisner, who ran PBSuccess, recommended that US officials say that they did not know whether the arms were intended for the army. Wisner explained that "this might be good as it might make the army mad."[75] In short, American officials were able to seize upon Árbenz's own attempts to deter regime change to further undermine him.

In June 1954, the CIA began its final push to convince the army to stand down and let Árbenz fall.[76] Part of these efforts included rallying the anticommunist opposition within Guatemala. A student anticommunist group harassed government officials and regime supporters as part of a CIA plan to provoke a government crackdown that would further reduce public support.[77] The CIA also barraged the Guatemalan public with anti-Árbenz and anticommunist propaganda through a radio station located in Nicaragua but allegedly broadcasting from within Guatemala. The finale was planned for mid-June, when Castillo Armas and his followers would launch an "invasion," during which radio broadcasts would describe the stunning success of Castillo Armas's Army of Liberation.[78] In reality, his army had only 250 men and would lose two of the three battles it was about to fight.[79] Its purpose, however, was merely "to create and maintain for a short time the *impression* of very substantial military strength" to convince the army to stay in its barracks.[80]

Neither Árbenz nor the army was duped. Both knew the rebels could be easily defeated. The greater fear was what might follow that defeat. As Árbenz told Fortuny, "The invasion is a farce. We can shoo them away with our hats. . . . [W]hat I'm afraid of is that if we defeat them right on the border, the Honduran government will manufacture a border incident, declare war on us, and the United States will invade."[81] The army also worried that defeating Castillo Armas would precipitate an American invasion.[82] But in contrast to the army, Árbenz was not ready to surrender. To avoid inciting a military revolt, he decided not to arm the peasants. Instead, he made an appeal to the United Nations, calling for a cease-fire and UN observers. This appeal, he hoped, would prevent the United States from manufacturing an incident to justify an invasion. Again faced with the threat of regime change, Árbenz sought to make himself more costly to remove.

Once more, the Eisenhower administration outmaneuvered Árbenz. It pressured both the British and French governments to withdraw their support for a Soviet proposal to send a UN mission.[83] The administration reminded its European allies that if they countered US interests by backing Guatemala's request, the United States would feel free to do the same with respect to their colonial interests.[84] The White House asserted that the matter should be referred to the OAS, where it would be quickly put to rest. This was not the first time the United States risked relations with its closest allies to remove Árbenz. Following the *Alfhem*'s arrival in Guatemala, the

United States had unofficially imposed a naval embargo, claiming the right to seize and inspect any ship, including those of its European allies. Eisenhower appeared less concerned with angering those with whom relations were good than risking US dominance over Latin America, where anti-American sentiment was much stronger.[85]

Interestingly, the White House authorized PBSuccess despite the CIA's own reservations about the odds of success. CIA reports reveal the agency's doubts during the course of Castillo Armas's "invasion" about whether the plan would work. Even after Árbenz learned that the army was refusing to fight, a CIA report asserted that there was "no evidence of defections from the Guatemalan army."[86] Yet, because it was a covert operation, the Eisenhower administration could afford to accept the lower odds of success and then deny involvement if the operation failed. The Americans never had to confront that possibility, however, because the operation succeeded in convincing the army to support a coup.

Days after Árbenz received word that the military would not fight the rebels, the army's commander, Colonel Carlos Enrique Díaz, and four fellow officers met with Ambassador Peurifoy to make a deal. They offered to assemble a military junta, force Árbenz out, and round up registered communists for exile if the United States would abandon its attempt to install Castillo Armas. Peurifoy agreed, and that evening Díaz and two other officers met with Árbenz to tell him the army would attack the presidential palace if he refused to surrender power. Díaz also assured Árbenz that Castillo Armas would not be installed as the new leader and that, although the junta would overturn Decree 900, it would not reverse the land expropriations already made. Árbenz agreed to step down and went into exile.

In the end, the United States succeeded in effecting full regime change by coercing the army to install Castillo Armas. Several officers were vying for the presidency, which Peurifoy used to his advantage. Over the next eleven days, various juntas formed with Peurifoy's encouragement, until the ambassador succeeded in obtaining a set of officers he could pressure to cede power to Castillo Armas. Peurifoy's efforts ensured that the external opposition (i.e., the elites), and not the army, which had ties to Árbenz, would rule. Castillo Armas reversed Decree 900, ordered the arrest and murder of communists, and deprived a majority of the population's voting rights by enforcing a literacy requirement. Though he was assassinated three years later, he was followed by a series of dictators who ruled with US support. His coup also laid the seeds for a guerilla movement that would develop into a thirty-six-year civil war marked by government-perpetrated mass killings and the disappearance of more than two hundred thousand Guatemalans.[87] Although the CIA considered PBSuccess a model covert operation, by the end of the Cold War, official assessments of it had changed.[88] In 1999, President Bill Clinton issued an apology for US actions in Guatemala.[89]

Alternative Arguments in the Guatemalan Case

Thus far, I have shown that Árbenz could not satisfy US interests without incurring significant domestic political costs. This gave him incentive to resist US pressure, which meant the United States would have had to strong-arm Guatemala through an oil embargo if it hoped to force Árbenz to concede. Rather than do this, the Eisenhower administration pursued covert regime change, which allowed it to avoid the diplomatic costs associated with coercion. There are, however, other potential explanations for the decision to topple Árbenz. These can be categorized according to whether they emphasize a psychological, bureaucratic/interest-group pressure, or rationalist approach. I consider each in turn.

PSYCHOLOGICAL BIAS

One alternative argument attributes US actions to the psychological biases of the individuals involved in the decision-making.[90] The Eisenhower administration was staffed with staunch anticommunists. Secretary of State Dulles, a devout Christian, frequently framed the Cold War as a battle between good and evil. He once opined that "there are two kinds of people in the world. There are those who are Christians and support free enterprise, and there are the others."[91] His brother, Allen Dulles, Director of Central Intelligence, who shared his anticommunist sentiments, had a long career in espionage dating back to World War I. The brothers' predilection for using covert action to topple suspected communists fit with Eisenhower's own foreign policy views. Though Eisenhower had abandoned his campaign advocacy of "rollback," a policy meant to overthrow communist regimes, he remained committed to using covert action to undermine Soviet-backed governments.[92]

The psychological biases of the Dulles brothers and Eisenhower can explain in part why they viewed Árbenz and his policies as a threat. However, as an explanation for the policy of regime change, a psychological approach runs into problems. First, the effort to overthrow Árbenz began with Truman, who is widely considered to have been more open to diplomacy and less dogmatic in his beliefs. Although the State Department had only half-heartedly supported PBFortune, Truman had given up on coercing Árbenz and, much like his successor, supported using covert action to oust the Guatemalan president. Antipathy toward the Guatemalan government also crossed party lines in the US Congress, where Democrats as well as Republicans routinely denounced Árbenz.[93] Skeptics might contend that the psychological bias influencing Eisenhower had affected Truman as well. But the Bolivia case discussed next in this chapter shows that neither Truman nor Eisenhower was so ideologically committed to overthrowing communist-supported leaders that they viewed regime change as the only solution. Both administrations used negotiation to convince Bolivia's MNR to cut ties to the communists within its ranks.

Another psychological approach might suggest that Árbenz's communist sympathies made him impossible to coerce. Influenced by his wife, who had turned to Marxism in reaction to her own upbringing among the Salvadoran elite, Árbenz reportedly hoped Guatemala would one day become a communist state.[94] However, Árbenz was not blind to the risks of challenging a more powerful nation.[95] He knew the United States would not tolerate a communist government and that Guatemala was vulnerable to an oil embargo. As a result, his land reform program was aimed at developing a capitalist economy. US policymakers knew this. One CIA report from October 1952 noted, "Rather than setting up a Communist state, Árbenz desires to establish a 'modern democracy' which would improve the lot of its people through paternalistic social reforms."[96] Árbenz's refusal to make concessions ultimately changed the CIA's evaluation of him. Yet his resistance to US pressure had more to do with his domestic political position. Árbenz could not give in to US demands without forsaking his political agenda and empowering his enemies, and he had no reason to take these steps as long as he doubted the United States could overthrow him.

BUREAUCRATIC AND INTEREST-GROUP PRESSURE

A second alternative argument attributes the Guatemalan coup to the pervasive influence of United Fruit within the Eisenhower administration. As an attorney, John Foster Dulles had helped United Fruit negotiate the acquisition of some of its Guatemalan landholdings. Allen Dulles had been a partner at the same firm. Walter Bedell Smith, who had headed the CIA under Truman and served as Eisenhower's undersecretary of state, was on United Fruit's board of directors.[97] Given these ties, early accounts of the coup suggested that the Eisenhower administration was acting principally to protect United Fruit.[98]

With the release of government documents, however, a consensus has emerged in the literature that the administration was far more concerned about communist influence in the Guatemalan government than about protecting United Fruit.[99] Indeed, the company had been more successful in influencing the Truman administration by generating unfounded alarm about the progressive policies of Árbenz's predecessor, Arévalo, whose labor code threatened United Fruit's access to cheap labor. By the time Árbenz was elected president in 1951, American embassy intelligence had improved, making it more difficult for the company to mislead embassy staff.[100] CIA and embassy reports show the Eisenhower administration knew the communists had little chance of seizing power in Guatemala. The fear was that communist influence would grow if left unchecked.

Although the Eisenhower administration protested what it called the "persecution" of American companies, it also recognized that United Fruit's privileged status in Guatemala could not last.[101] The US Department of Justice was already preparing an antitrust suit against United Fruit, which it filed after the coup.[102] In addition, a report by the IBRD confirmed what American embassy officials knew: United Fruit, along with the two American companies that controlled Guatemala's transportation and electric industries, was partly responsible for the semifeudal state of the Guatemalan economy.[103] Árbenz's reforms were modeled on the IBRD's recommendations.[104] However, from Washington's perspective, the problem was not land reform itself, but the influence Decree 900 conferred on the communists.

RATIONAL CHOICE ARGUMENTS

Finally, the two dominant rationalist explanations for conflict—the problems of incomplete information and credible commitment—offer only a partial explanation for the Guatemala case. The logic of an incomplete-information explanation would suggest that Árbenz doubted American threats and, therefore, pursued policies that antagonized the United States. But Árbenz had unusually good information; he knew the CIA was plotting against him. To be sure, Árbenz mistakenly believed he could outwit the

CIA. Yet, even if he had anticipated the CIA's success and made concessions, the Eisenhower administration might not have accepted them. Árbenz's domestic interests ran counter to US interests. Guatemalan communists were the only ones willing to help Árbenz liberate the peasantry, which he needed to do to break the power of the elite and transform the Guatemalan economy.

Although there is little evidence that incomplete information led Árbenz to resist, it does appear that the Guatemalan leader faced a commitment problem. Any concessions he might have made to limit the communists' power, he had incentive to overturn later on. Árbenz's commitment problem, however, did not make a settlement with him impossible. Both Árbenz and the Americans knew that Guatemala could not withstand an oil embargo. Had the United States been willing to threaten an embargo and maintain that threat, Árbenz might well have abandoned his political agenda and cut ties to the communists. But the Eisenhower administration was reluctant to bear the diplomatic costs of being seen as bullying a Latin American government. It was the sensitivity to these costs, not the impossibility of a settlement, that led the United States to pursue regime change.

The Case of Guatemala: Conclusions

The decision to overthrow Árbenz supports my argument's expectations (hypothesis $H1a_1$). Árbenz's domestic opposition gave him strong incentive to resist US demands to eliminate communist influence and overturn Decree 900. Had he complied, he would have empowered the Guatemalan elite while depriving himself of the opportunity to mobilize the indigenous population to fight on his behalf. Although Árbenz might have been convinced to abandon his political goals if threatened with a costly punishment, such as an oil embargo, the United States was unwilling to be seen as openly violating its Good Neighbor policy. The desire to avoid the costs of coercion drove the Eisenhower administration to use, as Truman had tried to do, Árbenz's opposition to overthrow him.

The Guatemala case also supports my hypotheses about how major powers implement regime change and how targeted leaders respond. Árbenz's weak external opposition would have required significant military assistance to counter him and his army. Instead, the Eisenhower administration pursued partial regime change by attempting to coerce the army to support a coup. This supports my hypothesis $H1a_5$, which holds that states seeking regime change are more likely to pursue coups when the external opposition is weak and the internal opposition is strong. Árbenz's response to the threat of regime change also supports $H1b_2$, which states that the target is more likely to adopt defensive actions when foreign powers threaten regime change but do not signal their intention to use direct force. Although he knew the United States was attempting to remove him, Árbenz refused to make concessions. He believed he could force the Americans to abandon their plans by making it more costly for them to force regime change.

In the next section, I show that, contrary to conventional wisdom, the Eisenhower administration was not so ideologically committed to ousting communists that it pursued regime change at all costs. Rather, when faced with a regime whose lack of domestic opposition made it less costly to coerce and also more costly to overthrow, the Eisenhower administration pursued a settlement instead.

Bolivia, 1954: Policy Change

On April 9, 1952, just weeks before Truman began to consider overthrowing Árbenz, the Movimiento Nacionalista Revolucionario seized power in Bolivia. Like the Guatemalan revolution eight years before, the Bolivian revolution that brought the MNR to power was inspired by an economic downturn and the injustices of a semifeudal system. As in Guatemala, the catalyst for the revolution was the ruling junta's attempt to cling to power, in this instance by nullifying the results of the 1951 presidential election.

The major difference between the two revolutions was that in Bolivia, the army's power had been almost completely destroyed. Workers' militias had joined with sympathetic police units to defeat the army, the longtime arbiter of the country's politics. When Víctor Paz Estenssoro, the MNR's leader and winner of the 1951 elections, assumed power in the wake of the uprising, he faced relatively little threat of a counterrevolution. This meant that Paz Estenssoro, in contrast to Árbenz, could more easily make concessions to the United States without fear of empowering his opposition. It also meant that the United States could not use the Bolivian army to overthrow him. As a result, rather than attempting to oust the MNR from power, US policy came to rest on dangling economic carrots to influence the course of the party's reforms. In the next section, I begin by explaining how Washington responded to the MNR's rise and the demands the United States placed on the new revolutionary government.

American Demands on the Bolivian Government

The Truman administration had serious reservations about the Bolivian government that seized power in 1952. Paz Estenssoro had been minister of finance under a previous government, but had been forced out in 1944, along with other MNR government officials, at Washington's behest.[105] The MNR's fiercely nationalistic policies, staunch opposition to foreign investment, and anti-Semitic tone had convinced American officials at the time that the MNR was fascist and sympathetic to the Axis.[106]

By 1952, the MNR had deemphasized its fascist sentiments, but its nationalist agenda and ties to communist factions worried the Truman administration. Writing roughly one month before the revolution, the Office of South American Affairs of the State Department observed, "The Junta is preferable to the sort of government which we fear the MNR would establish." Whereas the junta had accommodated US interests, the MNR was "intensely nationalistic and many of its supporters, if not all its leaders, [were] anti-U.S." The State Department elaborated, "the Junta is strongly anti-Communist, but the MNR has accepted Communist support and might collaborate with the Communists or even fall under their domination if it came to power."[107] Although Paz Estenssoro was considered a moderate, the Truman administration had believed the same of Árbenz, whose policies had become far more radical than Washington anticipated.

The Truman administration decided to delay recognition of the new Bolivian government.[108] The two most important concerns were the MNR's plans to nationalize Bolivia's tin mines and its alliance with labor. The United States wanted assurances that the MNR would not nationalize the tin industry immediately. If and when it did, the Americans wanted the MNR to compensate the mine owners.[109] Although Washington indicated some concern over the impact on US investors, who owned roughly 30 percent of Bolivia's largest mining company, the State Department was not concerned with protecting the mining companies, which it believed were "in large part responsible for their present predicament."[110] Rather, the main concern was the regional effect of nationalization.[111] As Secretary of State Dean Acheson explained in a memo, the State Department believed that Bolivia's "confiscatory nationalization" could have a "bad effect in other countries where US property rights are at stake." In particular, he noted, "Statements from Chile since recent election [regarding] possible nationalization [of] copper mines give us new cause for concern [on] this score."[112] As in Guatemala, US officials were mainly concerned about Bolivia's reforms spreading throughout the region.

The second major concern was the MNR's alliance with the left, especially the powerful workers' union known as the Central Obrera Boliviana (COB). Embassy officials described the COB leader and newly appointed minister of the mines, Juan Lechín Oquendo, as a "demagogic agitator" and "communist firebrand."[113] Although Washington recognized that Paz Estenssoro and his vice president, Hernán Siles Zuazo, were moderates, they understood that Paz Estenssoro owed Lechín a "great debt of gratitude for the mine workers' part in overcoming army resistance to the revolution."[114] Lechín was not the only controversial element within the COB. The Marxist Partido Comunista de Bolivia (PCB) and the Trotskyite Partido Obrero Revolucionario (POR) also wielded significant influence, and members of the pro-Moscow Partido de la Izquierda Revolucionario (PIR) were tied to the COB as well.[115] The COB's platform, which shared many POR and PCB demands, particularly alarmed the Americans with its calls for nationalization of the tin mines without compensation, nationalization of all transportation industries, a minimum wage, the breakup of large plantations, and worker control of the factories.[116] Based on its concerns, the United States delayed recognition, waiting for assurance that nationalization would bring compensation and that the party's "extreme radicals" could be controlled.[117]

Despite its reservations, the State Department soon concluded that nonrecognition was more likely to undermine than protect US interests. Acheson explained in a May 1952 memo to Truman that nonrecognition was unlikely to prevent nationalization and might have the opposite effect instead, "namely, that of strengthening the radical elements in the government."[118] To ensure the power of the "more sensible elements in the [government] such as Paz Estenssoro," Acheson recommended that the United States recognize the new government and restart negotiations over a contract for Bolivian tin.[119] These had broken off during the revolution. The United States formally recognized the MNR government on June 2, 1952, but pressured the MNR to limit reform, distance itself from communists, and provide compensation for the expropriated tin mines.

The Costs of Compliance Versus Resistance for the MNR

The MNR faced few reactionary threats when it came to power, but it did face threats from within its own ranks. The economic downturn and falling price of tin had already weakened the influence of the tin barons, and the army had been disgraced during the revolution. But the COB's political power made it almost impossible for MNR leaders to ignore its demands. Although aligned with the MNR, the COB functioned almost as a "government within a government."[120] It exercised control over the powerful labor movement and mining camps and retained the right to name the ministers of the mines, labor, and peasant affairs. The COB's power reflected the role the workers and unions had played during the revolution. Although the revolution had brought together an array of social classes, it was the workers militias that had helped defeat the army. Having seized weapons during the fighting, the militias emerged from the revolution stronger than before and were loyal to the COB. The COB's political and military power gave it significant influence over the MNR's reformist program, which put the MNR at odds with the United States.[121]

Bolivia's economic crisis, however, also made it difficult to ignore US demands. The Bolivian economy was almost entirely dependent on tin exports, more than 50 percent of which were traditionally sold to the United States.[122] By 1952, however, the American demand for Bolivian tin was drying up as higher-grade deposits in Asia and Africa became available. The United States had also stockpiled tin, which meant it not only had little need for more, but also could influence the price by selling its stockpiles.[123] In addition, the Bolivians had a limited customer base since the United States owned one of the only two smelters in the world capable of processing their tin. When the price dropped from a high of two dollars per pound in 1950 to eighty cents per pound in 1953, the economic crisis threatened to bring about the Bolivian government's collapse.[124] Tin sales provided 90 percent of government revenue and 40 percent of food imports.[125] A tin contract was, therefore, essential, both for the MNR's political survival and for avoiding famine.

The MNR responded to the competing pressures of the left's insistence on reform and the Americans' wariness of it by reassuring the United States in word but not in deed. Both publically and privately, Bolivian officials declared that the MNR was neither communist nor anticapitalist.[126] In a

May Day speech, Lechín held that "nationalization [was] not a Communist measure."[127] Vice President Siles declared publically, more than once, that the MNR was anticommunist, considered nationalization to be different from confiscation, and intended to respect Bolivia's international obligations.[128] Finally, the Bolivian ambassador to Washington, Víctor Andrade, used his extensive network in Washington to counteract the tin mine owners' efforts to paint the MNR as communist. He repeatedly stressed "genuine regret that nationalization became necessary" and insisted that Bolivia both needed and wanted "the help of outside capital."[129]

Given Bolivia's economic vulnerability, it is striking that the MNR did not make any major concessions to the United States in its first year other than unfulfilled promises to compensate the tin-mine owners. Instead, the MNR made concessions to its own left wing. In October 1952, it conceded to the left's demands for worker control of the mines. The arrangement was only for one year, but it had the effect of increasing the COB's influence in the mining camps by making it a central player in negotiations between workers and management.[130] Also, though the MNR had pledged roughly $20 million in compensation, it postponed discussions with the former mine owners on when and how it would be distributed. The Bolivian government had no funds to cover compensation, in part because the MNR had rehired thousands of mine workers who had been fired for union activities.[131] The MNR's attempts to ensure labor's support thus undercut its ability to placate the American demand for compensation.

A right-wing coup attempt on January 9, 1953, dramatically shifted the balance of power between the MNR's centrist leadership and the left wing of the party. This power shift would give Paz Estenssoro a greater ability to appease the United States. The right-wing faction responsible for the coup had grown alarmed by the president's concessions to the left and had acted to "free the president from Communist influence."[132] Although the coup had failed, it convinced many on the left that the revolution was still vulnerable. It also won the president greater popular support by casting him as a defender of the revolution.[133] Paz Estenssoro used his surging popularity to bring the left wing of the party under his control.[134] He capitalized on the divisions within the COB, particularly between Lechín and the POR, to force POR members from the leadership.[135] Lechín also increasingly sided with the centrists, attacking the communists in speeches and defending MNR policy.[136] Thus, in early 1953, the MNR's political costs of accommodating the United States by cracking down on the communists were beginning to decline.

Nevertheless, the MNR still could not afford to pay compensation to the mine owners without a long-term contract to sell tin to the United States. The Americans held that there would be no deal without compensation for the mine owners. The stalemate came to a head in March 1953, when the United States cancelled contract negotiations altogether.[137] Paz Estenssoro openly accused the Americans of attempting to use an economic crisis to overthrow the MNR.[138] But despite its rhetoric, the MNR soon began negotiating compensation with the largest of the mining companies. As I show in the next section, the MNR anticipated that its deeds would be rewarded by the United States.

The Costs to the United States of a Settlement with the MNR

My argument predicts that leaders who face few domestic threats will be less costly to coerce into settlements than leaders whose political power is more fragile. Although a leader's concessions still depend on the state's military and economic vulnerability, all else equal, the greater a leader's political power, the more concessions the leader can make, and the less incentive the foreign power must provide to obtain an agreement. After the January coup, Paz Estenssoro could crack down on communists without empowering the left. Compensating the tin-mine owners, however, remained financially and politically costly. Although the United States could pressure Paz Estenssoro by cancelling its tin contract, the MNR could not both pay compensation and survive politically. Given the MNR's communist ties and nationalist policies, offering it aid should have been a political impossibility in the United States. Paz Estenssoro's crackdown on communists and promises to pay compensation, however, would enable US policymakers to justify aid and thereby lower the political costs of it.

As the MNR shifted away from the left, the US embassy took notice and the Eisenhower administration's views evolved. The embassy reported in late February that "the party has . . . manifested its anti-communist orientation. A resolution passed by the Congress calls upon all MNR party members to collaborate with labor leaders in purging the COB and FSTMB [the Federation of Bolivian Mine Workers] of Communist elements. The Communists were characterized in the resolution as saboteurs of the MNR."[139] Although the MNR moved ahead with its land reform program in August 1953, the embassy noted that the Agrarian Reform Commission had put forward "relatively moderate proposals." It also reported that the commission had rejected the COB's "communist inspired" land reform proposal.[140] The embassy later observed that the government had removed "certain key communists from the trade union movement."[141] By October 1953, the embassy had concluded that "neither the MNR Party in the mass, nor its most important leaders, are Communists or crypto-Communist."[142]

The MNR's decision to negotiate compensation for the mine owners carried greater political costs for Paz Estenssoro than cracking down on the communists.[143] Because the government lacked budget reserves, it planned to pay compensation in installments through tin sales, which would reduce its ability to import food.[144] The MNR had three reasons for making this costly concession. First, the market price of tin had dropped drastically in early 1953, increasing the MNR's desperation for a tin contract from the United States at a potentially above-market price.[145] Second, although US officials had broken off talks, they indicated that a tin contract was still possible.[146] In response to anti-American speeches on May Day 1953, for example, the State Department advised the embassy to warn MNR officials that "such a campaign might so antagonize American people and Congress as to endanger substantial United States assistance already being given Bolivia and *future assistance such as term tin contract* which Bolivia desires."[147]

Third, and perhaps most importantly, the MNR knew that the United States had an interest in assisting it, because the only likely alternative to its continuation in power was a more radical leftist government.[148] In early October 1953, while awaiting a formal commitment of US aid, Paz Estenssoro accused the United States of intentionally delaying aid to facilitate a right-wing coup. He then warned the US ambassador that such a coup was unlikely to succeed. Referring to the Iranian coup, which the CIA had helped organize just two months prior, Paz Estenssoro noted that "an important difference in the analogy is that in Bolivia the 'shah's army' no longer existed; that the Bolivian government had the full, unqualified support of the vast majority of the people; that the new Bolivian army [was] loyal and pledged to support the people and the Government; and that there [was] no alternative [to the MNR] as was the case in Iran."[149] In short, the MNR could afford to take the costly step of compensating the mine owners because it knew the United States needed the MNR as much as the MNR needed the United States. This meant the United States was likely to reward Bolivian cooperation with a tin contract and economic aid to keep the MNR afloat.

The MNR was right to suspect its efforts would be rewarded. Shortly after the American government cancelled the tin contract talks in March 1953, State Department officials began working on plans for an economic aid package.[150] In June, the Bolivian government announced it would begin making compensation payments to the largest mining company, the only one with American stockholders.[151] Shortly thereafter, the State Department's aid proposal began gathering support. The president's brother, Dr. Milton Eisenhower, was one of its backers. In mid-June, President Eisenhower announced he would send his brother to Latin America on a good-will tour. US labor leaders and friends of Ambassador Andrade arranged for him to meet with Milton Eisenhower on June 17.[152] Whether Andrade's influence on the president's brother proved influential or merely confirmed what the State Department was already proposing remains unclear, but on June 22, the president indicated tentative support for a two-year contract for ten thousand tons of Bolivian tin.[153] He added that the tin contract would serve as "a lien to guarantee the proposed $10 million loan for agricultural development."[154] The formal aid package announced three months later would become just the first installment in roughly $327.7 million in aid the United States would send to the Bolivian government over the next decade.[155]

Given the US government's initial concerns over the MNR, the Eisenhower administration's decision to offer what would become the largest per capita aid program in the world at the time was remarkable. Although the financial costs to the United States were high, the political costs were relatively low. The MNR's efforts to appease the United States enabled the Eisenhower administration to justify sending funds. The State Department could point to the MNR's crackdown on communists to argue that the Bolivian government was "Marxist rather than Communist."[156] Indeed, when the assistant secretary of state for inter-American affairs, John Moors Cabot, announced the aid program in a speech, he drew an explicit contrast with Guatemala. Whereas Árbenz, he claimed, was "playing the communist game," the MNR was "sincere in desiring social progress and in opposing Communist imperialism."[157] The MNR's cooperative behavior lowered the political costs to the United States of reaching a settlement.

The United States might have forced the MNR to pay compensation earlier by threatening a tin embargo. Bolivia's dependence on American tin purchases made it highly vulnerable to coercion. However, the Eisenhower administration did not go that route because, as with Guatemala, it did not want to be seen as violating the Good Neighbor policy. A State Department report warned of "serious consequences should Latin America come to believe that the United States [was] attempting to bring about an economic crisis in Bolivia."[158] In addition, the Eisenhower administration feared an economic crisis might bring in a more radical leftist government.[159] As US ambassador Edward Sparks explained in a telegram, "Without assurance of US market for one half its tin production Bolivian descent to economic chaos with attendant political consequences [would] be accelerated."[160] Although the Americans knew a communist government was unlikely to emerge, they anticipated that a more radical regime would be open to working directly with the communists.[161] So when the Treasury Department argued against the tin contract, Cabot warned that "no one could say how long the situation in Bolivia would hold together."[162] As I will explain more fully, these concerns about the lack of a desirable alternative to the MNR were central in convincing the Eisenhower administration to negotiate rather than to overthrow the Bolivian government.

The Costs of Regime Change in Bolivia

The MNR's assurances that the party was neither communist nor hostile to foreign investment helped buy it time as it consolidated power during its first year.[163] Once it began to accommodate US demands after that, the United States had less reason to seek regime change. Yet the MNR's cooperative behavior was not the only factor that spared the party from FIRC. A major impediment to its overthrow was the simple fact that there was no feasible alternative to the MNR besides the party's own left wing.

The United States had reason to be patient with Paz Estenssoro since there was no other leader who could better contain the left. A January 1954 US embassy report observed that whatever reservations the Americans had about the MNR's "dark past and some of its de facto actions," policy had to be "influenced by possible alternatives to the present government." Here, the report noted, there was much "enigma," for although right-wing opposition parties made various claims about their ability to seize and maintain power, the facts suggested otherwise. The report's analysis concluded that, although the opposition had insisted that the indigenous population would accept any government imposed on it, "Even if their appraisal were correct with respect to 75 per cent of the adult Indian population, a misconception with respect to the remaining 25 per cent could be fatal insofar as political evaluation is concerned. Especially since this 25 per cent probably would include the armed workers militia—the most potent military force in Bolivia today."[164] Further, the indigenous population was already violently seizing property in the countryside. This contradicted the right's claim that the indigenous population would passively accept a return to the oligarchic control of Bolivia's elite.

The Falange Socialista Boliviana (FSB) was the most organized party on the right, and it attempted a coup on November 9, 1953. The FSB, however, had failed to rally support from any other opposition group. Moreover, as the embassy reported, the other right-wing opposition parties were effectively "moribund." The MNR had managed to "emasculate" them through shotgun arrests, control of the press, and threats of sanctions.[165] In terms of the FSB's supposed clandestine armed opposition force, the embassy reported that its odds of seizing power depended on an economic collapse and its ability to subvert the militias, the latter of which was unlikely. Indeed, the FSB's aborted coup showed it was no match for the MNR, which could call on an estimated fifteen thousand to forty thousand armed workers to fight in its defense.[166]

The MNR knew the lack of an organized opposition on its right gave it bargaining power. Bolivian officials frequently used American fears of a more radical leftist regime coming to power to pressure the Eisenhower, and later the Kennedy, administration for additional aid. The MNR added to this pressure with oblique references to contacts with the Eastern bloc. The State Department reported one exchange with Ambassador Andrade in which he stressed the difficulty of ignoring a Soviet loan offer of $60 million given that the "average Bolivian man in the street considered one dollar as good as another."[167] The pressure worked. Assistance from the United States dramatically increased between 1960 and 1962, from $15.3 million to $39 million.[168] During the Kennedy administration, Bolivia would become a centerpiece of the Alliance for Progress, a massive economic aid program designed to improve US–Latin American relations.[169]

Although the MNR was successful in exploiting America's Cold War fears to obtain aid, the United States was also successful in using its aid to shape Bolivian policy. In 1955, it threatened to cut off economic assistance unless Bolivia enacted a new petroleum code written by American lawyers.[170] The following year, high levels of inflation and rising prices in

Bolivia prompted Washington to press Paz Estenssoro to adopt a stabilization plan. The United States offered an additional $25 million in aid contin-
gent on the Bolivian government's adopting austerity measures that would
be particularly hard on workers.[171] The head of the American commission
overseeing the program, George Jackson Eder, later claimed that it brought
about the "repudiation, at least tacitly, of virtually everything the Revolutionary Government had done over the previous four years."[172] Thus, the
aid program shaped Bolivian policy in a way that was consistent with US
interests, thereby enabling the United States to achieve some of the same
goals it had in Guatemala but through a negotiated deal rather than regime
change.

American aid also led to the MNR's downfall. Because its conditions
targeted labor, the aid deepened the divide between the party's center and
its left wing. As the number of antigovernment demonstrations increased,
the MNR began asking for military assistance.[173] The United States
responded by offering both aid and military training. Between 1960 and
1964, US military aid summed to approximately $8.2 million.[174] As Paz
Estenssoro increasingly used the army to suppress strikes and demonstrations, his popularity waned.[175] On November 4, 1964, General René Bar-
rientos Ortuño staged a coup. Although there is no evidence that the
United States orchestrated it, US military assistance had been aimed explicitly at creating a force that would be pro-American.[176] Washington anticipated that if efforts to prop up the MNR failed, the military could seize
power to forestall a more radical regime.[177] Although the United States initially had no alternative to the MNR, it helped construct the alternative that
would eventually replace it.

Alternative Arguments in the Bolivian Case

My argument holds that the MNR was less costly for the United States to
negotiate with than to overthrow because of its strong base of domestic
political support. Many scholars, however, attribute the Eisenhower administration's approach to the MNR to a variety of other causes, including
psychological bias, bureaucratic or interest-group pressure, and information or commitment problems. I will show that, although some of these
arguments help us understand relations between the United States and the
MNR, they paint only a partial picture when it comes to explaining why
American policymakers came to support the MNR.

PSYCHOLOGICAL BIAS

A political-psychology explanation for the Eisenhower administration's dealings with the MNR might suggest the administration was predisposed to view the Bolivian government more favorably than the Guatemalan government. If actors only see what they expect, then they should be more willing to cooperate when they already have good relations with another party and more likely to use force when they do not. US relations were undoubtedly better with the MNR than they were with Árbenz. However, this was not always the case. During World War II, the Roosevelt administration had pressured the Bolivian government to purge itself of the MNR. When the MNR seized power in 1952, Truman at first denied it recognition due to its nationalist sentiments and communist ties. Washington only revised its views after the MNR began conceding to its demands. In contrast, the Americans were initially hopeful that Árbenz would temper Guatemala's revolution. Árbenz was seen as a moderate because he had been a former army colonel. It was only after the enactment of Decree 900 that the United States concluded he was helping the communists.

Furthermore, if the Eisenhower administration's policies were the product of psychological bias, we might have expected that bias to be stronger in the Bolivia case. For one thing, the Bolivian revolution was more complete than its Guatemalan counterpart. Change in Bolivia, writes Kenneth Lehman, "went deeper, came faster, and thus was more inherently destabilizing than change in Guatemala."[178] In addition, the Bolivian leadership periodically referred to the possibility of fostering trade and diplomatic ties with the Eastern bloc to elicit more aid from the United States. Árbenz, in contrast, never threatened to develop ties to the Soviet Union and only brokered the deal for Czech arms after learning of the CIA plot against him.[179] Ultimately, it was each government's response to US pressure that influenced American perceptions of it. Whereas Árbenz resisted concessions for fear of empowering the right, the MNR had no opposition on the right and so could make concessions that Árbenz could not. As a result, American policymakers came to view the MNR more favorably than Árbenz.

BUREAUCRATIC AND INTEREST-GROUP PRESSURE

Another explanation for the Eisenhower administration's different approach to Bolivia and Guatemala suggests that there were no bureaucrats or interest groups pushing a policy of regime change in Bolivia as there were in the Guatemalan case. There is some evidence to support this claim. Bryce Wood, for example, notes that it was easier to recompense Bolivia's tin mine owners than it was to compensate United Fruit for its massive loss of land in Guatemala under Decree 900.[180] United Fruit was also American owned, whereas American investors owned only 30 percent of Bolivia's largest mining company.

Although the MNR was more willing to make concessions, this was not necessarily because the owners of the tin mines were easier to compensate. United Fruit's claims may have been larger on an absolute scale, but the tin-mine owners' claims were large relative to what the Bolivian government could afford to pay. Bolivia was already in the grips of an economic crisis. Compensation for the tin-mine owners came at the direct expense of the government's ability to import food.[181] United Fruit may have also had more at stake in Guatemala than the small number of American investors had in Bolivia, but in both cases, US policymakers were more concerned about the regional effects of each country's reforms than the direct impact on American business interests. The fear that each government's plan to break up monopolies would be mimicked elsewhere motivated US policymakers to take action. The type of action taken depended on the relative ease of negotiating with versus overthrowing each government. In the Bolivian case, the MNR was not only more willing to offer compensation, because it faced little domestic opposition, it was also more difficult to overthrow, for the exact same reason.

Many accounts of the Bolivia case also suggest that the MNR was more effective in lobbying the White House than the Guatemalan government. There is evidence to support this claim as well. Ambassador Andrade cultivated an extensive network in Washington that helped him win access to such influential individuals as the president's brother. Whereas United Fruit could use its extensive ties to the Eisenhower administration to lobby against Árbenz, Andrade could use his ties to Republican Nelson Rockefeller and US labor leaders to lobby in favor of the MNR. Yet, Andrade's job was made easier by his own government's accommodating behavior. His assurances that the MNR opposed communism were made credible by Bolivia's purge of communists. Likewise, by the summer of 1953, he could point to ongoing negotiations to support his claims that his government would provide compensation. Notably, Andrade had less success in winning the trust of the United States during his first year, when the MNR was still beholden to the left. During this period, State Department and embassy memos show that US policymakers fretted over the MNR's communist ties and plans to seize the tin mines. Although Andrade's diplomatic skill and network likely helped to improve the MNR's image, it is unlikely they would have had the same effect had his government continued to resist US demands.

RATIONAL CHOICE ARGUMENTS

The two dominant rational choice theories would suggest that the MNR was either more trustworthy or better informed than Árbenz and thus could more easily reach a bargain with the United States. The Eisenhower administration did indeed have reason to believe the MNR would be a cooperative partner, as a credible-commitment approach would suggest. In addition to the party's concessions during its second year in office, Bolivia's dependence on US tin purchases may have assured the White House that the MNR would remain cooperative as long as its economic needs were satisfied. Yet there also remained ample reason for the United States to doubt Bolivian cooperation. In particular, the repeated references by the Bolivian government to trading with the Eastern bloc might well have signaled that it would stop cooperating with the United States if offered a better deal by others. But rather than convince the White House that the MNR was not to be trusted, the MNR's option of turning to the East won it more aid. Without an attractive alternative to the MNR, the United States had little choice but to induce its cooperation. Thus, it was not just the MNR's economic incentive to cooperate that facilitated a deal. It was also the high relative costs of regime change that made ousting the MNR infeasible and a deal preferable.

An incomplete-information approach might suggest that the MNR was better informed than Árbenz about the willingness of the United States to use force to attain its policy goals. The MNR, therefore, backed down, whereas Árbenz did not. The MNR was undeniably vulnerable to US economic pressure given its dependence on US tin purchases. Nevertheless, for its first year in office, the party appeased its left wing at the risk of angering the United States and losing a tin contract. The evidence shows that the January 1953 coup attempt led to the MNR's changes in policy that year. This event shifted the balance of domestic political power in Paz Estenssoro's favor and enabled him to appease the United States by cracking down on the left. Thus, there is little evidence that the MNR's concessions stemmed from its access to better information about US resolve.

Conclusion

The Guatemala and Bolivia cases are strikingly similar. In both countries, a popular revolution overthrew an elite-controlled government, which had aided and abetted the monopolies that controlled the nation's economy. Communist factions supported both rebellions, although the governments that emerged in both nations sought to build capitalist economies to replace semifeudalism. Even the leaders of these revolutions, Árbenz and Paz Estenssoro, were seen as relative moderates who would restrain the more radical elements of their respective parties. That impression of Paz Estenssoro lasted, but not that of Árbenz.

I argue that an important difference between the Guatemalan and Bolivian revolutions—a difference that accounts for the divergent US approaches to each case—was that the Bolivian revolution destroyed the power of the army and oligarchic elite, whereas the Guatemalan revolution did not. As such, Árbenz faced opposition on the right that both constrained his ability to make concessions and lowered the costs to the United States of imposing regime change. In contrast, the only opposition to the MNR came from the left. Although the left's political power constrained the MNR's ability to make concessions for a year, the MNR accommodated US demands once it consolidated its position in office. At the same time, the lack of an attractive alternative to the MNR increased the Americans' incentive to negotiate. These results show strong support for my hypothesis $H1a_1$, which holds that the probability of FIRC rests on the strength of the targeted leader's internal or external opposition.

The cases in this chapter also support my argument's predictions regarding the form of regime change and the leader's response to foreign pressure. In Guatemala, the United States initially sought full regime change by working with the external opposition, led by Castillo Armas. But when the CIA concluded Castillo Armas's rebels were too weak to seize power, the plan switched to partial regime change. As hypothesis $H1a_5$ predicts, the Eisenhower administration began pressuring the Guatemalan army to carry out a coup instead. Árbenz's attempts to publicize the CIA plot and to appeal to the United Nations also uphold my argument. Consistent with $H1b_2$, Árbenz adopted defensive actions because he recognized Eisenhower was reluctant to bear the diplomatic costs of using direct force and so believed he could thwart the operation by forcing Eisenhower to confront these diplomatic costs. Finally, Paz Estenssoro's response to US pressure also confirms $H1b_1$. Not only did he concede far more than Árbenz, who faced domestic opposition, but also Paz Estenssoro conceded more once his own domestic opposition abated.

In all, the Bolivia case shows that it was possible for the Eisenhower administration, despite its reputation for anticommunist zeal, to reach a settlement with a progressive, nationalist government with communist support. When dealing with a government that was willing to make concessions and costly to overthrow, Washington was open to negotiations. When faced with a leader whose domestic opposition made him more costly to coerce than to depose, however, Eisenhower opted for regime change.

CHAPTER 5

The Cold War

Soviet Policy Toward Poland and Hungary, 1956

The Polish and Hungarian crises of 1956 were crucial tests of Soviet hegemony in Eastern Europe. They were the first nationalist uprisings in which communist governments challenged Soviet domination. Yet the Soviet Union responded to each event very differently. Soviet leader Nikita Khrushchev initially threatened intervention in Poland but later accepted the return to power of Władysław Gomułka, who introduced political reforms and ousted Soviet officers from the Polish armed forces. In contrast, Khrushchev was initially receptive to changes in leadership and political reforms in Hungary but later ordered a massive invasion to remove Prime Minister Imre Nagy, who was ultimately tried and executed.

In this chapter, I argue that the central difference between the Polish and Hungarian crises was the domestic political opposition each targeted leader encountered. Gomułka faced almost no external opposition and only weak internal opposition. Although he needed to implement reforms to maintain his popularity, Gomułka was able to use that popularity to contain the unrest and implement limited reforms that would not challenge core Soviet security interests. At the same time, his lack of opposition made him more costly to remove, which increased Moscow's motivation to negotiate. In contrast, Nagy faced internal opposition within his Hungarian Workers' Party (HWP) and external opposition from various rebel factions. Both groups frustrated his attempts to bring a quick end to unrest, forcing Nagy to introduce reforms that he had initially opposed. As the Soviet leadership became increasingly concerned about the costs of a prolonged crisis, they used the divisions within the HWP to install an alternative leader more willing to support a Soviet crackdown.

Table 12. Controls for Confounding Variables: Hungary and Poland, 1956

	Hungary	*Poland*
Target's Characteristics		
Regime Type	One-party authoritarian regime	One-party authoritarian regime
Regime Ideology	National communism	National communism
Issues at Stake	Anti-Soviet riots, popular reforms	Anti-Soviet riots, popular reforms
Region	Eastern Europe	Eastern Europe
Foreign Power's Characteristics		
Decision Maker	Khrushchev	Khrushchev
Time Period	Cold War, 1956	Cold War, 1956
Outcome	Partial regime change	Settlement

The Hungary and Polish cases offer the chance to control for the same variables as in the previous chapter, as I illustrate in Table 12. The primary decision-maker for the stronger, foreign power was the same in both crises—Khrushchev. That he pursued two different strategies with two similar targets suggests that he was not ideologically inclined toward regime change. In addition, the target states were both Warsaw Pact members and thus strategically important to the Soviet Union. In fact, of the two, it was Poland to which Khrushchev assigned greater strategic value. The Kremlin needed a friendly government there to assure its lines of communication to Soviet troops in East Germany. During the crisis, Khrushchev remarked that, "Poland is not a Bulgaria or Hungary—together with [the USSR] it's the most important [country in the region]."[1] That Khrushchev chose to overthrow the Hungarian and not the Polish government suggests that his decision to impose regime change was not necessarily a function of strategic interest.

Another similarity between the two cases concerns the issues at stake and the ideological orientations of the two targeted leaders. The uprisings in both countries were partly a reaction to Khrushchev's "secret speech" in February 1956 at the 20th Congress of the Communist Party, during which the new Soviet leader denounced Stalin. Khrushchev was seeking to improve the Soviet Union's image and secure his own position vis-à-vis hardliners in the Kremlin. But by signaling a relaxation of Soviet control, Khrushchev's speech encouraged Hungarians and Poles to vent their anger toward their own Stalinist leaders. Although Gomułka and Nagy were committed Communists, they were also reformers, appointed to leadership positions to appease protestors. Their opposition to the Stalinists in their respective parties should have made them Khrushchev's ideological allies. Yet while Khrushchev had initially opposed Gomułka and accepted Nagy, he later overthrew Nagy and negotiated with Gomułka.

In this chapter, I also consider the evidence for arguments based on psychological bias, bureaucratic and/or interest-group politics, and the two dominant rational choice theories. If, for example, the psychological biases of the relevant actors explain why Hungary suffered FIRC but Poland did not, then we might expect to find that Nagy had a more contentious history with the Soviet leadership, one that primed Soviet leaders for a less cooperative approach. A bureaucratic-politics analysis would suggest that self-interested bureaucrats pushed Khrushchev to topple Nagy but encouraged him to negotiate with Gomułka. Finally, an incomplete-information focus would suggest that Gomułka was better informed than Nagy about Moscow's intentions and so backed down when coerced. A credible-commitment approach, meanwhile, would suggest that Khrushchev had greater confidence in Gomułka's promises to cooperate. I show that, although there is evidence to support some of these alternative arguments, they fall short in explaining why Khrushchev imposed regime change on Hungary but not Poland.

To evaluate the evidence for my own argument and these alternative explanations, I use both primary- and secondary-source historical materials. In particular, I use the minutes of the Central Committee of the Communist Party of the Soviet Union (CPSU CC) meetings, which were recorded by the head of the CPSU General Department, Vladimir N. Malin. These offer insight into deliberations within the Kremlin, making it possible to evaluate the rationale behind Soviet behavior.[2] I also consult the official correspondence between Moscow and the two Soviet emissaries in Budapest, Anastas Mikoyan and Mikhail Suslov. These letters, along with Malin's notes, have been translated into English and appear in *The 1956 Hungarian Revolution: A History in Documents*, edited by Csaba Békés, Malcolm Byrne, and János Rainer, as well as in various issues of the *Cold War International History Project Bulletin*.

Poland, 1956: Policy Change

In October 1956, following months of unrest that included a bloody uprising in the city of Poznań, the Polish United Workers' Party (PUWP) met to convene its Eighth Plenum. The agenda included the election of the popular former leader Władysław Gomułka as first secretary of the party. Gomułka was determined to enact significant reforms to restore order. Anticommunist and anti-Soviet sentiments had been widespread ever since late 1954, when a top official in the regime's security apparatus, Józef Światło, defected and exposed the abuses of Poland's Stalinist leaders. To win back public confidence, Gomułka planned to remove pro-Moscow hardliners from the Polish politburo. He also intended to pull Soviet officers, including the Polish-born, Soviet-installed defense minister Marshal Konstantin Rokossowski, from the Polish army.

In this section, I argue that Gomułka was successful in avoiding regime change because party hardliners had largely lost their influence before he came to power and so could not constrain or undermine his pursuit of reforms. This helped him maintain popularity, which he could then draw upon to convince the public to accept limited reform that would not threaten the Soviet-Polish alliance, Moscow's central concern. At the same time, the weakness of Gomułka's opposition made it costly for the Soviet Union to overthrow him, giving Khrushchev even greater reason to negotiate. I begin with a discussion of events leading to the October crisis and Soviet demands of the Polish leadership.

Soviet Demands in Poland

Światło's November 1954 revelation of the Polish government's corruption and abuse provided the spark for the demise of Poland's Stalinist regime.[3] Although Stalin had died in March 1953, it was not until Radio Free Europe began broadcasting Światło's disclosures that the regime's authority began to unravel. Światło had been a high-ranking official in the secret police. He provided details on the regime's routine arrests and torture of innocent people.[4] The disclosures caused a split in the PUWP between its reformist Puławy faction and its conservative Natolin faction. The two sides differed on how to respond to the allegations and mitigate the public's anger. The

Puławy faction advocated a radical break with Stalinism. The Natolin faction, in contrast, preferred to deflect criticism away from pro-Soviet Poles to a small clique that included two top aides to Poland's Stalinist leader, Bolesław Bierut.[5]

The Polish people's long-standing resentment of Soviet domination fed the unrest that followed the Światło revelations. Poles remained bitter about the Molotov-Ribbentrop Pact, which contained a secret agreement dividing Poland between Nazi Germany and Soviet Russia, itself a reminder of the eighteenth-century partition of Poland by Russia, Prussia, and Austria. The Soviet execution of some twenty-two thousand Polish nationals during World War II also fed resentment, as did Stalin's decision to let German troops crush the Warsaw Uprising.[6] Adding insult to injury, Rokossowski, whose troops had waited outside Warsaw during the uprising, was later named Poland's defense minister.[7] After the war, Bierut's government had hewed closely to Moscow's dictates, especially Soviet economic policies, which had proven disastrous for the Polish economy.[8]

After the Światło affair and ensuing unrest, the Polish Stalinist regime suffered another major blow in February 1956, when Khrushchev delivered his "secret speech" at the 20th Congress of the Communist Party. Khrushchev's denunciation discredited Stalin's associates not only in the Soviet Union, but also in the satellite states. Rumors of the speech circulated throughout Poland, where it aroused still more anger at the Polish government.[9] Then, in March, Bierut, who had attended the 20th Congress and was staying on in Moscow afterward, suddenly died. Popular suspicion that the Kremlin had ordered Bierut killed led to a brief surge in his popularity.[10] This, however, did little to restore the public trust in the PUWP.

Khrushchev approved the appointment of Bierut's successor, Edward Ochab, whom many saw as a Stalinist.[11] But Ochab gravitated toward the reformers. He relaxed censorship rules and released political prisoners. On May 1, Khrushchev made his opposition to Ochab's reforms clear. Confronting the Polish ambassador to Moscow, Khrushchev accused Ochab of going too far. "You have your sovereignty, but what you are doing today in Poland is against your sovereignty and against socialism." Khrushchev added, "Ochab has allowed anti-socialist elements to have their own way in Poland. They need to be rapped across the knuckles."[12] Yet Ochab's reforms, although indulgent from Khrushchev's perspective, did little to address the dire economic conditions contributing to the unrest in Poland.

The brewing resentment in Poland erupted into crisis on June 28, 1956. Dismal living conditions, increasing prices, and falling wages spawned riots in the city of Poznań.[13] Workers at the ZISPO locomotive factory protested increases in production norms and the cancellation of bonuses. Their strike evolved into a massive demonstration, during which protestors began shouting anti-Soviet and antigovernment slogans.[14] The demonstration quickly overwhelmed local security forces when protestors mounted attacks on public buildings, monuments, and infrastructure. The government ultimately responded with massive military force, sending in two armored and two infantry divisions, four hundred tanks and armored vehicles, and ten thousand soldiers.[15] In the ensuing crackdown, fifty-three died and hundreds were wounded.[16]

After Poznań, the Kremlin continued to insist that the Polish government resist pressures to reform. Soviet leaders were alarmed by reports that Gomułka would be appointed first secretary at the upcoming Eighth Plenum. They were even more dismayed by his plans to remove pro-Moscow Poles and Soviet officers from the Polish government and army.[17] By 1956, there were some fifty Soviet advisers in the Polish army.[18] From Moscow's perspective, the Soviet officers, particularly Rokossowski, who also held a position in the Polish politburo, assured Poland's commitment to the Warsaw Pact. They were being replaced by individuals that, in Khrushchev's view, were "anti-Soviet." As Khrushchev recounted in his memoirs, "The situation was such [that] we had to be ready to resort to arms. . . . The Soviet Union was being reviled with abusive language and the [Polish] government was close to being overthrown."[19]

Khrushchev arrived with a Soviet delegation in Warsaw on the morning of October 19, 1956, the day of the Eighth Plenum, determined to force the Polish leadership to delay Gomułka's election.[20] According to Gomułka's account, Khrushchev first greeted Rokossowski warmly before turning to the rest of the Polish leadership and declaring, "The treacherous activities of Comrade Ochab have become evident, this number won't pass here!"[21] After tense discussions during which Khrushchev threatened "to intervene brutally in [Polish] affairs," the Soviets agreed to allow for the announcement of Gomułka's election if the rest of the plenum were delayed until Soviet-Polish talks could be concluded.[22]

Khrushchev's primary goal was to keep the Polish-Soviet military alliance intact. As he explained in his memoirs many years later, he feared that anti-Soviet elements were taking control and that this would "threaten our lines of communication and access to Germany through Poland."[23] Negotiations between the Soviet delegation and Polish leaders continued at Warsaw's Belvedere Palace throughout October 19 and into the early morning hours of October 20. The Soviets protested "the abrupt removal of a group of comrades from the [PUWP] Politburo."[24] This group included members of the PUWP's conservative Natolin faction and, most critically, Rokossowski. The Soviets also opposed Gomułka's plan to remove Soviet advisers from the Polish armed forces. During the talks, Khrushchev ordered the mobilization of two Soviet divisions and Polish forces under Rokossowski's command, both of which began marching toward Warsaw as the Polish and Soviet delegations deliberated.

The Costs to Gomułka of Compliance Versus Resistance

My theory holds that concessions are less costly for leaders without domestic opposition, though their lack of opposition does not guarantee that they will concede to the foreign power. Even politically strong leaders may fear compliance will generate opposition and so resist if they have the military and economic power to do so. Nevertheless, given two leaders with similar levels of military and economic vulnerability, the leader without opposition should concede more than the leader with it. Gomułka had little opposition, but he faced a restive public insistent on reform. He, therefore, could not concede to Soviet demands entirely, because his popularity depended on reform. However, he was able to draw on this popularity to keep reform limited and assure the Soviets of their primary concern—Poland's commitment to the Warsaw Pact.

By the summer of 1956, a virtual cult of Gomułka had emerged.[25] Światło's revelations had not only discredited hardliners, they had also bolstered Gomułka's image. According to Światło, Gomułka had been spared a show trial because he had threatened to reveal that members of the Polish leadership had exposed Polish resistance members to the Gestapo during the war.[26] Gomułka, as leader of the first postwar Polish communist party, had advocated a "Polish road to development."[27] His opposition to the very policies that had weakened the Polish economy now led many to idealize his previous tenure. However, Gomułka's popularity was based more on expectations of what he might do than on concrete proposals of what he planned to do.[28]

At least two developments enabled Gomułka to preserve his popularity throughout the crisis. The first was the Polish government's initial reforms, which had helped prevent unrest from spiraling out of control.[29] Bierut had initiated these reforms following Światło's revelations by abolishing the Ministry of Public Security and purging the secret police.[30] Ochab then expanded them by granting amnesty to some thirty-five thousand political prisoners, relaxing censorship, and forcing Bierut's second in command, Jakub Berman, into retirement.[31] The government also admitted the party's "mistakes and shortcomings" after the Poznań riots and imposed only mild sentences on those arrested.[32] These attempts to placate the public helped to avoid an incident that might have spurred a wider rebellion. Gomułka thus assumed power at a time when protestors' demands were still restrained and when they remained willing to accept the government's authority. This would enable him to limit reforms.

The waning influence of the Natolin faction also strengthened Gomułka's domestic position. The conservative group had first attempted to co-opt Gomułka by offering him a seat in the politburo.[33] Gomułka refused to join unless he was made first secretary.[34] Although the Natolin rejected his demand, a shift in the balance of power on the Polish politburo soon enabled Gomułka to secure the party's top post. At the Seventh Plenum, ten days after Poznań, two reformers and a centrist were elected to the politburo, putting the Natolin in the minority.[35] Afterward, in a series of backroom deals, the reformers offered Gomułka the post of first secretary, to be formalized at the Eighth Plenum. Gomułka, along with Ochab, a fellow reformer, was also appointed to a three-member commission tasked with preparing a candidate list for the next round of elections. The group it named excluded the foremost hardliners. By pushing the hardliners aside, Gomułka was able to assure he would have the Polish politburo's full support as first secretary.[36]

Yet Natolin members still occupied positions of influence in the government. Rokossowski stayed on as defense minister and ostensibly had the military means to block Gomułka. In fact, rumors circulated that the Natolin faction was planning a coup to prevent Gomułka's expected election at the Eighth Plenum.[37] The problem for the Natolin, as I will explain shortly, was that Polish troops could not be relied upon to fight for a pro-Moscow regime.[38] The Natolin would need Soviet assistance to seize power. This would force Khrushchev to choose between negotiating with Gomułka and using Soviet forces to overthrow him.

The Costs to the Soviet Union of a Settlement with Gomułka

My theory suggests that settlements are less costly to obtain with leaders who can make concessions without imperiling their domestic political positions. Although leaders without opposition will not necessarily yield to a foreign power's demands, their lower domestic political cost of compliance means the foreign power has to invest less to coax their compliance. Gomułka's relatively strong position enabled him to assure the Soviets that the Polish-Soviet alliance would remain intact. However, he was not willing to abandon his plans to remove Rokossowski and the Soviet advisers because his popularity depended on it. This meant that a settlement would require Moscow to accept some change to the status quo. Khrushchev was initially unwilling to countenance any change; however, Gomułka's repeated assurances on the Polish-Soviet alliance would help convince the Soviet leader to settle rather than to take on the high costs of regime change.

Gomułka was both willing and able to keep Poland in the Warsaw Pact. He was willing to preserve the military alliance because he believed Poland needed the Soviet Union to help defend its borders against a possible revanchist Germany. During the Warsaw talks on October 19, he declared, "Poland needs friendship with the Soviet Union more than the Soviet Union needs friendship with Poland. . . . Without the Soviet Union we cannot maintain our borders with the West."[39] Yet, though Gomułka believed Poland should remain in the Warsaw Pact, he could also afford to take this position. Although Poles resented Soviet domination, Gomułka was not facing public pressure to withdraw from the Warsaw Pact. He was, therefore, able to insist Poland retain its military alliance with the Soviet Union without worrying about compromising his domestic standing or inviting political attacks. Khrushchev would later claim that it was Gomułka's emphatic assurance of Poland's commitment to the Polish-Soviet alliance that helped convince him to retain the Polish leader.[40]

Despite these later claims, at the time the Soviet leader continued demanding that the Polish leadership abandon reform. Around noon on October 19, as the talks between the two nations continued, the Polish leadership began hearing reports that Soviets troops stationed in northern and western Poland were advancing toward Warsaw.[41] At the same time, and unbeknown to top Polish leaders, Rokossowski ordered Polish units to meet the Soviet forces and march toward Warsaw as well.[42] The Soviet Baltic fleet was also patrolling the Bay of Gdańsk, and the Soviet air force began flying over Polish airspace.[43]

Though unclear whether these maneuvers were meant to force Gomułka into making concessions or to assist in a Natolin coup, they failed to change the Polish leader's position. Gomułka "vehemently" protested the mobilization. According to the notes of Polish politburo member Aleksander Zawadzki, there were "sharp clashes" between the Polish and Soviet leaders.[44] Gomułka later stated that he had told Khrushchev he would not continue the negotiations as long as the Soviets kept "a revolver on the table."[45] Yet the Polish leadership was also careful not to give Khrushchev reason to support Rokossowski's possible coup attempt. The Polish leadership ordered the Internal Security Corps (ISC) forces, whose commander was a recently installed Gomułka ally, to secure Warsaw. Although some officers insisted the ISC should be ready to battle the approaching Soviet and Polish forces, the diary of one commanding officer reveals the Polish leadership insisted on restraint. The ISC's main task was to maintain security to prevent popular protests from triggering a Soviet invasion.[46]

In the end, Khrushchev appeared to make concessions in Warsaw but did not entirely abandon the idea of a military intervention aimed, potentially, at Gomułka's removal. Khrushchev admitted during the talks that the Soviet delegation had come hoping to "influence" the Polish leadership, but that "[the Poles] will not entertain anything."[47] He indicated that the Soviets would "rather reluctantly" concede on the matter of the Soviet advisors. Nevertheless, Rokossowski's fate was not addressed and the Soviet forces did not return to their bases.[48] According to Gomułka, Khrushchev concluded the talks by saying, "It doesn't matter what you want, our view is such that we will have to restart the intervention."[49] Despite Gomułka's assurances, Khrushchev was not yet ready to accept the Polish leader's changes to the status quo.

In the days following the Warsaw talks, Gomułka continued to affirm his commitment to the Soviet-Polish alliance.[50] In a speech on October 24 that attracted a crowd of three hundred thousand, Gomułka carefully stressed the need for the relationship.[51] He also denounced any attempt to withdraw from the Warsaw Pact.[52] Some protestors demanded the government go further in its reforms, but Gomułka used the ISC to break up these demonstrations. When an initiative began among some Polish officers on October 23 to press for the removal of Soviet forces from Poland, Gomułka cut short the discussion.[53] To tamp down the widespread anger, he said publicly that the Soviet military maneuvers were an exercise.[54] Gomułka's ability to contain unrest further reassured the Soviets. Yet Khrushchev had another reason to accept a settlement—the high cost of removing the popular Gomułka.

The Costs of Regime Change in Poland

Upon returning to Moscow on October 20, 1956, Khrushchev indicated he was still considering military intervention. Despite his apparent concessions in Warsaw, he now told the CPSU CC Presidium, "There's only one way out—by putting an end to what is in Poland." But he also suggested that his decision to use force would rest on the Polish government's behavior. He noted that "if Rokossowski is kept, we won't have to press things for a while."[55] Malin's notes, although obscure on this issue, suggest that Khrushchev may have been making initial plans to oust Gomułka. The notes call for the formation of a committee, which historian Mark Kramer reports likely refers to a "provisional revolutionary committee" or provisional government, of the kind that was later assembled to replace Hungarian leader Imre Nagy.[56] By the next day, however, Khrushchev had adopted a more conciliatory tone. Meeting again with the presidium, he announced, "Taking account of circumstances, we should refrain from military intervention. We need to display patience." His view was unanimously approved, and on October 22, Khrushchev sent a letter to Gomułka approving the removal of Soviet advisors and officers.[57] The Rokossowski issue was not addressed.

Two types of cost considerations appear to have prompted Khrushchev's decision to finally concede on removing the Soviet advisors and officers. First, the high military costs of installing the Natolin faction in power proved a significant deterrent to regime change. Given the popular mood, a Natolin coup had the potential to spark a major rebellion. There were enough Soviet units to pacify Warsaw, but not enough to counter a nationwide uprising.[58] By Khrushchev's own account, he had planned to use Polish forces to suppress resistance. After meeting privately with Rokossowski in Warsaw, however, Khrushchev learned that the loyalty of the Polish forces could not be guaranteed. In his memoirs, he recounts their discussion:

Marshal [Ivan] Konev and I held separate consultations with Comrade Rokossowski, who was more obedient to us but had less authority than the other Polish leaders. He told us that anti-Soviet, nationalistic, and reactionary forces were growing in strength, and that if it were necessary to arrest the growth of these counterrevolutionary elements by force of arms, he was at our disposal. . . . But as we began to analyze the problem in more detail and calculate which Polish regiments we could count on to obey Rokossowski, the situation began to look somewhat bleak. Of course, our own armed strength far exceeded that of Poland, but we didn't want to resort to the use of our own troops.[59]

This account strongly suggests that Khrushchev was considering using Polish troops to install the Natolin faction but changed his mind after learning regime change would entail substantial military costs.

Khrushchev had additional reasons to fear the military costs of an intervention. ISC forces loyal to Gomułka were occupying strategic positions throughout Warsaw. The ISC was not ordered to fight off Soviet and pro-Moscow Polish forces, but it is unclear whether Khrushchev knew that. Rumors were circulating that the Poles were distributing arms to workers and students.[60] Although the Polish leadership had discouraged any steps that might provoke a Soviet intervention, Khrushchev later cited as fact the rumors of the Polish government's attempts to arm the population, suggesting he feared the potentially high costs of a military confrontation.[61] He told the CPSU CC Presidium on October 21 that "finding a reason for an armed conflict now would be very easy, but finding a way to put an end to such a conflict would be very hard."[62]

The high diplomatic costs of deposing Gomułka posed a second deterrent. Ousting a popular leader in an allied state was directly at odds with Khrushchev's attempt to remake the Soviet Union's image in the wake of Stalin's death. China, in particular, strongly opposed the Soviet Union's "great power chauvinism" and wanted to see the Polish crisis resolved peacefully. According to at least one source, Mao Zedong told the Soviet ambassador in a meeting on October 20 that China would "be vehement in its protests against [intervention]."[63] Khrushchev likely heard the Soviet ambassador's report either in Warsaw or soon after arriving back in Moscow on the 20th.[64] Four days later, two of Mao's most trusted advisers—Vice Chairman Liu Shaoqi and General Secretary Deng Xiaoping—arrived in Moscow to reinforce Beijing's view. Liu Shaoqi made a speech to the CPSU CC Presidium in which he referred to Soviet interference in its allies' domestic affairs and noted Soviet "shortcomings" in its relations with other socialist states.[65] Mao's opposition suggested the diplomatic costs of regime change might be high.

The same day, Khrushchev indicated he was finally willing to accept all of Gomułka's terms. He announced to the presidium, "Poland has now adopted a course that will eliminate the unpleasant state of affairs."[66] Four days later, he informed his colleagues that "with reference to Rokossowski, I told Gomułka that it is your (Polish) affair."[67] Some scholars note that the Hungarian uprising, which began on October 23, may explain the timing of Khrushchev's decision to concede to Gomułka's terms. Although the Kremlin was forced to turn its attention to Hungary, Khrushchev appears to have given up on the idea of regime change in Poland on the 21st, when he formally relented on the removal of the Soviet military advisors. By then, he had learned from Rokossowksi that an intervention would entail high military costs, and he knew, too, that China would oppose it, which meant high diplomatic costs as well. Whereas regime change was going to be costly, a negotiated settlement offered Khrushchev a chance to achieve his primary goal of keeping Poland in the Warsaw Pact at much lower cost.

Alternative Arguments in the Polish Case

I argue that Gomułka was willing to adhere to the Soviet-Polish military alliance in part because he faced little domestic opposition that might have forced him to adopt a more extreme position. The fact that he faced so little opposition also made him costly to overthrow. Consequently, Khrushchev abandoned his initial thoughts of regime change and turned to negotiation. There are, however, alternative explanations for this case.

PSYCHOLOGICAL BIAS

A psychological approach to understanding the Soviet decision to negotiate with, rather than overthrow, Gomułka would predict that the Polish leader had relatively good relations with the Soviet leadership prior to the crisis. If so, then Khrushchev would have been inclined to interpret Gomułka's policies as nonthreatening and been open to a settlement. The historical evidence, however, contradicts this expectation. Khrushchev's initial response to Gomułka was to threaten force. The October 20 minutes from the CPSU CC Presidium meeting in Moscow, during which the Soviet leader insisted on "putting an end to what is in Poland," indicate that Khrushchev's threats to intervene were sincere. His references to cobbling together an alternative government suggest further that he was considering regime change. Moreover, Khrushchev's memoirs indicate that he had considered backing a Natolin coup until informed that Polish troops could not be trusted to cooperate. Although one might have expected that Gomułka and Khrushchev's shared opposition to Stalinism would have made them natural allies, Khrushchev initially viewed Gomułka's reforms as a serious threat to Soviet security interests.

BUREAUCRATIC AND INTEREST-GROUP PRESSURE

Bureaucratic politics appears to have had very little impact on Khrushchev's response to the Polish crisis. Although Khrushchev did face domestic political pressure from hardliners in the Kremlin to assert Soviet dominance over the satellite states, this pressure did not lead to regime change in Poland. Khrushchev ultimately chose to settle with Gomułka. Further, the Malin notes indicate that CPSU CC Presidium members largely followed Khrushchev's lead and approved his decisions. There is also no evidence that Gomułka was manipulated by self-interested bureaucrats who pressured him to defy Moscow or that either leader was controlled by interest groups. Although Gomułka also had hardliners to contend with, he successfully pushed them aside.

RATIONAL CHOICE ARGUMENTS

An incomplete-information argument would suggest that Gomułka and Khrushchev were able to reach a settlement because each was well informed of the other's military capabilities and resolve to fight. The evidence for this argument is mixed. Both sides clearly understood that the Soviet Union had the military means to impose a government on Poland. Gomułka also appears to have believed the Soviet threat to intervene. The Polish leadership learned that the Soviets had mobilized their forces during the talks in Warsaw. Polish leaders also worried that unrest might provoke a Soviet intervention and so ordered ISC forces to prevent unrest. These actions suggest that Polish leaders took the threat of a Soviet intervention seriously.

Yet, an incomplete-information argument would predict that a target, once convinced of an opponent's will and ability to use decisive force, would back down. However, although the Polish leadership kept its reforms limited, it did not back down on them, despite Soviet threats. Gomułka appeared willing to run the risk of a Soviet military intervention so he could implement the reforms he believed necessary to reestablish the public's confidence in the PUWP and end the unrest. Gomułka was prioritizing his domestic political interests over appeasing the Soviets. He hoped his assurances on the Soviet-Polish alliance would satisfy Khrushchev, but he had no way of knowing if this would be adequate. The evidence thus suggests that the Polish crisis ended in a settlement in spite of Gomułka's resistance and not because he had sufficient information to know when to back down.

Finally, a credible-commitment argument would posit that Khrushchev believed Gomułka's promises to uphold the Soviet alliance and negotiated because he was confident the settlement would hold. There is evidence to support this claim. Gomułka was indeed a credible partner; he had strategic reasons for wanting to maintain the Soviet-Polish alliance. But a credible-commitment approach tells only part of the story. Gomułka could afford to be a credible partner, because he had strong domestic support. His popularity enabled him to appease the public with relatively modest reforms without endangering the Soviet-Polish alliance. He was also able to sustain his popularity throughout the crisis, because he faced few internal rivals who could stifle his reforms and undercut his popularity. Thus, Gomułka's lack of domestic opposition enabled him to reassure the Soviets of their primary security concerns.

Importantly, however, the evidence also indicates that the credibility of Gomułka's assurances was not enough to convince Khrushchev to forego regime change. The Soviet leader was still considering an intervention possibly aimed at regime change, even after his return to Moscow. He only abandoned the idea after learning that Polish troops were unlikely to fight on Moscow's behalf *and* that Mao vehemently opposed intervention. Khrushchev's concerns over the high military and diplomatic costs of regime change were, therefore, at least as important as his perception of Gomułka's credibility. It was both the expected low costs of a settlement and the high costs of regime change that led Khrushchev to negotiate.

THE CASE OF POLAND: CONCLUSIONS

The Polish case fits my theory's expectations (hypothesis $H1a_1$). The settlement reached between the Polish and Soviet leadership during the October 1956 crisis was facilitated by Gomułka's ability to command domestic support from both within the Polish politburo and the public at large.

Although my theory does not predict that leaders without domestic opposition will necessarily make full concessions, all else being equal, leaders without such opposition find it easier to make concessions than do leaders for whom compliance carries high political costs ($H1b_1$). The evidence in this case shows that Gomułka's lack of opposition made it easier for him to negotiate. He was able to trade on his popularity to keep reforms limited and discourage schemes to obtain greater autonomy from the Soviet Union. Although Gomułka favored the Polish-Soviet military alliance, had he faced stronger domestic political pressure, he might have been forced to implement more drastic reform that might have threatened Soviet security interests. Instead, his ability to implement modest reform allowed him to satisfy the Soviets on their foremost security goal—keeping Poland in the Warsaw Pact.

Khrushchev was at first unwilling to accept any change to the status quo and appears to have even considered regime change. But replacing the popular Gomułka was not going to be easy. He commanded the loyalty of the Polish military, which was expected to fight against a Soviet intervention. A military clash with Polish troops would have also put Moscow at odds with the Chinese, who made clear that they opposed the Soviets using force against a popularly supported ally. These high military and diplomatic costs, both a consequence of Gomułka's political power, convinced Khrushchev to negotiate with rather than overthrow the Polish leader.

Hungary, 1956: Partial Regime Change

In contrast to the Polish case, a similar crisis in Hungary became violent and ended with the execution of the Hungarian prime minister, Imre Nagy. Khrushchev initially supported Nagy, even as the Hungarian reformer made major concessions to protestors that included the creation of a multiparty electoral system. After a week, however, Khrushchev abruptly changed course and ordered a massive military invasion to depose Nagy and crush the rebellion. Nagy's fate was very different from Gomułka's because Nagy faced domestic opposition that his Polish counterpart did not. Although Nagy had popular support, his opponents within the various rebel factions and his own government frustrated his attempts to calm the rebellion. At the same time, Khrushchev was able to exploit the divisions within Nagy's government to convince centrists to overthrow him. The

Suez Crisis also helped trigger regime change by prompting Khrushchev to reconsider the costs of an invasion.[68] This event served as a catalyst for regime change by magnifying the effects of Nagy's domestic political vulnerability. It was not, however, a direct cause. As long as Nagy was unable to satisfy Soviet demands and his domestic opponents were willing to conspire against him, the Hungarian prime minister was likely to be overthrown.

Soviet Demands in Hungary

The Hungarian Revolution began on October 23, 1956. Although the protests were partly inspired by events in Poland, discontent had been growing in the country for several years. In 1953, Moscow had pressured Hungary's Stalinist leader, Mátyás Rákosi, to cede his post as prime minister to the reform-minded Nagy. Rákosi, however, was permitted to retain his other position as first secretary of the Hungarian Workers' Party (HWP). In contrast to Rákosi, Nagy supported a more gradual approach to collectivization and greater investment in consumer goods. During his tenure, he won popular support by liberating thousands of prisoners, restricting the widely despised secret police (the Államvédelmi Hatóság, or ÁVH), and increasing the standard of living by 15 percent.[69] In 1955, however, Rákosi convinced Moscow to replace Nagy as prime minister with the hardliner and Rákosi protégé András Hegedüs.[70] Nagy was later expelled from the party. In the ensuing years, he became a symbol of the opposition to Hungary's Stalinist regime.

In June, one day before the Poznań riots in Poland, the Petöfi Circle, an organization of intellectuals, criticized the government and issued a demand for reforms.[71] These reforms included reinstating Nagy to the party.[72] The Petöfi Circle's demand for Nagy's reinstatement was a clear challenge to the government's authority. CPSU CC Presidium member Anastas Mikoyan characterized the event as "an ideological Poznań without gunshots."[73]

In contrast to the Polish government's response to Poznań, the Hungarian government exacerbated its crisis. Although the Soviets had forced Rákosi to resign his post as first secretary in July, his replacement Ernő Gerő, was another of his protégés.[74] Gerő steadfastly rejected reform but attempted to appease the population by allowing the reburial of László Rajk, a prominent HWP member executed under Rákosi. Gerő, however, was out of the country on the day of the reburial, which attracted two hundred thousand people and soon developed into a demonstration.[75] When Gerő returned, he confessed to the Soviet ambassador that the situation had "become much worse and more turbulent than I had imagined."[76] Yet Gerő left the country again. He returned just hours before a massive demonstration in Budapest on October 23.[77] The protest turned violent when the ÁVH fired on unarmed protestors who were attempting to broadcast their demands from the main radio station in Budapest.[78] Hungarian soldiers that were mobilized to suppress the rebellion refused to fire on the civilians and, in some cases, joined them.[79] Later in the day, Gerő inflamed public opinion even more by delivering a harsh speech that condemned the protestors as counterrevolutionaries.[80]

With an uprising underway, Gerő asked Moscow to intervene militarily. The CPSU CC Presidium met on the 23rd to discuss the request. Although Khrushchev recommended sending troops, Mikoyan objected, arguing that Nagy should be reinstalled to contain the unrest.[81] "Without Nagy [the Hungarian communists] can't get control of the movement, and it's also cheaper for us," he argued. "We should try political measures, and only then send troops." Mikoyan was outvoted on the issue of sending troops, but his suggestion to use Nagy to regain control garnered support. Khrushchev concluded the discussion by suggesting, "We should recruit Nagy for political action."[82] The leadership agreed to send Mikoyan and Mikhail Suslov to Budapest to represent the Soviet position, report on events, and negotiate with the Hungarians.

Even the Hungarian hardliners accepted the idea of bringing Nagy back, hoping that his appointment would appease the protestors. In the early morning hours of October 24, Nagy assumed the post of prime minister, while Gerő retained his post as first secretary.[83] The introduction of Soviet troops, however, inflamed the situation even more. Soviet tanks lumbering down city streets without sufficient infantry became easy prey for Hungarian guerillas.[84] Upon arriving in Budapest, Mikoyan and Suslov reported to Moscow that the violence was causing "further panic among senior Hungarian officials, many of whom fled into underground bunkers."[85] On October 25, seventy-five unarmed protestors died and over two hundred were wounded when Soviet troops and ÁVH snipers fired on a large demonstration in Parliament Square. In the days after the massacre, there were several reported instances of crowds lynching members of the ÁVH.

Unable to suppress the uprising, the Soviets allowed Nagy to implement significant reforms over the next week to end the crisis. Nagy was initially reluctant to give in to many of the protestors' demands. He regarded demands for elections as "bourgeois democracy" and initially opposed calls for Soviet troop withdrawals.[86] By October 28, however, he had concluded that he needed to "lead" the revolution in order to contain it.[87] Nagy's concessions began that day with a cease-fire and amnesty, the withdrawal of Soviet troops from the city of Budapest, and a pledge to negotiate the withdrawal of Soviet troops from the country entirely. On the 30th, Nagy announced plans for multiparty elections that would include noncommunist parties. He also formed a new government that included members of those parties.[88] Notes from the meetings of the CPSU CC Presidium on the 30th show, remarkably, that the Soviet leadership approved these reforms, albeit reluctantly. On the same day that Nagy agreed to hold multiparty elections, for example, Khrushchev recommended that the Soviet government issue a declaration in support of Nagy. The Soviet leader noted that there were "two paths. A military path—one of occupation. A peaceful path—the withdrawal of troops, negotiations."[89] Khrushchev made clear he preferred the latter.

The Kremlin's willingness to accept Nagy's reforms reflected the Soviet leadership's primary goal—to end the rebellion. But it would not accept Hungary's withdrawal from the Warsaw Pact. Even Mikoyan, the most fervent opponent of intervention, insisted, "We simply cannot allow Hungary to be removed from our camp."[90] Keeping Hungary in the Warsaw Pact was a relatively modest goal by Soviet standards. Some rebel factions, however, were already calling for Hungary to declare its neutrality.[91] Having come to power in the midst of a rebellion, Nagy found himself needing to reconcile these more radical demands with Soviet security interests. As I show next, Nagy's domestic opposition would frustrate his attempts to do this.

The Costs to Nagy of Compliance Versus Resistance

Much like Gomułka in Poland, Nagy had broad popular appeal. Yet unlike Gomułka, Nagy was already facing a major rebellion when he took office. He also faced opposition from groups on both the right and the left. Within his government, he faced internal opposition from hardliners, who countered his decisions and attempted to undermine his popularity. Outside his government, he faced external opposition from some rebel factions, which sought to overthrow rather than merely reform the communist system. Together, these two sources of opposition served to intensify the rebellion, impeding Nagy's ability to convince Soviet leaders that he could manage it.

Whereas Gomułka had been able to purge his enemies before coming to office, Nagy was forced to contend with hardliners in the government for several days after assuming power. Gerő initially retained his post as first secretary but was soon ousted by the Soviets and replaced by János Kádár, a known centrist. Gerő and Hegedüs remained influential, however, as part of a committee to appoint the new government. From there, they were able to prevent some of Nagy's reformist allies from joining the leadership. Nagy's failure to oust the old guard disillusioned many of his supporters.[92]

The hardliners continued to advocate the use of force and, in some instances, directly undermined Nagy. Although the party leadership had agreed to a cease-fire to begin on October 28, hardliners secretly plotted with Soviet military officials and Hungarian officers loyal to Moscow to strike the main rebel factions that morning.[93] Rumors also surfaced that Nagy was responsible for the declaration of martial law on the 24th and the initial Soviet intervention that same day.[94] Although both had been ordered before Nagy assumed office, the rumors hurt his popularity. Nagy tried to rectify his image in a speech on the 27th. He insisted that hardliners had "tried to besmirch me by spreading the lie that I called in the Soviet troops."[95] On October 28, he finally gained Soviet approval to expel the hardliners and appoint a new government, but the damage had already been done. By undercutting Nagy's popular support, the hardliners complicated his efforts to control the rebellion.

Nagy faced opposition from various rebel factions, too. Although some of this stemmed from the hardliners' efforts to undercut him, Nagy hurt his own popularity with his initial reluctance to support the protestors' demands and signs of adherence to old communist ways. On October 23, for example, he drew jeers from a crowd of supporters when he addressed them as "comrades."[96] Although Nagy won back some support when he changed course and began introducing reforms, some rebel leaders remained determined to overthrow the communist government. Gergely Pongrátz, who led one of the strongest rebel factions, the Corvin Passage group, demanded Nagy hold free elections. Pongrátz agreed to recognize Nagy but would only continue supporting him if he were chosen via election.[97] A far more controversial rebel leader, József Dudás, reportedly insisted that Nagy make him the "sole legal representative of the armed rebel factions."[98]

As the crisis persisted, Nagy struggled against a tide of increasingly more radical rebel demands.[99] After the massacre of unarmed protestors in Parliament Square on October 25, he announced he would disband the ÁVH. Although a significant reform from Moscow's perspective, rebel groups demanded both exact dates for the ÁVH's dissolution and the withdrawal of Soviet troops. The Soviets insisted they could not withdraw as long as the rebels remained armed. But after the Soviet attack on the morning of the cease-fire, several rebel factions refused to surrender their arms until the Soviet troops withdrew.[100] The refusal of rebel groups to disarm also complicated the government's ongoing attempt to form a national guard, which was intended to bring the rebel factions under the government's control.

Radio Free Europe broadcasts also contributed to Nagy's difficulties in ending the rebellion. Although the Eisenhower administration had reassured the Kremlin that it had no interest in bringing Hungary into NATO, the president himself had made statements sympathetic to the Hungarians' cause and had offered aid.[101] The United States, United Kingdom, and France had also proposed discussing the crisis at the UN Security Council.[102] Radio Free Europe's program *Voice for Free Hungary* had an even more destabilizing effect. The program persistently denounced Nagy and instructed listeners on ways to conduct sabotage, such as destroying Soviet tanks.[103] One broadcast encouraged rebels to believe the United States would intervene. The announcer promised, "If the Soviet troops really attack Hungary . . . and Hungarians hold out for three or four days, then the pressure upon the government of the United States to send military help to the Freedom Fighters will become irresistible!"[104] These assurances fueled the rebel factions, some of which began to demand Hungary's neutrality and withdrawal from the Warsaw Pact.

Although Nagy had implemented significant reforms to placate the rebels, he was acutely aware throughout the crisis of the risk of antagonizing Moscow. On October 28, he warned the members of his government that if they did not take care, they would "be subjected to an intervention."[105] He routinely consulted with the Soviet representatives in Budapest, seeking Moscow's approval for his concessions. Nagy also carefully cultivated the support of the Hungarian Council of Ministers so he would not be blamed for acting unilaterally. He did not blindly challenge

Moscow by implementing reforms the Kremlin was bound to reject. Rather, he attempted to broker a compromise with the rebels that would end the uprising without triggering a Soviet invasion. Moscow was also mindful of the pressures on Nagy and, for the first week of the rebellion, accepted his reforms despite their costs. All this would change, however, on the morning of October 31, when Khrushchev ordered the second Soviet intervention, and with it, Nagy's removal.

The Costs to the Soviet Union of a Settlement with Nagy

Khrushchev had initially supported Nagy in part because he saw the military costs of regime change as high. Popular support in Hungary for the revolution was strong, which meant significant military force would be needed to crush it. Soviet leaders also feared that a second intervention would require a full military occupation. As Soviet premier Nikolai Bulganin warned, "This will drag us into a dubious venture."[106] Furthermore, Hungarian forces were expected to fight in defense of their country, not alongside Russian troops. Khrushchev knew the hardliners had little domestic support as well, and so could not easily be reinstalled. He had told Rákosi, who was in Moscow offering "help," that he would be in danger should he return home, for "the people will hang you there."[107]

The Soviet leader was also concerned about the diplomatic and reputational costs of appearing to be a "conqueror."[108] At the 20th Congress, Khrushchev had acknowledged that there were multiple forms of socialist development and had promoted peaceful coexistence as part of an effort to attract greater support in the Third World.[109] Crushing a nationalist uprising in an allied state would make it difficult to attract that support by suggesting that the Soviet Union could only keep allies through the use of force. Indeed, to avoid the perception of using force against an ally, Khrushchev had insisted on a formal request from the Hungarian government for the first Soviet intervention. When Nagy refused to provide one, Hegedüs, the previous prime minister, signed the document.[110]

Khrushchev was also concerned about how Soviet allies might perceive military intervention. The Soviet presidium members knew the crises in Poland and Hungary stemmed from anti-Soviet sentiments that were prevalent throughout the Eastern bloc. A crackdown threatened to exacerbate these sentiments. Mao's earlier opposition to the use of force in Poland also gave Khrushchev pause. Partly to allay Chinese concerns, the CPSU CC

Presidium decided to issue an October 30 declaration of its intentions to further strengthen "friendship and cooperation among the socialist countries" and to observe "the full sovereignty of each socialist state."[111] The declaration also announced Soviet plans to negotiate troop withdrawals from the satellites, in particular Hungary.

Yet, although the Chinese opposed the use of force against an ally, Mao had come to see intervention as necessary in Hungary. He was not, however, encouraging regime change. Rather, he was urging Khrushchev to wait for the Hungarian government to invite intervention. The Chinese leader believed that if the Soviets delayed, the "counter-revolutionaries" would reveal themselves.[112] Liu Shaoqi, one of Mao's most trusted advisers, explained to the Soviet ambassador after the crisis that if the Soviets had waited "seven or ten or even twenty days later, by that time the Hungarian people could have seen better the true face of the reaction, and could have understood better the role of the Soviet Army." Liu Shaoqi added that, by then, "[reactionary forces] would have driven away Imre Nagy . . . [and] would have come to power. . . . The real communists and other progressive people would have escaped to the Soviet troops."[113] By waiting for the Hungarians to request intervention, Mao's plan put Moscow firmly on the side of the Hungarian government. Rather than deposing Nagy, Moscow would be helping to restore him or a successor to power.

Khrushchev seriously considered Mao's plan.[114] Khrushchev and Liu Shaoqi, who was in Moscow during the crisis, deliberated into the night on October 30. Khrushchev recalls that Liu Shaoqi suggested they might wait for "the working class . . . to realize that the uprising was counterrevolutionary, and deal with it by itself."[115] But Khrushchev wondered whether the Hungarians could cope with the situation on their own.[116] By the end of the evening, the two had come to the decision not to use armed force.[117] By the next morning, however, the Soviet leader had changed his mind.[118]

Several scholarly accounts suggest that troubling news on October 30 led Khrushchev to change his mind and order an invasion the next day.[119] In an October 30th memo, Suslov and Mikoyan reported on a violent attack at the communist party headquarters in Budapest that occurred earlier that day. They also relayed details of a conversation with Nagy about the possibility of his declaring Hungary's neutrality. Some scholars suggest that Nagy's apparent inability to stop the violence and support for neutrality alarmed Soviet leaders and led to the invasion. However, despite the news that day, Khrushchev continued to support Nagy.[120] Khrushchev's memoirs confirm that after his discussions with Liu Shaoqi that evening, he went to bed still opposed to crushing the rebellion.[121] Furthermore, Mikoyan and Suslov's report also makes clear that Nagy had raised the prospect of neutrality in response to Soviet troop exercises, which Hungarian leaders took to be signs of an invasion. Although the two Soviet representatives warned of a potential "turning point" in Hungarian policy and recommended the Kremlin send Marshal Konev, the commander in chief of the Warsaw Pact forces, they also urged restraint.[122] In what appears to be a recommendation to avoid provocation, they wrote that the minister of defense should "cease sending troops into Hungary."[123]

Although it is difficult to know whether it merely took time for Khrushchev to decide that the events on October 30 warranted intervention, it appears more likely that the Suez Crisis, which began the morning of October 31, triggered the Soviet leader's policy reversal. My theory indicates that major events and crises can serve as a catalyst for regime change by prompting policymakers to reevaluate their policies and the costs of using force. As I explain in the next section, the Suez Crisis played precisely this role in Hungary.

The Costs of Partial Regime Change in Hungary

Faced with significant domestic opposition, Nagy had struggled to satisfy the Kremlin's central demand to end Hungary's rebellion. But until October 31, Khrushchev had regarded the military and diplomatic costs of deposing the Hungarian leader as high. However, after news that France and the United Kingdom had joined an Israeli attack on Egypt, a Soviet ally, Khrushchev's assessment of these costs changed. In particular, he feared a successful attack on Egypt would encourage the West to meddle in Hungary, which would increase the military costs of restoring order. In a CPSU CC Presidium meeting the morning of October 31, Khrushchev explained, "If we depart from Hungary, it will give a great boost to the Americans, English, and French—the imperialists. They will perceive it as weakness on our part and will go onto the offensive. We would then be exposing the weakness of our positions. Our party will not accept it if we do this. To Egypt they will then add Hungary. We have no other choice."[124] Although Khrushchev did not yet know the United States would oppose its allies in the crisis, he appears to have concluded that the military costs of waiting for Nagy to contain the rebellion were about to rise.

Khrushchev had reason to believe the West would interfere in Hungary. Although Eisenhower had indicated that the United States was not seeking to make Hungary a NATO ally, the United States might aid the rebels covertly.[125] In addition to Eisenhower's earlier statements on Hungarian neutrality, Radio Free Europe broadcasts were still urging the rebels to fight. The Kremlin also received reports of Hungarians returning to Budapest from Vienna.[126] The Soviets knew the United States had plans to build a corps of Eastern European émigrés to "support NATO."[127] These reports likely confirmed their fear that the United States would fan the flames of the rebellion.

The start of the Suez Crisis also eased Khrushchev's sensitivity to the diplomatic costs of using military force. It would be difficult for the key Western nations engaged in a war of aggression against Egypt to criticize the Soviet Union for similar behavior. According to Veljko Mićunović, the Yugoslav ambassador to Moscow, who recorded Khrushchev's discussion with Tito, the Soviet leader observed that an invasion of Hungary would cause "confusion and uproar in the West and the United Nations, but it would be less at a time when Britain, France and Israel were waging a war against Egypt."[128] Khrushchev was right. Although the Eisenhower administration had proposed discussing the Hungarian revolution at the United Nations, American attention promptly shifted to events in Egypt once the Suez Crisis began.

Khrushchev also had reason to think Soviet allies would support him, which lowered the diplomatic costs of military action still more. Although Mao was counseling Khrushchev to delay an intervention, he signaled that he would support one either way.[129] The satellite states were also warning that a failure to end the rebellion in Hungary would jeopardize their stability.[130] Reports of "mass confusion and unrest" in the Romanian cities of Cluj and Bucharest, prompted swift action by the Romanian government. In addition to sealing the border with Hungary, the Romanians created a general command staff with wide-ranging powers, including the ability to call a state of emergency and issue shoot-to-kill orders.[131] The Czechoslovakian government also warned Moscow that the Hungarian crisis was "having a deleterious psychological effect" on its citizens and that an "antisocialist mood" was developing among its troops sent to reinforce the border. Czechoslovakia also warned of possible "incursions by counterrevolutionary groups" if Soviet and Hungarian forces were withdrawn from northern Hungary.[132]

The potential for Western interference after the Suez Crisis also caused Khrushchev to reconsider the domestic political costs of delaying intervention. On November 3, Khrushchev told Tito in a meeting that losing Hungary would undermine his stand against the Stalinists in the Kremlin. According to Mićunović, who was present at the meeting, Khrushchev explained that "there were people in the Soviet Union who would say that as long as Stalin was in command everybody obeyed . . . but that now, ever since *they* had come to power . . . Russia had suffered the defeat and loss of Hungary." Khrushchev believed that the Soviet army, in particular, would react strongly if Hungary were lost.[133] Nagy's domestic political pressures had forced Khrushchev to absorb the high costs of Nagy's reforms, but the additional expense that he presumed would follow the Suez Crisis was too much.

Although the Suez Crisis appears to have played an important role in prompting Khrushchev to change course, most of the scholarly literature agrees that Moscow would have intervened even if the crisis had never occurred.[134] As long as Nagy remained unable to satisfy Moscow's central demand to end the rebellion, the Soviet Union would have looked to replace him with someone who could. Importantly, what made Nagy susceptible to regime change was his domestic opposition. His opponents on the right had undercut his popularity, while his opponents on the left refused to recognize his government. Had Nagy enjoyed the widespread support Gomułka had, the Suez Crisis might have had little effect. Nagy would have been not only better able to quell the rebellion but also more costly for the Soviet Union to replace.

Nevertheless, when it came to replacing Nagy, Khrushchev knew he could not rely on Hungarian hardliners. They lacked popular support. They were also no longer in government and so could not simply overthrow Nagy from within. My theory predicts that when the external opposition is too weak to overthrow the leadership, the stronger state will use the leader's internal opposition to effect partial regime change. Consistent with this prediction, Khrushchev used centrists within Nagy's government to topple him and construct a new administration. Khrushchev's first choice to replace Nagy was the interior minister Ferenc Münnich, with János Kádár as deputy premier.[135] Khrushchev had known Münnich since 1930, when they had shared a tent together during military training.[136] The hardliners, Rákosi, Gerő, and Hegedüs, who had fled to Moscow, also preferred Münnich.[137] Under Rákosi, Münnich had been ambassador to Moscow and

Belgrade.[138] During the crisis, Münnich was not only in direct contact with the Soviets but also appears to have advocated for a Soviet intervention.[139] On October 31, Khrushchev told the CPSU CC Presidium, "Münnich is appealing to us with a request for assistance. We are lending assistance and restoring order."[140]

But Khrushchev changed his mind about Münnich after Tito pointed out that Kádár was a better choice. Münnich had been ambassador to Moscow, Tito noted, while Kádár, a victim of Rákosi's purges, "had been in prison in Budapest. For every Hungarian this would be decisive in Kádár's favor." The Yugoslav leader warned that the new government would also have to denounce Rákosi and adopt a change of course to win political support.[141]

Kádár appears to have been less willing than Münnich to turn on Nagy. On November 1, Münnich encouraged Kádár to go with him to the Soviet embassy and then on to Moscow. Once there, Kádár and Münnich attended the November 2 CPSU CC Presidium meeting, during which Kádár initially defended the revolution and actions of the Hungarian government. He insisted that the insurgents were only "seeking the ouster of the Rákosi clique," and were fighting "for the withdrawal of troops and for the order of people's democracy."[142] Kádár also initially opposed a Soviet invasion. "The use of military force will be destructive and lead to bloodshed," he warned. "The morale of the Communists will be reduced to zero."[143] By the next day, however, Kádár had a very different view and agreed that a "counterrevolution" was underway. He was willing to blame Nagy too. "The counterrevolutionaries are killing [Communists]" he said, "and premier Nagy provides a cover."[144]

Kádár later claimed that he had consented to forming a new government because if he did not, someone else would have.[145] Having been tortured under Rákosi, Kádár likely knew the fate that awaited him if he stood by Nagy and a Rákosi acolyte took control.[146] Indeed, Khrushchev recalled many years later, that when he proposed withdrawing Soviet troops from Hungary, Kádár had shown little interest. Instead, Kádár insisted that his primary concern was that Moscow not return Rákosi to power. Khrushchev was surprised by Kádár's response, but reflected that there still "[existed] in Hungary people who sympathized with Rákosi . . . especially in the party."[147] Although there is no explicit evidence that Khrushchev threatened to reinstate the hardliners to coerce Kádár, the latter's concerns that hardliners would be returned to power gave Khrushchev an opening through which to drive a wedge between Nagy and the moderates in his government.

In sum, Nagy faced both external and internal opposition that ultimately led the Soviets to conclude he was more costly to work with than to replace. Khrushchev was initially reluctant to bear the military and diplomatic costs of using troops. The Suez Crisis prompted him to recalculate. The attack on Egypt increased Khrushchev's concern that the West would meddle in Hungary. With Western aid, greater military force would be needed to defeat the rebels. Khrushchev also feared that losing Hungary would cost him politically. Removing Nagy, in contrast, would allow the Soviet Union to reassert control at a time when the rest of the world was distracted by events in Egypt. Yet though the Suez Crisis helped precipitate the Soviet invasion, it was not decisive. Rather, it was Nagy's domestic opposition that simultaneously put him at odds with Moscow and left him vulnerable to regime change. Had he possessed a firmer grip on power, events in Egypt would have been less likely to trigger his overthrow.

Nagy's Response to the Threat of Regime Change

My theory suggests that a targeted leader's response to the threat of regime change depends on the immediacy of that threat. When threats are imminent, leaders are more likely to use partial or temporary compliance to deny the stronger state a reason to overthrow them. When the threat is more remote, targeted leaders will engage in more defiant behavior—such as securing another foreign power's protection or cracking down on their opposition—to protect their regimes.

Nagy's decision to declare Hungary's neutrality and appeal to the United Nations for help would seem to counter this prediction. Despite an imminent threat, the Hungarian leader responded with apparent defiance. But Nagy was not breaking off negotiations with the Soviets in an attempt to side with the West; instead, it appears he was hedging his bets. The Hungarian leadership had been receiving reports of Soviet troop movements over several days.[148] Nagy did not believe the West would intervene to aid Hungary, but he hoped that withdrawing from the Warsaw Pact would make plain that a Soviet invasion, if one was indeed occurring, should be understood as a hostile act.[149] The Soviets repeatedly reassured Nagy that the reports of an invasion were false, and Nagy continued to believe those assurances. As a result, he continued negotiating for a Soviet troop withdrawal until November 4, when Soviet troops reached Budapest.

Although Khrushchev had decided to use force on October 31, the Soviets stalled for time by proposing talks for Soviet troop withdrawals.[150] The plan appears to have been to dangle the possibility of a settlement to deny the Hungarian government a chance to organize a defense. The Soviet ambassador requested negotiations for November 2 but then postponed the meeting until the next day.[151] The Soviet delegation arrived that next day with a document listing the material conditions necessary for a withdrawal. The negotiators agreed to another round of talks that evening, and the Soviet representatives "promised that no new convoy transporting Soviet troops will cross the border."[152] At ten o'clock that night, the Hungarian delegation arrived at Soviet Army headquarters near Budapest for the second round of discussions. At eleven, KGB Chief Ivan Serov entered the room and ordered the arrest of the Hungarians. Almost simultaneously, Béla Király, commander of the Hungarian national guard, began receiving reports that Soviet forces were attacking Hungarian garrisons and disarming soldiers.[153] The invasion had begun.

By two in the morning, Király was urging Nagy to announce that the Soviet Union was at war with Hungary. Yet Nagy assured Király that "[Soviet] Ambassador Yuri Andropov is here in my study, and he stated that if there is any shooting . . . then it must be only a reply to Hungarian provocation."[154] Only after Király reported that Soviet tanks had arrived at the parliament building in Budapest did Nagy accept that there would be no agreement. Several hours later, Nagy announced that the Soviet Union was at war with Hungary. However, he never gave Király an order to fight. Király later concluded that Nagy knew he "could not in good conscience give any combat orders" because it was futile to resist.[155] Yet Nagy did not resign, nor did he urge Hungarian forces to lay down their arms. As Király writes, "Too much treachery had been committed in recent Hungarian history against men who had surrendered in good faith."[156] Having been deceived by the Soviets for three days, Nagy probably did not believe that his surrender would assure his own survival. Instead, he fled to the Yugoslav embassy.

As long as the Soviets were signaling interest in a political settlement, Nagy had continued to negotiate. As Király emphasizes, "the declaration of neutrality of Hungary was not the cause, but the effect of the already Soviet declaration [of an invasion] in the making."[157] Nagy remained in the Yugoslav embassy until November 22, when Kádár promised the Yugoslav government that Nagy and his followers would be allowed to return home if they left the embassy. Nagy did not trust Kádár but believed Kádár would not break his promise to Tito, who was at the time the only leader outside the Soviet bloc to recognize Kádár's government.[158] The group nevertheless was promptly arrested and deported to Romania.[159] Nagy was later charged with treason, secretly tried, and executed on June 16, 1958.

Alternative Arguments in the Hungarian Case

My argument holds that the intense domestic political pressure Nagy faced explains his overthrow. Khrushchev was at first understanding of Nagy's predicament but concluded after the Suez Crisis that the costs of waiting for Nagy to calm the rebellion or request intervention were higher than overthrowing him. I now will consider the evidence for alternative explanations based on psychological bias, bureaucratic pressure, and rational choice theories.

PSYCHOLOGICAL BIAS

One argument that has been advanced to explain Khrushchev's decision to overthrow Nagy suggests that misperception played a decisive role in Nagy's fate. Johanna Granville, for example, notes that Soviet decision makers displayed the common psychological tendency of attributing an enemy's behavior to internal factors, such as inherent personality traits, rather than external pressures. She writes that the Soviet leadership was supportive of Nagy as long as they approved of his behavior but later criticized him when they disapproved.[160] Yet the Malin notes show that even as Nagy introduced controversial reforms, which some Soviet leaders harshly criticized, the Kremlin leadership collectively agreed to support him. Indeed, Khrushchev continued supporting Nagy into the evening of October 30, despite learning he was threatening to declare neutrality if the Soviet Union invaded. It was not until the morning of the Suez Crisis on October 31 that Khrushchev changed his mind. Only after that, did he call Nagy a "traitor."[161] Thus, while the Soviet leadership did denounce Nagy, they did so only after deciding to overthrow him. Prior to that decision, they were critical but tolerant of his reforms, because they understood that his domestic pressures made them necessary.

Another possible psychological interpretation of the Hungarian case might suggest that Soviet leaders were inclined to view Nagy suspiciously because of a history of negative interactions with him, whereas they viewed Gomułka more favorably because of a less contentious relationship. There is little evidence to support this argument. First, Khrushchev was initially hostile toward Gomułka, with whom he later negotiated, and cooperative toward Nagy, whom he later overthrew. Second, of the two men, Nagy was the one with a history of loyalty to the Kremlin. He had lived in Moscow during the 1930s and served as an informer for the Soviet NKVD (Narodnyǐ Komissariat Vnutrennikh Del), the predecessor to the KGB. Named "Voldoya," Nagy was considered a "qualified agent" with great "initiative."[162] Although Nagy also had a reputation as a reformer, he sought Kremlin approval throughout the crisis. Khrushchev considered him the man "to cope with the storm."[163] Indeed, even after deciding to replace him with Kádár, Khrushchev left open the possibility that Nagy might later be brought into the new Hungarian government if he came to recognize it.[164] Thus, the Soviet leadership does not appear to have been biased against Nagy and inclined toward regime change.

BUREAUCRATIC AND INTEREST-GROUP PRESSURE

An alternative explanation for Moscow's decision to impose regime change on Hungary would suggest that Khrushchev's decision was the result of pressure from bureaucratic actors and/or interest groups. There is greater support for this interpretation. In his conversation with Tito, Khrushchev made clear that his decision to act in Hungary was related to domestic political concerns. He chiefly feared that the hardliners would blame him for "losing Hungary" and that the military, in particular, would oppose him. Given that Soviet hardliners would launch a coup attempt against Khrushchev within the year, his concern seems justified.

A bureaucratic-actor approach, however, leaves some pieces of the puzzle unexplained. For example, Khrushchev initially chose to support Nagy, despite the risk of upsetting hardliners. Stalinists, such as presidium members Vyacheslav Molotov and Kliment Voroshilov, were already criticizing Nagy for "speaking against us," and urging the Soviet leadership to "act decisively."[165] But their concerns did not alter Khrushchev's decision to support Nagy at this time. Furthermore, although Khrushchev feared that the hardliners would blame him for losing Hungary, other cost considerations also appeared to affect his decision. In particular, Khrushchev was initially concerned about the diplomatic costs of crushing a nationalist uprising in a Soviet ally. The Suez Crisis and the support of Soviet allies for intervention, however, altered this calculus, convincing Khrushchev that the diplomatic costs of *in*action were growing. Khrushchev may have been sensitive to the potential domestic costs of losing Hungary, but these were but one set of costs that he considered in deciding on regime change.

RATIONAL CHOICE ARGUMENTS

A credible-commitment approach to the Hungarian and Polish crises would suggest that the Soviets overthrew Nagy but not Gomułka because an enforceable bargain was attainable only with the latter. Nagy did indeed face a credibility problem. The Soviets wanted him to suppress the rebellion, but the prospect of American interference raised concerns that Nagy could not do so. Nagy's commitment problem sheds light on why the Soviets forcibly intervened to suppress the rebellion. It does not, however, necessarily explain why the Soviets removed Nagy. Rather than replacing him with Kádár, Khrushchev could have waited for Nagy to request a second Soviet intervention or coerced him to make such a request. Nagy's tenuous domestic position can help us understand why the Soviets opted instead to depose him. Had Nagy cast his lot with the Soviets by requesting their intervention, he would have lost what domestic support he had among reformers. Although Nagy could have relied on the Soviets to maintain his power, it took far less to convince the moderates to accept this option. Not only did some moderates, such as Münnich, already favor Soviet intervention, but they also stood to gain political power by collaborating with Moscow. Nagy, in contrast, faced the less appealing option of sacrificing the power he already had to become Moscow's puppet. Had Nagy known the fate that would befall him, he might have accepted this deal, but the Soviet leadership had little need to convince Nagy that resistance was futile as long as moderates were willing to replace him.

An incomplete-information approach would argue that Nagy doubted Khrushchev's resolve to use force and thus continued implementing reforms despite the risk. Several writers, for example, attribute Nagy's overthrow to his discussion of neutrality with Mikoyan and Suslov on October 30. They suggest that Nagy failed to appreciate the alarm this would cause in Moscow.[166] Jakub Zielinski offers a similar assessment but posits that Mikoyan and Suslov misled Nagy into believing his reforms would be accepted. Gomułka, in contrast, is said to have had better information because he negotiated directly with Khrushchev.[167]

Nagy's efforts to seek Soviet approval for his reforms, however, suggest
he was not defiantly pushing them because he doubted Soviet punishment.
In fact, according to George Heltai, Nagy's deputy foreign minister, Nagy
knew the Soviet Union would not tolerate Hungary's withdrawal from the
Warsaw Pact because Mikoyan and Suslov had communicated that clearly.[168]
In response, Nagy had told the Soviet representatives that Hungary would
only declare neutrality if attacked. The fact that, after learning of this discussion, Khrushchev continued to support Nagy until the start of the Suez Crisis
suggests that regime change was not driven by Nagy's defiance.

An incomplete-information argument also implies that if Nagy had not
provoked Moscow by discussing neutrality with the Soviet emissaries, then
Khrushchev might have refrained from deposing him. This may have been
true had Nagy been able to satisfy the Soviet leadership's central concern—
quelling the rebellion. Yet Nagy's domestic opposition hampered his ability
to do this, especially after the Suez Crisis raised the risk of greater Western
involvement. A parallel to the Hungary case is the 1968 Soviet invasion of
Czechoslovakia. The lesson Czech reformers drew from Hungary's experience was that Nagy's call for neutrality had prompted the Soviet invasion.
They concluded that if Czech leaders reassured the Soviet leadership that
Czechoslovakia would remain in the Warsaw Pact, Moscow would not
intervene.[169] They were wrong. Much like Nagy, Czech leader Alexander
Dubček faced opposition from both hardliners, who urged him to crack
down, and liberals, who pushed for greater reform.[170] Soviet leader Leonid
Brezhnev had little reason to accept the Prague Spring reforms as long as
he believed he could install Czech hardliners to overturn them. Though the
hardliners turned out to be too weak to oust Dubček, Brezhnev was able to
pressure the reformers to reverse course and later to replace Dubček with
the more malleable Husák. Thus, Dubček's removal, which occurred
despite his commitment to the Warsaw Pact, suggests that Nagy would have
been overthrown even if he had never mentioned neutrality. Nagy's tenuous political position both undermined his ability to placate Moscow and
offered the Soviet leadership a means by which to replace him.

Conclusion

The Polish and Hungarian cases support my hypothesis $H1a_1$, which holds
that domestic opposition in the target state drives the foreign power's decision to negotiate or impose regime change. In Poland, Gomułka faced a

very different domestic political landscape from that encountered by Nagy. The most dedicated Stalinists had already left the government by the time the PUWP turned to Gomułka for help. The party leader, Ochab, had also pursued a relatively moderate course that helped prevent a nationwide rebellion. When Gomułka assumed power, he was not facing rebel factions that rejected his authority. Moreover, the hardliners had lost their influence in Poland's politburo. Gomułka's strong political position enabled him to keep reform limited and reassure the Soviets that Poland would remain in the Warsaw Pact. Khrushchev initially rejected any reform, but after realizing the high costs of overthrowing Gomułka, he changed course and accepted the Polish leader's terms. Nagy, in contrast, came to power in the midst of a rebellion. He was forced to implement major reforms to restore order, even though he had initially opposed some of those reforms. Stalinist hardliners also initially retained their influence in the government. They were able to undercut Nagy and weaken his popular support, which further frustrated his attempts to contain the rebellion.

The evidence also supports hypothesis $H1b_1$, which holds that domestically strong leaders tend to make greater concessions than domestically weak ones, all else being equal. Although Gomułka, in this instance, did not concede to Khrushchev's demands to abandon reform, the Polish leader's reforms were significantly more modest than those of Nagy. Gomułka, therefore, could avoid making concessions, in part, because his reforms were modest to begin with. Had Gomułka faced domestic political pressure to overhaul the communist system and withdraw from the Warsaw Pact, as Nagy did, he would have been forced to take more drastic measures to restore the public's faith in the government. In short, Nagy's political vulnerability forced him to challenge Moscow's interests, while Gomułka's political strength enabled him to adopt a more moderate approach.

The evidence also supports my argument's expectations regarding how states impose regime change. Hungarian rebels were clearly opposed to the Soviets, while hardliners were too weak for Moscow to depend on. Instead, as hypothesis $H1a_5$ predicts, Khrushchev focused on pressuring moderates to break with Nagy to effect partial regime change. There is also qualified support for $H1b_2$, which holds that leaders faced with a credible threat of regime change will make concessions rather than adopt defensive measures. Although Nagy responded to initial reports of a Soviet invasion by declaring neutrality, he also attempted to negotiate with the Kremlin right up until the end, signaling his hopes of reaching a negotiated agreement.

Finally, the Suez Crisis played a contributing role by raising the costs of delaying intervention and simultaneously lowering the diplomatic costs of using force in Hungary. Khrushchev anticipated that a successful Western attack on Egypt, a Soviet ally, would embolden the West to interfere in Hungary. He also concluded that with the world's attention focused on Western intervention in Egypt, a Soviet parallel in Hungary would garner less notice. Consistent with hypothesis $H1a_3$, this event explains the timing and manner of regime change, not necessarily its occurrence. Scholars agree that the Soviet crackdown in Hungary would have likely occurred even without the Suez Crisis. As long as the rebellion continued to rage and Nagy refused Soviet intervention, Khrushchev would have likely reached the decision that keeping Nagy in power was more costly than removing him. By the same token, if Nagy had enjoyed Gomułka's political strength, it is unlikely the Suez Crisis would have had the same effect. Whereas Nagy was forced to contend with hardliners undercutting him and rebels making increasingly greater demands, Gomułka was able to push aside hardliners while convincing Poles to settle for modest reform. Without opposition, Nagy not only would have been better positioned to calm the Hungarian rebellion, but he also would have been more difficult to overthrow. In the end, it was Nagy's domestic political vulnerability that determined his fate, while the Suez Crisis helped determine the timing of that fate.

CHAPTER 6

The Post-9/11 Era

Regime Change and Rogues, Iraq 2003, Libya 2003, and Libya 2011

In his January 2003 State of the Union address, President George W. Bush made the case for regime change in Iraq. Characterizing Saddam Hussein as a menace to regional and international stability, the president argued that Saddam's suspected possession and use of weapons of mass destruction (WMD), his history of regional aggression, and his support for terrorism made him a threat.[1] The list of Saddam's transgressions, however, bore a striking resemblance to the record of Libya's Muammar Qaddafi, with whom Bush would reach a deal. Libya possessed active WMD programs and was believed to have used its chemical weapons during its war in Chad.[2] Qaddafi had also been a fervent sponsor of terror and had ordered attacks on Libya's neighbors as well as assassinations of foreign officials, including a US ambassador.[3] Yet, rather than overthrow Qaddafi, the administration negotiated with him, brokering a 2003 agreement in which Libya surrendered its WMD programs. In return, the United States normalized relations and renounced its long-standing policy of regime change for Libya.

At first glance, the reason the Bush administration overthrew Saddam but not Qaddafi in 2003 might appear straightforward. Saddam resisted US pressure throughout the 1990s, whereas Qaddafi became more willing to negotiate. Hoping to reconcile with the West, Qaddafi ended his support for terrorism and, after 2001, became an ally in the US global war on terror. A focus on each leader's behavior, however, cannot tell us why Qaddafi cooperated when Saddam did not. It also leaves unanswered the question of why Qaddafi's cooperation with the West failed to spare him from the 2011 NATO intervention that led to his overthrow. Ultimately, the question remains, why did the United States overthrow Saddam but negotiate with Qaddafi in 2003, only to overthrow Qaddafi eight years later?

The overthrows of Saddam and Qaddafi differ in several respects. The 2011 intervention in Libya was precipitated by a humanitarian crisis; the Iraq War was not.[4] Saddam's overthrow involved a major military invasion; the Libyan intervention was limited to an air campaign. Despite these differences, however, the two cases share an essential element—in both, US policymakers sought to obtain their aims by overthrowing rather than negotiating with the existing regime.

I argue that the key to understanding American policy with respect to Iraq and Libya lies in the very different domestic pressures that each leader confronted. Saddam faced a hostile domestic population, as well as neighbors who routinely sponsored rebellions among this population. His domestic and regional threats gave him incentive to resist UN-mandated weapons inspections, which threatened to reveal he no longer possessed the weapons he had used to safeguard his regime. Though Saddam had both domestic and regional enemies to fear, it was his domestic vulnerability that led American policymakers to seek his overthrow. Saddam's domestic threats not only drove his resistance to inspections, making him costly to coerce, but they also made him appear cheaper, by comparison, to overthrow. The notion that Saddam would be cheaper to topple than to contain was a conclusion reached not just by the George W. Bush administration. Both the George H. W. Bush and Clinton administrations also sought to overthrow Saddam, although they chose different methods to do it.

Qaddafi, in contrast, faced few domestic threats in 2003 and had reconciled with his regional enemies. His lack of an organized domestic opposition enabled him to accommodate US demands without fearing for his survival and also made him costly to overthrow. This was no longer true by 2011, when the Libyan uprising threatened his hold on power. Faced with an existential domestic threat, Qaddafi could not comply with UN demands without endangering his political position at home. Like Saddam, Qaddafi now faced domestic opposition that not only drove his defiance to foreign pressure, making him costly to coerce, but that also convinced the United States regime change would be comparatively cheap.

This chapter explains why US policymakers pursued regime change in each case and also why they chose the methods they did. In Iraq, the George H. W. Bush administration had used sanctions and covert aid to effect partial regime change. In late 1992, this policy shifted to full regime change

Table 13. Controls for Confounding Variables: Iraq 2003, Libya 2003, and Libya 2011

	Iraq 2003	*Libya 2003*	*Libya 2011*
Target's Characteristics			
Regime Type	Personalist authoritarian leader	Personalist authoritarian leader	Personalist authoritarian leader
Regime Ideology	Secular, Arab nationalism	Secular, Arab nationalism	Secular, Arab nationalism
Issues at Stake	Weapons of mass destruction	Weapons of mass destruction	Humanitarian crisis
Region	Middle East	North Africa	North Africa
Foreign Power's Characteristics			
Decision Maker	George W. Bush administration	George W. Bush administration	Barack Obama administration
Time Period	Post-9/11 era, 2003	Post-9/11 era, 2003	Post-9/11 era, 2011
Outcome	Full regime change	Settlement	Full regime change

as the United States began cooperating with exile groups representing Saddam's external opposition. These efforts expanded under the Clinton administration. As the decade wore on, however, American policymakers grew increasingly skeptical about their ability to overthrow Saddam through covert or indirect force. When George W. Bush was elected, his administration initially focused on revitalizing efforts to contain Saddam. After 9/11, however, US policy shifted dramatically to full regime change via a military invasion. Policy on Libya evolved too. From the outset, the de facto goal of the 2011 NATO intervention in Libya was regime change, but after a military stalemate set in, and the anticipated costs of regime change rose, US and NATO officials began considering a negotiated settlement.

The similarities among the Iraq and two Libya cases present another opportunity to control for several confounding variables, as illustrated in Table 13. In all three cases, the targeted leader was a secular personalist dictator who relied mainly on tribal, family, and clan support to maintain political power.[5] Although democratic peace theory suggests that democracies are prone to conflict with authoritarian leaders, Qaddafi not only reached a deal with the United States in 2003, but he also continued to broker deals with Western democracies while reversing Libya's modest political reform.⁶ The time periods and issues in the 2003 cases are also similar. Both occurred in the aftermath of 9/11, when officials in the Bush administration were especially concerned about WMD and terrorism. Although Qaddafi had ceased his support for terror, Libya possessed chemical weapons and was developing a nuclear weapons program.⁷

The differences across the three cases allow for controls as well. Although Iraq had greater strategic significance to the United States, Libya was not more strategically valuable in 2011, when the United States pursued regime change, than it had been in 2003, when it did not. In addition, although it might be argued that the Bush administration negotiated with Libya simply because it could not afford another war, US forces were still actively engaged in Afghanistan when the Obama administration pursued regime change in Libya.⁸ Finally, while the same set of decision makers chose very different policies with respect to Iraq and Libya in 2003, two very different decision makers chose very similar policies in Iraq in 2003 and Libya in 2011. This suggests that understanding the decision to pursue regime change requires going beyond the personalities or ideologies of the particular policymakers involved.

These controls do not eliminate every possible alternative explanation. In this chapter, I test the dominant narratives of the decisions leading to the Iraq War, which focus on psychological and bureaucratic influences. I argue that these interpretations can help us answer a number of important questions, such as why tensions persisted between the United States and Iraq and why US relations with Qaddafi deteriorated. They are also helpful in understanding why officials in both the Bush and Obama administrations failed to anticipate the high costs of regime change. Where these approaches fall short, however, is in their ability to predict regime change. As I will show, psychological bias and bureaucratic pressure can neither explain why previous administrations pursued regime change in Iraq nor why the Obama administration pursued it in Libya. My theory helps flesh out our understanding of these cases by explaining why policymakers with very different views, biases, and decision-making styles ended up pursuing the same policy.

I also test the traditional rationalist approaches, which suggest US bargaining with Iraq and Libya broke down because each side's doubts about the other made an enforceable deal impossible. The incomplete-information problem suggests that Saddam and Qaddafi's doubts about

American threats caused them to resist, which led to their undoing. The credible-commitment problem indicates that at least one or both sides' distrust of the other made it impossible for them to conclude a deal. I argue that although there is partial evidence to support these interpretations, neither can explain why costly signals and enforcement mechanisms were insufficient to overcome the information and commitment problems. To determine that, we must look to each leader's domestic political threats, which caused US policymakers to conclude that using signals, coercive force, and enforcement mechanisms to obtain a settlement would be more costly than regime change.

My research here draws on both secondary and primary sources. For the Iraq case, I use translated transcripts of recordings between Saddam and his top-level advisers that were captured in the aftermath of the Iraq War.[9] I also draw from special adviser Charles Duelfer's *Comprehensive Report of the Special Advisor to the Director of Central Intelligence on Iraq's WMD*, more commonly known as the Duelfer Report, which was compiled by the Iraq Survey Group, a CIA postwar fact-finding mission sent to examine evidence of Iraq's WMD programs.[10] The Iraq Survey Group, headed by Duelfer, also interviewed captured Iraqi officials, and I use these interviews, as well as the Federal Bureau of Investigation's debriefing of Saddam Hussein.[11] For both the Iraq and Libya cases, I draw from memoirs written by key players and also published interviews for insights into the policymaking process.[12] The first section of this chapter examines the decision to overthrow Saddam Hussein in 2003, the second explores the deal made with Qaddafi that same year, and the third addresses the overthrow of Qaddafi in 2011.

I begin each section by explaining the demands the United States placed on Saddam and Qaddafi and then describe how each leader's domestic costs of complying influenced his response. After that, I explain how each leader's resolve to resist affected the costs to the United States of reaching a deal and how these costs compared to those for regime change. I end each section with a consideration of alternative arguments.

Iraq, 2003: Full Regime Change

American and United Nations Demands in Iraq

The demands the United States placed on Saddam throughout the 1990s reflected the terms of the 1991 Gulf War cease-fire as formalized in UN

Security Council Resolutions 686 and 687. The first of these resolutions required Iraq to withdraw its claims on Kuwait, accept liability for losses and damages as a result of the war, and cease all hostilities.[13] The second resolution required Iraq to surrender its chemical, biological, and nuclear weapons programs and to destroy its ballistic missiles with a range greater than 150 kilometers. The resolution also authorized the creation of the UN Special Commission (UNSCOM) to verify the destruction of Iraq's WMD programs and establish a monitoring system to ensure continued compliance.[14] Days after the United Nations passed Resolution 687, it expanded its demands in response to a humanitarian crisis brought on by the Iraqi government's crackdown on Shi'a and Kurdish uprisings. Resolution 688 established the justification for Operation Provide Comfort, a humanitarian relief effort to assist Kurdish refugees. The resolution was also used to justify the creation of a Kurdish safe haven and the northern no-fly zone. In August 1992, the United States, the United Kingdom, and France also established a southern no-fly zone.[15]

US policy with respect to Iraq had two goals. The first and more immediate was containment, aimed at forcing Iraq to comply with the UN resolutions. Sanctions were designed to prevent Iraq from acquiring weapons or dual-use technology that would enable it to restart its programs. Inspections were conducted to ensure Iraq complied with the disarmament terms. The United States maintained a military presence in the Persian Gulf to patrol the no-fly zones, deter Iraq from regional aggression, and enforce compliance with the inspections. In the immediate aftermath of the war, this goal was shared by the other members of the UN Security Council.

The Americans' more long-range purpose, however, was regime change. On this issue, sharp divisions emerged between France, Russia, and China, on the one hand, and the United States and United Kingdom on the other.[16] President George H. W. Bush had made clear soon after Operation Desert Storm concluded in April 1991 that the United States would use sanctions to destabilize the Iraqi regime, declaring, "There will not be normalized relations with the US until Saddam Hussein is out of there. And we will continue economic sanctions."[17] The British foreign secretary, Douglas Hurd, also warned that Iraq would not be able to rejoin the community of nations as long as it had "a delinquent regime."[18] Both nations hoped that economic pressure would bring Saddam's ouster by depriving him of the oil revenue necessary to buy domestic political support and by giving the Iraqi military incentive to stage a coup.[19]

President Bill Clinton continued this dual tract policy of containment and regime change.[20] His administration expanded ties to Iraqi exile opposition groups and authorized covert operations in Iraqi Kurdistan. Over time, however, Clinton administration officials became increasingly skeptical of the likelihood of toppling the Iraqi regime. Saddam had proven himself highly capable of preempting and deterring coups. By the end of the 1990s, several officials in the Clinton administration had concluded that it would be necessary to reconcile with Saddam because air strikes were not going to force him out.[21]

The George W. Bush administration's initial approach to Iraq centered primarily on revitalizing containment. Sanctions were redesigned to reduce their humanitarian costs and pave the way for renewed international pressure.[22] Although the United States had not forsaken regime change as a goal, by the start of the new millennium, US efforts were aimed at forcing Saddam to uphold the Gulf War settlement terms to disarm and comply with inspections.

The Costs to Saddam of Compliance Versus Resistance

My argument holds that targeted leaders, when confronted with politically costly foreign demands, will resist as long as their domestic opposition remains more threatening than the foreign power making the demands. Inspections were politically costly for Saddam because they threatened to reveal he could no longer use chemical weapons to safeguard his regime. At the same time, the relatively mild punishment he faced for resisting gave him additional incentive to prioritize his domestic threats over the demands of the international community.

Saddam had long relied upon chemical weapons to defend himself from both his regional and domestic enemies. He began acquiring the weapons in the 1980s, specifically to counter Iran and Israel.[23] Top Iraqi officials believed the weapons, as well as Iraq's ballistic missiles, had forced Iran to negotiate an end to the Iran-Iraq War.[24] Saddam also believed Iraq's chemical weapons had deterred the United States from invading during the first Gulf War.[25] Saddam feared the consequences of revealing he no longer possessed WMD. According to his cousin Ali Hassan al-Majid (also known as Chemical Ali), Saddam admitted to his Revolutionary Command Council in the 1990s that Iraq no longer possessed WMD, but he refused to make this information public lest it prompt an Israeli attack.[26] In his later debriefing by the United States, Saddam justified his resistance to inspections by pointing to Iraq's regional threats. "The Persians have attacked Iraq regularly," he explained. "If they believe we are weak, they will attack. And it is well known that both the Israelis and Persians have nuclear bombs and chemical bombs and the biological weapons."[27]

Yet despite the many regional threats faced by Iraq, Saddam saw the risk of a domestic rebellion as still greater. This was in part because his regional enemies had long sponsored domestic rebellions among the Iraqi Shi'a and Kurdish populations, whose members comprised the regime's external opposition.[28] The United States, Iran, and Israel, for example, had funded a Kurdish rebellion in the 1970s to push Iraq into signing the Algiers Agreement.[29] After Iran's 1979 revolution, Ayatollah Khomeini called for an Iraqi Shi'a uprising and later aligned with Iraqi Kurds during the Iran-Iraq War. After the war, Iran continued to shelter the Supreme Council of the Islamic Revolution of Iraq (SCIRI), which Iraqi foreign minister Tariq Aziz considered one of the regime's greatest internal threats.[30] The United States had also helped stoke the Kurdish and Shi'a uprisings at the end of the Gulf War, when President George H. W. Bush urged Iraqis to topple Saddam.[31] Though the United States did not contribute to the rebellions, the US-patrolled no-fly zones prevented Saddam from fully reasserting control, while the Kurdish safe haven allowed for a de facto Kurdish state in the north.[32]

WMD played an important role in the regime's defense against these domestic threats, as well. In response to Kurdish support for Iran during the Iran-Iraq War, Saddam ordered a chemical attack that killed more than five thousand Kurdish civilians.[33] In 1991, when the regime faced massive rebellions, it again turned to chemical weapons. According to a former senior member of Iraq's chemical weapons program, "the Regime was shaking and wanted something 'very quick and effective' to put down the revolt."[34] It dropped sarin-filled bombs on a number of southern cities.[35] As the Duelfer Report observes: "That the Regime would consider this option with Coalition forces still operating within Iraq's boundaries demonstrates both the dire nature of the situation and the Regime's faith in 'special weapons.'"[36] Complying with inspections would have revealed that the Iraqi regime no longer possessed these weapons.

For Saddam, inspections were simply part of the United States' long-standing efforts to undermine him.[37] Throughout the 1990s, he routinely accused inspectors of spying for the United States and collecting intelligence that would be used later to bomb Iraq.[38] Although Saddam had initially been optimistic about improving relations with the Clinton administration, he ultimately concluded that the United States would never lift sanctions. He would reportedly ask his ministers, "We can have sanctions with inspectors or sanctions without inspectors; which do you want?"[39]

Saddam's suspicions about American intentions, however, did not make him impossible to coerce and contain. He repeatedly proved willing to back down when faced with a clear threat of costly punishment. For example, he ordered the destruction of Iraq's WMD in the summer of 1991 after the first round of inspections proved to be more intrusive than he had anticipated. After being caught in violation, Saddam concluded that some measure of compliance would be necessary to escape sanctions.[40] When he sent troops to the Kuwaiti border in 1994, he retreated after the United States mobilized forty thousand soldiers and 350 aircraft. As part of the resolution to the crisis, Saddam recognized the Kuwaiti border. However, Saddam also successfully mitigated his costs of compliance in many of these instances. When he destroyed Iraq's WMD in 1991, he did so without UNSCOM's supervision, as was required. And after his mobilization on the Kuwaiti border in 1994, he obtained a Russian promise to lobby the UN Security Council to lift sanctions.[41]

Although Saddam routinely conceded when resistance appeared costly, the problem was that the international community's threats to punish his resistance were seldom credible. Due to the divisions among its members, the UN Security Council was often unable to agree on a response to Iraqi resistance. After Iraq sent troops to the Kuwaiti border in 1994, for example, Saddam remarked with amazement that his punishment was a harshly worded UN memo. "It is really something, four nations, among them two of the greatest nations of the world: Russia and America. I mean, they have nuclear bombs, missiles, and so on. . . . They came to me and handed me a memo."[42] When Iraq obstructed inspections in 1997, France, Russia, and China blocked an American and British proposal for a travel ban on members of the Iraqi regime. The Security Council could only agree on a "firm intention" to impose the ban if Iraq did not comply by April 1998.[43] When Iraq's obstruction continued, the United States and United Kingdom responded with Operation Desert Fox, a four-day bombing campaign. But Saddam still ignored the subsequent UN resolution (Resolution 1284) demanding renewed inspections.[44] Thus, not only did compliance with inspections threaten his regime's survival, but also resistance to inspections entailed relatively mild costs.

The Costs to the United States of a Settlement with Saddam

My argument holds that it is more costly to reach settlements with leaders who fear the domestic political costs of compliance. Indeed, the more Saddam resisted inspections to keep his domestic opponents at bay, the more costly containment became for the international community, especially the United States. Economic, humanitarian, political, diplomatic, reputational, and military costs all rose.

To increase the costs to the international community of maintaining containment, Saddam deliberately cultivated allies on the UN Security Council. His aim was to sew divisions between its members to wear down the international community's will to enforce the Gulf War resolutions. In particular, he used economic incentives to ensure France, China, and Russia would come to support an end to Iraq's diplomatic and economic isolation.[45] Iraq already owed Russia $8 billion and France £5 billion.[46] To further ensure these countries would have an economic interest in seeing sanctions lifted, Saddam offered expensive trade and service deals, including a $40-billion contract to Russia for oil field exploration and the construction of a pipeline.[47] Direct bribes included one to the Russian foreign minister Sergei Primakov.[48] Russian, French, and Chinese individuals and oil companies also benefitted from Iraq's manipulation of the United Nations' oil-for-food program, by receiving oil vouchers that allowed them to sell Iraqi oil at a profit.[49]

International opposition to sanctions grew as the economic costs of sanctions mounted. In the UN Security Council, Russia, France, and China increasingly argued in favor of lifting sanctions. Russia became one of Baghdad's most ardent supporters on the council. It also alerted Iraq to surprise inspections and helped it avoid sanctions.[50] Smuggling routes began to open up along the Iraqi border, earning Saddam roughly $8 billion through illegal trade with Jordan, Turkey, Egypt, and Syria.[51] Prohibited goods and weapons, including 380 rocket engines, were also entering the country easily. According to the Duelfer Report, "Iraq was designing missile systems with the assumption that sanctioned material would be readily available."[52]

Sanctions also entailed humanitarian costs, which increased international opposition to them. Aid agencies repeatedly warned that the lack of medicine, sanitation, and clean water in Iraq was imperiling civilians, particularly children.[53] Prewar studies on child-mortality rates also suggested sanctions were having a dire effect. More recent analyses, however, now indicate that the Iraqi regime may have exaggerated these effects to increase the reputational costs to those countries pushing sanctions. Three postwar, UN-funded studies have reported childhood mortality rates for the sanctions era that are two to three times lower than prewar reports covering the same time period.[54] The major difference between the pre- and postwar studies is that the former relied on subjects and supervisors supplied by the Baathist regime. According to one Iraqi doctor interviewed after the invasion, the regime was attempting to exaggerate the humanitarian toll of sanctions. "We would get a shipment from the Ministry of Health of vaccines provided by the World Health Organization. But then we would be instructed not to use them until they had reached or even exceeded their sell-by date. Then the television cameras would come, and we would be told to lie and tell the public how the U.N. made ordinary Iraqis suffer."[55]

The perceived humanitarian costs of sanctions created international outrage. Two successive UN humanitarian coordinators for Iraq resigned in protest, with one calling the effect of sanctions a "true human tragedy."[56] The United Nations attempted to alleviate the suffering of the Iraqi people with the oil-for-food program. Under the program, Iraq was allowed to sell oil, the profits from which the United Nations managed in order to ensure Iraq could not buy goods for a weapons program. Saddam refused the program for over a year, claiming it violated Iraqi sovereignty.[57] Once he finally accepted it in 1996, however, he was able to exploit it, pocketing an estimated $1.7 billion through kickbacks and surcharges.[58]

The high humanitarian cost of sanctions generated not only diplomatic and reputational costs for the United States but also domestic political costs for its Middle Eastern allies. As reports of Iraqi suffering spread, Arab publics came to see the United States as the aggressor. The repeated American bombings of Iraq also increased sympathy for it. Under pressure at home, Arab leaders began publically opposing sanctions.[59] Although Saudi Arabia and Kuwait remained committed to a hardline approach, Qatar, the United Arab Emirates, and Bahrain began advocating reconciliation with Baghdad.[60] American critics of containment pointed to the domestic pressure on Arab regimes as evidence of its high political costs.[61] Others linked the growing Arab resentment of the United States to terrorism. Deputy Secretary of Defense Paul Wolfowitz, one of the foremost proponents of the war, insisted later that the "real price [of containment] was giving Osama bin Laden his principal talking point. . . . His big complaint is that *we* have

American troops on the holy soil of Saudi Arabia and that we're bombing Iraq."[62]

Whereas Middle Eastern nations linked to the United States bore political costs for being too hard on Iraq, American officials were more likely to incur them for appearing too soft. In fact, a June 1993 Gallup poll showed that 70 percent of Americans favored invading Iraq with ground troops.[63] Domestic support for a hardline on Iraq constrained American policy options in at least two respects. First, it made offering Saddam inducements politically untenable. When president-elect Bill Clinton indicated that he would be willing to negotiate with Saddam, there was a public uproar.[64] Vice president elect Al Gore issued a statement immediately afterward, insisting that the incoming administration was committed to regime change. On several occasions, Iraqi officials suggested privately to Americans that Iraq and the United States should open a dialogue, but American officials consistently refused to negotiate with Saddam.[65]

Second, domestic support for a hard line raised the political costs of containment by making the United States look weak every time Saddam defied it. Saddam's ability to emerge from a crisis with the United States seemingly unscathed offered political fodder for the Clinton administration's critics. In 1998, prominent Republicans, many of whom would later serve in the Bush administration, penned an open letter to President Clinton, pointing to Saddam's defiance as evidence that containment was ineffective.[66] The Republican-controlled Congress also pressured the president into signing the Iraq Liberation Act (ILA), which made regime change official US policy. That the bill passed the House of Representatives with 360 votes in favor and only 38 votes opposed, and passed the Senate unanimously, demonstrated the level of domestic support for a hard line toward Iraq.

Containment also entailed military expenses for the United States. During the mid-1990s, the United States stationed between fifteen thousand and twenty thousand military personnel in the region. After UN inspectors left in 1998, that number increased to between twenty thousand and twenty-five thousand.[67] Maintaining the no-fly zones required roughly thirty-four thousand flight missions a year, roughly a third of the missions flown in the Gulf War.[68] Saddam could also impose additional military expense on the United States by initiating crises.[69] During a December 1992 crisis, for example, the United States spent roughly $400 million on troop movements and air strikes. Saddam's 1994 mobilization along the Kuwaiti border cost the United States $257 million.[70] The total military expense of containment from 1991 until November 1998 was an estimated $6.9 billion. After 1998, Iraq stepped up challenges to the no-fly zones, which increased the average costs of containment to over $1 billion per year.[71]

The United States would also have to bear the costs of containment as long as Saddam retained an incentive to acquire WMD. And indeed, senior members of the Iraqi regime believed Saddam would attempt to revive Iraq's WMD programs once international pressure eased.[72] The growing clamor to end sanctions also meant that the United States and United Kingdom would be increasingly on their own in containing Iraq. This did not mean that containing Saddam would be impossible, but it would be costly. The crux of the problem was that Saddam would not comply unless coerced, but coercion was costly for those undertaking it. Charles Duelfer himself summarized this dilemma in a conversation with Clinton's national security advisor, Tony Lake, in the 1990s: "We, the United States, cannot sustain our forces around [Saddam] forever, and it is only under force that he accepts the inspections."[73]

In retrospect, the actual and projected costs of containment are dwarfed by the estimated $3 trillion the United States spent on the second Iraq War.[74] Nevertheless, in making the case for war, Bush administration officials could point to the diplomatic, reputational, humanitarian, political, and military costs of containment to argue that it was "a very, very costly strategy."[75] And, as I will show, US policymakers could simultaneously point to Saddam's domestic vulnerability to argue that he would be comparatively less costly to overthrow.

The Costs of Partial and Full Regime Change in Iraq

My argument indicates that strong domestic opposition to a targeted leader makes that leader appear not only costly to coerce but also cheaper to overthrow. Whether policymakers in the foreign power contemplating FIRC use external or internal opposition to overthrow the targeted leader depends on each opposition group's relative strength. However, if policymakers fear the target state could gain power and become more costly to coerce, they will prefer the external opposition, even if weak. My argument also holds that major events can influence the timing and manner of regime change by prompting policy reviews and increasing public support for military force.

Consistent with these expectations, I show in this section that US policy-makers initially favored partial regime change in Iraq but switched to supporting the external opposition when an internal coup began to appear unlikely. When doubts about the external opposition mounted, hopes for regime change began to fade, until 9/11. The attacks triggered the decision to impose full regime change via an invasion by heightening fears of the potential for Iraq to acquire WMD and transfer the weapons to terrorists. The attacks also increased public support for the use of military force.

The initial decision to overthrow Saddam Hussein dated back to the period after the first Gulf War. Officials in the George H. W. Bush administration believed Saddam's domestic opposition and diplomatic isolation made him highly vulnerable to regime change. But despite a massive uprising by his external opposition toward the end of the war, the administration was reluctant to impose full regime change.[76] Middle Eastern allies of the United States warned that empowering Iraqi Kurds or Shi'a would destabilize the region, leaving Iraq vulnerable to Iranian influence. American policymakers were also reluctant to bear the military and diplomatic costs of extending the war by involving US troops in Iraq's domestic uprising.[77] US officials also believed Saddam might fall on his own. As Secretary of State James Baker recalled, the United States' Arab allies had been assuring the administration that Saddam would be ousted in a coup within six to eight months.[78]

When this coup failed to materialize, the Bush administration pursued partial regime change, authorizing clandestine activities against Saddam in April 1991.[79] In mid-1992, the president asked Congress for an additional $40 million.[80] Meanwhile, the Americans and British publicly insisted sanctions would remain in place until Saddam left office. To entice Saddam's supporters to abandon him, US officials also suggested that the terms of the Gulf War cease-fire might be softened if a new government came to power.[81] But as prospects for an internal coup diminished, American policymakers increasingly shifted focus to working with the Iraqi external opposition among the Kurds and Shi'a.[82]

Although the Clinton administration formally pursued a policy of containment toward Iraq, it increased support for Saddam's external opposition. In 1994, it initiated CIA operations in northern Iraq. In both 1995 and 1996, the CIA allegedly encouraged coup attempts by the Iraqi National Congress (INC) and the Iraqi National Accord (INA).[83] Both failed disastrously. In 1998, under pressure from Republicans in Congress, Clinton signed the ILA, which granted $97 million to the Iraqi exile opposition.[84] Although Clinton had signed the bill reluctantly, the State Department later assigned a special representative to work with Iraqi exile opposition groups.[85] The exiles were committed to removing Saddam, but they also competed with one another.[86] Over time, these divisions caused Clinton administration officials to doubt that the opposition could topple Saddam. Equally problematic was that exile opposition leaders had spent many years outside Iraq and so lacked followers at home. As Clinton's national security advisor, Samuel R. "Sandy" Berger, concluded, "Saddam isn't going to be overthrown by a bunch of guys with briefcases in London."[87]

On coming to office in 2001, the George W. Bush administration focused mainly on refining sanctions. Though the policy of regime change in Iraq was not abandoned, the administration hoped to reinvigorate containment. Secretary of State Colin Powell worked to shore up consensus in the UN Security Council by limiting the scope of sanctions to strategic items, a move that would ease the impact of sanctions on Security Council members, US allies, and the Iraqi population. Although some members of the administration continued to push for regime change and later became vocal proponents of war, Powell's approach defined the administration's early policy on Iraq.[88]

The 9/11 terror attacks brought regime change back to the forefront of US policy. The 2001 attacks had two major effects. First, they reduced the anticipated costs of an invasion by offering the administration a means to rally domestic support for war. In public appearances, both the president and vice president drew implicit and explicit connections between Iraq and the attacks, citing what many in the intelligence community knew to be weak evidence.[89] In a September 26, 2002 speech, for example, Bush declared "there are al Qaeda terrorists inside Iraq."[90] Several other administration officials repeated the allegation that Iraq and al Qaeda were linked.[91] Polls consistently showed that roughly 70 percent of Americans believed Saddam Hussein was personally involved in the 9/11 attacks.[92] This translated into significant domestic support for war. Gallup polls showed that from 9/11 until the start of the Iraq War, a majority consistently supported an invasion, with approval rates hovering around 60 percent in the month before the war.[93]

Second, the 9/11 attacks increased the urgency with which officials viewed the Iraqi threat. Influential members of the Bush administration warned that Iraq, once armed with WMD, would be more difficult to contain and could directly threaten the United States by supplying terrorists with WMD.[94] Vice President Dick Cheney's "one percent doctrine" reflected these fears. He insisted that even a slim chance of al Qaeda acquiring a nuclear weapon necessitated preventive action.[95] Undersecretary of Defense for Policy Douglas Feith echoed these concerns when he defended the decision to go to war years later. According to Feith, fears that Iraq could acquire WMD and distribute the weapons to terrorists led administration officials to conclude that the costs of inaction (i.e., continuing with containment) outweighed the costs of action.[96]

Concerns that Iraq could one day directly threaten the United States led Bush administration officials to conclude that partial regime change would be insufficient and full regime change was, therefore, necessary.[97] An internal coup, officials concluded, would simply allow for "Saddamism without Saddam." According to Feith, the view inside the White House was that the international community would welcome a new Iraqi regime by relaxing pressure, which would then permit this new government to adopt "dangerous behavior of its own."[98] The administration also worried that American assistance to a new Sunni-dominated regime might require the United States to help it retain power by suppressing a Kurdish and/or Shi'a uprising.[99] Administration officials thus concluded that US military forces would have to invade Iraq even in the event of a coup to impose full regime change.[100] Several administration officials proposed installing INC leader Ahmad Chalabi. The plan the president approved shortly before the invasion, however, called for an Iraqi interim authority composed of both exiles and internal opponents to the Baathist regime.[101]

Several US government agencies remained skeptical of the administration's estimates of a low-cost regime change operation, but their warnings were largely dismissed. Both the State Department and the CIA issued reports warning of the potential for a costly postwar phase. These reports, however, were released after the summer of 2002. By that time, according to several sources, the president had already made the decision to invade.[102] In a July 2002 memo, for example, the chief of British foreign intelligence, Sir Richard Dearlove, reported that "military action was now seen as inevitable. Bush wanted to remove Saddam, through military action."[103] National Security Advisor Condoleezza Rice had also indicated in July that the decision to invade had already been made, according to Richard N. Haass, director of the policy-planning staff at the State Department.[104] In fact, as early as March 2002, Bush had declared "we're taking [Saddam] out" in a meeting between three US senators and Rice.[105] The decision to invade thus appears to have been made without a serious assessment of the opposition's ability to construct a stable postwar government.

The Bush administration's optimism rested on the assurances of Iraqi exile leaders, such as Chalabi. The head of the INC had been arguing since the 1990s that Iraqis would welcome Saddam's removal and that a democratic Iraq could be established with relatively little US support.[106] Though the State Department and CIA distrusted Chalabi, they had more faith in his rival, Iyad Allwai, a former Baathist, who broke with Saddam and headed the INA. Allawi also promoted the view that a stable post-Saddam Iraq was possible, as long as the United States relied on Iraqi forces to maintain security.[107] Even the Iran-backed SCIRI contended that a constitutional, parliamentary government could be constructed in Iraq and that the job should be left to Iraqis.[108]

The assurances of the exile opposition complemented the Pentagon's plan to limit the costs of regime change by swiftly transferring power to Iraqis after ousting Saddam. Secretary of Defense Donald Rumsfeld argued against a long-term military occupation, insisting that nation-building created a "culture of dependency" that would require US troops and personnel to administer Iraq indefinitely.[109] To keep the postwar costs low, he insisted, the United States should avoid sending a massive invasion force. Instead, it should opt for a light footprint, using a relatively small force of one hundred thousand to liberate the country. The United States could then withdraw and transfer power to Iraqis within months of the invasion.[110] This plan, however, was based on false assumptions that Iraq's bureaucratic agencies would continue to function and its security forces would maintain peace.[111] When these assumptions failed to hold up, the Pentagon had no plan to fall back on.[112]

The George W. Bush administration's willingness to believe the assurances of Iraqi exiles helps explain why the postwar phase was much more costly than anticipated. A different set of policymakers, particularly ones more skeptical of the Iraqi opposition, might have heeded the warnings that a military invasion would require a costly occupation. However, as I shall explain more fully, these warnings would have likely altered the way in which regime change was conducted, not the decision to undertake it. As long as Saddam's domestic vulnerability gave him incentive to resist inspections, he would remain costly to coerce. And as long as Saddam's domestic vulnerability made him appear susceptible to regime change, American policymakers would be tempted to overthrow him.

Saddam's Response to the Threat of Regime Change

My argument asserts that covert or indirect threats of regime change will prompt leaders to take defensive action (e.g., procuring powerful weapons and/or allies), while direct and imminent threats are more likely to prompt partial or temporary compliance. Saddam's behavior both during the 1990s and in the immediate run up to the 2003 Iraq War supports this interpretation. Saddam was fully aware of the George H. W. Bush and Clinton administrations' covert attempts to overthrow him. In response, he took measures to coup-proof his regime. He was already known for using a mix of fear and inducements to cultivate loyalty among his advisers.[113] Toward the end of the 1990s, he increasingly isolated himself, relying largely on family and clan members for advice and support.[114] Saddam also sought to cultivate powerful allies on the UN Security Council. By offering economic incentives, Saddam won the support of France, China, and Russia, which used their vetoes in the Security Council to lessen or block punishments for Iraq.

Given Saddam's general pattern of defiance, it is notable that he chose to comply with UN demands to eliminate Iraq's WMD in 1991. This decision would deprive him of the very means to make an invasion costly for the United States. Arguably, Saddam might have better protected himself by acquiring a nuclear deterrent, as North Korea would later do. His options for doing so, however, were limited at the time. With Iraq's military defeat in the Gulf War and internal uprising, Saddam was highly vulnerable. An attempt to quickly acquire a nuclear weapon in the aftermath of the war might have reignited hostilities and prompted the United States to swap its covert and indirect attempts to overthrow him for more direct ones. For Saddam, partial compliance was the quickest way to reduce the immediate foreign threat to his regime, so he could crack down on the internal one. As this foreign threat began to diminish, partial compliance also became a way for Saddam to win French, Chinese, and Russian support in the UN Security Council. Had he pursued a nuclear deterrent in these later years, he might have unified the Security Council against him. Lastly, Saddam's options were also constrained by UN sanctions, which limited his ability to quickly acquire a nuclear weapon.[115]

By the fall of 2002, as the United States amassed its troops in the Persian Gulf, Saddam was again facing a direct and imminent foreign threat. In response, he became more compliant. Kevin Woods and his coauthors argue that as the United States began massing troops in the Gulf for an invasion, "Saddam finally tilted towards pursuing policies designed to per-suade the international community that Iraq was cooperating with [UNS-COM] and that it was free of WMD programs."[116] In particular, he acquiesced to a new round of inspections and ordered Iraqi officials to cooperate with them. Saddam's cooperation at such a late hour was par-tially aimed at France and Russia, which he hoped would intercede on his behalf.[117] But he also decided to give inspectors full access so as "not to give President Bush any excuses to start a war."[118] Saddam believed the United States was too sensitive to casualties to fight a costly war and so could be convinced to settle for a bargain.[119] His son and other military officials reportedly urged him to mine the Gulf and take other deterrent actions, but Saddam refused.[120]

Initial reports concerning Saddam's level of cooperation with this last round of inspections were mixed. After Iraq submitted a roughly twelve thousand–page report detailing its compliance with UN demands, inspec-tors noted that the report had glaring omissions.[121] But subsequent reports by both the head of the UN inspections team, Hans Blix, and the director of the International Atomic Energy Agency, Mohamed ElBaradei, indicated that Iraq was, on the whole, complying.[122] Although questions remained regarding its accounting of certain weapons material, Blix observed that Iraq had taken the significant step of granting access to inspection sites without prior notice and permitting aerial surveillance.[123] ElBaradei also noted that, although Iraq initially offered only passive compliance, it was more cooperative by early March 2003. ElBaradei reported, "In the past three weeks, possibly as a result of ever-increasing pressure by the interna-tional community, Iraq has been forthcoming in its co-operation."[124] Thus, when faced with a direct and imminent threat of regime change, Saddam backed down.

The Bush administration, however, was no longer interested in Sad-dam's cooperation at this point. Indeed, when Saddam began sending out signals that he was interested in negotiating an exile deal, the Bush adminis-tration made clear that no such deal would be made. Allies of the United States in the Middle East reported that the Iraqi leader wanted financial remuneration and a guarantee of safety in exchange for leaving Iraq.[125] However, during a discussion with Egyptian President Hosni Mubarak's son in February 2003, Bush refused to guarantee Saddam's safety in exile. He also insisted that the United States would look unfavorably on any country offering Saddam protection.[126] It remains unclear whether

Saddam's alleged interest in exile was sincere or merely an attempt to stall for time. Regardless, given the Bush administration's refusal to negotiate, it is hardly surprising that Saddam rejected Bush's later ultimatum to leave Iraq or face war. He had nowhere to go.

Alternative Arguments in the Iraqi Case

Thus far, I have shown that the Bush administration, like its two predecessors, viewed Saddam as more costly to coerce than to overthrow. I argue that what drove this expectation was Saddam's domestic opposition, which both caused him to resist inspections and convinced American policymakers that Saddam was susceptible to being overthrown. There are, of course, a variety of alternative explanations for the war. As I explain in this section, these arguments offer potential answers to a number of important questions, including why the United States and Iraq viewed one another as enemies, why the Bush administration chose to use military force against Iraq, and why the effort to depose Saddam failed to establish a stable democracy. But there are also important questions these arguments cannot answer, in particular, why American policymakers, from the first Bush administration through to the second, saw regime change as the most effective way of dealing with Saddam. Below, I review the alternative arguments based on psychological bias, bureaucratic and/or interest-group pressure, and rational choice models. I explain what they can tell us about the war and what they cannot.

PSYCHOLOGICAL BIAS

One of the most common psychological arguments on the Iraq War holds that actors on both sides of the conflict were predisposed to fighting. One such argument suggests that after years of contentious relations with Saddam, which included an alleged attempt to assassinate George W. Bush's father, administration officials came to office convinced that the only way to deal with Iraq was through regime change.[127] Another version of this thesis contends that Saddam was predisposed to conflict with the United States because he was convinced that American policymakers were out to get him. There is evidence that leaders on both sides were inclined to distrust one another. Saddam, for example, had launched the first Gulf War at a time the first Bush administration was trying to engage him in cooperation.[128] His refusal to withdraw from Kuwait and, later, to cooperate fully with inspections, gave American officials additional reason to conclude that Saddam only understood the language of force. Likewise, Saddam had reason to distrust the United States because of its history of collaborating with his enemies.

Psychological arguments can help us understand why tensions between the United States and Iraq persisted, but they cannot explain why the American approach came to center on regime change. Certain officials in the Bush administration may have preferred regime change, but regardless of their views, the administration's initial policy focused on refining sanctions to revitalize containment.[129] Similarly, although Saddam clearly distrusted the United States, this distrust did not prevent him from backing down when he deemed it necessary. Saddam had ordered Iraq's WMD destroyed, because he believed doing so would enable him to escape sanctions. He also formally recognized the Kuwaiti border in 1994 and, when faced with the threat of an invasion in late 2002, accepted a new round of inspections with which he largely complied. Both sides may have been predisposed to conflict, but this predisposition did not make regime change inevitable.

A second common argument focuses on the psychological effects of the 9/11 attacks. Stressful events, according to Paul 't Hart, can trigger a groupthink mentality that causes policymakers to seek unanimity in their decision-making and shut out dissent.[130] Without debate, policymakers are prone to overestimating the benefits of their preferred policy and underestimating its costs. There is strong evidence that the psychological effects of 9/11 led policymakers to embrace a war plan without serious debate. Accounts show that after 9/11, there was little discussion within the administration on the merits of going to war. The president's closest advisers were quick to accept the assurances of Iraqi exile opposition leaders, despite the doubts of the State Department and CIA. Meanwhile, those who questioned the war or its cost estimates were marginalized or, in some cases, dismissed from their positions.[131]

Groupthink theory may offer insight into why the Bush administration so drastically underestimated the costs of regime change in Iraq, but it does not explain the choice to impose regime change. First, the theory is designed to explain why a consensus emerges around a particular policy; it does not tell us what the content of that policy will be. Policymakers might be just as likely to coalesce around a plan for limited air strikes as they would be to settle on a plan for regime change. Second, an argument that hinges on the effects of 9/11 cannot explain why American officials pursued regime change before 9/11. Finally, though groupthink may cause a policy to fail, this does not necessarily mean that groupthink drives the policy choice. Indeed, the fact that previous administrations, seemingly less prone to groupthink, also embraced regime change, suggests that a groupthink mentality was not necessary for regime change to occur.

BUREAUCRATIC AND INTEREST-GROUP PRESSURE

A second common argument on Iraq attributes the decision to invade to influential administration officials or interests groups who pushed policies designed to serve their own bureaucratic or personal interests. One such approach suggests that the decision to go to war was largely the consequence of a bureaucratic struggle for power in which the administration's hawks and neoconservatives dominated decision-making.[132] Rumsfeld, for example, was known for his skill in winning bureaucratic battles. He successfully contended with the military over how the war would be fought and the State Department over how the postwar phase would be managed.[133] A second approach sees the war as a result of pressure from interest groups, such as the oil industry, whose interests many Americans believe drove the decision to go to war. Another argument holds that pro-Israel administration officials and the Israeli lobby played a critical role in the decision to attack Iraq.[134]

Explanations citing bureaucratic and interest-group politics offer potential insight on why the Bush administration opted to use force against Iraq. But much like psychological bias arguments, they focus on the roles and interests of particular individuals within the George W. Bush administration and so cannot explain why previous administrations also pursued regime change. These arguments also imply that if individuals with different beliefs or interests had been in charge of decision-making, the United States might have abandoned its policy of regime change. But this is not necessarily the case. If Vice President Al Gore had won the 2000 presidential election, he would have faced the same dilemma as previous presidents—how to force Saddam, who was highly committed to resisting weapons inspections, to accept them indefinitely. Gore would have also faced the same domestic pressure as Clinton, particularly from Republicans in Congress, to take more assertive action on Iraq. After the traumatic events of 9/11, this pressure would have been especially intense, making it difficult to back away from the policy of regime change formalized in the Iraq Liberation Act. Although Gore might have continued the covert and indirect strategies of his predecessors, the high domestic political costs of negotiating with Saddam would have made it unlikely that Gore would have deviated from the long-standing policy of regime change.

Finally, arguments based on bureaucratic and interest-group politics are also unclear on why decision makers viewed regime change as the most effective way to fulfill their interests. If the Pentagon can be expected to push military solutions for the sake of its bureaucratic interests, then it might have been just as likely to support containment, which depended on the long-term use and threat of military force. Likewise, American oil companies had other ways to profit from Iraqi oil. They might have pressured the US government for sanctions relief to take advantage of Saddam's oil vouchers, which allowed the recipient to sell Iraqi oil at a profit.[135] Even Israel might have better secured its interests by pressuring the United States and its allies to continue isolating Iraq rather than undertaking a war that left Iraq weak and vulnerable to Iranian influence. Bureaucratic and interest-group models explain policy choice as a result of the interests of particular individuals or groups, but they do not explain why those individuals and groups believe a particular policy will advance their interests. By explaining how Saddam's domestic opposition made him appear both costly to coerce and susceptible to overthrow, my argument can explain why American policymakers chose regime change.

RATIONAL CHOICE ARGUMENTS

An approach focusing on commitment-problem logic suggests two possible interpretations of the decision to overthrow Saddam. The first is that the United States did not trust Saddam to disarm and so decided to depose him. There is evidence to support this claim. Saddam's obstruction of inspections caused American policymakers to conclude he must be hiding something. However, this explanation does not tell us why Saddam obstructed inspections, which could have proved his intention to disarm and spared him from regime change. Saddam's commitment problem may have compounded tensions between the United States and Iraq, but the question of why Saddam refused to take steps to resolve his commitment problem remains unanswered.

The second commitment-problem interpretation holds that Saddam feared his concessions would be used against him and so resisted American pressure. There is also evidence to support this claim. Saddam feared the United States was using inspectors to spy on his regime. However, if Saddam had known his obstructionism would cause the United States to invade and overthrow him, he would have had ample reason to comply with inspections to reduce, even if only slightly, the risk of an invasion. Although the inspection process entailed risk, the United States could have made it clear that noncompliance entailed greater risk. A commitment-problem argument, therefore, cannot explain why the United States did not simply increase its threat to force Saddam into making the concessions he was reluctant to make.

The incomplete-information approach offers a potential explanation for why the United States was unable to convince Saddam to accept the risks of compliance. Saddam simply did not believe American threats and so assumed he could resist with impunity. There is also strong evidence to support this interpretation. Indeed, Saddam had for years faced what he considered relatively mild punishments for noncompliance. He believed the Americans were too sensitive to casualties to fight a costly war and, according to many high-level Iraqis, remained convinced right up until the invasion that the Bush administration would merely launch air strikes.[136]

A focus on the issue of incomplete information, however, cannot explain why the United States failed to take the measures necessary to make its threat credible earlier. Saddam became more compliant in late 2002, as the United States began mobilizing for war. If the United States had taken these steps earlier, Saddam might have accepted inspections earlier. My argument explains why the United States failed to take these measures by pointing to their expense. The United States might have convinced Saddam to back down had it been willing to bear the costs of making a credible threat, but it was not, and so Saddam had no reason to back down. By the time the Bush administration was willing to prepare for war, the credibility of its threats no longer mattered, because the United States was seeking to overthrow Saddam, not to coerce him. In short, rational choice arguments, much like psychological and bureaucratic/interest-group actor arguments, can help us understand the conflict of interest between the United States and Iraq, but they do not explain why the United States chose to resolve that conflict with regime change.

The Case of Iraq: Conclusions

Saddam's domestic opposition not only drove his resistance to inspections, making him costly to contain, but also made him appear relatively less expensive to overthrow. For Saddam, reconciling with the United States required major concessions that threatened to empower his domestic enemies and regional rivals. The former were his primary concern, not only because he had previously faced major uprisings but also because his regional rivals had routinely backed these uprisings.[137] Saddam had no incentive to comply fully with inspections as long as he believed the punishment for resisting them would remain mild. Throughout the 1990s, Saddam had good reason to believe this, as his allies on the UN Security Council blocked harsh punishments. At the same time, Saddam's domestic vulnerability also convinced American policymakers, going back to the George H. W. Bush administration, that Saddam would be cheaper to overthrow than to contain. After 9/11, the George W. Bush administration became even less willing to bear the costs of containment as it became convinced that Saddam would become more costly to deal with once armed with WMD. Additionally, the popular support for war and the belief, pushed by Iraqi opposition leaders, that Iraqis could reconstruct Iraq on their own, encouraged the view that regime change would be cheaper than containing Saddam indefinitely.

Libya, 2003: Policy Change

In December 2003, the Bush administration announced it had successfully negotiated an agreement with Libya to end its WMD programs. The deal came after nearly a decade of signals from Libya that it was looking to reconcile with the West. Several scholars contend that Qaddafi's increasing domestic political threats, heightened by international pressure, explain his willingness to negotiate.[138] I show, however, that the Libyan leader, though interested in talks, refused to concede on the central issue at stake—the unconditional surrender of the Pan Am flight 103 bombing suspects—due to political costs.[139] Consistent with my theory's expectations, it was only after Qaddafi's domestic position improved and the United States and United Kingdom softened their demands that the Libyan leader began making significant concessions.

American Demands in Libya, 2003

An understanding of how the United States and Libya arrived at a deal in 2003 requires an examination of the three decades prior, during which US

policy went from treating Libya as a rogue state to embracing it as an ally
in the war on terror. US-Libyan relations passed through three distinct
phases as American demands gradually expanded.[140] In the first period,
from 1969 until 1991, the primary aim of US policy was to deter Qaddafi
from pursuing his aggressive foreign policy agenda. Within years of seizing
power in 1969, Qaddafi had become a major sponsor of terror, backing
myriad rebel and terrorist groups worldwide.[141] Evidence also linked Libya
to several high-profile attacks, including the murder of Israeli athletes at
the 1972 Summer Olympics in Munich and the 1973 assassination of the
US ambassador to Sudan.[142] By the 1980s, Libya was brazenly using its
embassies as bases from which to facilitate terrorist plots and assassinate
Libyan exiles. In the mid-1980s, Libya called for suicide attacks against
"U.S.-Zionist" embassies.[143] The Libyan regime was also engaged in efforts
to acquire a nuclear weapon and succeeded in amassing a chemicals weap-
ons stockpile.[144] Libya became involved in a nine-year intervention in the
Chadian civil war as well, and a 1977 plot to assassinate Egyptian president
Anwar Sadat.[145]

US-Libyan relations entered a second stage at the end of 1991, after
which the United States was no longer interested in merely deterring its
aggression but in compelling its compliance with a specific set of demands.
Although Qaddafi began modifying his behavior in the late 1980s and even
renounced terrorism, evidence emerged in 1991 that tied Libya to the
December 1988 Pan Am flight 103 bombing over Lockerbie, Scotland,
which left 270 dead. Libya was also implicated in the downing of UTA flight
772 over Niger in 1989, which left 171 dead.[146] In November 1991, the
United States and United Kingdom demanded Qaddafi turn over, without
condition, the two Libyan suspects tied to the Pan Am bombing. When
Qaddafi refused, the UN Security Council voted in March 1992 to impose
sanctions that included an aircraft ban, arms embargo, asset freeze, and a
prohibition on the sale of certain oil-industry expertise and equipment.[147]
Although the multilateral sanctions exacerbated Libya's economic problems, it would take seven years for Libya to surrender the suspects.

Libya's decision to turn over the Pan Am suspects marked the beginning
of a third phase in US-Libyan tensions, during which US demands
expanded. Although UN sanctions were suspended after Libya surrendered
the Pan Am bombing suspects, the US insisted Libya would have to accept
responsibility for the Pan Am bombing and compensate the families before
sanctions could be permanently lifted.[148] US sanctions would remain in

place until Libya surrendered its WMD programs. In May 1999, the Americans, British, and Libyans began secret talks focused on resolving the Pan Am issue. Although Libya offered to join the Chemical Weapons Convention, American officials still saw Libya's WMD programs as a relatively minor threat. They, therefore, insisted Libya resolve the Pan Am issue before the WMD issue could be addressed.[149]

The secret talks over the Pan Am bombing were suspended during the 2000 US presidential election but began again in the spring of 2001. In August 2002, as plans for the Iraq War began to take shape, British prime minister Tony Blair proposed to Bush the possibility of offering Qaddafi a quid pro quo by which the United States would normalize relations with Libya in exchange for relinquishing its WMD programs. Talks concerning Libya's WMD began in March 2003. In August 2003, Libya agreed to pay $2.7 billion to the families of the Pan Am bombing victims.[150] Roughly five months later, Qaddafi announced Libya was surrendering its WMD programs. The leader Reagan had once labeled the "mad dog of the Middle East" had conceded to US demands, even though they had steadily increased over the years.

The Costs to Qaddafi of Compliance Versus Resistance, 2003

My argument suggests that leaders who are coerced to make politically costly concessions will resist when their domestic threats are more pressing. In this section, I argue that during the first stage of US-Libyan tensions, Qaddafi was well insulated against foreign pressure and so defied the West, even though his political costs of compliance were low. In the second stage, Qaddafi's costs of resistance rose sharply, but so did his political costs of compliance. As a result, he resisted demands for the unconditional surrender of the Pan Am bombing suspects until his political position improved and the West agreed to a conditional surrender. During the third stage, Qaddafi's political position continued to improve, enabling him to make additional concessions to the West to capture the benefits of reintegration.

Qaddafi's belligerence during the first phase of US-Libyan tensions stemmed less from domestic political threats than from his desire to assert himself as a world leader. His attempt to construct an image as a champion of the weak was also a propaganda tool to rally popular support at home and throughout the Arab world.[151] Qaddafi's domestic political opponents played a small but relevant role in this foreign aggression. Paranoid about political threats, Qaddafi sent death squads after dissident leaders in exile.[152] That he was willing to risk relations with the countries in which these killings took place reveals the extent to which he was prepared to incur international costs to eliminate even minor political threats.

Qaddafi could afford to prioritize these negligible domestic threats because the costs of defying the West were even more inconsequential.[153] At least three factors kept his costs of resistance low. First, the Libyan regime could use its oil wealth both to fund its foreign adventures and to buy off or eliminate any potential domestic opposition.[154] Second, when the United States imposed an oil boycott in 1982, Libya was able to avoid the economic impact by increasing sales to Europe. The United Kingdom, for example, increased imports of Libyan oil by 350 percent in the first eighteen months of the US ban. Germany, Italy, and, later, Brazil and Turkey became reliable customers.[155] European countries also publicly opposed the Reagan administration's efforts to ratchet up pressure on Qaddafi and isolate him diplomatically.[156] Finally, as Libya's relations with the United States deteriorated in the 1970s, Qaddafi expanded ties with Moscow. By the time the Reagan administration took office in January 1981, the Soviet Union had become a major arms supplier to Libya and was using Libyan bases.[157]

By the end of the 1980s, however, Qaddafi's defense against Western pressure began to erode. Libya's ailing economy made it increasingly difficult for Qaddafi to buy domestic political support. The regime's system of massive government dependence was plagued by corruption and incompetence. Government wages were low, often paid late, and frozen from 1982 to 2003.[158] With 75 percent of government spending coming from the oil industry, falling oil prices in the 1980s led to severe government shortfalls.[159] From 1985 to 1986, the price of oil dropped from $26.92 per barrel to $14.44 per barrel.[160] In addition, after the United States launched a bombing raid on Tripoli in 1986, European countries imposed diplomatic sanctions and an arms embargo on Libya, as well.[161] Finally, the collapse of the Soviet Union left Libya bereft of its superpower ally and arms supplier.[162]

As Qaddafi became more vulnerable to Western pressure, Libya's foreign and domestic policy began to change. The Libyan regime not only introduced domestic reforms to appease the public but also sought to repair its relations with neighboring states.[163] It withdrew its forces from Chad in 1987, essentially accepting defeat.[164] More significantly, Qaddafi declared that Libya would no longer support terrorism. Reagan administration officials concluded that the 1986 bombing raid had convinced Qaddafi to abandon terrorism.[165] But a spate of terrorist attacks immediately following the bombing, as well as evidence linking Libya to the Pan Am and UTA bombings, suggests otherwise. These bombings aside, Libya eventually did reduce its involvement in terrorism. Qaddafi's terrorist activity had never been critical to his domestic power; he could, therefore, abandon it without incurring political costs. The costs of defying the West, meanwhile, were beginning to mount as the conditions that had once shielded his regime began to disappear.[166]

In 1991, the US-Libyan standoff entered its second stage, during which Qaddafi faced a new set of demands, specifically the unconditional surrender of the Pan Am bombing suspects. He began signaling an interest in talks with the West but nevertheless refused to surrender the suspects unconditionally. He resisted this demand even though resistance was becoming more costly for him. UN sanctions, imposed in April 1992, compounded Libya's economic troubles. Within a year, Libya's GDP growth rate was negative 30 percent, and within two years, inflation had jumped to 50 percent. Unemployment hovered between 20 and 30 percent in the mid-1990s, and the value of the dinar plunged, causing wages to fall 35 percent a year.[167]

As the standard of living declined, the Libyan regime began to face an increasing number of domestic political challenges. The military tried several times to pull off a coup.[168] In 1993, officers from the Werfella tribe, which dominated the military, coordinated an attempt with the exile opposition group, the National Front for the Salvation of Libya.[169] Islamists, however, posed the most formidable challenge. The regime had conducted mass arrests to stamp out extremist cells in the late 1980s, but as Libyan fighters returned from Afghanistan in the early 1990s, the movement rebounded.[170] Islamist rebel organizations such as the Libya Martyrs' Movement and the Libyan-Islamic Fighting Group (LIFG) orchestrated a string of attacks that left an estimated six hundred dead.[171]

Although Qaddafi was eager to escape sanctions, the demand to surrender the Pan Am bombing suspects carried too high a price. One of the suspects, Abdelbaset al-Megrahi, was a member of the powerful Megraha tribe, which the regime depended upon for political support.[172] In addition, hardliners within the regime staunchly opposed surrendering the suspects. In particular, the revolutionary committees, which were populated by ideologues, opposed surrendering the suspects.[173] Regime insiders, such as Qaddafi's brother-in-law, 'Abdallah al-Sanusi, and 'Abd al-Salam Jallud, an influential member of the Megraha tribe, also advocated defiance.[174] Finally, popular opinion opposed surrendering the suspects.[175] Qaddafi himself referred to these domestic concerns when he claimed that if he relinquished the suspects, "the Libyan people would say 'these two men are our compatriots. . . . You cannot take them and give them to another country. We are not sheep that he [Qaddafi] would dispose of us in this way.'"[176] Finally, Qaddafi also feared the United States and United Kingdom might use a public trial to humiliate him and undermine his regime.[177]

Two conditions appear to have led to Qaddafi's ultimate decision to remand the suspects in 1999. First, his domestic political position at home began to improve. By the end of the 1990s, the regime had largely defeated the Islamist opposition. In 1998, the LIFG announced an end to its struggle and went into exile. Mass arrests had all but incapacitated the Muslim Brotherhood as well.[178] Second, the United States and United Kingdom modified their demands. Qaddafi had already proposed a number of compromises. In 1994, he suggested a trial at the International Court of Justice (ICJ) under Scottish jurisdiction.[179] The United States and United Kingdom refused, but by the end of the decade, diminishing international support for sanctions led them to agree. In 1998, they proposed a trial at a specially convened court in The Hague under Scottish jurisdiction, essentially the same plan as Qaddafi's 1994 proposal.[180] Nevertheless, Qaddafi still feared the domestic consequences of compliance and so demanded and received a series of assurances to protect his political power.[181] In short, although resistance was costly for Qaddafi, the high domestic political costs of surrendering the Pan Am suspects appear to have led him to resist until the United States and United Kingdom agreed to a conditional surrender.

During the third stage of US-Libyan relations, US demands expanded again to include compensation for the families of the Pan Am bombing victims and, later, the surrender of Libya's WMD. Although international pressure on Qaddafi had diminished by this point with the lifting of UN sanctions, the Libyan leader continued making concessions. Accounts that attribute Qaddafi's surrender of the Pan Am bombing suspects to his fear of losing domestic power have difficulty explaining these concessions, because his political position was, by this time, improving.[182] The regime achieved military victories over its Islamist opposition in the late 1990s. The Libyan economy had also rebounded. Oil prices increased from $12 a barrel in 1998 to $28 a barrel in 2003.[183] Inflation subsided and foreign reserves increased too.[184]

Consistent with the predictions of my theory, as Qaddafi's domestic position improved, his compliance costs decreased, enabling him to expand cooperation with the West. Talks over compensation for the Pan Am victims' families began shortly after the suspects were handed over in April 1999 and resumed in 2001 after the US presidential election. According to an American official participating in the talks, the United States and United Kingdom essentially "presented the Libyans with a 'script,'" which they accepted.[185]

In August 2002, Tony Blair proposed to Bush the basis for what would become the 2003 WMD deal. The United States would offer normalized relations in exchange for Qaddafi's relinquishing his WMD programs. Blair had good reason to believe Qaddafi would be receptive. The Libyan government had already offered to surrender its chemical weapons program during the 1999 talks.[186] The new round of formal negotiations began in March 2003 but stalled over the timing of inspections. In September, the interdiction of the *BBC China*, a German-owned ship carrying centrifuge parts, revealed that Libya still had an active nuclear weapons program.[187] Reports from inside Libya, however, suggest that this program was part of a back-up plan, meant to deter an American attack if rapprochement failed.[188] Two weeks after the interdiction, Libya agreed to a timeline for inspections.[189] By December, the Libyan government formally announced its decision to abandon its WMD programs.

My argument indicates that politically strong leaders are better positioned to make concessions but that the size of their concessions still depend on their vulnerability to economic and military pressure and the amount of pressure. Qaddafi's diminishing domestic threats lowered his compliance costs, but negative and positive incentives from the West also influenced his decision to surrender Libya's WMD. American sanctions, for example, prevented Libya from modernizing its oil industry.[190] With its oil reserves declining, Libya was looking for new investment in both oil and gas technology, which necessitated access to the American market.[191] In addition, the regime's technocrats, led by Qaddafi's reform-minded son, Saif al-Islam Qaddafi, insisted that Libya's WMD programs sapped the country's resources. As future Libyan prime minister Shukri Ghanem later explained, "For a small country like Libya . . . your thinking is to defend yourself by all means. . . . But then you find out that [your weapons are] eating all your money."[192]

The invasion of Iraq may have also facilitated the 2003 deal. Although the Libyan regime had been reaching out to the West for over a decade,

Qaddafi himself said that the Iraq War had influenced his decision.[193] Saif, however, later claimed that the Iraq War was more an opportunity than a warning. It gave Libya a chance to break out of isolation. "We knew the Americans would not find yellowcake in Iraq—as we warned them—but that there was yellowcake in Libya, and that this card was worth something," Saif explained. "I saw WMD as a card in our hands" and the Iraq invasion was "the best time to play" it.[194] Saif also insisted that Western officials had offered Libya security guarantees, as well as "access to sensitive technology" and "defensive weapons."[195]

Whether positive or negative incentives influenced Qaddafi's ultimate decision, his stronger domestic position played a crucial role in paving the way for the 2003 deal. Although he had initially resisted turning over the Pan Am bombing suspects, once his domestic position improved, his compliance with US demands did as well. He no longer needed to worry that his concessions would weaken him politically and so could make major concessions without fearing they would empower his domestic enemies.

The Costs to the United States of a Settlement with Qaddafi, 2003

During the first phase of US-Libyan relations, the United States responded to Qaddafi's radicalism by increasing pressure designed to change the Libyan leader's behavior.[196] Though coercing Qaddafi entailed some costs for the United States, these were only moderate. In fact, the Reagan administration had chosen to target Libya rather than other state sponsors of terrorism because it saw Qaddafi as an easier target. According to a CIA report written by then deputy director Robert Gates, the agency had considered leaning on Iran and Syria, but "Iran proved to be 'too hard,'" while Syria entailed the risk of a confrontation with the Soviet Union. "So the process of elimination brought [the] CIA to Libya."[197]

The costs of coercing Qaddafi were higher for European countries, whose leaders argued that a hardline approach would only antagonize him.[198] From the US perspective, however, Europe's economic interests were the real reason it opposed coercing Qaddafi. Whereas the United States began buying oil from other sources after cutting ties with Qaddafi, Europe still relied heavily on Libyan oil. Libya was also the 16th most important buyer of European Community exports. Libya had also racked up European debt; it owed Italy roughly $800 million.[199] As one National

Security Council staff paper put it, NATO allies, "compete with each other for profitable Libyan contracts while pronouncing the convenient rationale that it is better to collaborate with Qaddafi than to isolate him."[200]

Europe's reluctance to cut ties to Libya explains, in part, why US efforts to coerce Qaddafi had little effect during this period.[201] But the United States could not pressure its European allies to apply greater pressure without incurring diplomatic costs itself. At first, the Reagan administration was reluctant to risk its relations with Europe.[202] Even after Libya's involvement in the terrorist attacks on the Rome and Vienna airports in December 1985, the administration's initial response was to increase economic rather than military pressure. But after that failed to alter Qaddafi's behavior, the administration ordered naval maneuvers off the coast of Libya in March 1986. Soon after, a bomb exploded at the La Belle discotheque in Berlin. The United States claimed it had evidence of Libyan involvement and launched Operation El Dorado Canyon, the April 1986 bombing raid on Tripoli.

Libya was the principal target of El Dorado Canyon, but Europe was the second one. The Reagan administration hoped the operation would convince its European allies to increase pressure on Libya by demonstrating that the United States would employ unilateral force if left to act alone.[203] In this respect, the strategy worked. The raid brought additional European measures, including an arms embargo and the expulsion of a number of Libyan diplomatic personnel and businessmen from Europe.[204] But the Europeans refused to support the raid itself. France and Spain, for example, denied the United States overflight access, which forced US pilots to fly an additional six thousand miles round-trip to bases in the United Kingdom.[205] British prime minister Margaret Thatcher, the only European leader to support the raid, incurred substantial domestic criticism for doing so.[206]

During the second stage of US-Libyan interactions, the diplomatic costs of pressuring Qaddafi were originally low for the United States, but rose steadily over the decade. Evidence of Libyan involvement in the Pan Am and UTA bombings initially generated international support for UN sanctions. This support, however, would wane over time, leaving the United States increasingly at odds with some of its European allies. Although Europe had agreed to apply sanctions, the countries dependent on Libyan oil—Italy, Spain, and Germany—refused a full oil embargo, diminishing the sanctions' effect.[207] As the decade wore on, countries with the strongest trade ties to Libya gradually lost interest in upholding sanctions. France and Italy began secretly trading with Libya, and in 1997, Italy announced it would reestablish diplomatic relations.[208] Europeans were also angered when, in 1996, the US Congress passed legislation imposing penalties on foreign firms violating UN sanctions.[209] As with Iraq, the humanitarian toll of sanctions further diminished international support for them. By 1998, both the Arab League and the Organization of African Unity were threatening to violate sanctions, and widespread criticism of the humanitarian costs suggested others might follow suit.[210]

The growing diplomatic costs of coercing Qaddafi to relinquish the Pan Am suspects led the United States and United Kingdom to change course. In 1998, US policymakers grew concerned that international pressure on Libya would disappear entirely when the ICJ ruled that it had jurisdiction over the Pan Am case. American and British officials worried that the court would rule in favor of Libya, further undermining their ability to pressure Qaddafi. As Secretary of State Madeleine Albright explained, "As our prospects for maintaining sanctions dimmed . . . we began to consider other options."[211] The United States and United Kingdom soon agreed to a compromise deal similar to Qaddafi's earlier proposal.[212]

By the third phase of US-Libyan tensions, Qaddafi's more cooperative behavior had dramatically lowered the costs to the United States of obtaining a negotiated agreement with him. Although US sanctions remained in place, these carried little cost to the United States, which had cut its economic ties to Libya years before. Qaddafi's willingness to settle with the Pan Am families also lowered the domestic political costs to US policymakers of openly negotiating with him. Unlike Saddam, Qaddafi was no longer seen as a dangerous pariah. Although his compliance on WMD was inconsistent, as the *BBC China* incident demonstrated, Qaddafi quickly accepted inspections just two weeks after the incident. In all, the costs to the United States of concluding an agreement with Qaddafi were low because Qaddafi's political costs were low, which enabled him to respond to US pressure and inducements without fear of jeopardizing his domestic power.

The Costs of Full Regime Change in Libya, 2003

Though coercing Qaddafi forced the United States to incur diplomatic costs during the first phase of US-Libyan tensions, these costs were insufficient to convince American policymakers to fully embrace regime change. Because

Qaddafi's Western-oriented opposition was weak and disorganized, replacing him would be hard to do. Although the Reagan administration did authorize a covert program in the 1980s to encourage a coup, this was part of a larger campaign to deter Libya from terrorism.[213] The administration consistently signaled it would be open to negotiating if Qaddafi changed his behavior, which meant its primary goal was not regime change, but policy change.

Even these modest covert efforts to threaten Qaddafi's political power, however, came to an end as officials concluded Qaddafi's opposition was too weak to be effective. In the year before funding for covert operations was approved, CIA Deputy Director John N. McMahon had opposed a similar plan, calling Qaddafi's exile opposition "Boy Scouts" with little chance of success.[214] The State Department's intelligence branch also questioned the plan's feasibility, noting that it failed to take account of "Qaddafi's enduring popularity."[215] One of the proposed plans for removing Qaddafi entailed collaborating with Egypt to provoke a conflict that would allow military action. Egyptian President Hosni Mubarak, however, rejected the idea, and subsequent efforts to undermine Qaddafi remained focused on funding exiles.[216]

Operation El Dorado Canyon was emblematic of US strategy at this time. Although officials hoped Qaddafi might be killed in the attacks, regime change was not the primary goal.[217] The attacks targeted the Aziziyah barracks, where Qaddafi had a residence, but US bombs did not have the payload to penetrate Qaddafi's bunker.[218] Some administration officials also warned that deliberately attempting to kill Qaddafi could turn him into a martyr. Although most US officials readily agreed that they would not be disappointed if Qaddafi happened to be killed, they saw the primary purpose as coercing Libya to abandon its support for terrorism.[219]

During the second phase of US-Libyan relations, Qaddafi experienced an increasing number of domestic political threats. Given that the diplomatic costs to the United States of coercing Qaddafi began to rise as international opposition to UN sanctions grew, the United States might have resorted to regime change during this period. Yet the Bush and Clinton administrations remained committed to coercing rather than overthrowing Qaddafi. Although there are unconfirmed reports of both American and British attempts to assist the exile opposition in a coup, there was no explicit policy aimed at regime change. This was largely because Qaddafi's most powerful domestic opposition was Islamist and hostile to the West.[220]

The Western-oriented Libyan opposition remained weak and disorganized. As such, the costs of regime change remained high.

By the start of the third phase, Libyan and American interests began to intersect, making regime change unnecessary. Not only had Qaddafi conceded on the Pan Am bombing and WMD issues, but Libya had also become an ally in the global war on terror. Qaddafi had also become stronger domestically than he had been during the mid-1990s. The Libyan economy had rebounded and his domestic threats were largely eliminated. Thus, even had the United States wanted to overthrow him at this point, no opposition group had the strength to assist the United States in imposing regime change.

Alternative Arguments in the Libyan Case, 2003

The evidence supports my argument that the 2003 deal was a product of Qaddafi's strong domestic political position, which made him relatively easy to negotiate with and hard to overthrow. Next, I consider the evidence for alternative arguments based on psychological bias, bureaucratic and/or interest-group pressure, and the two dominant rational choice models. As in the Iraq case, there is evidence to support the claims of many of these arguments, but they leave the central question of why the United States opted to negotiate with rather than overthrow Qaddafi unanswered.

PSYCHOLOGICAL BIAS

A psychological approach to understanding the decision to negotiate with Qaddafi would suggest that US policymakers had better relations with him than Saddam and were, therefore, more inclined to negotiate with the Libyan leader. By 2003, this was true. Qaddafi was seeking to reconcile with the West during the 1990s, but Saddam remained defiant until late 2002. Moreover, Qaddafi responded to 9/11 by offering the United States assistance with counterterrorism. The Iraqi government, in contrast, criticized the United States. An official government statement declared, "The American cowboys are reaping the fruit of their crimes against humanity."[221]

Yet a psychological approach cannot explain how Libya and the United States overcame their longstanding mutual distrust. Qaddafi, for example, claimed his family had been injured in the 1986 bombing of Tripoli and that his adopted daughter had been killed. Some considered the bombing of Pan Am flight 103 two years later to be an act of vengeance.[222] If Qaddafi's experience with the United States colored his views and influenced his policy choices, he should have appeared more defiant after the 1986 raid, not less so. US policymakers also had reason to question Qaddafi's intentions, given his past transgressions and ongoing attempts to acquire WMD. As one Reagan administration official had put it, Qaddafi was known for lulling people to sleep by appearing cooperative and then "doing whatever he please[d]."[223] In fact, Qaddafi had first called for a ban on WMD in 1988, just after starting his chemical weapons program. His regime was also caught importing components for a nuclear weapons program during the 2003 WMD talks. Yet, despite these reasons for distrust, the United States and Libya continued to negotiate. A psychological approach may be able to explain why US officials viewed Qaddafi more favorably than Saddam, but it cannot explain why Qaddafi was more cooperative than Saddam.

BUREAUCRATIC AND INTEREST-GROUP PRESSURE

An explanation focusing on the role of bureaucratic politics suggests that influential members of the George W. Bush administration shaped the president's policy decisions to align with their own interests. The literature on the Iraq case suggests that both hawks and neoconservatives held considerable sway in the administration after 9/11. If true, we would expect the president to have hewed closely to their policy preferences. Yet Secretary of Defense Rumsfeld and Deputy Secretary Wolfowitz, both of whom played major roles in the decision to invade Iraq, opposed negotiating with Qaddafi. They argued that the United States should continue to insist Libya reform politically and respect human rights and wanted US policy to remain focused on changing the Libyan regime.[224] Bush's decision to ignore these recommendations appears to have been in response to British pressure. British officials reportedly insisted the White House keep some of the most vocal proponents of regime change out of the talks with Libya.[225] Bush thus pursued a negotiated settlement, though some of the most influential members of his administration opposed it.

RATIONAL CHOICE ARGUMENTS

An incomplete-information argument would suggest that Qaddafi was more convinced than Saddam that resisting US pressure was costly and, therefore, was more willing to concede. There is evidence to support this claim. UN sanctions, for example, hurt the Libyan economy at a time when Qaddafi was facing an increasing number of domestic threats. Qaddafi also had the benefit of learning from Saddam's experience. He even acknowledged that the Iraq War had influenced his decision to abandon his WMD programs.[226]

A closer look at Qaddafi's record of compliance, however, reveals that it does not fit the pattern that an incomplete-information approach would predict. First, despite the pain UN sanctions caused him during the 1990s, Qaddafi refused to release the Pan Am bombing suspects until the end of the decade. By then, however, it appeared his costs of resistance were set to drop because the international consensus on sanctions was fraying. Thus, Qaddafi appeared to surrender more as the ability of the United States to threaten a costly punishment diminished. Second, though the Iraq War may have revived the credibility of US threats, Qaddafi was making major concessions before the war and had previously offered to surrender Libya's chemical weapons. It, therefore, does not appear that Qaddafi's concessions were driven solely by his beliefs about the credibility of US threats.

Finally, a credible-commitment problem would suggest that the United States and Qaddafi both had greater incentive to trust one another than did the United States and Saddam. It is true that Qaddafi's increasingly cooperative behavior from the late 1990s on gave the Americans reason to believe he would remain cooperative. But as the *BBC China* incident demonstrated, Qaddafi was also still actively engaged in attempts to acquire a nuclear weapons program. Although he soon agreed to allow inspections, it remains unclear why American policymakers believed he would remain cooperative. He could have, for example, agreed to inspections and then obstructed them, much as Saddam had done. Qaddafi also had reason to distrust the United States. There was little way to guarantee a future administration would not overturn the deal and use Libya's newfound vulnerability against it, as would ultimately occur. Thus, both sides had reason to doubt the intentions of the other, and yet each was willing to strike a deal. A credible-commitment approach indicates that the greater levels of trust between the United States and Libya helped engender cooperation, but it does not tell us where that trust came from. My argument, in contrast, holds that Qaddafi's improving domestic position lowered his compliance costs, which in turn lowered the costs to the United States of reaching a deal with him.

The Case of Libya, 2003: Conclusions

Over the roughly three decades the United States put pressure on Libya, Qaddafi backed down only when the political costs of doing so were low and the costs of resistance were high. During the 1980s, he faced few domestic threats. But international economic and political conditions shielded him from American attempts to coerce him, enabling his defiance. By the 1990s, Qaddafi was much more vulnerable domestically, which led him to resist surrendering the Pan Am bombing suspects to avoid losing face at home. Although the United States might have partnered with his opposition to depose him, Qaddafi's opposition consisted mainly of Islamist groups. As a result, the Clinton administration chose instead to soften its demands to facilitate a deal. In the late 1990s, Qaddafi's domestic position improved, making him harder to overthrow. But with his political costs of concessions also falling, there was less need to overthrow him. Qaddafi's greater willingness to make concessions paved the way for talks on Libya's WMD. By 2011, however, Qaddafi's domestic political situation had changed, and with it, US policy.

Libya, 2011: Full Regime Change

On March 28, 2011, nine days after NATO initiated an intervention in Libya, President Obama clarified in a speech his reasons for supporting military action. "To brush aside America's responsibility as a leader—and more profoundly—our responsibilities to our fellow human beings under such circumstances would have been a betrayal of who we are," he explained. "And as president, I refused to wait for the images of slaughter and mass graves before taking action."[227] The president's words emphasized one of the intervention's critical goals, to prevent what many Western leaders believed would be a massacre in the Libyan city of Benghazi. The UN Security Council passed Resolution 1973 on March 17 to authorize member states to use "all necessary measures" to protect Libyan civilians. What those measures would be, however, remained unclear.

The decision to conduct a humanitarian intervention in Libya was distinct from the choice to pursue regime change. The president had insisted that, although he wanted to see the Libyan dictator removed from power, "broadening our military mission to include regime change would be a mistake."[228] This suggested that the Libyan mission might resemble the NATO interventions in Bosnia and Kosovo, which ended with cease-fire agreements.[229] Yet, from the start of the Libyan intervention, NATO members refused to negotiate with Qaddafi, despite his calls for a cease-fire. They also supplied Libyan rebels with arms, training, and military assistance. As the Libyan intervention progressed, it became increasingly clear that regime change was the de facto goal of the NATO mission.

In this section, I address why the Obama administration decided to take action in Libya and why it ultimately pursued regime change. Understanding the decision-making that led to the NATO intervention is crucial to explaining Qaddafi's fall from power. Libyan forces were on the verge of crushing the rebellion when the United Nations authorized action, which meant that Qaddafi might have otherwise survived.[230] I focus on the US decision to push for an "all necessary measures" UN resolution, as this was critical in allowing regime change to become the de facto goal. Although France and the United Kingdom actively lobbied for stepping in, their proposals were limited to a no-fly zone, which was unlikely to precipitate regime change. Given that pro-Qaddafi troops and mercenaries on the ground posed the greatest danger to civilians, a no-fly zone was unlikely to stop even the violence. Thus, the Obama administration's decision to expand the British and French proposal for a no-fly zone marked the beginning of the decision to pursue regime change.

American and United Nations Demands in Libya, 2011

In negotiating the 2003 deal, the Bush administration had decided to focus its demands on Libya's WMD programs, not on political reform. Although Qaddafi had permitted some modest reforms prior to the deal, these were gradually reversed in the years following it. Meanwhile, Western governments, eager to access Libya's oil and secure its cooperation on illegal immigration and counterterrorism, expanded their cooperation with the regime. The end of the European Union arms embargo in 2004 paved the way for a series of deals that not only denied Qaddafi incentive to reform but also helped him extract concessions from the West.[231] Libya, for example, brokered an arms deal with French president Nicolas Sarkozy, in what critics alleged was a quid pro quo for the release of six Bulgarian medics.[232] In 2007, the British negotiated a $165-million deal for the defense contractor General Dynamics to train and supply forces charged with the regime's protection.[233] In 2008, Italy authorized the sale of $500 million in surveillance equipment to Libya to stem illegal immigration.[234] Qaddafi's success at exploiting Western interests to strengthen his regime was perhaps most evident in the 2009 release of jailed Pan Am bombing suspect al-Megrahi.

Qaddafi was said to have threatened to withhold British Petroleum oil contracts to force al-Megrahi's release.[235]

Intelligence agencies in the United States and United Kingdom also
worked closely with Libya's security services on counterterrorism, further
reducing pressure on the Libyan regime to respect human rights. The CIA,
for example, transferred eight suspects into Libyan custody, one of whom
was Ibn al-Shaykh al-Libi. Under torture in Egypt, al-Libi had supplied
information he later recanted that tied Iraq to al Qaeda.[236] Another was the
head of the LIFG, Abdelhakim Belhaj. Although the LIFG was focused on
fighting the Libyan regime, it was put on the State Department's list of
terrorist organizations for alleged ties to al Qaeda. Thus, Libya's collaboration in counterterrorism efforts ensured the regime American assistance in
rounding up its own Islamist opponents.[237]

Despite the collaboration of their intelligence services, relations between
the United States and Libya cooled toward the latter part of the decade.
Qaddafi criticized the United States for taking two years to remove Libya
from the State Department terror list.[238] He also claimed that he was promised more than he was given for surrendering Libya's WMD programs.[239]
Just weeks before the Libyan uprising in early 2011, relations hit a low point
when WikiLeaks published reports by the US ambassador to Libya, who
detailed the regime's corruption and cronyism. These reports reflected US
ambivalence toward a regime that had failed to embrace any meaningful
democratic reforms and whose leader was still considered "mercurial and
eccentric."[240] Nevertheless, Libya's failure to reform politically might not
have caused more than disappointment in the West had it not been for the
Arab Spring uprisings, which spread to Libya in early 2011.

The Libyan uprising began in Benghazi on February 15, following the
arrest of a prominent local activist, Fathi Terbil. Although Terbil was
released that evening, demonstrations continued, with protestors firing
shots in the streets and throwing rocks and petrol bombs at government
buildings.[241] On February 17, protestors converged for what they called a
"Day of Rage" in Benghazi. Activists reported that government security
forces attacked the crowd with knives and guns, while protestors set fire to
police and security headquarters.[242] Some reports since the intervention
have charged that Western media accounts exaggerated the nature of the
violence and death toll.[243] But the regime's reputation for human rights
abuse helped fuel concerns it would use any means to preserve power.[244]

Qaddafi's own televised pledge to "cleanse Libya inch by inch" furthered the impression of the regime's brutality.[245]

Qaddafi's rhetoric, as well as media reports of atrocities, helped build momentum for a humanitarian intervention. On February 26, the UN Security Council adopted Resolution 1970, which called for an "immediate end to the violence" and demanded the Libyan regime take "steps to fulfill the legitimate demands of the population." It also urged Libya to lift media restrictions, respect human rights, and ensure safe passage for humanitarian aid agencies.[246] To enforce its demands, the United Nations imposed an arms embargo and froze the assets of Qaddafi family members and top Libyan officials. The European Union also imposed its own arms embargo and an asset freeze. In addition, the UN resolution referred the Libyan regime to the International Criminal Court (ICC) for investigation.[247] On March 17, 2011, the UN Security Council, in Resolution 1973, reiterated its demand for an immediate end to the violence and authorized member nations to take "all necessary measures" to protect civilians and civilian populated areas.[248]

Western leaders also began calling on Qaddafi to step down. As early as February 25, France's Sarkozy declared, "Mr. Gaddafi must leave."[249] On March 3, President Obama said that Qaddafi had "lost the legitimacy to lead and he must leave."[250] But even as Western leaders were calling for regime change, they were simultaneously signaling that they would not pursue it through the use of force. UN Resolution 1973, for example, explicitly forbade "a foreign occupation force of any form on any part of Libyan territory."[251] President Obama continued to promise that the United States would not use military force to impose regime change in Libya.[252] Nevertheless, the calls for Qaddafi to step down suggested that any cease-fire terms would likely include demands for a political transition.

The Costs to Qaddafi of Compliance Versus Resistance, 2011

Qaddafi's response to the two UN resolutions and the ensuing NATO intervention reflected the high costs to him of complying with even the most basic of UN demands to end the violence. Irrespective of the larger demand for regime change, complying with UN demands to respect human rights, lift media restrictions, and ensure safe passage to aid agencies would have impaired the regime's ability to reassert control.

The speed and intensity of the rebellion in early February 2011 meant that Qaddafi could not meet UN demands without relinquishing control over large parts of the country. Within five days of the first major protest, rebel forces controlled Benghazi, Baida, and Tobruk. Anti-Qaddafi government councils were soon administering each city.[253] Libya's representatives to the United Nations defected on February 18, calling Qaddafi a "tyrant" and urging the army to overthrow him.[254] The most significant defection came from the minister of the interior, Abdul Fatah Younis Al-Obeidi, on February 22. Younis had been part of the coup that brought Qaddafi to power and was considered a member of the Libyan leader's inner circle.[255] Sporadic and disorganized protests also took place in Tripoli. By February 26, rebels had taken control of Misrata, Ajdabiya, Zintan, Zuwara, and Zawiya, the last a mere thirty kilometers from Tripoli.[256] Rebel training camps set up in Benghazi were reportedly turning out approximately three hundred volunteers per day.[257]

By the middle of March, Qaddafi had even less incentive to comply with UN demands because his forces were on the verge of victory. His compliance would have allowed the rebel movement to survive. The regime had launched a counteroffensive on March 6 and had racked up a string of victories within ten days. Loyalist forces had retaken Zawiya and Zuwara in the West and moved east, establishing themselves on the outskirts of Benghazi.[258] Qaddafi's son, Saif, who sided with his father against the reformers he had once sponsored, announced on March 16 that the rebellion would be over in forty-eight hours.[259] On the 17th, the day the UN Security Council voted on Resolution 1973, Qaddafi defiantly declared that his forces were on their way to Benghazi, where they would show "no mercy" to rebel fighters.[260]

Before Resolution 1973, the cost to Qaddafi of resisting UN demands had been relatively low. UN sanctions and the European Union arms embargo had little impact on his ability to prosecute the war.[261] Although France, the United Kingdom, and even the Arab League were calling for a no-fly zone by March 12, reports indicate that neither Qaddafi nor Saif believed those countries could secure the necessary UN Security Council votes to authorize intervention.[262] By the 17th, however, the Security Council had done so, making clear that the regime's costs of resistance were set to rise.

Faced with imminent intervention, Qaddafi changed course and called for a cease-fire. Western leaders, however, noting that fighting continued, questioned Qaddafi's sincerity. President Obama expanded US demands by insisting Qaddafi "withdraw his forces from rebel-held cities."[263] That meant Qaddafi would have to let rebels claim still-contested cities, which would give them an advantage in subsequent negotiations and a larger base from which to continue attacks. The cost to Qaddafi would have been large, especially as the rebel council indicated it planned to continue its hostilities and encourage those in occupied cities to rebel. "If [Qaddafi] shoots people for standing for freedom, then he will be back at war, and the West will take action," a spokesman for the rebels declared.[264] Qaddafi, therefore, could not concede to foreign demands without threatening his regime's survival.

Hypothetically, Qaddafi could have gone into exile. Rebels had indicated they would only negotiate if Qaddafi and his family left Libya. Yet even a deal for exile would have involved potentially high compliance costs. Qaddafi faced the possibility of ICC prosecution. Although the United States could have offered him amnesty in a state not party to the Rome Statute, which established the ICC, Qaddafi still faced the possibility that his domestic enemies might seek retribution.[265] There also remained the possibility that the United States might later press for prosecution, as it did with Liberian leader Charles Taylor.[266] Given the risks associated with leaving power, Qaddafi had little reason to accept a potentially costly exile deal as long as he believed NATO would not forcibly remove him.

Qaddafi had good reason to doubt NATO would forcibly remove him. Germany, Poland, and Turkey, each NATO members, had voiced opposition to intervention.[267] Germany, a nonpermanent member of the UN Security Council, had even abstained from the vote on Resolution 1973, as did Russia, China, Brazil, and India. Divisions within the coalition also emerged within the first few days of the bombing. Arab League members backed away from their initial pledges of support, and Turkey and Italy clashed with France over the latter's attempts to assert a leadership role.[268] There was also little domestic appetite for war even in the nations that were leading the intervention. A Pew Center poll released on March 14, showed that only 44 percent of Americans favored a no-fly zone. The American public was decidedly against bombing Libyan air defenses (77 percent opposed), providing arms to rebels (69 percent), or sending troops into Libya (82 percent).[269] Qaddafi, therefore, had reason to think that resistance would cost him less than compliance and that he could win simply by holding out.[270] As my theory predicts, Qaddafi's more serious domestic threat led him to resist foreign pressure.

The Costs to the United States of a Settlement
with Qaddafi, 2011

Qaddafi's determination to hold out ensured that pushing him to accept anything other than the status quo ante would be costly for the United States. The Obama administration could have responded to Qaddafi's resistance in three ways. The first was to do nothing other than evacuate American citizens from Libya.[271] The second was to adopt a coercive strategy aimed at obtaining a cease-fire, as NATO had done in Bosnia and Kosovo. This would have likely been followed by talks aimed at a political settlement. Finally, there was regime change. Half measures like a no-fly zone might have relieved international pressure but would have done little to resolve the conflict.

When France and the United Kingdom began pushing for a no-fly zone in late February 2011, divisions emerged in the Obama administration over whether and how to respond. Early advocates for intervention, including US ambassador to the United Nations Susan Rice and National Security Council staff member Samantha Power, proposed that the United States had an obligation to uphold the United Nation's Responsibility to Protect norm, which obliges member states to act when governments commit mass atrocities.[272] However, opponents, who included Secretary of Defense Robert Gates, argued in favor of staying out of Libya. Gates cautioned that an intervention would not be the "short, easy fight" advocates expected.[273] He also warned that the White House had "no idea how many resources will be required" and that an intervention would distract attention from Iraq and Afghanistan. Moreover, if the United States used troops to "liberate" Libyans, US forces might end up becoming the target of aggression in a country with little strategic value.[274] Most importantly, Gates warned, a no-fly zone was unlikely to work. No-fly zones in Iraq, he observed, had "never prevented Saddam from slaughtering his people."[275] The case for doing nothing thus rested on the idea that half measures would be ineffective and more extensive ones would be too costly.

As international momentum for a no-fly zone increased, however, the Obama administration grew increasingly sensitive to the diplomatic costs of the do-nothing approach. The president had pledged a "new beginning between the United States and Muslims" in a much-heralded speech in Cairo in 2009, but as the Arab Spring uprisings swept the region, the slow response from the United States drew criticism.[276] Vice President Joe Biden denied that Egyptian president Hosni Mubarak was a dictator just two days after thousands of protestors marched through Cairo.[277] France and the United Kingdom had also been slow to support the uprisings, but they had changed course and were now pushing the United States to do the same. When the Arab League also voted in favor of a no-fly zone on March 12, the diplomatic and reputational costs to the United States of doing nothing rose further, as America was now seen as at odds with the Arab world.[278]

Secretary of State Hillary Clinton became the principal proponent of the argument that inaction entailed high costs. Initially an intervention skeptic, she changed her mind after a March 14 meeting in which Arab states said they would contribute militarily to a no-fly zone. From that point on, Clinton argued that intervention "would increase US standing in the Arab world, and it would send an important signal for the Arab Spring movement."[279] A failure to act, however, she warned, might risk relations with the new regimes in those countries or destabilize them by subjecting them to a refugee crisis.

Clinton also warned that the United Kingdom and France might act on their own if the United States did nothing. During a decisive meeting with Obama and the National Security Council on March 15, she cautioned that the United States might be dragged in later. Calling from Paris, she reportedly told the president, "You don't see what the mood is here, and how this has a kind of momentum of its own. And we will be left behind, and we'll be less capable of shaping this."[280] Obama came to accept Clinton's argument that the costs of inaction would be high.[281] During the meeting, he concluded that "if we don't act, if we put brakes on this thing, it will have consequences for US credibility and leadership, consequences for the Arab Spring, and consequences for the international community."[282]

Although the argument for doing something had gained the president's support, what that something would be remained unclear. Even if the United States could persuade the rebels to accept a cease-fire, Qaddafi retained a strong incentive to violate it in order to safeguard his political position. This meant that any cease-fire agreement would require a peacekeeping force to uphold it. During the March 15 meeting, Gates continued to warn about the potential for a long-term and costly commitment. NATO forces were still in Kosovo some fifteen years after that conflict ended, and in Iraq, the United States had spent over a decade enforcing a no-fly zone.[283]

With the American public strongly opposed to sending ground troops, and NATO allies ambivalent about intervention, President Obama wanted to avoid a settlement that would require a long-term, costly commitment. The desire to avoid a peacekeeping role, which would require such a commitment, appears to have led to the decision to pursue regime change. In the end, the administration concluded that "NATO and its allies weren't going into Libya as peacekeepers to referee a protracted stalemate between loyalist and rebel forces, and they couldn't pretend that was their role. To solve the problem, Qaddafi had to go."[284] That meant that the United States would need an "all necessary measures" UN resolution that would free NATO to use the force required to facilitate regime change. If France, the United Kingdom, and the Arab League wanted action, the president said, they would have to authorize a broader mandate.[285] In short, the high costs of enforcing a cease-fire indefinitely was at the heart of the decision to pursue regime change.

The Costs of Regime Change in Libya, 2011

The decision to pursue regime change also rested on the view that it could bring about a pro-Western, democratic government in Libya at little cost to the United States. Although the notion that rebels could establish a stable, democratic government later seemed like wishful thinking, American policymakers believed regime change to be feasible at the time for several reasons. First, Qaddafi was militarily vulnerable. He had weakened his military over the years to prevent a coup and had surrendered his once sizable chemical weapons arsenal. He had also alienated most Arab leaders and had no powerful allies to protect him.[286] Second, Libya appeared to lack the deep sectarian divisions that plagued Iraq. Several US allies also strongly favored action. As State Department official Derek Chollet later explained, "I thought, all right, we've got a small population, six million people, we have tremendous energy resources that had been underdeveloped, we had the international community that is extraordinarily unified and invested in Libya's success. I mean, this is the opposite of Iraq in every way."[287]

Third, the strength and makeup of Qaddafi's opposition also suggested the Libyan leader could be replaced by a regime sympathetic to the West. Early on during the uprising, the State Department had established legitimate local leadership as a criterion for intervention.[288] The United States found this leadership in the National Transitional Council (NTC), the political wing of the rebel movement. The NTC's membership included activists and regime reformers known both within and outside Libya.[289] The

NTC chairman, former justice minister Mustafa Abdul Jalil, was a known supporter of human rights. Jalil had encouraged families of victims massacred at the infamous Abu Salim prison to file court claims.[290] The NTC's youth minister, Fathi Terbil, was the lawyer for those families. His arrest had triggered the first major protest.[291] The NTC's foreign representatives were two probusiness reformers, Mahmoud Jibril, the former head of the Economic Development Board, and Ali Issawi, the former ambassador to India.[292] After meeting with Jibril in Paris on March 14, Secretary Clinton remarked that because of his government experience, Jibril, "seemed to understand how much work would be necessary to rebuild a country devastated by decades of cruelty and mismanagement." After the meeting, she thought "there was a reasonable chance the rebels would turn out to be credible partners."[293]

Fourth, the large number of regime defections also suggested Qaddafi's fall was imminent. That his long-time allies, and not just reformers, left his side suggested that he was losing the support of the people who might have otherwise helped him maintain power. The most significant defections came from former interior minister Younis and spy chief Musa Kusa, both members of Qaddafi's inner circle.[294] By May 30, 120 top officials had defected, including at least five former cabinet ministers.[295] Distrust between defectors and longtime regime opponents would later lead to divisions in the rebel movement.[296] Although Obama administration officials arguably might have anticipated these divisions, in the early stages, the defections were seen as a sign of the strength of the rebel movement, not a potential source of division within it.

Some of the problems that later arose in erecting a government to replace Qaddafi were avoidable. But many had more to do with the way in which regime change was pursued than the decision to pursue it. For example, when the NATO intervention began, Islamist influence in the rebel movement was minimal.[297] Qaddafi had nearly defeated the strongest Islamist groups in the late 1990s.[298] Those that remained lost additional members and money when Libyan security services partnered with Western governments after 9/11. Qaddafi's son, Saif, had also sponsored an amnesty program that released over a thousand militants in return for high-profile Islamists pledging to remain neutral in politics. LIFG leader Belhaj even penned a public apology to Qaddafi in 2009. The regime also gave government positions and money to former leaders of the Muslim Brotherhood.[299] However, Islamist influence in the rebellion grew after the intervention began largely as a result of Qatar's influence. Qatar began supplying Islamists with arms and training; it also pressured the NTC to grant them greater control.[300] The Obama administration had initially approved Qatar's arms shipments, which allowed the United States to avoid a direct role in Qaddafi's overthrow.[301] But, by doing so, it lost the ability to influence which groups would come out on top in the post-Qaddafi phase. The White House later attempted to reign in Qatar's role, but by then, Islamist influence in the rebellion had already grown.

As a stalemate between rebel and regime forces emerged in April 2011, the administration's estimated costs of regime change began to rise. One White House source, expressing the administration's dismay, said, "We thought it was going to be quick."[302] Although the Americans continued to demand publicly that Qaddafi step down, by the end of July, both the United States and NATO were seeking options for negotiations.[303] On July 16, the assistant secretary of state for Near Eastern affairs, Jeffrey D. Feltman, met with members of the Libyan regime in Tunisia. He proposed a deal that would require Qaddafi to step down but allow him to remain in Libya.[304] Rebels rejected the deal. By August 23, however, the issue of a settlement was mooted by the fall of Tripoli. Two months later, Qaddafi was captured. Consistent with my theory's expectations, as the opposition's ability to oust Qaddafi came into doubt, the Obama administration began looking to negotiate Qaddafi's departure, although it had initially refused to do so when Qaddafi had appeared more vulnerable.

Alternative Arguments in the Libyan Case, 2011

My argument holds that the high costs of coaxing Qaddafi from power and enforcing a cease-fire caused the Obama administration to choose regime change, which it believed would be relatively cheap to bring about. Qaddafi's domestic threats both ensured that the Libyan leader would be costly to coerce into a settlement and simultaneously caused US policymakers to conclude he would be relatively cheap to remove. As in the other cases discussed in this volume, alternative arguments can offer insight on a number of questions, but those arguments do not offer a clear explanation for why the United States pursued regime change in Libya.

PSYCHOLOGICAL BIAS

A political-psychology approach suggests that a history of negative interactions creates distrust that causes actors to reject negotiation. In accordance with this argument, the United States' relationship with Qaddafi had in fact begun to cool by the end of the 2000s. Qaddafi, for example, believed the United States had failed to live up to some of its promises in the 2003 deal. Meanwhile, American policymakers viewed Qaddafi as "erratic."[305] Yet, despite this growing disenchantment, Obama does not appear to have been predisposed to overthrowing Qaddafi. In fact, Obama indicated he was ambivalent about intervention. In a private conversation, the president told Gates that "the Libyan military operation had been a 51–49 call for him."[306]

Another psychological interpretation suggests that actors tend to cling to their beliefs when confronted with crises over which they have little information.[307] The Obama administration relied principally on Western media reports and opposition leaders for information on developments within Libya during the uprising.[308] This lack of credible information increased the opposition's influence on the administration's views, but it does not appear to have prompted the president to embrace an ideological commitment to humanitarian intervention. Obama was initially reluctant to intervene and appears to have been more swayed by Hillary Clinton's strategic rationale for intervention than the argument that the Responsibility to Protect norm compelled the United States to act. Furthermore, humanitarian intervention does not require regime change. Humanitarian interventions can end with cease-fire agreements, as in Bosnia and Kosovo. The president's beliefs may have influenced his decision to take military action, but they did not necessarily dictate his decision to pursue regime change.

BUREAUCRATIC AND INTEREST-GROUP PRESSURE

A bureaucratic-politics explanation suggests that actors in the Obama administration convinced the president to pursue FIRC for their own professional or personal interests.[309] Interestingly, in this case, officials with the greatest bureaucratic incentive to promote the use of force—the secretary of defense and the chairman of the Joint Chiefs of Staff—opposed intervention.[310] Instead, it was the secretary of state, Clinton, who favored intervention. However, it was the president, and not Clinton, who pushed for the more aggressive UN Security Council resolution that enabled regime change to become the de facto goal. If politically influential members of the administration controlled the decision-making, then we might also have expected to find that proponents of intervention shut out opponents during policy discussions. Accounts of the decisive March 15 meeting show, however, that Obama heard from both camps. Thus, there is little evidence that the president's decision to back regime change in Libya was the result of bureaucratic pressure.

Incomplete-information logic suggests that FIRC occurs when targeted leaders resist a stronger state because they doubt its threats. Prior to the NATO decision, Qaddafi did indeed doubt the United States would intervene; however, his doubts were not the consequence of incomplete information. The Libyan leader had good reason to doubt the international community's threats to intervene because there was considerable reluctance within the international community to do so. Key NATO allies remained doubtful about intervention while some, such as Germany, refused to participate. A majority of the American public was also opposed to taking any action in Libya beyond a no-fly zone. The reluctance of NATO members to bear significant military costs meant that the coalition was unlikely to use the full extent of its military capabilities, which gave Qaddafi good reason to hold out.

A credible-commitment approach suggests that neither the United States nor Qaddafi could trust the other to uphold a peace deal. Although Qaddafi might have feared his concessions would be used against him, NATO had the military capability to convince him that resistance would lead to a far worse outcome. If Qaddafi had believed resistance would ensure him a fate similar to that of Saddam, he would have had a strong incentive to make concessions, no matter how risky. Qaddafi's reluctance to trust the United States, thus, did not make a deal impossible.

Qaddafi's commitment problem could also be overcome. Although NATO leaders had reason to doubt he would uphold a cease-fire, they could have enforced that cease-fire with a peacekeeping mission. The problem was that NATO members and the American public were unlikely to support a long-term peacekeeping mission because of the costs. A credible-commitment approach, much like the incomplete-information approach, can tell us why it was difficult for the United States and Libya to strike a bargain, but these arguments do not tell us why both sides failed to use measures that would have helped them achieve a settlement. As I have shown, it was the costs of these measures, specifically the costs of a peacekeeping mission, that appears to have been central to the US decision to pursue regime change.

Conclusion

For all its determination to avoid the mistakes of the Bush administration, the Obama administration based its decision to depose Libya's Muammar Qaddafi on logic that was strikingly similar. In both cases, American policymakers anticipated that the costs of reaching and maintaining a settlement with each leader would be high. Yet the difficulty of reaching a settlement did not make an agreement impossible in either case. Although US policymakers had reason to doubt Saddam and Qaddafi would comply, enforcement mechanisms could have mitigated these trust issues. Had Saddam complied with the inspections process or had Qaddafi accepted a peacekeeping force, each leader might have denied the United States reason to impose regime change. Yet, neither Saddam nor Qaddafi had reason to bow to US demands as long as the political costs of doing so were high and the penalty for resistance appeared low.

The United States might have invested more resources to convince Saddam and Qaddafi that the penalty for resistance would be high. Yet, consistent with the predictions of my hypothesis $H1a_1$, the same domestic political threats that drove each targeted leader's resistance also convinced American policymakers that the costs of regime change would be comparatively low. Because both targeted heads of state lacked popular support, the Bush and Obama administrations concluded the local populations would welcome regime change. Both presidents also believed that relying on opposition groups would make it easier to construct a more legitimate government without a costly occupation. In each case, skeptics warned that the costs of regime change would be much higher than proponents argued. Yet the Libya case shows that cost miscalculation is not necessarily the result of groupthink or powerful bureaucrats dictating policy, as is often argued in the Iraq case. Instead, opposition leaders in both nations played an important role by reassuring American officials that regime change could be effected at relatively low cost to the United States.

The evidence in these cases is also consistent with my argument's expectations about how leaders respond to the threat of regime change (hypothesis $H1b_2$). During the 1990s, the United States pursued regime change in Iraq through covert and indirect methods. Saddam responded by coup-proofing his regime and seeking favor with other major powers to prevent the United States from deposing him. Similarly, before the United Nations adopted the resolution authorizing intervention, Qaddafi was defiant. He ignored the earlier UN resolution insisting that his regime negotiate with rebels and even publicly boasted he would show them no mercy. Once faced with a credible threat of intervention, however, both leaders' behavior changed. Saddam accepted a new round of inspections, with which he was largely complying in early 2003. Qaddafi, likewise, called for a cease-fire as soon as the United Nations authorized the NATO intervention. Although he continued to fight, he had little option to do otherwise. Both the rebels and the United States made clear they were unwilling to negotiate.

My argument's expectations concerning how states impose regime change are also upheld. As hypothesis $H1a_5$ suggests, the George H. W. Bush administration concluded that Saddam's external opposition would be too costly to impose, and so looked to encourage a coup to effect partial regime change. Once it became apparent that a coup was unlikely, American policymakers shifted to funding the external opposition but continued to use indirect and covert methods. After 9/11, however, officials in the George W. Bush administration became concerned that Iraq would not only acquire WMD but also supply them to terrorists, making Iraq much more costly to contain. Hypothesis $H1a_7$ predicts that when policymakers fear a target will become too costly to coerce, they will impose the external opposition, even if weak, because they expect it to be more politically reliable. Consistent with this hypothesis, administration officials concluded that US troops would have to invade, even in the event of a coup, because partial regime change would simply put another Saddam in power.

My theory also predicts that exogenous events, such as 9/11, can serve as a catalyst for regime change, though not necessarily a cause (see hypothesis $H1a_3$). The United States had been trying to topple Saddam since 1991. Although regime change was a long-standing policy, the terrorist attacks changed how it was pursued. The fear that Iraq would become too costly to contain prompted Bush administration officials to prefer full regime change, which would transfer power to Saddam's external opposition and make it unlikely that another Saddam would come to power. The attacks also lowered the domestic political costs of military action by offering a way for the Bush administration to rally the public to war.

The United States might have avoided the long-term costs of forcing Saddam and Qaddafi to comply with a settlement by negotiating an exile deal with each leader. But even an exile deal would have been costly to attain. First, both leaders had strong incentive to resist one because they would be vulnerable to attacks from their political enemies once out of power. They also faced the risk that the United States might later renege on its amnesty guarantee. These costs and risks did not make a deal impossible, but convincing Saddam and Qaddafi to accept the price of exile required convincing them that they would be deposed if they did not.[311] It would also have required ensuring that they could never again return to power or meddle in the politics of their home states from abroad. Although both actions were technically feasible, US policymakers had no reason to undertake them as long as they believed each leader (and their respective associates) could be eliminated and replaced with a democratic government. In short, even though exile deals are aimed at securing regime change, as with any other deal that might be made, they can be costly to attain. In both Iraq and Libya, American policymakers saw the costs of an exile deal as high and the relative costs of full regime change as low. In Libya, consistent with hypothesis $H1a_6$, it was only after the projected costs of full regime change rose that the United States became open to negotiations.

My argument is designed to explain why American policymakers, some with very different political views, interests, biases, and decision-making styles, pursued a policy of regime change, first in Iraq and later in Libya. It also explains why the very same policymakers, who endeavored to topple Saddam Hussein, chose to strike a deal with Muammar Qaddafi. I do not contend that the alternative arguments on these cases are wrong. Rather, some perform well, explaining important questions such as why tensions persisted between the United States and these leaders and why American policymakers encountered greater costs than they expected when attempting to overthrow these leaders. But arguments explaining why tensions persist cannot necessarily explain why those tensions are resolved with regime change. Likewise, arguments that shed light on why a chosen policy fails cannot necessarily tell us why that particular policy was chosen. In short, my argument, when paired with these other interpretations, offers a more complete understanding of these cases by helping to clarify why American policymakers viewed regime change as the most effective way to achieve their policy aims.

Conclusion

In 1839, Lord Auckland, the governor-general of British India, launched a disastrous war to replace Afghanistan's emir with a new leader willing to block Russian expansion in the region. The United Kingdom's ill-fated endeavor ended in a bloodbath. Afghan tribesman picked off the forty-five hundred retreating British and Indian troops, as well as their twelve thousand civilian followers, massacring all but a handful, as the group struggled to reach Jalalabad. The British army chaplain in that city, G. R. Gleig, later characterized the First Anglo-Afghan War as one "begun for no wise purpose, carried on with a strange mixture of rashness and timidity, brought to a close after suffering and disaster."[1] And yet thirty-six years later, British India's new viceroy, Lord Lytton, replayed that war. Far from being deterred by Auckland's experience, Lytton was confident he could install a more accommodating emir. Lytton would have greater success in securing control over Afghanistan, but only after encountering several rebellions, incurring high casualties, and abandoning his initial aim of establishing a British mission in Kandahar.[2]

The high costs the United Kingdom incurred in attempting to subdue Afghanistan did little to dissuade other foreign powers from attempting the same task. Roughly a century later, Soviet leader Leonid Brezhnev would launch another invasion of Afghanistan, once again convinced that an accommodating government could be imposed on Kabul. The Soviets would ultimately be forced to withdraw after a bloody ten-year war. Just over a decade after that, the George W. Bush administration would initiate its own attempt at regime change in Afghanistan, where, after nearly two decades, billions of dollars, and over twenty-three hundred American service member deaths, the United States remains caught in what some have come to call a "forever war."[3]

It might seem that only policymakers misled by their own biases and ideological convictions, or by biased advisors, would pursue regime change despite its potentially high costs. Indeed, much of the literature on the

2003 Iraq War implies precisely this conclusion. But the tendency to resolve disputes with foreign leaders by replacing them is pervasive. In fact, just about every American president since World War II has undertaken regime change.[4] Even policymakers who might have been deterred by direct personal experience or that of their predecessors have endeavored to overthrow foreign leaders. President Kennedy, for example, authorized a plan to topple Fidel Castro just sixteen months after the humiliating failure of the Bay of Pigs invasion.[5] As a presidential candidate, George W. Bush had decried Bill Clinton's nation-building efforts for their high costs and scant rewards, but as president, Bush launched what would become two of the most ambitious and costly nation-building projects since World War II. Obama, too, criticized his predecessor's decision to impose regime change on Iraq but later backed regime change in Libya. Even after Libya's collapse, officials both within and outside the Obama administration continued to insist that the United States should do more to overthrow Syria's Bashar al-Assad.

Despite its questionable record of success, FIRC has a long history. This study counts 133 attempts in the last two centuries alone, but regime change extends back even further. Ever since the creation of the Westphalian state system, states have attempted to exact policy change in others by changing those states' policymakers. Yet regime change is arguably a costly enterprise. Rather than bear the costs of installing a new government, states could bargain with the existing one. They could use coercion and/or inducement to obtain favorable settlements or relax their terms to arrive at more neutral deals. They could also accept the status quo, in essence accepting a deal on the targeted leader's terms. No matter how they achieve it, a deal with the targeted leader would allow the foreign power to avoid the costs of installing a new one. Why then pursue regime change?

To attribute regime change to the poor judgment of individual policymakers would be to ignore the conditions that make regime change a constant temptation for them all. As I have shown in this book, even rational actors, who can hypothetically see past the biases and bureaucratic pressures that can cause misperception, may have incentive to pursue regime change. They do so when they anticipate that negotiating a deal with a foreign leader will be more costly than replacing that leader. What causes them to believe this is the effect that the targeted leader's domestic opposition has on their expected costs of negotiation and regime change.

Domestic opposition in the target state can make a deal costly for a foreign power to achieve by causing the leader of that state to resist the foreign power's demands. Whether the leader is a populist, like Nagy or Árbenz, or a dictator, like Saddam or Qaddafi, acceding to a politically costly foreign demand can empower the leader's domestic opposition, enabling it to seize power. The more compliance threatens the leader's political survival, the more incentive that leader will require to concede to a politically costly demand. In such situations, the foreign power has a choice. It can either use greater coercive force (and/or inducements) to convince the targeted leader to accept and abide by a deal, or it can use the domestic opposition to overthrow the leader. Both options entail costs. But if the domestic opposition is strong enough to reduce the foreign power's costs of regime change and is also more willing to accommodate its demands, then regime change may appear to be the cheaper option. Lytton, for example, saw Afghanistan's Sher Ali as unpopular and easy to replace.[6] When the Afghan emir refused Lytton's demands for a British diplomatic mission, Lytton looked to install Sher Ali's more pliable son rather than increase his threats to force the emir to concede.

My argument not only explains why regime change occurs but also why it occurs most often where it should least be necessary. FIRC has generally been a weapon used by the strong against the weak. On the one hand this is unsurprising because the weak make easy targets. Yet, on the other hand, we might expect that militarily weak leaders would be more likely to make concessions and thus less prone to regime change. The domestic threats these leaders face can partially explain their resistance. But equally significant is the fact that a strong state's threats are not inherently credible. To convince a targeted leader to acquiesce, the strong must demonstrate their intention to use force, both to secure the leader's acquiescence, and to enforce it. They can do so by using costly signals and coercive force to obtain an agreement, and constructing enforcement mechanisms to ensure it lasts. But these measures also entail a variety of costs, ranging from political and diplomatic to reputational and military. If the targeted leader's domestic vulnerability convinces the foreign power that regime change will be comparatively cheap, the foreign power may never give the targeted leader reason to concede. Instead, it may bypass bargaining altogether and go straight to regime change.

The cases explored in this book illustrate the dilemma faced by targeted leaders. They can either capitulate to the demands of a foreign power and risk being overthrown by their domestic enemies, or resist and risk being overthrown by the foreign power. The more powerful their domestic enemies, the more likely targeted leaders will choose the latter approach to safeguard their domestic power. Had Guatemala's Jacobo Árbenz capitulated to US pressure, he would have been forced to accept the possibility that Guatemala's elite and army would eventually overthrow him and overturn his country's revolution. To Árbenz, the only way to assure the revolution's success and his own political survival was to mobilize the peasants by working with the communists to carry out land reform. Similarly, had Libya's Muammar Qaddafi accepted a ceasefire in late February 2011, as the United Nations demanded, rebels opposing him could have used the lull in fighting to arm, organize, and recruit. Qaddafi would have also missed the chance to defeat them, which his forces were poised to do just before the NATO intervention. Likewise, in Iraq, Saddam Hussein could not comply with the Gulf War resolutions without revealing that his regime lacked the chemical weapons it had relied on to deal with both domestic and regional threats. As it would have for Árbenz and Qaddafi, compliance would have threatened Saddam's political power.

A targeted leader's incentive to resist does not necessarily make a deal with that leader impossible. If the stronger nation is willing to make a sufficiently credible threat (or offer other incentives), it may be able to obtain its policy objectives through bargaining. The United States could have subjected Árbenz to the oil embargo he most feared in order to convince him to abandon the communists. NATO could have mobilized an invasion force to convince Qaddafi to accept a cease-fire and used a peacekeeping force to maintain it. And in Iraq, the United States could have pressured the international community to maintain sanctions or, potentially, offered Iraq a deal to induce its cooperation. Even if Iraq eventually acquired WMD, the United States could have used threats of force to deter it from using them.[7] In each of these instances, opportunities existed for a deal with the current leader. Regime change was unnecessary.

Yet in each of these instances, a variety of costs also prevented policymakers from employing the measures necessary to secure a modus vivendi with the targeted leader. Eisenhower, for example, knew Guatemala would be vulnerable to an oil embargo, but he wanted to avoid the diplomatic expense of blatantly violating the Good Neighbor policy. He was, of course, willing to violate the policy in practice but wanted to maintain at least the illusion that the United States was a good neighbor to avoid jeopardizing US relations throughout the region. The Obama administration likewise sought to avoid the military, diplomatic, and domestic political costs of a long peacekeeping mission in Libya. Obama was looking to end the wars in Iraq and Afghanistan, not commit to an indefinite peacekeeping operation. In the Iraq case, the George W. Bush administration insisted that containment entailed military, diplomatic, humanitarian, and reputational costs. After 9/11, it also concluded that containing Saddam would only get harder once he acquired WMD.

Regime change can, of course, entail some of the very same expenses as the measures necessary to obtain a settlement. These costs can also mount over time if the stronger power must prop up its protégé. But whereas domestic opposition can increase the costs of obtaining an agreement with a foreign leader, it can simultaneously decrease the expected costs of overthrowing that leader. This is because the foreign power can use the opposition to topple the leader. The opposition causing the leader to resist need not be the same as the one the foreign power uses to oust the leader. Foreign powers can choose to partner with an external opposition group or an internal one. In either event, the stronger that opposition group is, the greater the burden it can carry in helping to impose regime change. Eisenhower, for example, sought to avoid the diplomatic costs of a confrontation with Árbenz by using covert methods to convince the army to overthrow him. Even though US support for the rebels became an open secret, the Eisenhower administration was still able to deny involvement. In Libya, the Obama administration looked to circumvent a long-term peacekeeping mission by helping rebels depose Qaddafi and turning the task of constructing a new democratic regime over to them. And in Iraq, the George W. Bush administration also believed it could avoid the long-term costs of containment, as well as the long-term costs of an occupation, by ousting Saddam and letting Iraqis manage the postwar phase.

In some instances, major events or crises help trigger regime change by prompting policymakers to reevaluate their existing approach to the targeted leader. Such occurrences can also lower the estimated costs of taking action and/or increase the expected costs of inaction. In Hungary, for example, the Suez Crisis lowered Khrushchev's diplomatic costs of an invasion by drawing the international community's attention elsewhere. The crisis also convinced the Soviet leader that the military and domestic costs of delaying intervention were much higher than he had previously believed. If the West were successful in Egypt, he feared, it might interfere in Hungary, at which point the rebellion could spiral out of control and he would be blamed. In much the same way, the 9/11 attacks helped trigger the invasion of Iraq. Although regime change had been US policy since 1991, the attacks lowered the domestic political costs of launching a military invasion. The 9/11 attacks also increased policymakers' concerns that Iraq might transfer its WMD to terrorists and thereby become too costly to contain.

Events such as the Suez Crisis and 9/11, however, are catalysts, not causes. Though they magnify the effects of the targeted leader's domestic opposition, those same events might have a different effect without that opposition. The 9/11 attacks, for example, increased the Bush administration's willingness to use force against Saddam, but not Qaddafi, whose stronger domestic position made him both more willing to cooperate and harder to overthrow. Events and crises are not necessary for regime change to occur. The Suez Crisis may have raised concern in Moscow that the West would interfere in Hungary, but when the Soviets invaded Czechoslovakia twelve years later, there was no similar event stoking fears of Western interference. Major events and crises can affect the timing of regime change and the decision to use force, but whether regime change occurs still depends on the strength of the targeted leader's domestic opposition.

My argument also explains how states impose regime change. Policymakers can pursue either full regime change, in which they install new political institutions, or partial regime change, in which they remove only the leader. Which method they choose depends on the relative strength of the leader's external and internal opposition. External groups are disadvantaged by the existing political system. Their incentive to overturn it makes them useful allies for states seeking full regime change. External opposition groups also depend on different supporters from the leader and so may be able to accept the foreign power's demands without losing support. In Guatemala, Carlos Castillo Armas's elite-backed rebels shared American policymakers' disdain for communism. They also favored an authoritarian system that would allow them to impose policies favorable to their own interests and those of the United States. In Libya, reformers and human rights activists in the National Transitional Council shared Western goals for a democratic regime. Although some Islamist rebels did not, they were minor players during the early stages of the uprising.[8] In all, external opposition groups often willingly collaborate with foreign powers to see a political system that provides them no benefit replaced with one that does.

External opposition groups may be more willing collaborators, but by virtue of their exclusion from power, they often require greater military assistance to seize it. If the external opposition is too weak (or opposes the foreign power altogether), then the foreign power may use the internal opposition to carry out partial regime change. In some instances, the leader's rivals may willingly abandon the leader, but in others, they may have to be coerced or induced to do so. The CIA, for example, knew Castillo Armas was too weak to topple Árbenz. As a result, the Eisenhower administration coerced the otherwise loyal Guatemalan army to turn against the president. Khrushchev also knew Hungarian hardliners were too unpopular to be restored to power. So, he coerced the more moderate János Kádár into replacing Nagy. Though the leader's internal rivals are often easier to install, they can be less reliable allies. They rely on the same supporters and institutions as the leader, and so they too may find the political costs of compliance to be high. For this reason, partial regime change operations are more likely to produce lasting policy change when insiders, once installed, transform the political coalitions and institutions sustaining their power. The Guatemalan army, for example, had intended to keep some of Árbenz's reforms, but once Castillo Armas was in control, he gutted Guatemala's democratic institutions.

When insiders remain loyal to the leader, foreign powers may still attempt regime change by pressuring the leader to resign. Though a seemingly simple task, the leader's resignation can be difficult to obtain because it tends only to be pursued when the leader is in a relatively strong position—that is, when the internal opposition is weak and the external opposition requires military aid that the foreign power is reluctant to provide. Under these conditions, the foreign power's threat to remove the leader holds little credibility, which means the leader has little incentive to leave power. Only when conditions change—as when either the foreign power decides to forcibly install the external opposition or insiders begin defecting—does leader resignation tend to work. That is, a resignation becomes easier to obtain as the leader's political power wanes. But once this happens, the foreign power seldom needs nor wants to negotiate the leader's exit. Doing so would only leave open the possibility that the leader or the leader's supporters could preserve their political influence. As a result, states tend to pursue the leader's resignation only when looking for a quick-fix, low-cost solution to a crisis. These instances tend to arise when the foreign power faces domestic or international pressure to act but lacks a strategic motive to commit to forcibly removing the leader.

Although foreign powers typically look for other, less costly options when the external opposition is too weak to carry out full regime change, an exception arises when the target state is poised to gain or regain power rapidly. If the target state were to remain weak, the foreign power could take the risk of installing the less reliable internal opposition. To incentivize its continued cooperation, the foreign power could simply use military and economic inducements or pressure. If, however, the target state is expected to acquire or reacquire the military means to resist, the foreign power may have to offer much greater incentives to ensure the new regime's continued compliance. Rather than pay these long-term enforcement costs, the foreign power may prefer the higher up-front costs of installing the weak, though more reliable, external opposition. Franklin Roosevelt, for example, refused to partner with Prussian elites in overthrowing Hitler because he doubted they would honor a postwar settlement once Germany recovered. Likewise, the George W. Bush administration concluded that any Baath Party leader would rule much as Saddam had, and so would also be more costly to contain once armed with WMD. Bush, therefore, insisted that US forces would invade and occupy Iraq, even in the event of a coup. In these instances, the anticipated high costs of ensuring that insiders continued cooperating once in power led to full regime change.

Alternative Arguments

Although the literature on the causes of FIRC is sparse, two kinds of potential explanations permeate both historical interpretations of individual cases and the broader analytic literature. The first of these emphasizes the misperceptions that can lead decision makers into costly wars, whereas the second shows why rational actors might end up in costly wars, which they could avoid by negotiating peace. Among the former, two of the most common explanations suggest regime change stems from the psychological biases of the decision makers or the bureaucratic and interest-group pressures they face.

Arguments focused on psychological bias or bureaucratic and interest-group pressures can offer insight on a number of questions related to regime change. They may, for example, explain why tension persists between two states for so long. They can also shed light on why regime change sometimes fails. Where these arguments fall short, however, is in explaining why a state would reject bargaining and pursue regime change instead. The statistical results in Chapter 3 show that even when bias and bureaucratic or interest-group pressures should play influential roles, regime change is no more likely to occur. One might expect, for example, that policymakers' biases would lead them to overthrow leaders with whom they have ideological differences. Yet states are no more likely to pursue regime change against targets with different authority structures, which represent beliefs on how power should be distributed in a society. The evidence that regime change stems from democracies waging ideological wars against nondemocracies is also weak. And although we might expect that a history of conflict would cause policymakers to malign the opposing leader and seek regime change, the data show that the number of militarized interstate disputes over the previous decade has little substantive effect on the probability of FIRC. Military governments may have a bureaucratic incentive to promote FIRC, but the data show that they are no more likely than civilian governments to attempt regime change. Finally, high levels of trade do not correlate with regime change, despite the expectation that the beneficiaries of that trade would push for regime change to protect their commercial interests.

Psychological bias and bureaucratic or interest-group pressure can, of course, be difficult to measure quantitatively. These influences could also lead to FIRC in ways other than those controlled for in the statistical chapter. However, their ability to explain the decision-making on FIRC in the case studies is also limited. In many instances, bias and/or pressure from domestic actors existed, but these influences did not necessarily cause policymakers to choose regime change. A common explanation for Árbenz's overthrow in Guatemala, for example, holds that officials in the Eisenhower administration pushed for regime change because of their ties to the United Fruit Company.[9] In contrast, there was no equivalent American firm demanding special protection in the Bolivia case. However, the argument that United Fruit caused the Eisenhower administration to overthrow Árbenz exaggerates the company's influence. American policymakers knew United Fruit's business practices were problematic and filed an antitrust suit against it after the change in the Guatemalan government. The documentary evidence shows that American policymakers were more concerned about how Árbenz's Decree 900 would empower communists than about protecting United Fruit's landholdings.

In the case of Hungary, one explanation for Nagy's overthrow holds that psychological bias caused Soviet leaders to misinterpret his actions. Rather than attributing his reforms to domestic pressure, Soviet leaders are said to have blamed his personal shortcomings. Yet although Soviet leaders did denounce Nagy, they were not initially biased against him. In fact, they had conceded that his reforms were necessary to quell the rebellion. Even after learning Nagy might declare neutrality, Khrushchev still supported him. It was not until the next day, after the Suez Crisis had begun, that Khrushchev changed his mind.

In the Iraq case, psychological bias and bureaucratic pressure also appear to play important roles in explaining why the George W. Bush administration launched an ill-conceived war. They offer an incomplete explanation, however, when it comes to the question of why that war was focused on regime change. The president and his advisors may have personally despised Saddam, and some officials may have had a bureaucratic or personal incentive for war; however, regime change was not a new policy. Both the George H. W. Bush and Clinton administrations had also professed a commitment to overthrowing Saddam, though they opted for different methods. A bureaucratic-politics approach also cannot explain why some of the very same individuals commonly credited with pushing the president toward regime change in Iraq were unable to convince him to abandon negotiations with Qaddafi. Rumsfeld and others argued that the United States should press for political change in Libya, rather than simply settle for the surrender of its WMD. But while regime-change advocates dominated policy on Iraq, they were shut out of the decision-making on Libya.

Both psychological-bias models and models based on bureaucratic and/ or interest-group influence also struggle to explain why Obama, who advocated a more diplomatic approach to foreign policy, ultimately eschewed Bush's diplomatic approach to Libya and overthrew Qaddafi. Obama was neither personally nor ideologically motivated to impose regime change, as some accounts explain George W. Bush's approach to Saddam. Unlike Bush, Obama also solicited advice from both opponents and proponents of intervention in his administration. Additionally, it was Obama, and not his advisors, who pushed for the "all necessary measures" UN resolution (Resolution 1973) that paved the way for regime change in Libya. Psychological-bias and bureaucratic/interest-group arguments should not be dismissed. They can still account for various aspects of these cases, such as why each side viewed the other as a threat and why regime change entailed greater costs than expected. Yet, my theory can flesh out our understanding of these cases by answering a question these other approaches cannot, namely, why the United States ended up overthrowing Saddam and Qaddafi when it was possible to coerce and contain them.

The two dominant rational choice arguments, which consider the problems of incomplete information and credible commitment, constitute an alternative approach to the causes of imposed regime change. They show that one side's doubts about the other's threats or promises can make an enforceable agreement unobtainable. They offer significant insight into why bargaining is hard, and evidence of their claims arises in many of the cases examined in this volume. Both Qaddafi and Saddam, for example, doubted the resolve of the United States to take military action, as an incomplete-information argument would suggest. In accordance with a commitment problem, American policymakers also distrusted Saddam's and Qaddafi's promises to cooperate. The two leaders also had reason to fear that their concessions might be used against them.

Information and commitment problems, however, paint only a partial picture. They do not explain why actors fail to take measures to resolve the doubts that cause bargaining failure. If the target doubts the foreign power's resolve to use force, the foreign power should be able to signal its resolve by using actions that less committed actors would avoid. Saddam, for example, had reason to doubt US threats because American reprisals had never gone beyond air strikes prior to 9/11. Had the US threat to remove him been more immediate and credible, he might have offered greater concessions to avoid a far worse fate, despite his fears that concessions would be used against him. Although the United States was better positioned to signal its resolve to use force after 9/11, by that point, Bush administration officials had concluded that overthrowing Saddam would be cheaper than containing him indefinitely. Similarly, US policymakers had good reason to suspect Qaddafi would violate a cease-fire, but this commitment problem did not make a negotiated settlement impossible. Had NATO been willing to introduce peacekeepers, it could have enforced a cease-fire. A peacekeeping mission, however, would have entailed political, military, diplomatic, opportunity, and potentially reputational costs that the Obama administration was unwilling to bear.

Information and commitment problems imply that one side's doubts about the other's threats and promises can make a bargain impossible. But if states are willing to use costly signals, coercive force, and enforcement mechanisms to attain deals, a bargain may very well be possible. It is the price of that bargain that may cause states to pursue regime change instead.

Implications for Policy and Theory

Dealing with Rogue Regimes

One of the most important policy implications of my argument is that a foreign power's threats or attempts to impose regime change can make a "rogue" regime more costly to remove and more difficult to control. If foreign powers are truly committed to overthrowing a regime, they may fare better when pursuing immediate and direct action. When foreign powers make idle threats or use covert or indirect methods, their targets often have the time to take defensive measures that could make both regime change and coercion more difficult. Throughout the 1990s, for example, Saddam feared that the United States intended to use UN weapons inspections to undermine his regime. Accordingly, he sought to coup-proof his regime by surrounding himself with family and clan members. He also cultivated ties with Russia, France, and China to secure their support on the UN Security Council and prevent the United States from obtaining UN resolutions to use force against Iraq. Similarly, when Árbenz learned of the CIA plot against him, he attempted to convince the United Nations to intervene. He hoped he could raise the diplomatic costs to the United States of removing him by appealing to the international community for assistance. Albania's Enver Hoxha responded similarly to Yugoslav and Soviet attempts to overthrow him by eliminating internal opponents and seeking foreign patrons that could provide him protection (see Chapter 1).

Not all attempts to impose regime change will drive the target to adopt defensive measures. When a foreign power's threat to impose regime change is imminent and direct, and as a result, more credible, the targeted leader may offer partial or temporary compliance to dissuade the foreign power from attacking. In these cases, because the leader has fewer options available to raise the foreign power's costs of regime change, the leader may hope to convince the foreign power to negotiate instead. Even though Nagy declared Hungary's neutrality after hearing reports of a possible Soviet invasion, he still attempted to make a deal with the Soviets because he was led to believe they were interested as well. Similarly, Saddam responded to the large buildup of US forces in the Persian Gulf by accepting and largely complying with a new round of inspections. In Libya, Qaddafi also offered partial compliance, calling for a cease-fire just after the United Nations authorized the NATO intervention.

Although a targeted leader may offer up last-minute concessions when faced with a visible, credible threat of regime change, these concessions will not necessarily dissuade the foreign power from imposing regime change. Even if the targeted leader concedes entirely, the foreign power would still end up bearing the costs of enforcing the leader's continued compliance over the long term. Otherwise, the targeted leader might renege to win back domestic political support. Knowing this, the foreign power is more likely to use the leader's opposition to effect regime change.

In sum, policymakers would do well to carefully consider the conditions under which they threaten regime change. Idle threats meant to mollify domestic constituents or covert and indirect attempts to effect regime change can backfire. Although covert and indirect methods are often more appealing than overt ones because they can entail lower costs, they can also cause the target to take defensive measures that make regime change harder to achieve and coercion less effective. Fidel Castro's ability to rely on Soviet aid, for example, made him not only more difficult for the United States to overthrow but also more difficult to coerce.

Nevertheless, renouncing regime change will not necessarily induce a target's compliance. Leaders with a strong domestic incentive to resist will continue to resist unless their domestic position improves or the foreign power gives them sufficient reason to acquiesce. The important point remains that targeted leaders are more likely to make concessions when given incentive (positive or negative) to acquiesce rather than reason to take defensive action.

Predicting Coercion Success and Failure

The coercion literature has long sought to explain why coercive bargaining appears to have a high failure rate and, when it does succeed, what accounts for that success. Some of the arguments in this literature share my conclusion that domestic political pressure in the target state can cause leaders to resist a foreign power's threats, but surprisingly few of these arguments incorporate the effects of strategic interaction. The strategies actors choose may be driven by their expectations of what their opponents will do. If these expectations were to change, outcomes might change. By incorporating strategic interaction, my argument suggests at least two implications that can help us understand why coercion succeeds when it does and why it appears prone to failure.

First, my research indicates that, all else being equal, coercion is more likely to succeed when the targeted leader is domestically strong rather than weak.[10] Domestically strong leaders are better equipped to withstand a domestic challenge and so can run the risk of concessions in a way that their domestically weak counterparts cannot. Poland's Gomułka, for example, could afford to keep his reforms limited because he had staunch popular support and faced little domestic pressure for more radical change. Hungary's Nagy, in contrast, was struggling to maintain his popularity and so could not afford to limit reforms for the sake of appeasing Moscow's security interests.

The conventional wisdom suggests that politically weak leaders are more sensitive to foreign pressure because it hinders their ability to fend off their domestic opponents. Indeed, for many scholars and policymakers, the 2003 WMD deal with Libya serves as evidence that "rogues" can be tamed if coercive pressure is used to threaten the stability of their regimes.[11] Accounts often stress that UN sanctions exacerbated Libya's economic woes and threatened Qaddafi's political survival, causing him to seek reconciliation with the West to strengthen his political position. This interpretation, however, misses the crucial point that, despite Qaddafi's eagerness to talk to the West, he consistently refused its demand to surrender the suspects in the bombing of Pan Am flight 103. He feared that the surrender of the two suspects would cost him politically. It was only in the late 1990s, when Qaddafi's domestic political position improved, that he relinquished them. Leaders without domestic opposition will not necessarily make concessions. Indeed, Qaddafi waited for the United States and United Kingdom to soften their demands to surrender the Pan Am suspects, though his political position had begun to improve. However, convincing domestically secure leaders to comply will still require less of a foreign power than convincing a leader for whom compliance is akin to political (or actual) suicide.

Second, my research offers insight into why coercion appears to fail more often than it succeeds. Even studies with very positive findings about the effectiveness of coercion conclude that it succeeds less than half the time.[12] By taking account of strategic interaction, my argument shows that the tendency for coercion to fail may reflect not its own limitations but the conditions under which it is pursued. Two insights lead to this conclusion. First, strong states tend to pursue negotiations when they are either unwilling or unable to impose regime change. Their targets, anticipating that they are unlikely to use overwhelming military force, resist as a result. Coercion may, therefore, fail in these instances for good reason. The strong state tends to fall back on coercion only when it lacks the resolve to make a sufficiently credible threat and the weak state knows this.

Second, by the time the strong state acquires the resolve to make a sufficiently credible threat, it may no longer be interested in the leader's concessions. As the various costs associated with coercion mount, the stronger state may acquire greater resolve to use force. But this greater resolve will not necessarily result in a bargain. If the foreign power believes the target's opposition is strong enough to make the leader relatively cheap to overthrow, it may simply pursue regime change, instead. As a result, the targeted leader may never have the chance to make the concessions he or she might have made once convinced of the foreign power's resolve. Coercive bargaining may, therefore, appear to fail, though a bargain might have been attained had the foreign power been willing to pursue it. Saddam, for example, had good reason to doubt US threats throughout the 1990s because American policymakers could not credibly threaten to invade Iraq. Once they could, however, American policymakers were no longer interested in containing him but in using military force to depose him. In sum, the high rate of coercion failure may reflect not just the tendency of states to use coercion when it is least likely to work (i.e., when their threats to the target state lack credibility) but also their tendency to abandon coercion when it is most likely to work (i.e., when their threats are credible).

Predicting the Success or Failure of Regime Change

Recent US pursuits of regime change have encouraged the view that regime change either fails outright or, at best, turns into a costly quagmire. This has led many scholars and pundits to conclude that the decision-making leading to it must be flawed. Although there is little doubt that US policymakers underestimated the costs of regime change in Iraq, Afghanistan, and Libya, and that the benefits to the United States appear modest, these errors do not mean that all regime change turns out poorly or is the result of flawed decision-making. If success is defined by the creation of a reliable (but not necessarily democratic) ally, then the United States was largely successful in imposing regimes on Germany, Japan, Grenada, and Panama. Even the covert operations in Iran, Guatemala, and Chile, though disastrous for human rights and social progress in those countries, created the anticommunist allies the United States wanted at the time. The Soviet

Union's invasion of Hungary helped Moscow attain its objective of keeping Hungary within the Warsaw Pact, as did the invasion of Czechoslovakia in 1968. France accomplished a similar goal in Spain in 1823 when it overthrew that country's liberal government and restored the Bourbon monarch, as did Prussia in Baden and Saxony. Regime change does not always fail.[13] We should, therefore, avoid inferring from high-profile failures that regime change is necessarily the result of poor judgment.

My argument is based on policymakers' expectations about the relative costs of regime change and bargaining. I do not claim that policymakers get these costs right. Sometimes they do, and sometimes they do not. Yet, although my argument is not designed to explain when cost expectations will be accurate, it does suggest certain conditions under which policymakers may be more likely to launch regime-change operations that ultimately entail higher costs or fewer benefits than anticipated. First, foreign powers may be more likely to misjudge costs when they rely on the targeted leader's domestic opposition for information. The opposition has an incentive to exaggerate its abilities so that the foreign power will aid its cause. One of the consequences of isolating Iraq during the 1990s and early 2000s was that the United States lost opportunities to gather its own intelligence.[14] This increased its reliance on third parties, such as the opposition in exile. Although some US agencies were skeptical of the information they received, the lack of reliable intelligence networks in Iraq made refuting it difficult. In Guatemala, the Truman administration was also initially misled by both the Guatemalan elite and the United Fruit Company. As US intelligence improved, American policymakers came to realize that, contrary to what they had been told, a communist takeover was not imminent and the elite-backed rebels were weak and disorganized.[15]

Foreign powers are especially likely to rely on the opposition for intelligence when they believe they need to act quickly and lack the time to develop more reliable sources. In Libya, for example, the Obama administration wanted to preempt a massacre in Benghazi that many Western leaders believed to be imminent. The United States relied heavily on Western media reports that used protesters as sources and, in some instances, mischaracterized the scale of the ongoing violence. One popularly circulated report, for example, indicated that Qaddafi's forces had used live ammunition during the first day of the rebellion, but the source for that information was later revealed to be a video posted online the year before.[16]

Second, my argument also suggests that the way in which regime change is imposed can influence the odds of success. The stability and cooperation of the new regime will depend on the amount of domestic opposition it faces. If remnants of the former regime continue to pose a threat, the new regime will require foreign aid to consolidate power. Without it, the new regime may either fall or attempt to appease its opposition by adopting policies contrary to the foreign power's interests. One implication of this is that regime change may be more likely to succeed when it is imposed after long wars that end with the former regime's decisive military defeat. In such cases, members of the former regime are more likely to be disorganized, demoralized, discredited, or dead. By the time the Allies occupied Germany in World War II, for example, the Nazi Party had been defeated and discredited, making it difficult for Nazi loyalists to reconsolidate power. Quick military victories will not necessarily produce the same results. If the opposition merely retreats, it may be able to harass the new regime for years to come. Vietnam, for example, ousted Cambodia's Khmer Rouge within two weeks, but the Khmer Rouge continued fighting the Vietnamese-backed government in Phnom Penh for another decade.

When targeted leaders and their supporters cannot be eliminated, foreign powers that choose to co-opt the opposition may produce more stable and cooperative regimes. The collaboration of the Japanese emperor, for example, played an important role in ensuring the cooperation of the Japanese population with the American occupation after World War II.[17] Similarly, by installing centrists like Janos Kádár in Hungary, the Soviets were able to increase the odds that Hungarians would accept the new regime. Co-optation can, however, carry a price. Because the regime includes those tied to the former one, it may be less cooperative than it would have been without them. The trade-off for a more politically viable regime in Hungary was Moscow's accepting a new government whose policies were more moderate than it might have otherwise preferred. Under Kádár's "goulash communism," the Hungarian government relaxed censorship, lifted foreign trade restrictions, and allowed for some market reforms—not Soviet ideals.

Third, my argument also suggests that success may depend on the type of regime the foreign power seeks to install. Establishing a stable democratic regime is typically far more complicated than establishing a dictatorship. Popularly supported leaders must appeal to a broad array of domestic constituents, but the societies they lead may be too fractured for them to form stable governing coalitions. Furthermore, establishing a stable democracy is even more difficult when members of the former regime survive the transition. Survivors of the old rule can exploit a democratic regime's greater liberties and restraint to plot against it. Consequently, the foreign power may find itself forced to send in its own troops to defend the new regime until a loyal and capable military can be established to eliminate these threats.

In contrast, when a foreign power seeks to install an authoritarian regime, the requirements for installing a reliable ally are often more easily met. The foreign power seldom needs to locate leaders who can attract a broad array of supporters or broker compromises among diverse political coalitions. Instead, it often needs only to ensure that the military is either part of the new regime or at least not a threat to it, and that the new regime has the capabilities to employ repression. If the new regime has these capabilities, members of the former regime may not have the chance to organize in opposition. They may be killed, jailed, or exiled as soon as the new regime seizes power. Authoritarian regimes are not necessarily more stable. A dictator's repression could inspire an insurgency over time, as occurred in Guatemala. The foreign power, however, may still regard sending aid to shore up a dictator's forces as less costly than sending its own troops to defend a newly democratic regime. The unfortunate implication of this is that states may be more successful at installing pliant authoritarian regimes than democratic ones.

Importantly, even when regime change is more costly than anticipated, the foreign power would not necessarily have chosen to bargain if its estimates had been more accurate. Indeed, foreign powers may still choose regime change even when they know it will be costly. What matters most is the *relative* cost of regime change, compared to that of attaining and enforcing a settlement. Khrushchev, for example, knew the Hungarian military was likely to resist a Soviet invasion and that crushing the Hungarian revolution would be costly as a result. Nevertheless, he also believed that keeping Nagy in power and waiting for him to suppress the rebellion or request a Soviet intervention would entail costs too. If the United States were to stoke the rebellion further, the ensuing chaos might not only spread to other Warsaw Pact states but also cost Khrushchev politically at home. Keeping Nagy in power, Khrushchev concluded, would be more costly than ousting him.

When foreign powers anticipate high costs, they may devise alternative ways to overthrow their targets rather than abandon regime change altogether. When the CIA learned that Castillo Armas's band of Guatemalan exiles was weak, the Eisenhower administration shifted from a goal of full to partial regime change, focusing instead on convincing the Guatemalan army to abandon Árbenz. Similarly, the US experience in Iraq did not dissuade Obama from helping rebels overthrow Qaddafi in Libya. Rather, it convinced him he should avoid sending American troops and establishing a military occupation. Future research on the success and failure of regime-change operations would benefit from consideration of both the conditions under which foreign powers impose regime change and how the strategies and goals they adopt during a regime-change attempt affect their likelihood of success.

The Enduring Appeal of Regime Change and War

My argument has important implications for our understanding of war more generally. Much of the conflict literature treats war as ex post inefficient. That is, if both sides suffer some cost they could have avoided by negotiating, then each could have secured a more efficient outcome by reaching an enforceable bargain.[18] Yet the measures necessary to reach an enforceable bargain might also entail costs. Mine is not the first study to highlight the so-called costs of peace.[19] What the existing scholarship does not do, however, is identify what would cause a state's costs of negotiating a bargain to rise precisely as its costs of fighting fall. By pointing to a leader's domestic opposition as the mechanism that simultaneously drives up the foreign power's bargaining costs while driving down the costs of regime change, my argument specifies the conditions under which war, or more specifically, regime change, can be considered an efficient outcome.

The difficulty of negotiating with leaders who have strong domestic incentives to resist foreign pressure is one of the main reasons FIRC has endured as a foreign policy tool and likely will continue to do so. The very feature that makes a regime costly to bargain with—the domestic opposition—can also tempt foreign powers to overthrow it. Policymakers need not be blinded by their own biases or hoodwinked by self-interested bureaucrats to believe it more costly to settle with a foreign government than to overthrow it. Indeed, one implication of my argument is that even with more cautious and judicious policymakers in power, regime change would still occur. Good judgment offers no insurance against a regime-change policy. In fact, even policymakers who have criticized their predecessors for pursuing it have gone on to pursue regime change themselves.

Militarily weak and politically unstable foreign leaders are ubiquitous. As long as their domestic insecurity gives them reason to resist a foreign power, while giving the foreign power reason to believe overthrowing them will be comparatively cheap, even rational actors will be tempted to pursue regime change. Though we may desire more cautious and judicious policy-makers for a variety of other reasons, electing them will not rid the world of FIRC.

Although regime change is likely to endure, there is little doubt that it can sometimes turn out to be more costly than anticipated. Too often, the difficulty of negotiating bargains with recalcitrant foreign leaders, compared to the apparent ease of overthrowing them, causes policymakers to conclude that peace cannot be achieved when, in fact, it is possible. If policymakers were willing to bear the political, reputational, military, economic, and opportunity costs that are often required to negotiate sustainable bargains, they might be able to avoid the sometimes higher costs of regime change.

Yet, though regime change should not be necessary, a negotiated agreement will not always be preferable. Such agreements require policymakers to do things they often do not want to do. A negotiated agreement may require them to jeopardize their diplomatic relations, their reputations, or even their own domestic political power. In all, the costs associated with coercive bargaining and with regime change are a significant part of the reason both foreign policy tools appear so prone to failure. Policymakers are often reluctant to bear the costs of the measures necessary to make them work. In the end, it is not so much the tools themselves that are problematic, but the underlying purpose that both are meant to serve. The act of forcing another state's policies to align with one's own is an inherently ambitious objective and one that can seldom be achieved without great cost.

Foreign-Imposed Regime Change, 1816–2007

Table 14. Foreign-Imposed Regime Change

Case No.	Year	Target	Imposer	Imposer Major Power?	Target Major Power?
1	1821	Two Sicilies	Austria	Yes	No
2	1823	Spain	France	Yes	No
3	1828	Portugal	United Kingdom	Yes	No
3	1828	Portugal	Prussia	Yes	No
3	1828	Portugal	Austria	Yes	No
3	1828	Portugal	Russia	Yes	No
4	1848	Modena	Austria	Yes	No
5	1848	Tuscany	Austria	Yes	No
6	1849	Baden	Prussia	Yes	No
7	1849	Saxony	Prussia	Yes	No
8	1849	Piedmont-Sardinia	Austria	Yes	No
9	1849	Roman Republic	France	Yes	No
9	1849	Roman Republic	Spain	No	No
9	1849	Roman Republic	Austria	Yes	No
9	1849	Roman Republic	Sicily	No	No
10	1851	Argentina	Brazil	No	No
11	1859	Modena	France	Yes	No
11	1859	Modena	Piedmont	No	No
12	1862	Mexico	France	Yes	No
13	1864	Paraguay	Brazil	No	No
13	1864	Paraguay	Argentina	No	No
14	1870	France	Prussia	Yes	Yes
15	1876	El Salvador	Guatemala	No	No
16	1881	Peru	Chile	No	No
17	1882	Peru	Chile	No	No
18	1882	Egypt	United Kingdom	Yes	No
19	1906	Cuba	United States	Yes	No
20	1907	Honduras	Nicaragua	No	No
21	1909	Nicaragua	United States	Yes	No
22	1910	Nicaragua	United States	Yes	No

Table 14. (Cont.)

Case No.	Year	Target	Imposer	Imposer Major Power?	Target Major Power?
23	1911	Honduras	United States	Yes	No
24	1912	Dominican Rep.	United States	Yes	No
25	1914	Dominican Rep.	United States	Yes	No
26	1914	Mexico	United States	Yes	No
27	1914	Belgium	Germany	Yes	No
28	1915	Haiti	United States	Yes	No
29	1915	Serbia	Austria	Yes	No
30	1916	Dominican Rep.	United States	Yes	No
31	1916	Albania	Italy	Yes	No
32	1917	Cuba	United States	Yes	No
33	1917	Greece	United Kingdom	Yes	No
33	1917	Greece	France	Yes	No
34	1917	Russia	United States	Yes	Yes
34	1917	Russia	United Kingdom	Yes	Yes
34	1917	Russia	France	Yes	Yes
34	1917	Russia	Italy	Yes	Yes
34	1917	Russia	Japan	Yes	Yes
35	1918	Belgium	United States	Yes	No
35	1918	Belgium	United Kingdom	Yes	No
35	1918	Belgium	France	Yes	No
36	1918	Germany	United States	Yes	Yes
37	1919	Hungary	France	Yes	No
37	1919	Hungary	Romania	No	No
38	1919	Latvia	Germany	No	No
39	1921	Mongolia	Soviet Union	Yes	No
40	1924	Honduras	United States	Yes	No
41	1926	Nicaragua	United States	Yes	No
42	1928	China	Japan	Yes	No
43	1936	Spain	Portugal	No	No
43	1936	Spain	Germany	Yes	No
43	1936	Spain	Italy	Yes	No
44	1936	Ethiopia	Italy	Yes	No
45	1937	China	Japan	Yes	No
46	1939	Albania	Italy	Yes	No
47	1940	Netherlands	Germany	Yes	No
48	1940	Belgium	Germany	Yes	No
49	1940	Luxembourg	Germany	Yes	No
50	1940	Estonia	Soviet Union	Yes	No
51	1940	Latvia	Soviet Union	Yes	No
52	1940	Lithuania	Soviet Union	Yes	No
53	1940	Norway	Germany	Yes	No
54	1941	Yugoslavia	Germany	Yes	No
55	1941	Greece	Germany	Yes	No
56	1941	Ethiopia	United Kingdom	Yes	No
57	1941	Iran	United Kingdom	Yes	No
57	1941	Iran	Soviet Union	Yes	No

58	1941	Iraq	United Kingdom	Yes	No
59	1943	Germany	United States	Yes	Yes
59	1943	Germany	United Kingdom	Yes	Yes
59	1943	Germany	Soviet Union	Yes	Yes
60	1943	Japan	United States	Yes	Yes
61	1944	Luxembourg	United States	Yes	No
61	1944	Luxembourg	United Kingdom	Yes	No
62	1944	France	United States	Yes	No
62	1944	France	United Kingdom	Yes	No
63	1944	Hungary	Germany	Yes	No
64	1944	Bulgaria	Soviet Union	Yes	No
65	1945	Netherlands	United States	Yes	No
65	1945	Netherlands	Canada	No	No
65	1945	Netherlands	United Kingdom	Yes	No
66	1945	Norway	United States	Yes	No
66	1945	Norway	United Kingdom	Yes	No
67	1945	Denmark	United States	Yes	No
67	1945	Denmark	United Kingdom	Yes	No
68	1946	Albania	Yugoslavia	No	No
69	1947	Hungary	Soviet Union	Yes	No
70	1947	Romania	Soviet Union	Yes	No
71	1948	Czechoslovakia	Soviet Union	Yes	No
72	1949	Albania	United States	Yes	No
73	1950	North Korea	United States	Yes	No
73	1950	North Korea	United Kingdom	Yes	No
74	1953	Iran	United States	Yes	No
75	1954	Guatemala	United States	Yes	No
76	1956	Hungary	Soviet Union	Yes	No
77	1956	Egypt	United Kingdom	Yes	No
77	1956	Egypt	France	Yes	No
77	1956	Egypt	Israel	No	No
78	1957	Indonesia	United States	Yes	No
79	1959	Laos	North Vietnam	No	No
80	1960	Congo	Belgium	No	No
81	1961	Cuba	United States	Yes	No
82	1963	South Vietnam	United States	Yes	No
83	1964	Gabon	France	Yes	No
84	1965	Dominican Rep.	United States	Yes	No
84	1965	Dominican Rep.	Honduras	No	No
84	1965	Dominican Rep.	Brazil	No	No
85	1968	Czechoslovakia	Soviet Union	Yes	No
86	1970	Jordan	Syria	No	No
87	1973	Chile	United States	Yes	No
88	1974	Cyprus	Greece	No	No
89	1974	Cyprus	Turkey	No	No
90	1975	Angola	Zaire/DRC	No	No
90	1975	Angola	South Africa	No	No
91	1978	Cambodia	Vietnam	No	No
92	1979	C. African Rep.	France	Yes	No
93	1979	Uganda	Tanzania	No	No

Table 14. (Cont.)

Case No.	Year	Target	Imposer	Imposer Major Power?	Target Major Power?
94	1979	Afghanistan	Soviet Union	Yes	No
95	1980	Nicaragua	United States	Yes	No
96	1980	Iran	Iraq	No	No
97	1982	Iraq	Iran	No	No
98	1983	Grenada	United States	Yes	No
99	1983	Chad	Libya	No	No
100	1984	Mongolia	Soviet Union	Yes	No
101	1986	Afghanistan	Soviet Union	Yes	No
102	1989	Panama	United States	Yes	No
103	1989	Comoros	France	Yes	No
104	1992	Tajikistan	Russia	Yes	No
104	1992	Tajikistan	Uzbekistan	No	No
105	1994	Haiti	United States	Yes	No
106	1994	Lesotho	South Africa	No	No
107	1995	Comoros	France	Yes	No
108	1997	Zaire/DRC	Uganda	No	No
108	1997	Zaire/DRC	Rwanda	No	No
109	1998	Sierra Leone	Guinea	No	No
109	1998	Sierra Leone	Ghana	No	No
109	1998	Sierra Leone	Nigeria	No	No
110	2001	Afghanistan	United States	Yes	No
111	2003	Iraq	United States	Yes	No
111	2003	Iraq	United Kingdom	Yes	No
112	2003	Liberia	United States	Yes	No
Total				**Total**	**Total**
150				**113**	**11**

Table 15. Cases Excluded by Correlates of War Data Set

Case No.	Year	Target	Imposer	Imposer Major Power?	Target Major Power?
113	1831	Modena	Austria	Yes	No
114	1831	Parma	Austria	Yes	No
115	1837	Peru	Argentina	No	No
115	1837	Peru	Chile	No	No
116	1839	Afghanistan	United Kingdom	Yes	No
117	1843	Uruguay	Argentina	No	No
118	1848	Parma	Austria	Yes	No
119	1855	Honduras	Guatemala	No	No
120	1863	Honduras	Guatemala	No	No
120	1863	Honduras	Nicaragua	No	No
121	1863	El Salvador	Guatemala	No	No
122	1864	Paraguay	Uruguay	No	No
123	1864	Uruguay	Brazil	No	No
123	1864	Uruguay	Argentina	No	No
124	1871	El Salvador	Honduras	No	No
125	1872	Honduras	Guatemala	No	No
125	1872	Honduras	El Salvador	No	No
126	1874	Honduras	Guatemala	No	No
126	1874	Honduras	El Salvador	No	No
127	1876	Honduras	Guatemala	No	No
128	1878	Afghanistan	United Kingdom	Yes	No
129	1894	Honduras	Nicaragua	No	No
130	1907	Korea	Japan	Yes	No
131	1916	Montenegro	Austria	Yes	No
132	1943	Denmark	Germany	Yes	No
133	1944	Belgium	United States	Yes	No
133	1944	Belgium	Canada	No	No
133	1944	Belgium	United Kingdom	Yes	No
Total **28**				**Total** **10**	**Total** **0**

A Game Theoretic Model of Regime Change

In this appendix, I use a formal model to illustrate how a targeted leader's opposition affects a foreign power's choice to pursue a settlement or regime change. To begin, I construct a model of coercion wherein one state chooses either to coerce a target that faces a domestic adversary or to accept the status quo. This model shows that domestically weak leaders, *ceteris paribus*, are more costly to coerce.[1] I then expand the model by giving the foreign power the option to back an opposition group to attain its aims. This model shows that as a leader's strength declines, relative to the opposition, regime change is more likely to result.

The Coercion Game

I start with a basic take-it-or-leave-it bargaining game, in which Side 1 (S_1) first chooses to accept the status quo or coerce the target, S_2, into accepting a policy change, which is on the interval $r \in [0,1]$. Assume S_2 prefers a policy outcome close to $r = 1$ and S_1 and prefers a policy outcome close to $r = 0$. After S_1 chooses to coerce, it mobilizes for war and selects a mobilization level of cost $m \geq 0$.[2] Mobilization costs are sunk, meaning that once m is chosen, S_1 incurs this cost no matter what. I assume that $m > 0$ will increase S_1's probability of victory. I follow Branislav Slantchev in defining S_1's probability of victory as $0 < p(m) < 1$, where $p(m) = \dfrac{M_1 + m}{M_1 + M_2 + m}$ and M_1 and M_2 represent the current mobilization levels for S_1 and S_2, respectively.[3]

After observing m, S_2 can choose to resist or accept the policy change. If S_2 resists, S_1 initiates conflict. If S_2 accepts the policy change, an opposition group, S_3, launches an attack.[4] I assume that under the status quo, S_3

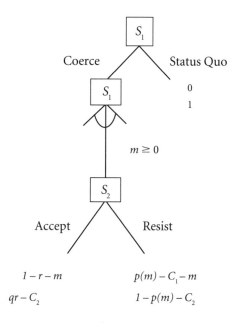

Figure 6. The Coercion Game

will not challenge S_2. However, when S_2 accepts the policy change, its probability of defeating S_3 is reduced by $r < 1$, which encourages S_3 to attack.

The payoffs for the game are as follows. If S_1 accepts the status quo, then S_2 keeps $r = 1$, which gives S_1 a payoff of 0. If S_1 chooses to coerce and S_2 accepts the policy change, then S_1 gets $1 - r$, but pays cost m. Side 2 gets r with probability $0<q<1$, but pays costs of fighting $C_2 > 0$. If S_2 resists, then both sides go to war. If Side 1 wins the war, which it does with probability $p(m)$ and with cost of fighting $C_1 > 0$, it can set $r = 0$. However, because the costs of the signal are sunk, S_1 also pays cost, m, which makes its payoff $p(m) - C_1 - m$. Side 2's utility for conflict is $1 - p(m) - C_2$. To reduce the number of parameters in the model, I assume S_2's costs of fighting are the same no matter who it fights. Introducing a different set of costs will affect the value of m but will not alter the effect of q, the main parameter of interest. The extensive form of the model is pictured in Figure 6.

By backward induction, the leader acquiesces when $(m) \geq 1 - qr \equiv p(m)^*$. As long as S_1 chooses a mobilization level, m^*, that will make $p(m) \geq p(m)^*$, then S_2 will acquiesce. Substituting p^* and solving for m, we can locate the boundary $m^* = \frac{M_2}{qr} - (M_1 + M_2)$, above which S_2 will always play accept. If S_2 accepts, S_1 will set $m = m^*$, since there is no need for it to incur additional expense if S_2 will accept for sure. If S_2 will resist, however, then S_1 will simply set $m = 0$, since it knows S_2 will resist no matter what. The game has four subgame perfect equilibria (Settlement, Limited War, Status Quo 1, and Status Quo 2), which I describe here.

1. **Settlement:** If, $m \geq m^*$, S_2 plays accept. If S_2 plays accept, S_1 plays coerce and sets $m = m^*$ if $1 - r - m^* > 0$, which is true when $q > \frac{M_2}{r(1-r+M_1+M_2)}$.

2. **Limited War:** If $m < m^*$, S_2 plays resist. If S_2 plays resist, then S_1 plays coerce and sets $m = 0$ if $p(m) - C_1 > 0$, which is true when $p(m) > C_1$.

3. **Status Quo 1:** If $m \geq m^*$, S_2 plays accept. If S_2 plays accept, S_1 will choose the status quo if $1 - r - m^* < 0$, which is true when $q < \frac{M_2}{r(1-r+M_1+M_2)}$.

4. **Status Quo 2:** If $m < m^*$, S_2 plays resist. If S_2 plays resist, then S_1 will choose the status quo and set $m = 0$ if $p(m) - C_1 < 0$, which is true when $p(m) < C_1$.

The most important takeaway from the coercion game is that a settlement is more likely the stronger S_2 is relative to its domestic opposition (i.e., as q increases). Conventional wisdom holds that coercion is more likely to succeed against leaders who are domestically weak. This line of thinking rests on the idea that domestically weak leaders are forced into making concessions to preserve their political power. But, as q decreases, S_2's payoff for accepting S_1's demand decreases. This forces S_1 to increase its threat and assume greater costs, m, to convince S_2 to accept. Thus, increases in q enable S_1 to spend less to obtain a settlement.

In the next game, the regime change game, I examine what would happen if instead of using coercive force, S_1 could attempt regime change by backing S_2's opposition, S_3.

The Regime Change Game

In the regime change game, S_1 can now choose between coercing the leader into accepting some policy along the interval $r \in [0,1]$ or installing the

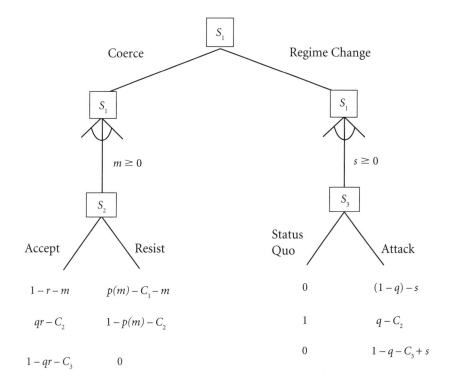

Figure 7. The Regime Change Game

leader's opposition, S_3. In this game, I assume that S_3 shares S_1's policy preference, $r = 0$. Recall that S_3 will not attack under the status quo. To induce S_3 to attack, S_1 must give it aid, which costs $s \geq 0$.

The game begins with S_1 choosing to coerce the leader or pursue regime change by paying S_3 to attack. If S_1 chooses to coerce, then the game is the same as the coercion game. If S_1 chooses regime change, then it offers aid in the amount of $s \geq 0$ to S_3, which then decides to attack S_2 or do nothing. If S_3 does nothing, then the status quo attains, in which case, S_1 and S_3 get nothing and S_2 gets 1. If the opposition chooses to fight, then S_1 gets 1, but only if the opposition wins. Side 1 also pays costs, s. The target, S_2, defeats the opposition with probability q and pays costs C_2. Finally, S_3 wins with probability $1 - q$, while getting s from S_1, but pays costs of fighting $C_3 > 0$. Figure 7 illustrates the game.

As in the coercion game, S_2 will acquiesce when $m \geq m^\star = \frac{M_2}{qr} - (M_1 + M_2)$. To induce S_3 to fight, S_1 needs to offer $s \geq s^\star \equiv q + C_3 - 1$.

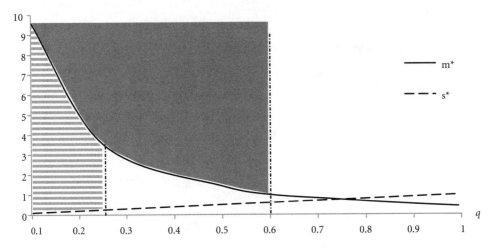

Figure 8. Conditions Supporting the Regime Change Equilibria

The game has eight subgame perfect equilibria, which I detail at the end of this section. However, to demonstrate the effect of q on the likelihood of FIRC, I focus on the conditions supporting the two regime change equilibria. Figure 8 shows the lines m^* and s^* as functions of q, based on the following assumed values: $r = .1$, $M_1 = .5$, $M_2 = .1$, $C_3 = 1$, $C_1 = .5$. In this scenario, Side 1 demands a policy outcome, r, close to its own preference point. It also has a clear military advantage over Side 2. Given costs of fighting $C_1 = .5$, Side 1 has a positive utility for limited war, as long as it has a greater than 50 percent chance of defeating Side 2. This means Side 1 has a credible threat to attack Side 2, even without paying additional costs, m.

With Side 1's military capabilities being five times greater than those of the target, the conventional wisdom would suggest that Side 1 would be successful in coercing Side 2 into a bargain. Yet, despite its military advantage, Side 1 will increasingly prefer regime change over a bargain as Side 2's probability of defeating Side 3 (q) decreases. The shaded regions in Figure 8 depict the two cases in which a regime change equilibrium holds. The first occurs when $m \geq m^*$ and $s \geq s^*$. In this case, S_1 will choose regime change when $1 - r - m^* < (1 - r)(1 - q) - s$, which is true when $M_2 > qr (M_1 + M_2 + C_3 - 1 + 2q - r)$. When substituting the values for r, M_1, M_2, C_1, and C_3 listed earlier, the inequality holds when $q < .6$.

This means that Side 1 will pursue regime change in the solid-shaded region above the lines m^* and s^*, and to the left of the vertical line, $q = .6$. When $q > .6$, however, Side 1 will seek a bargain with Side 2. In the second case, Side 1 will pursue regime change when $m < m^*$ but $s \geq s^*$, and $p(m) - C_1 < (1 - q) - s$, which is true when $q < 1 + \frac{C_1 - p(m) - C_3}{2}$. In this instance, Side 1 knows Side 2 will resist and so sets $m = 0$, because Side 1 gains nothing from setting $m > 0$. Again, when substituting the values for M_1, M_2, C_1, and C_3 as above, the condition, $q < 1 + \frac{C_1 - p(m) - C_3}{2}$, holds when $q < .25$. This means that the regime change equilibrium will also occur below the line m^*, but above the line s^*, and to the left of the line $q = .25$ (see lined-region in Figure 8). As q increases beyond .25, however, Side 1 will choose to bargain. In all, these results show that FIRC becomes more likely to occur the weaker Side 2 is relative to its domestic opposition, Side 3.

The subgame perfect equilibria for the regime change game are as follows:

1. **Settlement 1:** If $m \geq m^*$ and $s < s^*$, then S_2 plays accept and S_3 chooses the status quo. If S_2 plays accept, S_1 plays coerce and sets $m = m^*$ and $s = 0$, if $1 - r - m^* > 0$, which is true when $q > \frac{M_2}{r(1 - r + M_1 + M_2)}$.

2. **Settlement 2:** If $m \geq m^*$ and $s \geq s^*$, then S_2 plays accept and S_3 chooses to attack. If S_2 plays accept, S_1 will choose to coerce if $1 - r - m^* > (1 - q) - s$, which is true when $M_2 < qr (M_1 + M_2 + C_3 - 1 + 2q - r)$.

3. **Regime Change 1:** If $m \geq m^*$ and $s \geq s^*$, then S_2 plays accept and S_3 chooses to attack. If S_2 plays accept, S_1 will choose regime change if $1 - r - m^* < (1 - r)(1 - q) - s$, which is true when $M_2 > qr (M_1 + M_2 + C_3 - 1 + 2q - r)$.

4. **Regime Change 2:** If $m < m^*$ and $s \geq s^*$, then S_2 plays resist and S_3 chooses to attack. In this event, S_1 will choose regime change and set $m = 0$ and $s = s^*$ when $p(m) - C_1 < (1 - q) - s$, which is true when $q < 1 + \frac{C_1 - p(m) - C_3}{2}$. Because $q < 1$, S_1 will always choose regime change if $p(m) < C_1 - C_3$.

5. **Limited War 1:** If $m < m^*$ and $s \geq s^*$, then S_2 plays resist and S_3 chooses to attack. In this event, S_1 will choose to coerce and set

$m = 0$ and $s = s^*$ when $p(m) - C_1 < (1 - q) - s$, which is true when $q > 1 + \frac{C_1 - p(m) - C_3}{2}$. Because $q < 1$, for this inequality to hold, it must be true that $p > C_1 - C_3$.

6. **Limited War 2**: If $m < m^*$ and $s < s^*$, then S_2 plays resist and S_3 chooses the status quo. In this event, S_1 will choose to coerce and set $m = 0$ and $s = 0$ if $p(m) - C_1 > 0$, which is true when $p(m) > C_1$.

7. **Status Quo 1**: If $m < m^*$ and $s < s^*$, then S_2 plays resist and S_3 chooses the status quo. In this event, S_1 will choose regime change but set $m = 0$ and $s = 0$ if $p(m) - C_1 < 0$, which is true when $p(m) < C_1$.

8. **Status Quo 2**: If $m \geq m^*$ and $s < s^*$, then S_2 plays accept and S_3 chooses the status quo. If S_2 plays accept, S_1 plays regime change and sets $m = m^*$ and $s = 0$, if $1 - r - m^* < 0$, which is true when $q < \frac{M_2}{r(1 - r + M_1 + M_2)}$.

NOTES

Introduction

1. "Transcript: Obama's Speech Against the Iraq War," National Public Radio, January 20, 2009, http://www.npr.org/templates/story/story.php?storyId = 99591469.

2. On civil war and democratization, see Goran Peic and Dan Reiter, "Foreign Imposed Regime Change, State Power, and Civil War Onset, 1920–2004," *British Journal of Political Science* 41 (2011): 453–75; Andrew J. Enterline and J. Michael Greig, "Beacons of Hope? The Impact of Imposed Democracy on Regional Peace, Democracy, and Prosperity," *Journal of Politics* 67 (2005): 1075–98; Andrew J. Enterline and J. Michael Greig, "Against All Odds? The History of Imposed Democracy and the Future of Iraq and Afghanistan," *Foreign Policy Analysis*, 4 (2008): 321–47; and Alexander Downes and Jonathan Monten, "Forced to Be Free: Why Foreign-Imposed Regime Change Rarely Leads to Democratization," *International Security* 37 (2013). One study indicates that conflict is less likely to reignite after FIRC: Nigel Lo, Barry Hashimoto, and Dan Reiter, "Ensuring Peace: Foreign-Imposed Regime Change and Postwar Peace Duration, 1914–2001," *International Organization* 62 (2008): 717–36. A more recent one contends FIRC has no effect on the probability of a dispute: Alexander B. Downes and Lindsey A. O'Rourke, "You Can't Always Get What You Want: Why Foreign-Imposed Regime Change Seldom Improves Interstate Relations," *International Security* 41 (2016): 43–89.

3. Examples include John M. Owen IV, *The Clash of Ideas in World Politics: Transnational Networks, States, and Regime Change, 1510–2010* (Princeton, N.J.: Princeton University Press, 2010); Elizabeth N. Saunders, *Leaders at War: How Presidents Shape Military Interventions* (Ithaca, N.Y.: Cornell University Press, 2011); Martha Finnemore, *The Purpose of Intervention: Changing Beliefs About the Use of Force* (Ithaca, N.Y.: Cornell University Press, 2003); Suzanne Werner, "Absolute and Limited War: The Possibility of Foreign-Imposed Regime Change," *International Interactions* 22 (1996): 67–88; and Mark Peceny, *Democracy at the Point of Bayonets* (University Park, Pa.: Pennsylvania State University Press, 1999).

4. Although inducement can also be used, strong states often adopt coercive methods because they can exploit their military advantage when dealing with weak states. Accordingly, throughout this book, I focus primarily on coercive methods, although the costs associated with them can apply to inducement as well.

5. On weak states and intervention, see Stephen D. Krasner, *Sovereignty: Organized Hypocrisy* (Princeton, N.J.: Princeton University Press, 1999), 155; Andrew M. Dorman and Thomas G. Otte, *Military Intervention: From Gunboat Diplomacy to Humanitarian Intervention* (Aldershot, UK: Dartmouth Publishing, 1995); J. H. Leurdijk, *Armed Intervention in International Politics: A Historical and Comparative Analysis* (Nijmegen, The Netherlands: Wolf Legal

Publishers, 2006), 6; John M. Owen, "The Foreign Imposition of Domestic Institutions," *International Organization* 56, no. 2 (2002): 392–93; Marc Trachtenberg, "Intervention in Historical Perspective," in *Emerging Norms of Justified Intervention*, ed. Carl Kaysen and Laura Reed (Cambridge, Mass.: American Academy of Arts and Sciences, 1993), 44; and Werner, "Absolute and Limited War," 75–79.

6. Data on FIRC collected by author; see Appendix 1. The term *major power* includes the fourteen states identified as such by the Correlates of War Project's data set; see Correlates of War Project, "State System Membership List, v2008.1," 2008, http://correlatesofwar.org/data -sets/state-system-membership. Some FIRC cases do not meet the criteria for statehood in the Correlates of War data set. These are listed separately in Table 15 in Appendix 1.

7. Capabilities calculated using the National Material Capabilities data set, version 4.0. David J. Singer, Stuart Bremer, and John Stuckey, "Capability Distribution, Uncertainty, and Major Power War, 1820–1965," in *Peace, War, and Numbers*, ed. Bruce Russett (Beverly Hills, Calif.: Sage, 1972), 19–48; David J. Singer, "Reconstructing the Correlates of War Dataset on Material Capabilities of States, 1816–1985," *International Interactions*, 14 (1987): 115–32.

8. Unlike many rational choice theories, I do not assume that states are unitary actors. Although I refer to the side imposing regime change as a "foreign power" or "the stronger state" throughout this book, my theory allows for the possibility that domestic political costs affect the choice to negotiate or impose regime change.

9. As a rational choice explanation, my theory assumes that actors calculate their utility for a particular strategy based on estimated probabilities and costs, using information available to them at the time. These estimations may differ from the actual costs. Actors can also vary in their willingness to accept risk, and so risk-acceptant actors may act on probability and cost estimates that would deter risk-adverse ones. James D. Morrow, *Game Theory for Political Scientists* (Princeton, N.J.: Princeton University Press, 1994), 17, 36.

10. On postwar regime change, see Werner, "Absolute and Limited War"; Dan Reiter, *How Wars End* (Princeton, N.J.: Princeton University Press, 2009); Alex Weisiger, *Logics of War: Explanations for Limited and Unlimited Conflicts* (Ithaca, N.Y.: Cornell University Press, 2013); and Bruce Bueno de Mesquita et al., *The Logic of Political Survival* (Cambridge, Mass.: MIT Press, 2003). On covert operations, see Lindsey A. O'Rourke, "Secrecy and Security: U.S.-Orchestrated Regime Change During the Cold War" (PhD diss., University of Chicago, 2013). On institutional FIRC, see Owen, *Clash of Ideas*.

11. For example, John J. Mearsheimer and Stephen M. Walt, "An Unnecessary War," *Foreign Policy* 134 (February 2003): 50–59; Richard N. Haass, *War of Necessity, War of Choice: A Memoir of Two Iraq Wars* (New York: Simon and Schuster, 2010): 10–11.

12. A common neorealist assumption is that all states are functionally the same, regardless of who rules them. Although neorealists do not necessarily reject the notion that domestic politics can influence a state's policies, they consider this relevant to the realm of foreign policy rather than international politics. Kenneth N. Waltz, *Theory of International Politics* (Reading, Mass.: Addison-Wesley, 1979), 65–73. For defensive realists, domestic politics can best explain anomalous events, such as overexpansion. See, for example, Jack L. Snyder, *Myths of Empire* (Ithaca, N.Y.: Cornell University Press, 1991). Neoclassical realism affords a greater role to domestic politics, but major works remain focused on explaining foreign policy. Gideon Rose, "Neoclassical Realism and Theories of Foreign Policy," *World Politics* 51 (1998): 144–172; Steven E. Lobell, Norrin M. Ripsman, and Jeffrey W. Taliaferro, *Neoclassical Realism, the State, and Foreign Policy* (New York: Cambridge University Press, 2009).

13. Thomas C. Schelling, *Arms and Influence* (New Haven, Conn.: Yale University Press, 1966), 5, 72–73.

14. Schelling, 4.

15. Schelling, 7.

16. Studies on intervention and FIRC that focus on motivations include: Werner, "Absolute and Limited War"; Saunders, *Leaders at War*; Finnemore, *Purpose of Intervention*; Owen, *Clash of Ideas*; O'Rourke, "Secrecy and Security"; Stephen Kinzer, *Overthrow: America's Century of Regime Change from Hawaii to Iraq* (New York: Times Books/Henry Holt, 2006); Jon W. Western, *Selling Intervention and War: The Presidency, the Media, and the American Public* (Baltimore: Johns Hopkins University Press, 2005); Frederic S. Pearson, Robert A. Baumann, and Jeffrey J. Pickering, "Military Intervention and Realpolitik," in *Reconstructing Realpolitik*, ed. Frank W. Wayman and Paul F. Diehl (Ann Arbor: University of Michigan Press, 1994), 205–25; Tony Smith, *America's Mission* (Princeton, N.J.: Princeton University Press, 1994); Leurdijk, *Armed Intervention*; and Dorman and Otte, *Military Intervention*.

17. Bureaucratic-politics and interest-group arguments do not necessarily assume actors are irrational. Rather, they reject the assumption that states are unitary actors, wherein a single leader makes policies in support of the national interest. Because bureaucratic-politics and interest-group arguments help explain why leaders would adopt policies that seemingly violate the state's interests, I group them here with political-psychology theories. For political-psychology hypotheses that offer potential insight into why states might overthrow foreign leaders, see Robert Jervis, "Hypotheses on Misperception," *World Politics* 20, no. 3 (1968): 454–79; Robert Jervis, *Perception and Misperception in International Politics* (Princeton, N.J.: Princeton University Press, 1976); Yaacov Y. I. Vertzberger, *Risk Taking and Decisionmaking: Foreign Military Intervention Decisions* (Stanford, Calif.: Stanford University Press, 1998); Steve A. Yetiv, *National Security through a Cockeyed Lens: How Cognitive Bias Impacts U.S. Foreign Policy* (Baltimore: Johns Hopkins University Press, 2013); and Jeffrey W. Taliaferro, *Balancing Risks: Great Power Intervention in the Periphery* (Ithaca, N.Y.: Cornell University Press, 2004), 14–18. On accounts attributing foreign policy decisions to either bureaucratic politics or interest-group pressure, see Graham T. Allison, "Conceptual Models and the Cuban Missile Crisis," *American Political Science Review* 63, no. 3 (1969): 689–718; Snyder, *Myths of Empire*.

18. These arguments are more common in the literature on specific cases of FIRC. See, for example, Amatzia Baram, "Deterrence Lessons from Iraq," *Foreign Affairs* 91 (2012): 76–90.

19. T. Edward Damer, *Attacking Faulty Reasoning* (Boston: Wadsworth, 2012), 93.

20. On success and failure, see Downes and Monten, "Forced to Be Free"; David Edelstein, *Occupational Hazards: Success and Failure in Military Occupation* (Ithaca, N.Y.: Cornell University Press, 2008); Lo, Hashimoto, and Reiter, "Ensuring Peace"; Patricia L. Sullivan, *Who Wins? Predicting Strategic Success and Failure in Armed Conflict* (Oxford, UK: Oxford University Press, 2012); Peic and Reiter, "Foreign Imposed Regime Change"; Enterline and Greig, "Against All Odds?"; and Downes and O'Rourke, "You Can't Always Get What You Want."

21. Jaromír Navrátil, *The Prague Spring 1968: A National Security Archive Document Reader* (New York: Central European University Press, 2006), 352.

22. Dana G. Munro, "Dollar Diplomacy in Nicaragua, 1909–1913," *Hispanic American Historical Review* 38, no. 2 (1958): 213.

23. James D. Fearon, "Rationalist Explanations for War," *International Organization* 49 (1995): 379–414. Fearon notes that although the two sides could simply tell each other their private information, each has incentive to exaggerate its value for war to gain more in negotiations.

24. Robert Powell shows that a third approach, the indivisibility problem, is a type of commitment problem. Robert Powell, "War as a Commitment Problem," *International Organization* 60 (2006): 169–203.

25. Reiter, *How Wars End*, 25–34. See also Alexander Downes, "The Causes of Foreign-Imposed Regime Change in Interstate Wars" (paper, American Political Science Association 2008 Annual Meeting, Boston, Mass., August 28–31, 2008); Weisiger, *Logics of War*, 26–33; Alexandre Debs and Nuno P. Monteiro, "Known Unknowns: Power Shifts, Uncertainty, and War," *International Organization* 68 (2014): 1–31.

26. Bueno de Mesquita et al., *Logic of Political Survival*, 439–41.

27. Although these arguments are not explicitly based on a rational choice framework, their emphasis on the target's doubts about the stronger side's resolve suggest private information is central to the cause of war. T. V. Paul, *Asymmetric Conflicts: War Initiation by Weaker Powers* (New York: Cambridge University Press, 1994), 27–28; James J. Wirtz, "The Balance of Power Paradox," in *Balance of Power: Theory and Practice in the 21st Century*, ed. James J. Wirtz, T. V. Paul, and Michael Fortmann (Stanford, Calif.: Stanford University Press, 2004), 129, 132–34. Wirtz also argues that strong states expect weak states to back down and so do not always threaten the level of coercive force necessary to make them back down.

28. James Fearon, "Signaling Foreign Policy Interests: Tying Hands Versus Sinking Costs," *Journal of Conflict Resolution* 41 (1997): 68–90; Kenneth A. Schultz, "Domestic Opposition and Signaling in International Crises," *American Political Science Review* 92 (1998): 829–44.

29. Virginia Page Fortna, *Peace Time: Cease-Fire Agreements and the Durability of Peace* (Princeton, N.J.: Princeton University Press, 2004); Barbara F. Walter, *Commiting to Peace: The Successful Settlement of Civil Wars* (Princeton, N.J.: Princeton University Press, 2002). Todd Sechser points out that foreign powers also have a commitment problem. Leaders may resist because they fear inviting additional demands.Todd S. Sechser, "Goliath's Curse: Coercive Threats and Asymmetric Power," *International Organization* 64, no. 4 (2010): 627–60.

30. Branislav L. Slantchev, *Military Threats: The Costs of Coercion and the Price of Peace* (Cambridge: Cambridge University Press, 2011), 84–95.

31. Robert Powell, "Bargaining in the Shadow of Power," *Games and Economic Behavior* 15, no. 2 (1996): 255–89; Powell, "War as a Commitment Problem": 192–94; Andrew Coe, "Costly Peace: A New Rationalist Explanation for War" (working paper, School of International Relations, University of Southern California, Los Angeles, 2011). Phil Haun also argues that powerful states may abandon bargaining because they see war as cheaper. Phil M. Haun, *Coercion, Survival, and War: Why Weak States Resist the United States* (Stanford, Calif.: Stanford University Press, 2015). Although these arguments similarly conclude that the expected costs of bargaining can exceed those for conflict, they do not identify a mechanism that can cause bargaining costs to rise and expected war costs to fall at the same time.

32. Andrew Mack, "Why Big Nations Lose Small Wars: The Politics of Asymmetric Conflict," *World Politics* 27 (1975): 175–200.

33. This contrasts notably with US policy with respect to Iraq, where US officials repeatedly emphasized that they would continue their efforts to topple Saddam Hussein irrespective

of his behavior. Brian L. Davis, *Qaddafi, Terrorism, and the Origins of the U.S. Attack on Libya* (New York: Praeger, 1990), 121–23; Robert Litwak, *Regime Change: U.S. Strategy through the Prism of 9/11* (Washington, D.C.: Woodrow Wilson Center Press, 2007), 174.

34. Ian Dear and M. R. D. Foot, eds., *The Oxford Companion to World War II* (Oxford: Oxford University Press, 1995), 42. I include the World War I case because President Woodrow Wilson demanded "authentic representatives of the German people" as a precondition for armistice negotiations in 1918. Although he did not explicitly demand Kaiser Wilhelm II's abdication, Wilson, at the very least, wanted the kaiser stripped of his political power. Lamar Cecil, *Wilhelm II, Vol. 2: Emperor and Exile, 1900–1941* (Chapel Hill: University of North Carolina Press, 1996), 283.

35. Prior to the war, Iran meddled in Iraq by aiding both Kurdish and Shi'a opposition groups, but despite its rhetoric, these efforts do not appear part of a concerted effort to remove Saddam Hussein from power. Dilip Hiro, *The Longest War: The Iran-Iraq Military Conflict* (New York: Routledge, 1991), 35. Iraq, however, backed an unsuccessful coup attempt by Iranian exiles just two months before launching its invasion. On the coup attempt and Iranian goals after Iran's counterinvasion, see F. Gregory Gause III, *The International Relations of the Persian Gulf* (Cambridge: Cambridge University Press, 2010), 63–64, 73; Gary Sick, "Trial by Error: Reflections on the Iran-Iraq War," *Middle East Journal* 43, no. 2 (1989): 236.

36. This follows Downes and Monten, "Forced to Be Free," 111.

37. Robert L. Willett, Jr., *Russian Sideshow: America's Undeclared War, 1918–1920* (Washington, D.C.: Potomac Books Inc., 2005), 267.

38. For a similar coding rule, see Downes and Monten, "Forced to Be Free," 109–10.

39. Stephen Van Evera, *Guide to Methods for Students of Political Science* (Ithaca, N.Y: Cornell University Press, 1997), 23–24.

40. Though Saddam and Qaddafi ultimately suffered similar fates, the United States chose to negotiate with Qaddafi in 2003 but not Saddam, despite similarities in their leadership style. Both leaders are coded as personalist dictators in Barbara Geddes' data on authoritarian regime types. Personalist dictators control both access to and the rewards from political power. Barbara Geddes, "What Do We Know about Democratization after Twenty Years?" *Annual Review of Political Science* 2 (1999): 121.

41. Nick Cullather, *Secret History: The CIA's Classified Account of Its Operations in Guatemala, 1952–1954* (Stanford, Calif.: Stanford University Press, 1999); Susan Holly, ed., *Foreign Relations of the United States, 1952–1954, Guatemala* (Washington, D.C.: United States Government Printing Office, 2003); N. Stephen Kane and William F. Sanford Jr., eds., *Foreign Relations of the United States, 1952–1954, The American Republics, Volume IV* (Washington, D.C.: United States Government Printing Office, 1983).

42. Csaba Békés, Malcolm Byrne, and János M. Rainer, eds., *The 1956 Hungarian Revolution: A History in Documents* (New York: Central European University Press, 2002); Mark Kramer, "Special Feature: New Evidence on Soviet Decision-Making and the 1956 Polish and Hungarian Crises," *Cold War International History Project Bulletin* 8/9 (1996): 358–84.

43. Saddam Hussein Regime Collection, Conflict Records Research Center, National Defense University, Fort McNair, D.C.

44. Kevin Young, "Purging the Forces of Darkness: The United States, Monetary Stabilization, and the Containment of the Bolivian Revolution," *Diplomatic History* 37 (2013): 513.

Chapter 1

1. George Lenczowski, ed., *Iran Under the Pahlavis* (Stanford, Calif.: Hoover Institution Press, 1978), xix; Nikki R. Keddie and Yann Richard, *Modern Iran: Roots and Results of Revolution* (New Haven, Conn.: Yale University Press, 2006), 105. Both the United Kingdom and Soviet Union also alleged there was the potential for a pro-German coup. However, these alleged coup plans, along with Reza Shah's pro-German sentiments, may have been exaggerated as part of a post-hoc justification for the invasion. Nikolay A. Kozhanov, "The Pretexts and Reasons for the Allied Invasion of Iran in 1941," *Iranian Studies* 45 (2012): 486.

2. Richard A. Stewart, *Sunrise at Abadan: The British and Soviet Invasion of Iran, 1941* (New York: Praeger, 1988), 190.

3. Stewart, 201.

4. Stewart, 198, 201.

5. Stewart, 200.

6. Mohammad Gholi Majd, *August 1941: The Anglo-Russian Occupation of Iran and Change of Shahs* (Lanham, Md.: University Press of America, 2012), 67–68.

7. Stewart, *Sunrise at Abadan*, 184.

8. Stewart, 208.

9. Majd, *August 1941*, 68.

10. Stewart, *Sunrise at Abadan*, 211. Quoted in Bruce Bueno de Mesquita et al., *The Logic of Political Survival* (Cambridge, Mass.: MIT Press, 2003), 425.

11. This section draws from Bueno de Mesquita et al.'s selectorate theory. An internal rival is akin to the authors' concept of a "challenger" within the selectorate. Bueno de Mesquita et al., *Logic of Political Survival*, 38–39.

12. Bueno de Mesquita et al., 415.

13. Robert D. Putnam, "Diplomacy and Domestic Politics: The Logic of Two-Level Games," *International Organization* 42 (1988): 427–60; Powell, "War as a Commitment Problem," *International Organization* 60 (2006): 189–92.

14. In fact, after ultranationalists murdered the former Serbian king and queen in 1903, the Serbian government came under foreign pressure to remove the ultranationalists from influential posts. But because of their role in the coup, King Peter resisted moving against them. Vladimir Dedijer, *The Road to Sarajevo* (New York: Simon and Schuster, 1966), 377–80; Barbara Jelavich, "What the Habsburg Government Knew About the Black Hand," *Austrian History Yearbook* 22 (1991): 134–38.

15. According to Bruce Bueno de Mesquita and his coauthors, groups most likely to undertake antigovernment actions include both disenfranchised groups and members of the selectorate left out of the leader's winning coalition. Bueno de Mesquita et al., *Logic of Political Survival*, 330–36.

16. Democracies and nondemocracies typically use both coercive and inclusive measures to manage external threats. Dictators, for example, may offer the opposition token bureaucratic appointments or hold fraudulent elections to buy off opposition. Democracies, meanwhile, use the police and military to manage threats from groups seeking to topple the government. Jennifer Gandhi and Adam Przeworski, "Cooperation, Cooptation, and Rebellion Under Dictatorships," *Economics and Politics* 18 (2006): 1280; Philip Roessler, "The Enemy Within: Personal Rule, Coups, and Civil War in Africa," *World Politics* 63, no. 2 (2011): 300–346; Guillermo A. O'Donnell et al., eds., *Transitions from Authoritarian Rule:*

Comparative Perspectives (Baltimore: Johns Hopkins University Press, 1986), 7–8, 23–33; and Daniel N. Posner and Daniel J. Young, "The Institutionalization of Political Power in Africa," *Journal of Democracy* 18 (2007): 126–40.

17. On the Reagan administration's negotiations with Noriega, see Kevin Buckley, *Panama: The Whole Story* (New York: Simon and Schuster, 1991), 102–45.

18. Philip Roessler argues that the threat of a coup has led some African leaders to abandon power-sharing agreements. Roessler, "Enemy Within," 308–11.

19. The Polish Workers' Party had a "negligible" membership at the end of the war, but with Moscow's help, came to dominate Polish politics after the 1947 election. Norman Davies, *God's Playground: A History of Poland, 1795 to the Present, Volume II* (New York: Columbia University Press, 2005), 548–49, 568–70.

20. On domestic political threats motivating resistance to foreign pressure see, for example, Benjamin A. Valentino, *Final Solutions: Mass Killing and Genocide in the Twentieth Century* (Ithaca, N.Y.: Cornell University Press, 2004), chap. 3; Steven R. David, *Choosing Sides: Alignment and Realignment in the Third World* (Baltimore: Johns Hopkins University Press, 1991); H. E. Goemans, *War and Punishment: The Causes of War Termination and the First World War* (Princeton, N.J.: Princeton University Press, 2000); and Chiozza and Goemans, *Leaders and International Conflict*.

21. Goemans, *War and Punishment*, 20–21, 37.

22. Robert Johnson, *The Afghan Way of War: How and Why They Fight* (New York: Oxford University Press, 2011), 101; Brian Robson, *The Road to Kabul: The Second Afghan War 1878–1881* (London: Arms and Armour, 1986), 45–46.

23. As I note later, concessions and inducements can entail costs similar to coercion. To simplify the discussion, I focus on coercion costs because strong states, due to their military advantage, often adopt coercive methods when dealing with weaker states.

24. Paul, *Asymmetric Conflicts*, 25–28; James J. Wirtz, "The Balance of Power Paradox," in *Balance of Power: Theory and Practice in the 21st Century*, ed. James J. Wirtz, T. V. Paul, and Michael Fortmann (Stanford, Calif.: Stanford University Press, 2004), chap. 5; and Daryl Press, *Calculating Credibility: How Leaders Assess Military Threats* (Ithaca, N.Y.: Cornell University Press, 2005), 20–28.

25. James D. Fearon, "Rationalist Explanations for War," *International Organization* 49 (1995): 379–414.

26. On costly signals, see James D. Fearon, "Domestic Political Audiences and the Escalation of International Disputes," *American Political Science Review* 88 (1994): 577–92; James D. Fearon, "Signaling Foreign Policy Interests: Tying Hands Versus Sinking Costs," *Journal of Conflict Resolution* 41 (1997): 68–90; Branislav L. Slantchev, "Military Coercion in Interstate Crises," *American Political Science Review* 99 (2005): 533–47.

27. Branislav L. Slantchev, *Military Threats: The Costs of Coercion and the Price of Peace* (Cambridge: Cambridge University Press, 2011), 75, 84–95.

28. I bracket discussion of the effectiveness of these measures to focus on how the overall costs of coercion could cause a foreign power to abandon it altogether. On the relative effectiveness of coercive bargaining strategies, see Karl Mueller, "Strategies of Coercion: Denial, Punishment, and the Future of Air Power," *Security Studies* 7 (1998): 182–228; Robert A. Pape, *Bombing to Win: Air Power and Coercion in War* (Ithaca, N.Y.: Cornell University Press, 1996); and Robert A. Pape Jr., "Coercion and Military Strategy: Why Denial Works and Punishment Doesn't," *Journal of Strategic Studies* 15 (1992): 423–75.

29. Daniel Byman and Matthew C. Waxman, *The Dynamics of Coercion: American Foreign Policy and the Limits of Military Might* (Cambridge: Cambridge University Press, 2002), 50–82; Daniel R. Lake, "The Limits of Coercive Airpower: NATO's 'Victory' in Kosovo Revisited," *International Security* 34 (2009): 83–112.

30. According to Ivan Arreguin-Toft, strong states that use brutal methods, such as scorched-earth tactics, against weaker adversaries using the same tactics are more likely to win due to their greater military capabilities. Ivan Arreguin-Toft, "How the Weak Win Wars: A Theory of Asymmetric Conflict," *International Security* 26 (2001): 93–128.

31. Fearon, "Domestic Political Audiences," 579; Fearon, "Signaling Foreign Policy Interests," 70–71.

32. Even settling for the status quo involves costs, as the foreign power may be forced to accept conditions that endanger its security or anger its public.

33. Nicholas Khoo, *Collateral Damage: Sino-Soviet Rivalry and the Termination of the Sino-Vietnamese Alliance* (New York: Columbia University Press, 2011), 124.

34. Not all signals impose up-front costs. Verbal threats can carry political costs that are incurred only if the leader later backs down. However, if the leader's domestic public opposes force, then verbal threats of force could also entail political costs up front.

35. Thomas Donnelly, Margaret Roth, and Caleb Baker, *Operation Just Cause: The Storming of Panama* (New York: Lexington Books, 1991), 48.

36. Kathleen H. Hicks and Lisa Sawyer Samp, eds., *Recalibrating U.S. Strategy Toward Russia: A New Time for Choosing* (Washington, D.C.: Center for Strategic and International Studies, 2017), 28.

37. I prove this point formally in Appendix 2.

38. Goemans argues that leaders may prolong war to avoid paying the domestic political costs of a defeat. Goemans, *War and Punishment*, 36–51. Paul notes that weaker states may hold out in a war of attrition, believing that their stronger adversary will not use the full extent of its military capabilities due to the political and military costs of doing so. Paul, *Asymmetric Conflicts*, 25.

39. Kathryn Weathersby, "'Should We Fear This?' Stalin and the Danger of War with America," (working paper #39, Cold War International History Project Working Paper Series, Woodrow Wilson International Center for Scholars, Washington, D.C., 2002), 9–12, https://www.wilsoncenter.org/sites/default/files/ACFAEF.pdf

40. Peter Liberman, *Does Conquest Pay? The Exploitation of Occupied Industrial Societies* (Princeton, N.J.: Princeton University Press, 1996), 92–93. The author notes that while this passive-resistance campaign lasted, France and Belgium earned nothing from the occupation; however, when the passive resistance campaign later collapsed, the occupiers began to turn a profit.

41. Samantha Power, *"A Problem from Hell": America and the Age of Genocide* (New York: Basic Books, 2002), 368–69.

42. Karen Dawisha, *The Kremlin and the Prague Spring* (Berkeley: University of California Press, 1984), 327–29; Jaromír Navrátil, *The Prague Spring 1968: A National Security Archive Document Reader* (New York: Central European University Press, 2006), 395.

43. Roughly thirty-five hundred Brazilians and fifteen hundred Uruguayans fought alongside Urquiza's troops. John Lynch, *Argentine Caudillo* (Wilmington, Del.: Rowman and Littlefield Publishers, 2001), 143, 156.

44. Liberman, *Does Conquest Pay?*, 144–45.

45. Giacomo Chiozza and H. E. Goemans, *Leaders and International Conflict* (Cambridge: Cambridge University Press, 2011), chap. 5.

46. Daniel G. Acheson-Brown, "The Tanzanian Invasion of Uganda," *International Third World Studies Journal and Review* 12 (2001): 4.

47. Acheson-Brown, 8; Tony Avirgan and Martha Honey, *War in Uganda: The Legacy of Idi Amin* (London: Zed Press, 1982), 233.

48. Stephen J. Morris, *Why Vietnam Invaded Cambodia: Political Culture and the Causes of War* (Stanford, Calif.: Stanford University Press, 1999), 111; Thu-Huong Nguyen-Vo, *Khmer-Viet Relations and the Third Indochina Conflict* (Jefferson, N.C: McFarland, 1992), 128; and Khoo, *Collateral Damage*, 124.

49. Acheson-Brown, "Tanzanian Invasion of Uganda," 8.

50. Operation Valuable, later named Project BGFIEND, ended in debacle; many of the Albanian operatives were killed almost as soon as they entered the country. Sarah-Jane Corke, *US Covert Operations and Cold War Strategy* (New York: Routledge, 2007), 98–100.

51. Andrew Roadnight, *United States Policy Towards Indonesia in the Truman and Eisenhower Years* (New York: Palgrave, 2002), 141–63.

52. Mark J. Gasiorowski, "The 1953 Coup d'Etat in Iran," *International Journal of Middle East Studies* 19 (1987): 263, 271–72, 274.

53. Robert C. Grogin, *Natural Enemies: The United States and the Soviet Union in the Cold War, 1917–1991* (Lanham, Md.: Lexington Books, 2001), 133–34.

54. Stephen Kinzer, *Overthrow: America's Century of Regime Change from Hawaii to Iraq* (New York: Times Books/Henry Holt, 2006), 69–70.

55. Peter Kornbluh, *The Pinochet File: A Declassified Dossier on Atrocity and Accountability* (New York: New Press, 2004), chaps. 2, 3.

56. I prove this point formally in Appendix 2.

57. Eytan Gilboa, "The Panama Invasion Revisited," *Political Science Quarterly* 110 (1995): 548, 552–54.

58. James Addison Baker and Thomas M. DeFrank, *The Politics of Diplomacy* (New York: G.P. Putnam's Sons, 1995), 189.

59. Buckley, *Panama*, 225.

60. Artemy Kalinovsky, "Decision-Making and the Soviet War in Afghanistan: From Intervention to Withdrawal," *Journal of Cold War Studies* 11 (2009): 50.

61. Michael C. Reed, "Gabon: A Neo-Colonial Enclave of Enduring French Interest," *Journal of Modern African Studies* 25 (1987): 297.

62. Don Oberdorfer and Robert Carlin, *The Two Koreas: A Contemporary History*, 3rd ed. (New York: Basic Books, 2013), 395–403.

63. Nicholas C. Pano, *The People's Republic of Albania* (Baltimore: Johns Hopkins Press, 1968), 92.

64. Pano, 92.

65. China remained Albania's major trading partner until the US-China rapprochement. Although Hoxha initially followed China's example, he reversed course in 1973 after the end of the Cultural Revolution for fear of empowering his domestic opponents. As relations cooled with China, Hoxha renewed relations with Yugoslavia. Teresa Rakowska-Harmstone, ed., *Communism in Eastern Europe*, 2nd ed. (Bloomington: Indiana University Press, 1984), 220; Elez Biberaj, *Albania: A Socialist Maverick* (Boulder, Colo.: Westview Press, 1990), 26.

66. See, for example, Suzanne Werner, "Absolute and Limited War: The Possibility of Foreign-Imposed Regime Change," *International Interactions* 22 (1996); Elizabeth N. Saunders, *Leaders at War: How Presidents Shape Military Interventions* (Ithaca, N.Y.: Cornell University Press, 2011); Martha Finnemore, *The Purpose of Intervention: Changing Beliefs About the Use of Force* (Ithaca, N.Y.: Cornell University Press, 2003); John M. Owen IV, *The Clash of Ideas in World Politics: Transnational Networks, States, and Regime Change, 1510–2010* (Princeton, N.J.: Princeton University Press, 2010); Lindsey A. O'Rourke, "Secrecy and Security: U.S.-Orchestrated Regime Change During the Cold War" (PhD diss., University of Chicago, 2013); Kinzer, *Overthrow;* Jon W. Western, *Selling Intervention and War: The Presidency, the Media, and the American Public* (Baltimore: Johns Hopkins University Press, 2005); Frederic S. Pearson, Robert A. Baumann, and Jeffrey J. Pickering, "Military Intervention and Realpolitik," in *Reconstructing Realpolitik,* ed. Frank W. Wayman and Paul F. Diehl (Ann Arbor: University of Michigan Press, 1994), 205–25; Tony Smith, *America's Mission* (Princeton, N.J.: Princeton University Press, 1994); J. H. Leurdijk, *Armed Intervention in International Politics: A Historical and Comparative Analysis* (Nijmegen, The Netherlands: Wolf Legal Publishers, 2006); and Andrew M. Dorman and Thomas G. Otte, *Military Intervention: From Gunboat Diplomacy to Humanitarian Intervention* (Aldershot, UK: Dartmouth Publishing, 1995).

67. Robert Jervis, *Perception and Misperception in International Politics* (Princeton, N.J.: Princeton University Press, 1976), 143. Also see Leon Festinger, *A Theory of Cognitive Dissonance* (Stanford, Calif.: Stanford University Press, 1962), 7–10, 22; Ole R. Holsti, "Cognitive Dynamics and Images of the Enemy," *Journal of International Affairs* 21 (1967): 17.

68. Robert Jervis, "Hypotheses on Misperception," *World Politics* 20, no. 3 (1968): 455–56.

69. Jervis, *Perception and Misperception,* 388–89.

70. Deborah Welch Larson, *Anatomy of Mistrust: U.S.-Soviet Relations During the Cold War* (Ithaca, N.Y.: Cornell University Press, 2000), 23–24.

71. Weisiger argues that when states are attacked they are more likely to pursue regime change in war, because the attack convinces them that their adversary is an implacable enemy. Although Weisiger argues this mistrust is part of a commitment problem, his argument implies that the attack has a psychological effect, causing policymakers to attribute the adversary's behavior to intrinsic qualities rather than conditions. Alex Weisiger, *Logics of War: Explanations for Limited and Unlimited Conflicts* (Ithaca, N.Y.: Cornell University Press, 2013), 26–33.

72. Graham T. Allison, "Conceptual Models and the Cuban Missile Crisis," *American Political Science Review* 63, no. 3 (1969), 707–15. See also Graham Allison and Philip Zelikow, *Essence of Decision: Explaining the Cuban Missile Crisis,* 2nd ed. (New York: Longman, 1999), 255–300; Morton H. Halperin, Priscilla Clapp, and Arnold Kanter, *Bureaucratic Politics and Foreign Policy* (Washington, D.C.: Brookings Institution, 1974); James Wilson, *Bureaucracy: What Government Agencies Do and Why They Do It* (New York: Basic Books, 1991); and Jeffrey Pfeffer, *Power in Organizations* (Marshfield, Mass.: Pitman Publishing, 1981).

73. Scott D. Sagan and Kenneth N. Waltz, *The Spread of Nuclear Weapons: An Enduring Debate,* 3rd ed. (New York: Norton, 2012), chap. 2; Scott D. Sagan, *The Limits of Safety* (Princeton, N.J.: Princeton University Press, 1995), 271–73. On organization theory, see James G. March and Herbert A. Simon, *Organizations,* 2nd ed. (Cambridge, Mass.: Wiley-Blackwell,

1993), 51, 186; Charles Perrow, *Complex Organizations: A Critical Essay* (Brattleboro, Vt.: Echo Point Books and Media, 2014).

74. Jack L. Snyder, *Myths of Empire* (Ithaca, N.Y.: Cornell University Press, 1991), 1–2, 14–20.

75. Dan Reiter, *How Wars End* (Princeton, N.J.: Princeton University Press, 2009), 25–34. See also Weisiger, *Logics of War*, 26–33.

76. Bueno de Mesquita et al., *Logic of Political Survival*, 439–41.

77. Sechser observes that the challenger could compensate the target for the risk associated with compliance, but because the challenger's intentions are private, the two sides are likely to disagree on what constitutes adequate compensation. Todd S. Sechser, "Goliath's Curse: Coercive Threats and Asymmetric Power," *International Organization* 64, no. 4 (2010): 627–60.

78. Kenneth A. Schultz, "The Enforcement Problem in Coercive Bargaining," *International Organization* 64 (2010): 281–312.

79. Tanisha M. Fazal, *State Death: The Politics and Geography of Conquest, Occupation, and Annexation* (Princeton, N.J.: Princeton University Press, 2007), 37–42.

Chapter 2

1. On covert operations, see Lindsey A. O'Rourke, "Secrecy and Security: U.S.-Orchestrated Regime Change During the Cold War" (PhD diss., University of Chicago, 2013). On regime change following interstate war, see Dan Reiter, *How Wars End* (Princeton, N.J.: Princeton University Press, 2009); Alex Weisiger, *Logics of War: Explanations for Limited and Unlimited Conflicts* (Ithaca, N.Y.: Cornell University Press, 2013); and Bruce Bueno de Mesquita et al., *Logic of Political Survival* (Cambridge, Mass.: MIT Press, 2003), chap. 9.

2. See, for example, John M. Owen IV, *The Clash of Ideas in World Politics: Transnational Networks, States, and Regime Change, 1510–2010* (Princeton, N.J.: Princeton University Press, 2010), 274.

3. Bueno de Mesquita et al., *Logic of Political Survival*, 419–21.

4. Paul W. Schroeder, *The Transformation of European Politics, 1763–1848* (Oxford: Clarendon Press, 1994), 777–78; Priscilla Smith Robertson, *Revolutions of 1848: A Social History* (Princeton, N.J.: Princeton University Press, 1952), 356–59.

5. Bueno de Mesquita et al., *Logic of Political Survival*, 38–39.

6. Edward Luttwak, *Coup d'Etat: A Practical Handbook* (Cambridge, Mass.: Harvard University Press, 1979), 27.

7. Bueno de Mesquita et al. term this set of supporters the leader's "winning coalition." They argue that leaders with large coalitions are more prone to FIRC because they cannot buy off their internal rivals. It is, therefore, harder for them to accommodate foreign demands while competing with their internal rivals for power. In contrast, I argue that the nature of the foreign power's demands determines the type of leader targeted. A demand for elections, for example, is more difficult for a leader with a small coalition to accommodate, which puts these leaders at higher risk for FIRC. Although I bracket discussion of the determinants driving the foreign power's demands, my argument implies that both types of leaders are prone to FIRC. Bueno de Mesquita et al., *Logic of Political Survival*, 51–55, 439–41.

8. Kennedy later wavered because he was concerned the generals lacked a sufficient following to succeed. Yet, after signaling his initial support, he did little to dissuade the generals; and on the day of the coup, US personnel provided the plotters with $40,000 while the

American ambassador encouraged Diem to surrender. John Prado, "JFK and the Diem Coup," National Security Archive, Electronic Briefing Book No. 101, posted November 5, 2003 (accessed August 15, 2015), http://nsarchive.gwu.edu/NSAEBB/NSAEBB101/.

9. The assumption that leaders are primarily interested in maintaining power is common in the literature. See, for example, Ross A. Miller, "Domestic Structures and the Diversionary Use of Force," *American Journal of Political Science* 39 (1995): 763; Bueno de Mesquita et al., *Logic of Political Survival*, 8.

10. Abel Escribà-Folch and Joseph Wright, *Foreign Pressure and the Politics of Autocratic Survival* (Oxford: Oxford University Press, 2015), 78–80, chap 5.

11. Peter Kornbluh, "Chile and the United States: Declassified Documents Relating to the Military Coup, September 11, 1973," National Security Archive, Electronic Briefing Book No. 8, accessed August 15, 2015, http://nsarchive.gwu.edu/NSAEBB/NSAEBB8/nsaebb8.htm.

12. Jonathan Haslam, *The Nixon Administration and the Death of Allende's Chile* (London: Verso, 2005), 78.

13. Allende's own policies also led to his loss of support. See Haslam, *Nixon Administration*, chap. 5. On the US role in the coup, see Peter Kornbluh, *The Pinochet File: A Declassified Dossier on Atrocity and Accountability* (New York: New Press, 2004), chap. 2.

14. Karen Dawisha, *The Kremlin and the Prague Spring* (Berkeley: University of California Press, 1984), 327–29.

15. Jaromír Navrátil, *The Prague Spring 1968: A National Security Archive Document Reader* (New York: Central European University Press, 2006), 505, 509, 530.

16. Eytan Gilboa, "The Panama Invasion Revisited," *Political Science Quarterly* 110 (1995): 556, 558–59.

17. Risa A. Brooks, "Military Defection and the Arab Spring," *Oxford Research Encyclopedia of Politics*, published February 27, 2017 (accessed November 19, 2017), http://politics.ox fordre.com/view/10.1093/acrefore/9780190228637.001.0001/acrefore-9780190228637-e-26; Holger Albrecht, "Does Coup-Proofing Work? Political-Military Relations in Authoritarian Regimes amid the Arab Uprisings," *Mediterranean Politics* 20 (2015): 36–54; and Michael Makara, "Coup-Proofing, Military Defection, and the Arab Spring," *Democracy and Security* 9 (2013): 334–59.

18. Susan Hannah Allen, "The Determinants of Economic Success and Failure," *International Interactions* 31 (2005), 124; Risa A. Brooks, "Sanctions and Regime Type: What Works, and When?" *Security Studies* 11 (2002): 1–50; Jonathan Kirshner, "The Microfoundations of Economic Sanctions," *Security Studies* 6 (1997), 32–64; William H. Kaempfer, Anton D. Lowenberg, and William Mertens, "International Economic Sanctions Against a Dictator," *Economics and Politics* 16 (2004): 29–51; and Daniel W. Drezner, "Sanctions Sometimes Smart: Targeted Sanctions in Theory and Practice," *International Studies Review* 13 (2011): 100.

19. Jack Snyder and Leslie Vinjamuri, "Trials and Errors: Principle and Pragmatism in Strategies of International Justice," *International Security* 28 (2004): 14.

20. Philippe R. Girard, *Clinton in Haiti: The 1994 U.S. Invasion of Haiti* (New York: Palgrave Macmillan, 2004), 3–6. The Clinton administration also used inducements to secure the junta's cooperation. Raul Cédras, the leader of the junta, was offered amnesty and the equivalent of $1 million in nonmonetary benefits. Kenneth Freed, "U.S. Gives Cedras a Lucrative Deal to Get Out of Haiti," *Los Angeles Times*, October 14, 1994, http://articles.latimes .com/1994–10–14/news/mn-50281_1_white-house.

21. Girard, *Clinton in Haiti*, 135.

22. Colin M. Waugh, *Charles Taylor and Liberia: Ambition and Atrocity in Africa's Lone Star State* (London: Zed Books, 2011), 279.

23. Noriega claimed he preferred "being a pain in the rear" of the United States. Kevin Buckley, *Panama: The Whole Story* (New York: Simon and Schuster, 1991), 142–45.

24. Girard, *Clinton in Haiti*, 110–20.

25. Alex Dupuy, *The Prophet and Power: Jean-Bertrand Aristide, the International Community, and Haiti* (Lanham, Md.: Rowman and Littlefield Publishers, 2007), 168–72; Girard, *Clinton in Haiti*, xvi, 62.

26. Dupuy, *Prophet and Power*, 171–73.

27. Margaret MacMillan, *Paris 1919: Six Months that Changed the World* (New York: Random House, 2002), chap. 14.

28. France's reparations policy has been the subject of much debate. Long portrayed as vindictive, France's policy, revisionist historians argue, was aimed primarily at obtaining British and American cooperation in stabilizing Europe. France's failure to do so led to its occupation of the Ruhr. Walter A. McDougall, "Political Economy Versus National Sovereignty: French Structures for German Economic Integration after Versailles," *Journal of Modern History*, 51 (1979): 4–23; Marc Trachtenberg, *Reparation in World Politics: France and European Economic Diplomacy, 1916–1923* (New York: Columbia University Press, 1980).

29. Elspeth O'Riordan, "British Policy and the Ruhr Crisis 1922–24," *Diplomacy and Statecraft* 15 (2004): 226; and Sally Marks, "The Myths of Reparations," *Central European History* 11 (1978): 236.

30. The timing of Roosevelt's declaration was meant to reassure Soviet leader Joseph Stalin of the West's commitment to the war, but the belief that Germany could not be trusted to uphold a settlement was widely held at the time. Reiter, *How Wars End*, 113–14; Weisiger, *Logics of War*, 124.

31. Anne Armstrong, *Unconditional Surrender* (New Brunswick, N.J.: Rutgers University Press, 1961), 209–12; Peter Hoffmann, *The History of the German Resistance, 1933–1945* (Cambridge, Mass: MIT Press, 1977), 227.

32. Theodore S. Hamerow, *On the Road to the Wolf's Lair: German Resistance to Hitler* (Cambridge, Mass: Belknap Press of Harvard University Press, 1997), 40–41.

33. Makoto Iokibe, "American Policy Towards Japan's 'Unconditional Surrender,'" *Japanese Journal of American Studies* 1 (1981): 32; Bradley F. Smith and Elena Aga Rossi, *Operation Sunrise: The Secret Surrender* (New York: Basic Books, 1979), 6, 9–13. Both Winston Churchill and Joseph Stalin were more willing to talk to anti-Nazi Germans than Roosevelt. However, after the failed coup of July 20, 1944, Churchill adopted the US policy of nonrecognition. Stalin's encouragement of anti-Nazi Germans appears to have been aimed at merely weakening the Nazis rather than a sincere attempt to negotiate. Armstrong, *Unconditional Surrender*, 55–58.

34. One study concludes that coercive diplomacy succeeds roughly 32 percent of the time. Robert J. Art and Patrick M. Cronin, *The United States and Coercive Diplomacy* (Washington, D.C.: United States Institute of Peace Press, 2003), 405. One of the most comprehensive studies on the effectiveness of sanctions estimates a similar success rate of roughly 34 percent. Gary Clyde Hufbauer et al., *Economic Sanctions Reconsidered* (Washington, D.C.: Peterson Institute for International Economics, 2009), 93. Deterrence, a form of coercion, is

often viewed as more effective. See Paul Huth and Bruce Russett, "Deterrence Failure and Crisis Escalation," *International Studies Quarterly* 32 (1988): 29–46; James D. Fearon, "Signaling Versus the Balance of Power and Interests: An Empirical Test of a Crisis Bargaining Model," *Journal of Conflict Resolution* 38 (1994): 236–69; and James D. Fearon, "Selection Effects and Deterrence," *International Interactions* 28 (2002): 5–29. On coercion more generally, see Alexander L. George, William E. Simons, and David Kent Hall, *The Limits of Coercive Diplomacy*, 2nd ed. (Boulder, Colo.: Westview Press, 1994); Peter Viggo Jakobsen, "Pushing the Limits of Military Coercion Theory," *International Studies Perspectives* 12 (2011): 153–70; Korina Kagan, "The Failure of Great Powers to Coerce Small States in the Balkans, 1875–1877 and 1914," in *Strategic Coercion*, ed. Lawrence Freedman (Oxford: Oxford University Press, 1998); Robert A. Pape, "Why Economic Sanctions Do Not Work," *International Security* 22 (1997): 90–136; T. Clifton Morgan and Valerie L. Schwebach, "Fools Suffer Gladly: The Use of Economic Sanctions in International Crises," *International Studies Quarterly* 41 (1997): 27–50; and Daniel Byman and Matthew C. Waxman, *The Dynamics of Coercion: American Foreign Policy and the Limits of Military Might* (Cambridge: Cambridge University Press, 2002).

35. Stephen T. Hosmer, *The Conflict over Kosovo: Why Milosevic Decided to Settle When He Did* (Santa Monica, Calif.: Rand, 2001), 17–18, chap. 5.

36. Daniel G. Acheson-Brown, "The Tanzanian Invasion of Uganda," *International Third World Studies Journal and Review* 12 (2001): 7–9.

37. Stephen J. Morris, *Why Vietnam Invaded Cambodia: Political Culture and the Causes of War* (Stanford, Calif.: Stanford University Press, 1999), 98–100.

38. Stephen C. Pelletiere, *The Iran-Iraq War: Chaos in a Vacuum* (New York: Praeger, 1992), 35.

39. Carl H. Bock, *Prelude to Tragedy* (Philadelphia: University of Pennsylvania Press, 1966), 196, 343–45.

40. Bock, 196.

41. Daniel Dawson, *The Mexican Adventure* (London: G. Bell and Sons LTD, 1935), 57.

42. Michele Cunningham, *Mexico and the Foreign Policy of Napoleon III* (New York: Palgrave, 2001), 37.

43. Cunningham, 45.

44. Able to rally thousands of followers, the Buddhist movement became a powerful political force from 1964 to 1966. Robert J. Topmiller, *The Lotus Unleashed: The Buddhist Movement in South Vietnam, 1964–1966* (Lexington: University Press of Kentucky, 2002), 4–5; James McAllister, " 'Only Religions Count in Vietnam': Thich Tri Quang and the Vietnam War," *Modern Asian Studies* 41 (2007): 1–31.

45. Azam Ahmed and Matthew Rosenberg, "Karzai Arranged Secret Contacts with the Taliban," *New York Times*, February 3, 2014, http://www.nytimes.com/2014/02/04/world/asia/karzai-has-held-secret-contacts-with-the-taliban.html.

46. This may partly explain a recent finding that FIRC rarely improves relations with the target. Alexander B. Downes and Lindsey A. O'Rourke, "You Can't Always Get What You Want: Why Foreign-Imposed Regime Change Seldom Improves Interstate Relations," *International Security* 41 (2016): 43–89.

47. Although American policymakers disagreed on whether to accommodate or oppose the Buddhist movement, American Ambassador to Vietnam, Henry Cabot Lodge, had considerable influence and came to support the crackdown that ultimately led to the movement's defeat. McAllister, "Only Religions Count in Vietnam," 781.

48. Buckley, *Panama*, 258–59.

49. Major-General William Elphinstone, the British commander in chief in Kabul during the first war, for example, was elderly, ill, and widely seen as incompetent. William Dalrymple, *Return of a King: The Battle for Afghanistan, 1839–42* (New York: Vintage, 2014), xxi.

50. James M. Scott, *Deciding to Intervene: The Reagan Doctrine and American Foreign Policy* (Durham, N.C.: Duke University Press, 1996), 16.

51. Morris, *Why Vietnam Invaded Cambodia*, 216.

Chapter 3

1. J. H. Leurdijk, *Armed Intervention in International Politics: A Historical and Comparative Analysis* (Nijmegen, The Netherlands: Wolf Legal Publishers, 2006), 11. Studies that suggest a link between FIRC and domestic opposition in the target include Suzanne Werner, "Absolute and Limited War: The Possibility of Foreign-Imposed Regime Change," *International Interactions* 22 (1996): 67–88; Leurdijk, *Armed Intervention*; and John M. Owen, "The Foreign Imposition of Domestic Institutions," *International Organization* 56, no. 2 (Spring 2002): 375–409.

2. Werner, "Absolute and Limited War," 73.

3. Focusing solely on regime-change events can be useful for theory building, but non-events are needed to test theory. See, for example, Leurdijk, *Armed Intervention*; Owen, "The Foreign Imposition of Domestic Institutions."

4. These 133 cases include 112 cases that involve states listed in the Correlates of War dataset, as well as an additional 21 cases involving states not included in the Correlates of War dataset. Correlates of War Project, "State System Membership List, v2016," 2017, http://www.correlatesofwar.org/data-sets/state-system-membership.

5. The data sets I drew from include those found in Alexander Downes and Jonathan Monten, "Forced to Be Free: Why Foreign-Imposed Regime Change Rarely Leads to Democratization," *International Security* 37 (2013): 90–131; Werner, "Absolute and Limited War"; Leurdijk, *Armed Intervention*; Owen, "Foreign Imposition of Domestic Institutions"; Hein Goemans, Kristian Skrede Gleditsch, and Giacomo Chiozza, "Introducing Archigos: A Data Set of Political Leaders," *Journal of Peace Research* 46 (2009): 269–83; Patrick M. Regan, *Civil Wars and Foreign Powers: Interventions and Intrastate Conflict*, 2nd ed. (Ann Arbor, Mich.: University of Michigan Press, 2002); Andrew J. Enterline and J. Michael Greig, "Beacons of Hope? The Impact of Imposed Democracy on Regional Peace, Democracy, and Prosperity," *Journal of Politics* 67 (2005): 1075–98; Nigel Lo, Barry Hashimoto, and Dan Reiter, "Ensuring Peace: Foreign-Imposed Regime Change and Postwar Peace Duration, 1914–2001," *International Organization* 62 (2008): 717–36; Goran Peic and Dan Reiter, "Foreign Imposed Regime Change, State Power, and Civil War Onset, 1920–2004," *British Journal of Political Science* 41 (2011): 453–75; and Frederic S. Pearson, "Geographic Proximity and Foreign Military Intervention: 1948–67," *Journal of Conflict Resolution* 18 (1974): 432–60.

6. Paul W. Schroeder, *The Transformation of European Politics, 1763–1848* (Oxford: Clarendon Press, 1994); Peter N. Stearns and William L. Langer, *The Encyclopedia of World History*, 6th ed. (Boston: Houghton Mifflin, 2001); Alex P. Schmid and Ellen Berends, *Soviet Military Interventions Since 1945* (New Brunswick, N.J.: Transaction Books, 1985); and Michael Grow, *U.S. Presidents and Latin American Interventions: Pursuing Regime Change in the Cold War* (Lawrence: University Press of Kansas, 2008).

7. My definition follows closely that used by Downes and Monten and differs mainly with respect to my inclusion of attempted regime change. Downes and Monten, "Forced to Be Free," 111.

8. Examples of ad hoc attempts include the various alleged CIA plots to assassinate Cuba's Fidel Castro, such as the poisoning of his cigars with botulinum. More serious plans to overthrow Castro continued to be developed after the Bay of Pigs invasion, though they were not fully implemented and appear to have been abandoned after the Cuban missile crisis. Aiyaz Husain, "Covert Action and US Cold War Strategy in Cuba, 1961–62," *Cold War History* 5 (2005): 23–53.

9. For data on sanctions aimed at regime change, see Gary Clyde Hufbauer et al., *Economic Sanctions Reconsidered*, 3rd ed. (Washington, D.C.: Peterson Institute for International Economics, 2009), 67–69, 80.

10. Panayiotis J. Vatikiotis, *The History of Modern Egypt: From Muhammad Ali to Mubarak* (Baltimore: Johns Hopkins University Press, 1991), 253.

11. Data compiled using the Expected Utility Generation and Data Management Program (EUGene), version 3.204. D. Scott Bennett and Alan Stam, "EUGene: A Conceptual Manual," *International Interactions* 26, no. 2 (2000): 179–204.

12. I exclude North Korea's invasion of South Korea for the same reason.

13. Data were imported from EUGene, version 3.204. Bennett and Stam, "EUGene: A Conceptual Manual."

14. Douglas Lemke and William Reed, "The Relevance of Politically Relevant Dyads," *Journal of Conflict Resolution* 45 (2001): 126–44. Because minor powers seldom impose regime change on major powers, I also test Model 1 on politically relevant dyads in which only Side 1 can be a major power. The results are consistent with those reported here.

15. James P. Klein, Gary Goertz, and Paul F. Diehl, "The New Rivalry Data Set: Procedures and Patterns," *Journal of Peace Research* 43 (2006): 339. I use Klein, Goertz, and Diehl's data set here because it has a lower threshold for dispute severity and, therefore, identifies a larger number of interstate rivals than does William Thompson and David Dreyer's rivalry data set. This allows me to incorporate more FIRC events into the analysis. See also William R. Thompson and David Dreyer, *Handbook of International Rivalries, 1494–2010* (Washington D.C.: Congressional Quarterly Press, 2011).

16. Only 49 of the 148 FIRC events occur between rivals.

17. This population of cases includes 76 FIRC events.

18. Arthur S. Banks and Kenneth A. Wilson, Cross-National Time-Series Data Archive, (Jerusalem, Israel: Databanks International, 2015), http://www.databanksinternational.com.

19. James Honaker, Gary King, and Matthew Blackwell, "Amelia II: A Program for Missing Data," *Journal of Statistical Software* 45 (2009): 1–47.

20. The Minorities at Risk data set, for example, reports on the size of disadvantaged minority groups, but data are only available for the period 1990–99. Minorities at Risk Project, Minorities at Risk Dataset (College Park: Center for International Development and Conflict Management, University of Maryland, 2009), http://www.mar.umd.edu/. Data on ethnolinguistic and religious divisions, such as the Fractionalization data, also only cover more recent time periods. Alberto Alesina et al., "Fractionalization," *Journal of Economic Growth* 8 (2003): 155–94.

21. H. E. Goemans, *War and Punishment: The Causes of War Termination and the First World War* (Princeton, N.J.: Princeton University Press, 2000). See also Scott Gates et al.,

"Institutional Inconsistency and Political Instability: Polity Duration, 1800–2000," *American Journal of Political Science* 50 (2006): 893–908.

22. Abel Escribà-Folch and Joseph Wright, *Foreign Pressure and the Politics of Autocratic Survival* (Oxford: Oxford University Press, 2015), 127–41.

23. On the effects of time on leader tenure, see Giacomo Chiozza and H. E. Goemans, "International Conflict and the Tenure of Leaders: Is War Still Ex Post Inefficient?," *American Journal of Political Science* 48 (2004): 607; Joseph Wright, "To Invest or Insure? How Authoritarian Time Horizons Impact Foreign Aid Effectiveness," *Comparative Political Studies* 41 (2008): 971–1000; and Bruce Bueno de Mesquita and Randolph M. Siverson, "War and the Survival of Political Leaders: A Comparative Study of Regime Types and Political Accountability," *American Political Science Review* 89 (1995): 251–84. On the "liability of newness," see Arthur L. Stinchcombe, "Social Structure and Organizations," in *Handbook of Organizations*, ed. James March (Chicago: Rand McNally, 1965), 148; John Gerring et al., "Democracy and Economic Growth: A Historical Perspective," *World Politics* 57 (2005): 323–64.

24. Gerring et al., "Democracy and Economic Growth"; Philip Keefer, "Clientelism, Credibility, and the Policy Choices of Young Democracies," *American Journal of Political Science* 51 (2007): 804–21.

25. The authors show that regimes transitioning to democracy *and* to autocracy are more prone to interstate conflict as a result. Edward D. Mansfield and Jack L. Snyder, *Electing to Fight: Why Emerging Democracies Go to War* (Cambridge, Mass.: MIT Press, 2005), 72, 146–47, 156–58. See also William R. Thompson and Richard Tucker, "A Tale of Two Democratic Peace Critiques," *Journal of Conflict Resolution* 41 (1997): 428–54; Erich Weede et al., "Democratization and the Danger of War," *International Security* 20 (1996): 5–38; and Michael D. Ward and Kristian S. Gleditsch, "Democratizing for Peace," *The American Political Science Review* 92 (1998): 51–61.

26. Kurt Dassel and Eric Reinhardt, "Domestic Strife and the Initiation of Violence at Home and Abroad," *American Journal of Political Science* 43 (1999): 56–85; Lars-Erik Cederman, Simon Hug, and Lutz F. Krebs, "Democratization and Civil War: Empirical Evidence," *Journal of Peace Research* 47 (2010): 377–94.

27. Goemans, Gleditsch, and Chiozza, "Introducing Archigos."

28. Goemans, Gleditsch, and Chiozza, "Introducing Archigos," 7.

29. For a similar approach, see Thompson and Tucker, "A Tale of Two Democratic Peace Critiques"; Ward and Gleditsch, "Democratizing for Peace." On the Polity IV data, see Monty G. Marshall, Ted Robert Gurr, and Keith Jaggers, "Polity IV Project: Political Regime Characteristics and Transitions, 1800–2016, (unpublished manuscript, Center for Systemic Peace, 2017), http://www.systemicpeace.org/inscr/p4manualv2016.pdf. Polity IV dataset version 2016, available at http://www.systemicpeace.org/inscrdata.html.

30. Marshall, Gurr, and Jaggers, "Polity IV Project," 8.

31. Marshall, Gurr, and Jaggers explain: "For example, Country X has a POLITY score of -7 in 1957, followed by three years of -88 [a missing value] and, finally, a score of $+5$ in 1961. The change ($+12$) would be prorated over the intervening three years at a rate of per year, so that the converted scores would be as follows: 1957 -7; 1958 -4; 1959 -1; 1960 $+2$; and 1961 $+5$." Marshall, Gurr, and Jaggers, "Polity IV Project," 17.

32. See, for example, Guillermo A. O'Donnell, *Bureaucratic Authoritarianism: Argentina, 1966–1973, in Comparative Perspective* (Berkeley: University of California Press, 1988); Guillermo A. O'Donnell et al., *Transitions from Authoritarian Rule: Comparative Perspectives* (Baltimore: Johns Hopkins University Press, 1986); Juan J. Linz and Alfred C. Stepan, eds., *The*

Breakdown of Democratic Regimes (Baltimore: Johns Hopkins University Press, 1978); Gordon Richards, "Stabilization Crises and the Breakdown of Military Authoritarianism in Latin America," *Comparative Political Studies* 18 (1986): 449–85; and David Collier, ed., *The New Authoritarianism in Latin America* (Princeton, N.J.: Princeton University Press, 1979).

33. Maddison Project Database, version 2013. J. Bolt and J. L. van Zanden, "The Maddison Project: Collaborative Research on Historical National Accounts," *Economic History Review*, 67, no. 3 (2014): 627–51, working paper, https://www.rug.nl/ggdc/historicaldevelopment/maddison/releases/maddison-project-database-2013

34. National Material Capabilities data set, version 4.0. David J. Singer, Stuart Bremer, and John Stuckey, "Capability Distribution, Uncertainty, and Major Power War, 1820–1965," in *Peace, War, and Numbers*, ed. Bruce Russett (Beverly Hills, Calif.: Sage, 1972), 19–48; David J. Singer, "Reconstructing the Correlates of War Dataset on Material Capabilities of States, 1816–1985," *International Interactions*, 14 (1987): 115–32.

35. Bennett and Stam, "EUGene"; Gary L. Fitzpatrick and Marilyn J. Modlin, *Direct-Line Distances* (Metuchen, N.J.: Scarecrow Press, 1986).

36. Correlates of War Formal Interstate Alliance v4.1 data. Douglas Gibler, *International Military Alliances, 1648–2008* (Washington, D.C.: CQ Press, 2009).

37. Nathaniel Beck, Jonathan N. Katz, and Richard Tucker, "Taking Time Seriously: Time-Series–Cross-Section Analysis with a Binary Dependent Variable," *American Journal of Political Science* 42 (1998): 1260–88.

38. Charles S. Gochman and Zeev Maoz, "Militarized Interstate Disputes, 1816–1976: Procedures, Patterns, and Insights," *Journal of Conflict Resolution* 28 (1984): 585–616.

39. These variables could also be compatible with a credible-commitment explanation. Each side distrusts the other because each expects the other to resort to arms, as in the past.

40. Werner, "Absolute and Limited War," 71.

41. Michael W. Doyle, "Liberalism and World Politics," *American Political Science Review* 80 (1986): 1161–62.

42. Werner, "Absolute and Limited War," 74–75.

43. Ted Robert Gurr, Polity II: Political Structures and Regime Change, 1800–1986 (Ann Arbor, Mich.: Inter-university Consortium for Political and Social Research [distributor], 1990), https://doi.org/10.3886/ICPSR09263.v1. Werner uses the following Polity II variables: XRREG, which refers to executive recruitment; XRCOMP, which refers to executive competitiveness; and XROPEN, which refers to executive openness. The Euclidean distance is calculated as follows: difference between Side 1's and Side 2's political authority structures $=$ $[(XRREG(S1) - XRREG(S2))^2 + (XRCOMP(S1) - XRCOMP(S2))^2 + (XROPEN(S1) - XROPEN(S2))^2]^{0.5}$ Werner, "Absolute and Limited War," 85.

44. This variable (AUTH_DIFF_L) correlates with the Polity 2 interaction variable (POL1xPOL2_L) in the model ($\varrho = -.61, p < .000$). To examine whether the difference in authority structure mediates the effect of the Polity interaction variable, I test the model both with and without the authority structure variable. The results remain the same.

45. Banks and Wilson's cross-polity survey provides data on military and military-civilian governments. The latter are civilian governments controlled by the military. Unlike the data on political instability in the cross-polity survey, this variable (MILITARY) does not have a large number of missing observations. Banks and Wilson, Cross-National Time-Series Data Archive. This variable is only marginally correlated with the Polity score for Side 1 ($\varrho = -.22$)

46. Trade data were imported from EUGene. Katherine Barbieri, Omar Keshk, and Brian Pollins, "Trading Data: Evaluating Our Assumptions and Coding Rules," *Conflict Management and Peace Science* 26 (2009): 471–91; Katherine Barbieri and Omar Keshk, *Correlates of War Project Trade Data Set Codebook*, version 3.0, 2012, http://www.correlatesofwar.org/data-sets/bilateral-trade.

47. The trade variables are highly correlated (ϱ = .8270) with one another. I also test their effects separately. The results are consistent with those reported here.

48. Bruce Bueno de Mesquita, *The Logic of Political Survival* (Cambridge, Mass.: MIT Press, 2003), 51–55.

49. Bueno de Mesquita et al. also create an S score, which measures the size of the selectorate, the group of people eligible to select the leader. The authors incorporate the S score because, in corrupt regimes, the selectorate may be large, but the winning coalition size is small. Because the size of the winning coalition should determine whether states pursue regime change, I use only the W score.

50. The W scores are highly correlated with the Polity 2 scores (ϱ = .8762, p < .000) from the Polity IV dataset. A bivariate regression of Side 1's Polity 2 score on its W score returns an R-squared of .65. The variance inflation factor is also high for the W scores when included in the model with the Polity 2 scores, suggesting the W scores are redundant. For this reason, I test the W scores without the Polity 2 scores in the model and report the results here. Results when both are simultaneously tested remain similar.

51. Kenneth A. Schultz, "The Enforcement Problem in Coercive Bargaining," *International Organization* 64 (2010): 281–312.

52. This variable (CONTIGUITY) is correlated with distance (ϱ = −.7381). I also run the model with each indicator separately. Contiguity is significant without distance in the model but not when distance is included, which suggests distance is more important.

53. Tanisha M. Fazal, *State Death: The Politics and Geography of Conquest, Occupation, and Annexation* (Princeton, N.J.: Princeton University Press, 2007).

54. Fazal, *State Death*, 1–2.

55. I use Thompson and Dreyer's data set for the RIVAL_L variable rather than the data from Klein, Goertz, and Diehl, which I use to identify rivalry dyads. The RIVAL_L variable is meant to capture cases in which Side 1 imposes regime change on Side 2 to preempt a rival from doing so. Thompson and Dreyer's data are appropriate for this variable because they rely on elite perceptions of rivalry and, therefore, can better identify cases in which both states regard one another as a peer competitor. Klein, Goertz, and Diehl's data, in contrast, use a broader definition, and so include dyads of asymmetric military power, such as the United States and the Dominican Republic, that do not necessarily view one another as rivals. This is helpful for identifying disputatious dyads but not necessarily peer competitors. Thompson and Dreyer, *Handbook of International Rivalries*; Klein, Goertz, and Diehl, "New Rivalry Data Set."

56. James D. Fearon, "Domestic Political Audiences and the Escalation of International Disputes," *American Political Science Review* 88 (1994): 577–92.

57. Variables containing an "L" at the end of their name have been lagged.

58. Results discussed in this chapter but not reported in the tables are available in the online appendix, which can be accessed at http://www.uvm.edu/~mmwillar/.

59. I also use a Wald test to examine whether the variables measuring domestic opposition (POLCHG5_L, IRREG10_L, IRREG10_L, and ECONCHG5_L) are different from zero.

The p-value associated with each chi-squared is .0000, indicating that these variables do improve model fit.

60. David W. Hosmer Jr., Stanley Lemeshow, and Rodney X. Sturdivant, *Applied Logistic Regression*, 3rd ed. (Hoboken, N.J.: Wiley, 2013), 158–60. See also Scott Menard, *Applied Logistic Regression Analysis*, 2nd ed. (Thousand Oaks, Calif: Sage, 2001), 23.

61. J. Scott Long and Jeremy Freese, *Regression Models for Categorical Dependent Variables Using Stata*, 2nd ed. (College Station, Tex.: Stata Press, 2006), 84.

62. William Shawcross, *The Quality of Mercy: Cambodia, Holocaust and Modern Conscience* (New York: Simon and Schuster, 1985), 115–16, 124.

63. Stephen J. Morris, *Why Vietnam Invaded Cambodia: Political Culture and the Causes of War* (Stanford, Calif.: Stanford University Press, 1999), 107.

64. Haiti's Jean-Claude Duvalier (1986), Leslie Manigat (1988), Henri Namphy (1988), and Jean Bertrand Aristide (1991) were all removed from power by the Haitian military. Prosper Avril left power after popular protest in 1990. Goemans, Gleditsch, and Chiozza, "Introducing Archigos."

65. The unit of measurement for determining GDP used by Maddison is 1990 international dollars. Maddison Project Database, version 2013. Bolt and van Zanden, "The Maddison Project."

66. Predicted probabilities were calculated using the Clarify software. The covariates are held at the values for each country in the year in which regime change was initiated. Gary King, Michael Tomz, and Jason Wittenberg, "Making the Most of Statistical Analyses: Improving Interpretation and Presentation," *American Journal of Political Science* 44 (April 2000): 341–55; Michael Tomz, Jason Wittenberg, and Gary King, "CLARIFY: Software for Interpreting and Presenting Statistical Results," *Journal of Statistical Software* 8 (2003): 1–29, http://j.mp/2oSx5Pc.

67. I use Model 1 to calculate the effect of this variable.

68. As I will show, the (Ln)MILCAP_L variable is also significant when tested on regional dyads and imputed data.

69. I test the target's relative military capability independently in the model because the scholarly consensus holds that asymmetric military power correlates with FIRC independent of other effects. However, I also test this variable when interacted with the proxies for domestic opposition. It remains insignificant, which suggests that military vulnerability may not be as important as domestic vulnerability when it comes to FIRC.

70. Multiple imputation rests on the assumption that the data are missing at random and can be predicted from the observed data. Gary King et al., "Analyzing Incomplete Political Science Data: An Alternative Algorithm for Multiple Imputation," *American Political Science Review* 95 (2001): 46–69.

71. Matthew Blackwell et al., "CEM: Coarsened Exact Matching in Stata," *The Stata Journal* 9 (2009): 524–46. On the benefits of matching over other possible controls for bias, such as Heckman selection models, see Beth A. Simmons and Daniel J. Hopkins, "The Constraining Power of International Treaties: Theory and Methods," *American Political Science Review* 99 (2005): 623–31.

72. Owen, "Foreign Imposition of Domestic Institutions," 379–80.

73. Downes and Monten, "Forced to Be Free," 111.

74. Werner, "Absolute and Limited War" 73.

75. Lo, Hashimoto, and Reiter, "Ensuring Peace," 725.

76. For politically relevant dyads, Werner's data have twenty-eight FIRC events and Lo et al.'s data have twenty-four FIRC events.

77. When using politically relevant dyads, Owen's data include 102 FIRC events and Downes and Monten's data include 98 events. Owen, "Foreign Imposition of Domestic Institutions"; Downes and Monten, "Forced to Be Free."

78. After removing duplicate cases coded with different years, there are 217 FIRC events.

Chapter 4

1. Eisenhower authorized the operation during a meeting of the National Security Council. Nick Cullather, *Secret History: The CIA's Classified Account of Its Operations in Guatemala, 1952–1954* (Stanford, Calif.: Stanford University Press, 1999), 129.

2. David A. de Lima to Department of State, December 8, 1950, Decimal File 724.00(W)/12–850, Box 3309, Department of State (DOS) Central Files, Record Group (RG) 59, National Archives and Records Administration (NARA), College Park, Md. See also, James Dunkerley, *Rebellion in the Veins: Political Struggle in Bolivia, 1952–82* (London: Verso, 1984), 15–16. On the size of the Bolivian aid program, see Cole Blasier, *The Hovering Giant* (Pittsburgh, Pa.: University of Pittsburgh Press, 1976), 144; Kevin Young, "Purging the Forces of Darkness: The United States, Monetary Stabilization, and the Containment of the Bolivian Revolution," *Diplomatic History* 37 (2013): 513; and Laurence Whitehead, *The United States and Bolivia: A Case of Neo-colonialism* (London: Haslemere, 1969), 22.

3. James Siekmeier, for example, credits the Bolivian ambassador in Washington with cultivating a network of influential supporters who helped him gain access to officials in the Eisenhower administration. James F. Siekmeier, *The Bolivian Revolution and the United States, 1952 to the Present* (University Park: Pennsylvania State University Press, 2011), 66–67.

4. Siekmeier, 53; Blasier, *Hovering Giant*, 134.

5. Cullather, *Secret History*; Susan Holly, ed., *Foreign Relations of the United States, 1952–1954, Guatemala* (Washington, D.C.: United States Government Printing Office, 2003).

6. The State Department reports come from Record Group (RG) 59, National Archives and Records Administration (NARA), College Park, Md.; hereafter cited as RG 59, NARA. N. Stephen Kane and William F. Sanford Jr., eds., *Foreign Relations of the United States, 1952–1954, The American Republics, Volume IV* (Washington, D.C.: United States Government Printing Office, 1983).

7. Richard H. Immerman, *The CIA in Guatemala* (Austin: University of Texas Press, 1982), 52, 63.

8. Immerman, 28.

9. Jim Handy, " 'The Most Precious Fruit of the Revolution': The Guatemalan Agrarian Reform, 1952–54," *Hispanic American Historical Review* 68 (1988): 685.

10. Piero Gleijeses, "The Agrarian Reform of Jacobo Arbenz," *Journal of Latin American Studies* 21 (1989): 461.

11. Handy, "Most Precious Fruit," 685.

12. Kane and Sanford, *Foreign Relations, 1952–1954, American Republics*, Document 422.

13. Piero Gleijeses, *Shattered Hope: The Guatemalan Revolution and the United States, 1944–1954* (Princeton, N.J.: Princeton University Press, 1991), 143.

14. Holly, *Foreign Relations, 1952–1954, Guatemala*, Document 6.

15. Holly, Document 35, pp. 70–78.

16. The exception was Costa Rica, whose president, José Figueres, considered Árbenz a communist and supported his removal. Gleijeses, *Shattered Hope*, 239.

17. Kane and Sanford, *Foreign Relations, 1952–1954, American Republics*, Document 424. See also, Cullather, *Secret History*, 24–27.

18. Holly, *Foreign Relations, 1952–1954, Guatemala*, Document 51.

19. Immerman, *CIA in Guatemala*, 8.

20. Cullather, *Secret History*, 26.

21. Handy, "Most Precious Fruit," 680.

22. Cullather, *Secret History*, 51–52; Gleijeses, *Shattered Hope*, 248–49.

23. Árbenz was directly involved in foiling Arana's coup plot as part of a group sent by Arévalo to arrest Arana. The circumstances surrounding Arana's death remain unclear. Some witnesses claim Arana and his group were fired upon, while others report that members of Arana's group fired first. Gleijeses, *Shattered Hope*, 64–67.

24. Jim Handy, *Revolution in the Countryside: Rural Conflict and Agrarian Reform in Guatemala, 1944–1954* (Chapel Hill: University of North Carolina Press, 1994), 185–86.

25. Gleijeses, *Shattered Hope*, 202.

26. Gleijeses, 175.

27. Gleijeses, 200–202.

28. Immerman, *CIA in Guatemala*, 26.

29. Handy, *Revolution in the Countryside*, 27.

30. Immerman, *CIA in Guatemala*, 26.

31. Gleijeses, *Shattered Hope*, 12.

32. Gleijeses, 193.

33. As the embassy's deputy chief, Bill Krieg stated in an interview many years later, "The revolutionary parties were groups of bums of the first order; lazy, ambitious, they wanted money, were hangers-on. Those who could work, had a sense of direction, ideas, knew where they wanted to go, were Fortuny and his PGT friends; they were very honest, very committed. This was the tragedy: the only people who were committed to hard work were those who were, by definition, our worst enemies." Gleijeses, 193.

34. Gleijeses, 145–47.

35. Gleijeses, 126. See quote from Richard C. Patterson Jr. to United Fruit in Immerman, *CIA in Guatemala*, 106.

36. Gleijeses, *Shattered Hope*, 144.

37. He also believed that a capitalist stage was a necessary first step in the development of a communist system. Gleijeses, 145–48. See also Handy, *Revolution in the Countryside*, 36–39.

38. Holly, *Foreign Relations, 1952–1954, Guatemala*, Document 27.

39. Kenneth Lehman, "Revolutions and Attributions: Making Sense of Eisenhower Administration Policies in Bolivia and Guatemala," *Diplomatic History* 21, no. 2 (1997): 195.

40. Gleijeses, *Shattered Hope*, 227.

41. Holly, *Foreign Relations, 1952–1954, Guatemala*, Document 6, p. 8.

42. Gleijeses, *Shattered Hope*, 264–65.

43. Holly, *Foreign Relations, 1952–1954, Guatemala*, Document 6, p. 8.

44. Gleijeses, *Shattered Hope*, 322.

45. Venezuela, a potential alternative supplier of oil, was ruled by a staunch US ally, while Mexico, which might have been more sympathetic to Guatemala, was also susceptible to US pressure. Gleijeses, 322, 376.

46. Bryce Wood, *The Dismantling of the Good Neighbor Policy* (Austin: University of Texas Press, 1985), 160.

47. John C. Hill Jr., second secretary of the US embassy in Guatemala, cited in Gleijeses, *Shattered Hope*, 247n86.

48. There are reports that the United States attempted to bribe Árbenz but to no avail. John Stephen Zunes, "Decisions on Intervention: United States Response to Third World Nationalist Governments, 1950–1957" (PhD diss., Cornell University, 1990), 115.

49. This hostility was in part a result of the efforts of United Fruit. I address United Fruit's role in my discussion of alternative arguments at the end of this section. Gleijeses, *Shattered Hope*, 130–31.

50. Gleijeses, 177.

51. Gleijeses, 229; Cullather, *Secret History*, 27–31.

52. Holly, *Foreign Relations, 1952–1954, Guatemala*, Document 51.

53. Holly, Document 12.

54. Holly, Document 23, Document 113. See also Cullather, *Secret History*, 27–31; Gleijeses, *Shattered Hope*, 229–31. State Department officials later gave the impression that this support was never given. Kane and Sanford, *Foreign Relations, 1952–1954, American Republics*, Document 413.

55. Cullather, *Secret History*, 29.

56. Cullather, 30–31.

57. The moment of silence for Stalin was not Árbenz's doing. Rather, members of the Guatemalan congress routinely engaged in anti-US rhetoric and symbolic gestures to win popular support. Handy, *Revolution in the Countryside*, 177; Gleijeses, *Shattered Hope*, 180.

58. Holly, *Foreign Relations, 1952–1954, Guatemala*, Document 47.

59. Kane and Sanford, *Foreign Relations, 1952–1954, American Republics*, Document 3.

60. Cullather, *Secret History*, 36.

61. Kane and Sanford, *Foreign Relations, 1952–1954, American Republics*, Document 422.

62. Kane and Sanford, Document 422.

63. Gleijeses, *Shattered Hope*, 247.

64. Holly, *Foreign Relations, 1952–1954, Guatemala*, Document 51.

65. Holly, Document 51, pp. 104, 107, 108. See also, Gleijeses, *Shattered Hope*, 246.

66. Cullather, *Secret History*, 38; Kane and Sanford, *Foreign Relations, 1952–1954, American Republics*, Document 424.

67. Quoted in Gleijeses, *Shattered Hope*, 254.

68. Quoted in Gleijeses, 254.

69. Gleijeses, 256, 270.

70. Gleijeses, 247.

71. Gleijeses, 258–59.

72. Gleijeses, 283.

73. Gleijeses, 266.

74. Cullather, *Secret History*, 58. Dulles recognized that the "major interest of the Latin American countries at this conference would concern economics whereas the chief United States interest is to secure a strong anti-Communist resolution against Guatemala." Immerman, *CIA in Guatemala*, 145.

75. Gleijeses, *Shattered Hope*, 300. See also, Immerman, *CIA in Guatemala*, 154.

76. Cullather, *Secret History*, 74.

77. Gleijeses, *Shattered Hope*, 317. The plan worked. At the end of May, with Castillo Armas's invasion just weeks away, the government initiated a violent crackdown that left seventy-five dead.

78. Gleijeses, 295.

79. Gleijeses, 320, 326–27, 333. The only battle the rebels won was that in which the army had eagerly surrendered.

80. Holly, *Foreign Relations, 1952–1954, Guatemala*, Document 214. Emphasis in the original.

81. Cited in Gleijeses, *Shattered Hope*, 324.

82. Gleijeses, 328, 338.

83. Gleijeses, 330.

84. Gleijeses, 331.

85. Eisenhower even took the risk of revealing US involvement by resupplying the rebels with two planes lost during the "invasion." Given that the United States had already dodged accusations by the Guatemalan government, Eisenhower probably assumed he could dodge a new round of allegations. Gleijeses, 339.

86. Gleijeses, 337.

87. Cullather, *Secret History*, 173.

88. Cullather, 110.

89. John M. Broder, "Clinton Offers His Apologies to Guatemala," *New York Times*, March, 11, 1999, http://www.nytimes.com/1999/03/11/world/clinton-offers-his-apologies-to -guatemala.html.

90. The psychological biases of US policymakers is a persistent theme in historical accounts of the Guatemala case. See, for example, Gleijeses, *Shattered Hope*, 116, 126, 131; Immerman, *CIA in Guatemala*, 16. Lehman explains the psychological bias that caused US policymakers to attribute Árbenz's behavior to "dispositional unfriendliness," and the MNR's behavior to situational constraints. Similar to the argument made here, Lehman points to Árbenz's domestic position to explain his resistance to US pressure. Lehman, "Revolutions and Attributions," 196.

91. Stephen Kinzer, *The Brothers: John Foster Dulles, Allen Dulles, and Their Secret World War* (New York: Times Books, 2013), 320–21.

92. Jim Newton, *Eisenhower: The White House Years* (New York: Doubleday, 2011), 128–29; Stephen G. Rabe, *Eisenhower and Latin America* (Chapel Hill: University of North Carolina Press, 1988), 55, 58.

93. Gleijeses, *Shattered Hope*, 366–67.

94. Gliejeses writes that although Árbenz was not a PGT member, he was more than a "fellow traveler," as the State Department believed. Lehman notes that Gliejeses's conclusions regarding the depths of Árbenz's commitment to communism rest mainly on interviews with Árbenz's wife and the PGT's Fortuny, who may have been inclined to see his views in harmony with their own. Yet, whether he was a communist or not, Árbenz's political program was squarely focused on the development of a capitalist economy. Lehman, "Revolutions and Attributions," 190n13; Gleijeses, *Shattered Hope*, 147.

95. Holly, *Foreign Relations, 1952–1954, Guatemala*, Document 27; Gleijeses, *Shattered Hope*, 145–48.

96. Indeed, this report contends that Árbenz's ties to communists were mostly opportunistic: "President Árbenz is still convinced that he is 'using' Communism to further his own ends and in no sense is he dictated to by Communist elements although he often plays into their hands in his attempts to use them and the Party line of world Communism." Holly, *Foreign Relations, 1952–1954, Guatemala*, Document 27.

97. Stephen Kinzer, *Overthrow: America's Century of Regime Change from Hawaii to Iraq* (New York: Times Books/Henry Holt, 2006), 130. Kinzer also notes that John Moors Cabot, the assistant secretary of state for inter-American affairs, was a large shareholder in United Fruit, while his brother, Thomas Dudley Cabot, who was director of international security affairs at the State Department, was United Fruit's former president. The head of the National Security Council, General Robert Cutler, was also a former chairman of the board; and the president of the IBRD, John J. McCloy, was also a former board member. These ties likely biased members of the Eisenhower administration against Árbenz. But, as I argue, even without these ties, the Eisenhower administration would have overthrown Árbenz because coercing him was deemed more costly than overthrowing him.

98. Stephen C. Schlesinger and Stephen Kinzer, *Bitter Fruit: The Untold Story of the American Coup in Guatemala* (Garden City, N.Y: Anchor Books, 1984).

99. Stephen G. Rabe, "The U.S. Intervention in Guatemala," *Diplomatic History* 28 (2004): 787; Stephen M. Streeter, "Interpreting the 1954 U.S. Intervention in Guatemala," *History Teacher* 34 (2000): 61–74; Handy, *Revolution in the Countryside*, 173.

100. Gleijeses, *Shattered Hope*, 363.

101. Gleijeses, 85.

102. Cullather, *Secret History*, 19; Gleijeses, *Shattered Hope*, 361.

103. Cullather notes that the CIA reports show officials were concerned that feudal agriculture would become an issue around which communists could attract greater support. Cullather, *Secret History*, 26. See also Holly, *Foreign Relations, 1952–1954, Guatemala*, Document 35; Immerman, *CIA in Guatemala*, 63; G. E. Britnell, "Problems of Economic and Social Change in Guatemala," *Canadian Journal of Economics and Political Science* 17, no. 4 (November 1951): 477; and Gleijeses, *Shattered Hope*, 86–87.

104. Immerman, *CIA in Guatemala*, 51.

105. Blasier, *Hovering Giant*, 48–49.

106. Blasier, 48–49; Dunkerley, *Rebellion in the Veins*, 31.

107. Zunes, "Decisions on Intervention," 132.

108. Department of State, Miller to Maleady, April 21, 1952, Entry 1130, Box 2, Bolivia Folder, DOS Central Files, RG 59, NARA.

109. Zunes, "Decisions on Intervention," 147.

110. Kane and Sanford, *Foreign Relations, 1952–1954, American Republics*, Document 136.

111. Sparks to Department of State, April 11, 1953, Decimal File 724.00/4–1153, DOS Central Files, RG 59, NARA.

112. Kane and Sanford, *Foreign Relations, 1952–1954, American Republics*, Document 140. See also, Zunes, "Decisions on Intervention," 152.

113. De Lima to Department of State, December 8, 1950, RG 59, NARA. Lechín had once called for a "dictatorship of the proletariat." AmEmbassy La Paz to Department of State, p. 2, December 8, 1950, Decimal File 724.00(W)/12–850, DOS Central Files, RG 59, NARA.

See also AmEmbassy La Paz to Department of State, April 18, 1952, Decimal File 724.00(W)/ 4–1852, DOS Central Files, RG 59, NARA, and AmEmbassy La Paz, For Maleady from Miller, April 21, 1952, Central Decimal File 1950–54, Box 3309, RG 59, NARA, and Sparks to Miller, p. 3, April 23, 1952, Central Decimal File 1950–54, Box 3309, RG 59, NARA.

114. Kane and Sanford, *Foreign Relations, 1952–1954, American Republics,* Document 136.

115. MNR centrists were particularly wary of the PIR, which had joined with extreme right-wing factions to overthrow the previous MNR-supported government. James M. Malloy, "Revolutionary Politics," in *Beyond the Revolution: Bolivia Since 1952,* ed. James M. Malloy and Richard S. Thorn (Pittsburgh, Pa.: University of Pittsburgh Press, 1971), 123.

116. Siekmeier, *Bolivian Revolution,* 44. US officials were also concerned about the COB's right wing, which had close ties to Argentina's Juan Perón. Shortly after the MNR came to power, embassy officials reported that "many fear Bolivia may become 'another province' of Argentina." AmEmbassy La Paz to Department of State, April 18, 1952, RG 59, NARA.

117. Kane and Sanford, *Foreign Relations, 1952–1954, American Republics,* Document 136.

118. Kane and Sanford, Document 136.

119. Kane and Sanford, Document 136, p. 492.

120. Malloy, "Revolutionary Politics," 123.

121. Dunkerley, *Rebellion in the Veins,* 13; Malloy, "Revolutionary Politics," 122–23.

122. Rabe, *Eisenhower and Latin America,* 79.

123. A memo sent to Secretary of State Acheson from the Assistant Secretary of State for Economic Affairs, Willard L. Thorp, and the Assistant Secretary of State for Inter-American Affairs, Edward G. Miller, Jr., notes that, "We have, in effect, used our stockpile to force that price down, since in the absence of the stockpile we could never have held out as long as we did." Kane and Sanford, *Foreign Relations, 1952–1954, American Republics,* Document 134.

124. Rabe, *Eisenhower and Latin America,* 79. See also, Kane and Sanford, *Foreign Relations, 1952–1954, American Republics,* Document 134.

125. Siekmeier, *Bolivian Revolution,* 69–70. Food imports accounted for one-quarter of the Bolivian diet. Blasier, *Hovering Giant,* 133.

126. Blasier, *Hovering Giant,* 87.

127. The embassy noted that these words were probably added at Paz Estenssoro's behest. AmEmbassy to Department of State, May 9, 1952, Decimal File 724.00/5–952, RG 59, NARA.

128. Cole Blasier, "The United States and the Revolution," in *Beyond the Revolution: Bolivia Since 1952,* ed. James M. Malloy and Richard S. Thorn (Pittsburgh, Pa.: University of Pittsburgh Press, 1971), 64.

129. Blasier, 70.

130. Dunkerley, *Rebellion in the Veins,* 64; Malloy, "Revolutionary Politics," 121.

131. Víctor Andrade, *My Missions for Revolutionary Bolivia, 1944–1962* (Pittsburgh, Pa.: University of Pittsburgh Press, 1976), 131, 155–56; Dunkerley, *Rebellion in the Veins,* 60.

132. Dunkerley, *Rebellion in the Veins,* 64.

133. Malloy, "Revolutionary Politics," 129.

134. Dunkerley, *Rebellion in the Veins,* 64.

135. Dunkerley, 65.

136. Zunes, "Decisions on Intervention," 193–94.

137. The Eisenhower administration was looking to avoid the domestic political costs of negotiating a contract for tin, which the United States did not need. Kane and Sanford, *Foreign Relations, 1952–1954, American Republics*, Document 152.

138. Kane and Sanford, Document 156.

139. Zunes, "Decisions on Intervention," 217.

140. AmEmbassy to Department of State, July 31, 1953, Decimal File 724.00(W)/7–3153, RG 59, NARA.

141. AmEmbassy La Paz, "Bolivian Highlights 1953," January 13, 1954, Decimal File 724.00/1–1354, RG 59, NARA.

142. AmEmbassy to Department of State, "Opposition Views on the MNR Government," October 23, 1953, Decimal File 724.00/10–2353, RG 59, NARA.

143. Andrade, *My Missions*, 175.

144. Kane and Sanford, *Foreign Relations, 1952–1954, American Republics*, Document 147.

145. Between March and July 1953 the tin price dropped by one-third. Zunes, "Decisions on Intervention," 160.

146. Officials in the State Department's Office of South American Affairs began developing plans for aid in late April 1953. See, for example, William P. Hudson to Mr. Atwood, "A Suggested Approach to the Bolivian Problem," April 30, 1953, Decimal File 824.00/4–3053, RG 59, NARA.

147. Emphasis added. Kane and Sanford, *Foreign Relations, 1952–1954, American Republics*, 527n2. The embassy noted that while the party's leaders had been making "anti-imperialistic—and presumably anti-United States—public statements" since at least July 1952, they appeared to stop doing so after May 1, 1953. AmEmbassy to Department of State, "Opposition Views," October 23, 1953, RG 59, NARA.

148. Rowell to Department of State, February 6, 1953, Decimal File 724.00(W)/2–653, Box 3309, RG 59, NARA. See also, Zunes, "Decisions on Intervention," 186.

149. Zunes, "Decisions on Intervention," 228. The United States denied any role in the Iranian coup, but Paz Estenssoro's warning that the United States would not succeed in orchestrating a similar coup in Bolivia demonstrates just how widely CIA involvement in the Iranian coup was suspected.

150. Hudson to Atwood, "A Suggested Approach," April 30, 1953, RG 59, NARA. For discussion of the program, see Kane and Sanford, *Foreign Relations, 1952–1954, American Republics*, Document 157.

151. Kane and Sanford, Documents 155, 156, pp. 526–28.

152. Andrade, *My Missions*, 172–73; Lehman, "Revolutions and Attributions," 203.

153. Blasier, *Hovering Giant*, 73.

154. Kane and Sanford, *Foreign Relations, 1952–1954, American Republics*, Document 158.

155. Dunkerley, *Rebellion in the Veins*, 85.

156. Lehman, "Revolutions and Attributions," 193. As Lehman notes, in the era of McCarthyism, this was a surprisingly subtle distinction.

157. Lehman, 186.

158. Kane and Sanford, *Foreign Relations, 1952–1954, American Republics*, Document 151.

159. AmEmbassy to Department of State, "Opposition Views," October 23, 1953, RG 59, NARA. Kane and Sanford, *Foreign Relations, 1952–1954, American Republics*, Document 153.

160. Kane and Sanford, *Foreign Relations, 1952–1954, American Republics*, Document 153.

161. Young, "Purging the Forces of Darkness," 534.

162. Kane and Sanford, *Foreign Relations, 1952–1954, American Republics*, Document 158.

163. Lehman, "Revolutions and Attributions," 186.

164. AmEmbassy La Paz, "Bolivian Highlights," January 13, 1954, RG 59, NARA.

165. AmEmbassy La Paz, "Bolivian Highlights," January 13, 1954, RG 59, NARA.

166. AmEmbassy La Paz, "Bolivian Highlights," January 13, 1954, RG 59, NARA.

167. "Current Status of Bolivian Problems," December 29, 1958, Entry 1132, Box 1, RG 59, NARA. See also, La Paz to Secretary of State, November 22, 1960, Decimal File 724.5-MSP/11–2260, RG 59, NARA.

168. Siekmeier, *Bolivian Revolution*, 98.

169. Malloy, "Revolutionary Politics," 139.

170. Dunkerley, *Rebellion in the Veins*, 112; Siekmeier, *Bolivian Revolution*, 51; Zunes, "Decisions on Intervention," 168; and Whitehead, *United States and Bolivia*, 11.

171. Dunkerley, *Rebellion in the Veins*, 87.

172. Cited in Zunes, "Decisions on Intervention," 171.

173. "Memorandum of Conversation Regarding Military Assistance to the Bolivian Armed Forces," April 1, 1960, Decimal File 724.5-MSP/4–160, RG 59, NARA.

174. Blasier, "United States and the Revolution," 93.

175. Siekmeier, *Bolivian Revolution*, 99–100.

176. Although the Bolivian station CIA chief, Lt. Col. Edward Fox, is believed to have played a role in the coup, there is no evidence of an explicit US policy aimed at the MNR's overthrow. Whitehead, *United States and Bolivia*, 24–25; Dunkerley, *Rebellion in the Veins*, 108, 113, 114–15.

177. Siekmeier, *Bolivian Revolution*, 99.

178. Lehman, "Revolutions and Attributions," 189.

179. For the MNR's allusions to working with the Eastern bloc, see, for example, Rowell to Department of State, November 14, 1952, Decimal File 724.00(W)/11–1452, Box 3309, RG 59, NARA, and Rowell to Department of State, May 8, 1953, Decimal File 724.00(W)/5–853, Box 3309, RG 59, NARA. Even after receiving aid, the Bolivians continued to allude to the possibility of establishing contacts with the Soviet Union; see Memorandum of Conversation, December 29, 1958, Entry 1162, Box 1, RG 59, NARA. An October 1952 CIA report noted, "[Árbenz] definitely would prefer US domination to Soviet domination. The best example of this is the fact that throughout his bluffing of US interests he has never used the potential weapon of proposed trade treaties with Soviet bloc countries, although it seems logical to assume that such commercial overtures have been made to him." Holly, *Foreign Relations, 1952–1954, Guatemala*, Document 27.

180. Wood, *Dismantling*, 150–51.

181. Kane and Sanford, *Foreign Relations, 1952–1954, American Republics*, Document 147.

Chapter 5

1. L. W. Gluchowski, "Poland, 1956: Khrushchev, Gomułka, and the 'Polish October,'" *Cold War International History Project Bulletin* 5 (1995): 42.

2. Malin's notes are published in the following sources: Csaba Békés, Malcolm Byrne, and János M. Rainer, eds., *The 1956 Hungarian Revolution: A History in Documents* (New York: Central European University Press, 2002); Gluchowski, "Poland, 1956"; and Mark Kramer, "Special Feature: New Evidence on Soviet Decision-Making and the 1956 Polish and Hungarian Crises," *Cold War International History Project Bulletin* 8/9 (1996): 358–84.

3. Tony Kemp-Welch, "Khrushchev's 'Secret Speech' and Polish Politics," *Europe-Asia Studies* 48 (1996): 18; Pawel Machcewicz, *Rebellious Satellite*, trans. Maya Latynski (Washington, D.C.: Woodrow Wilson Center Press, 2009), 15.

4. Konrad Syrop, *Spring in October: The Story of the Polish Revolution, 1956* (New York: Praeger, 1957), 22.

5. Leszek W. Gluchowski, "The Soviet-Polish Confrontation of October 1956: The Situation in the Polish Internal Security Corps" (working paper no. 17, Cold War International History Project Working Paper Series, Woodrow Wilson International Center for Scholars, Washington, D.C., April 1997), 16–23. See also Michael Checinski, *Poland, Communism, Nationalism, Anti-Semitism* (New York: Karz-Cohl Publishers, 1982), 94, 99–100.

6. Syrop, *Spring in October*, 4.

7. Syrop, 7. Stalin explained his determination to dominate Poland at the 1944 Yalta Conference, noting that the orientation of the future Polish regime was "a question of security of the [Soviet] state not only because we are on Poland's frontier but also because throughout history Poland has always been a corridor for attack on Russia." Bryton Barron, ed., *Foreign Relations of the United States, Diplomatic Papers, Conferences at Malta and Yalta, 1945* (Washington, D.C.: United States Government Printing Office, 1955), p. 679, https://history.state.gov/historicaldocuments/frus1945Malta/pg_679.

8. These included the nationalization of industry, expropriation of large tracts of privately owned land, and rapid collectivization of agriculture. Although Bierut had been slower to impose political controls than other Warsaw Pact leaders, by the early 1950s, these were firmly in place too. It was during this period that Gomułka, who had opposed Stalin on rapid collectivization and the break with Yugoslavia, was jailed, and in 1953 the popular Catholic dissident, Cardinal Wyszyński, was also detained. Machcewicz, *Rebellious Satellite*, 12–13.

9. On the public's knowledge, see Kemp-Welch, "Khrushchev's 'Secret Speech,'" 196–202.

10. Machcewicz, *Rebellious Satellite*, 49–51.

11. In March 1956, Khrushchev had traveled to Warsaw to attend Bierut's funeral but stayed on to influence decisions on the party's new leadership. Kemp-Welch, "Khrushchev's 'Secret Speech,'" 6.

12. Kemp-Welch, 16.

13. Machcewicz, *Rebellious Satellite*, 139.

14. Jakub Karpinski, *Countdown, the Polish Upheavals of 1956, 1968, 1970, 1976, 1980* (New York: Karz-Cohl, 1982), 49–53; Machcewicz, *Rebellious Satellite*, 113–15.

15. Machcewicz, *Rebellious Satellite*, 117.

16. Mark Kramer, "Hungary and Poland, 1956: Khrushchev's CPSU CC Presidium Meeting on East European Crises, October 24, 1956," *Cold War International History Project Bulletin* 5 (1995): 50.

17. Krzysztof Persak, "The Polish-Soviet Confrontation in 1956 and the Attempted Soviet Military Intervention in Poland," *Europe-Asia Studies* 58 (2006): 1291.

18. Gluchowski, "Poland, 1956," 49.

19. Nikita S. Khrushchev, *Khrushchev Remembers: The Last Testament*, trans. and ed. Strobe Talbott (Boston: Little, Brown, 1974), 199–200.

20. Syrop, *Spring in October*, 95. The composition of the delegation was telling. Although led by the more moderate Khrushchev and Anastas Mikoyan, the delegation also included the Stalinist Vyacheslav Molotov and Lazar Kaganovich, as well as the commander in chief of the Warsaw Pact forces, Marshal Ivan Konev. There were also unconfirmed reports that the Soviet commander in chief, Marshal Georgy Zhukov, was part of the delegation, but there were also reports that Zhukov was in Moscow participating in talks with the Japanese. Persak, "Polish-Soviet Confrontation," 1290n11.

21. Gluchowski, "Poland, 1956," 40.

22. Gluchowski, 44.

23. Khrushchev, *Khrushchev Remembers: Last Testament* (1974), 199–200.

24. Gluchowski, "Poland, 1956," 42.

25. Machcewicz, *Rebellious Satellite*, 365.

26. Syrop, *Spring in October*, 22. Syrop notes that this does not explain why Gomułka was not secretly executed. Światło claimed Gomułka's popularity helped save him from execution and that Bierut lacked the "courage to deal with him." See also, L. W. Gluchowski, "The Defection of Jozef Swiatlo and the Search for Jewish Scapegoats in the Polish United Workers' Party, 1953–1954," *Intermarium* 3, no. 2 (1999): 12, http://www.columbia.edu/cu/ece/research/intermarium/vol3no2/gluchowski.pdf.

27. Syrop, *Spring in October*, 18.

28. Machcewicz, *Rebellious Satellite*, 39.

29. Machcewicz, 200.

30. Syrop, *Spring in October*, 24–25.

31. Gomułka was released by Bierut in December 1955, although his release was not made public until Ochab announced it in 1956. Kemp-Welch, "Khrushchev's 'Secret Speech,'" 15. The third Stalinist in command behind Bierut, Hilary Minc, would not be removed until early October; however, he was ill at this time and had less influence. Syrop, *Spring in October*, 84.

32. Machcewicz, *Rebellious Satellite*, 163; Syrop, *Spring in October*, 54, 76.

33. Initially, the Puławy faction, many of whom had participated in Gomułka's arrest, had feared Gomułka might seek vengeance. After Poznań, however, the faction came to accept Gomułka as the only communist leader with the popularity to save the party. Andrzej Werblan, "The Polish October of 1956—Legends and Reality," in *The Polish October 1956 in World Politics*, ed. Jan Rowiński (Warsaw: Polish Institute of International Affairs, 2007), 23.

34. Syrop, *Spring in October*, 65.

35. Persak, "Polish-Soviet Confrontation," 1286; Syrop, *Spring in October*, 63.

36. What precisely transpired in these backroom negotiations remains unclear; however, the political changes made over the next few months likely reflect what Gomułka demanded.

These changes included the appointment of General Wacław Komar, a Gomułka ally, as head of the Internal Security Corp on August 24. They also included Gomułka's appointment to a three-member committee that determined the candidate list for the next election. Syrop, *Spring in October*, 82.

37. Persak, "Polish-Soviet Confrontation," 1290.

38. Khrushchev, *Khrushchev Remembers: Last Testament* (1974), 203.

39. Nikita Sergeevich Khrushchev, *Khrushchev Remembers: The Glasnost Tapes*, trans. and ed. Jerrold L. Schecter with Vyacheslav V. Luchkov (Boston: Little, Brown, 1990), 115; Gluchowski, "Poland, 1956," 41.

40. Nikita S. Khrushchev, *Memoirs of Nikita Khrushchev*, ed. Sergei Khrushchev, vol. 3, *Statesman, 1953–1964* (University Park: Pennsylvania State University, 2004), 630–31.

41. Persak, "Polish-Soviet Confrontation," 1294.

42. For Gomułka's own account of the crisis, see the notes from his discussion with Zhou Enlai in Gluchowski, "Poland, 1956," 44.

43. Persak, "Polish-Soviet Confrontation," 1295.

44. Gluchowski, "Poland, 1956," 43.

45. Gluchowski, 40.

46. Gluchowski, "Soviet-Polish Confrontation," 46.

47. Gluchowski, "Poland, 1956," 43–44.

48. Gluchowski, 45. The Soviet forces would not return to their bases for another five days. Persak, "Polish-Soviet Confrontation," 1303.

49. Gomułka gave this account to Zhou Enlai in January 1957. Gluchowski, "Poland, 1956," 43–44.

50. Gluchowski, 45.

51. Khrushchev responded positively to Gomułka's speech, saying, "This speech by comrade Gomułka gives hope that Poland has now adopted a course that will eliminate the unpleasant state of affairs." Persak, "Polish-Soviet Confrontation," 1306.

52. Kramer, "Hungary and Poland, 1956," 51.

53. Gluchowski, "Soviet-Polish Confrontation," 68–70.

54. Gluchowski, 30; Werblan, "Polish October of 1956," 28–29.

55. It is unclear whether Khrushchev meant Rokossowski's position in the politburo or his status as defense minister.

56. Malin's minutes simply state: "Maneuvers. Prepare a document. Form a committee." As Kramer notes, the meaning of these points is not entirely clear, but "a committee" may refer to a "provisional revolutionary committee," or an alternative government. Rumors suggested that PUWP politburo member Franciszek Mazur, who was in the Soviet Union at the time, was the Kremlin's pick to replace Gomułka. Mark Kramer, "The 'Malin Notes' on the Crises in Hungary and Poland, 1956," *Cold War International History Project Bulletin* 8/9 (1996): 388–401; Persak, "Polish-Soviet Confrontation," 1301.

57. Gluchowski, "Poland, 1956," 45–46.

58. Werblan, "Polish October of 1956," 27.

59. Khrushchev, *Khrushchev Remembers: Last Testament* (1974), 203.

60. Kramer, "New Evidence," 361.

61. Gluchowski, "Soviet-Polish Confrontation," 41–42. On Khrushchev's belief that arms were distributed, see Kramer, "Malin Notes," 5. See also Khrushchev, *Memoirs*, 3:629.

62. Kramer, "Hungary and Poland, 1956," 54.

63. Persak, "Polish-Soviet Confrontation," 1298.

64. Persak, 1298.

65. Persak, 1304.

66. Gluchowski, "Poland, 1956," 54.

67. Gluchowski, "Soviet-Polish Confrontation," 81.

68. Sergeï Khrushchev, *Nikita Khrushchev and the Creation of a Superpower* (University Park: Pennsylvania State University Press, 2000), 185.

69. Charles Gati, *Failed Illusions* (Washington, D.C.: Woodrow Wilson Center Press, 2006), 56–57; Johanna Granville, "Imre Nagy, aka 'Volodya'—A Dent in the Martyr's Halo?," *Cold War International History Project Bulletin* 5 (1995): 34.

70. The decision to remove Nagy was also a reflection of Soviet internal politics. Khrushchev, who had by this time successfully assumed leadership, sought to overturn his predecessor's policies towards the satellites states. Kramer, "New Evidence," 362.

71. Although the Petöfi Circle had been created by Rákosi to control political debate, after Khrushchev denounced Stalin at the 20th Congress of the Communist Party, the Petöfi Circle became the center of opposition to Rákosi. Kramer, "New Evidence," 363–64; Johanna C. Granville, *The First Domino: International Decision Making During the Hungarian Crisis of 1956* (College Station: Texas A&M University Press, 2004), 39.

72. Gati, *Failed Illusions*, 132; Kramer, "New Evidence," 363.

73. Granville, *First Domino*, 50.

74. Békés, Byrne, and Rainer, *1956 Hungarian Revolution*, 145; Granville, *First Domino*, 34.

75. Granville, *First Domino*, 35.

76. Kramer, "New Evidence," 365.

77. Mark Kramer, "The Soviet Union and the 1956 Crises in Hungary and Poland: Reassessments and New Findings," *Journal of Contemporary History* 33 (1998): 182.

78. Kramer, "New Evidence," 366.

79. William Lomax, *Hungary 1956* (New York: St. Martin's Press, 1976), 113–14.

80. Granville, *First Domino*, 56.

81. Gati, *Failed Illusions*, 152.

82. Békés, Byrne, and Rainer, *1956 Hungarian Revolution*, 217–18.

83. Gerő retained his post as first secretary but was soon forced by the Soviets to resign in favor of János Kádár.

84. Granville, *First Domino*, 78; Victor Sebestyen, *Twelve Days: The Story of the 1956 Hungarian Revolution* (New York: Pantheon Books, 2006), 139.

85. Kramer, "New Evidence," 367.

86. Sebestyen, *Twelve Days*, 108, 114.

87. On October 28, Nagy announced to the Hungarian Political Committee: "There are two options: if we look upon this movement, backed up by such substantial forces, as a counterrevolution then we have no choice but to subdue it with tanks and artillery. This is a tragedy. . . . If we're not careful we will be subjected to an intervention. We should lean on and lead the huge national forces that are on the move." Cited in Granville, *First Domino*, 84.

88. Békés, Byrne, and Rainer, *1956 Hungarian Revolution*, 205; Granville, *First Domino*, 79.

89. Kramer, "New Evidence," 393.

90. Paul Lendvai, *One Day That Shook the Communist World: The 1956 Hungarian Uprising and Its Legacy* (Princeton, N.J.: Princeton University Press, 2008), 120.

91. Tibor Méray, *Thirteen Days That Shook the Kremlin* (London: Thames and Hudson, 1959), 187.

92. Gati, *Failed Illusions*, 152.

93. Granville, *First Domino*, 83. Soviet forces would attack, although half-heartedly. Upon learning that Soviet forces were on their way to launch a strike, Nagy phoned Khrushchev and threatened to resign. The Soviets ended up withdrawing a third of their force but then proceeded to attack until ultimately forced to withdraw. Sebestyen, *Twelve Days*, 174–75.

94. Radio Free Europe, which was owned and operated by the United States, reported that Nagy had called in Soviet forces. Gerő may have contributed to this rumor as well as. Imre Mező, a Nagy ally, had earlier informed Nagy that Gerő was waiting for an opportunity to attack him. Johanna C. Granville, "Imre Nagy, Reluctant Revolutionary," *Cold War International History Project Bulletin* 5 (1995): 27. Gerő, along with the Soviet ambassador, also pressured Nagy to sign the formal request for the first Soviet intervention, but Nagy refused. Gati, *Failed Illusions*, 151. Nagy later explained during his interrogation that someone else had ordered a curfew in his name. Granville, *First Domino*, 81.

95. Sebestyen, *Twelve Days*, 222.

96. Méray, *Thirteen Days*, 80.

97. In an interview many years later, Pongrátz recounted, "The whole revolution was against the communist system. But the 28 of October, we had a big meeting in the Korvin; many high officers and from the Government people involved. And I made a compromise: I said, 'All right, we accept Imre Nagy to be the Prime Minister until the elections. And if the Hungarian people will elect Imre Nagy, we accept him.' " Pongrátz also noted that he and his fighters, many of whom were only twelve to fourteen years old, expected US assistance. Gergely Pongrátz, interview, *The Cold War*, "Episode 7: After Stalin," CNN, aired March 29, 1998, https://www.cnn.com/2014/01/02/world/the-cold-war-landmark-documentary/index.html; transcript, "Interview with Gergely Pongracz—17/6/96," available on National Security Archive website, http://nsarchive.gwu.edu/coldwar/interviews/episode-7/pongracz2.html.

98. Sebestyen, *Twelve Days*, 225–26.

99. In one exchange on October 29 with revolutionaries who had come to demand free elections, Nagy snapped, "There must be an end. . . . It is intolerable that the authority of the government should be sapped by demands that are constantly changing." Sebestyen, 194.

100. Méray, *Thirteen Days*, 110–14; Békés, Byrne, and Rainer, *1956 Hungarian Revolution*, 205; Granville, *First Domino*, 83, 85.

101. Eisenhower offered $20 million in aid to Hungary. Méray, *Thirteen Days*, 115, 199. Once in office, the Eisenhower administration backed away from its policy of "rollback," aimed at overturning communist governments; nevertheless, its campaign rhetoric had encouraged many Hungarians to believe the United States would assist their cause. Granville, *First Domino*, 180.

102. Fearful of a potential nuclear confrontation over a country that mattered little to US security interests, the Eisenhower administration never seriously considered intervening militarily. The United States attempted to make its lack of interest in Hungary clear to the Soviets in an October 27 speech by Secretary of State John Foster Dulles, in which Dulles

declared, in reference to the Soviet satellites, that the United States does "not look upon these nations as potential military allies." Békés, Byrne, and Rainer, *1956 Hungarian Revolution*, xxxviii, 127, 209.

103. Békés, Byrne, and Rainer, 286–89.

104. Békés, Byrne, and Rainer, 468.

105. Granville, *First Domino*, 84.

106. Békés, Byrne, and Rainer, *1956 Hungarian Revolution*, 267.

107. Veljko Mićunović, *Moscow Diary*, trans. David Floyd (Garden City, N.Y.: Doubleday, 1980), 136. In later discussions concerning the postinvasion government, Khrushchev characterized Rákosi as "hardline" and Gerő as "hapless." He said the two had done "many stupid things." Kramer, "New Evidence," 398.

108. Zhihua Shen and Yafeng Xia, *Mao and the Sino-Soviet Partnership, 1945–1959: A New History* (Lanham, Md.: Lexington Books, 2015), 175.

109. Donald S. Zagoria, *Sino-Soviet Conflict, 1956–1961* (Princeton, N.J.: Princeton University Press, 2015), 40, 50.

110. Nagy had argued he could not sign the order because he was not premier at the time the decision was made. Although Hegedüs later signed the backdated order, when the Soviet ambassador read the request out loud at a meeting of the UN General Assembly, he omitted Hegedüs's name. Békés, Byrne, and Rainer, *1956 Hungarian Revolution*, 272. See also Kramer, "New Evidence," 366.

111. At the October 30th CPSU CC Presidium meeting, during which Khrushchev voiced support for a troop withdrawal and negotiations, Soviet foreign minister Dimitri Shepilov declared, "The course of events reveals the crisis in our relations with the countries of people's democracies. Anti-Soviet sentiments are widespread." And Soviet commander in chief Zhukov observed, "There is a lesson for us in the military-political sphere." Békés, Byrne, and Rainer, *1956 Hungarian Revolution*, 294, 297, 301; Shen and Xia, *Mao and the Sino-Soviet Partnership*, 172.

112. Péter Vámos, "Sino-Hungarian Relations and the 1956 Revolution" (working paper no. 54, Cold War International History Project Working Paper Series, Woodrow Wilson International Center for Scholars, Washington, D.C., November 2006), 26, https://www.wilsoncenter.org/sites/default/files/WP54_Final2.pdf. Indeed, this was the approach Mao later adopted during the Hundred Flowers campaign. Shen and Xia, *Mao and the Sino-Soviet Partnership*, 174.

113. Péter Vámos contends the Chinese did not encourage the Soviets to undertake an immediate invasion. Although years later (after the Sino-Soviet split) Beijing claimed it had urged the Soviets to act, the Soviets gave their own interpretation of events on November 5, 1960. This interpretation is consistent with the Malin notes, which suggest the Chinese urged the Kremlin to keep Soviet troops in Hungary but did not advocate an immediate invasion. Cited in Vámos, "Sino-Hungarian Relations," 16.

114. Khrushchev may have had reason to believe Mao's plan might work. Mikoyan and Suslov had previously reported on October 26 that Nagy would not oppose another Soviet military intervention. Granville, *First Domino*, 22.

115. Khrushchev, *Memoirs*, 3:650.

116. Békés, Byrne, and Rainer, *1956 Hungarian Revolution*, 292.

117. During their discussion, Liu Shaoqi contacted Mao by phone. Khrushchev said Mao was willing to approve either decision. He writes, "We ended our all-night session with the decision not to use force." Khrushchev, *Memoirs*, 3:650.

118. Khrushchev recounts, "When I climbed into bed that morning, I found I was still too preoccupied with the whole problem to rest. It was like a nail in my head and it kept me from being able to sleep." Nikita S. Khrushchev, *Khrushchev Remembers*, trans. and ed. Strobe Talbott (Boston: Little, Brown, 1970), 418.

119. See, for example, Kramer, "New Evidence," 369; Granville, *First Domino*, 72; Békés, Byrne, and Rainer, *1956 Hungarian Revolution*, 210; and Gati, *Failed Illusions*, 153.

120. Békés, Byrne, and Rainer note that the new developments in Budapest on October 30 "did not immediately change the view of the CPSU Presidium." Békés, Byrne, and Rainer, *1956 Hungarian Revolution*, 292.

121. Khrushchev, *Memoirs*, 3:650.

122. Békés, Byrne, and Rainer, *1956 Hungarian Revolution*, 292.

123. Békés, Byrne, and Rainer, 292.

124. All the presidium members present agreed, except for the first deputy premier, Maksim Saburov, who argued the decision would "vindicate NATO." When Mikoyan returned to Moscow on November 1, he also voiced his opposition. He too favored giving the Hungarian government more time. Kramer, "New Evidence," 393–94.

125. Méray, *Thirteen Days*, 199.

126. "On whose planes from Vienna did agents of capitalist countries and reactionary Hungarian emigres return to the country? Who was helping [the insurgents]? I'll say it bluntly: of course there was sponsorship and sympathy, and aid was provided." Khrushchev, *Memoirs*, 3:658.

127. In 1950, the US Congress authorized $100 million for the creation of military units composed of Eastern European émigrés to "support NATO." The plan for a Volunteer Freedom Corps was meant to attract defectors for the purposes of intelligence and propaganda aimed at detaching the satellite states from the Soviet Union. Soviet officials denounced the congressional bill. After witnessing the brutal Soviet crackdown in Hungary, Eisenhower abandoned the plan. Granville, *First Domino*, 182–87.

128. Mićunović, *Moscow Diary*, 134.

129. Khrushchev, *Memoirs*, 3:650–51.

130. Khrushchev, 3:650.

131. Kramer, "Soviet Union and the 1956 Crises," 194.

132. Sebestyen, *Twelve Days*, 218; Kramer, "Soviet Union and the 1956 Crises," 194.

133. Mićunović, *Moscow Diary*, 134. Italics in the original.

134. See, for example, Kramer, "New Evidence," 370; Gati, *Failed Illusions*, 153.

135. Khrushchev even held out the possibility that Nagy himself might later join the government. Kramer, "New Evidence," 393.

136. Khrushchev, *Memoirs*, 3:647.

137. The trio's names appear in Malin's notes from the CPSU CC Presidium meeting on October 31. It is unclear whether they were present or consulted during the meeting. Kramer, "New Evidence," 394.

138. Sebestyen, *Twelve Days*, 165.

139. Gati, *Failed Illusions*, 190.

140. Kramer, "New Evidence," 393.

141. Kádár was in fact both Rákosi's accomplice and victim. It was Kádár who had convinced his friend László Rajk to make a false confession, on the basis of which Rajk was executed. Rákosi later turned on Kádár. Granville, *First Domino*, 126–27.

142. Kramer, "New Evidence," 396.

143. Kramer, 396.

144. Kramer, 397.

145. Sebestyen, *Twelve Days*, 256; Lendvai, *One Day That Shook*, 142–43; Khrushchev, *Memoirs*, 3:670; Miklós Molnár, *Budapest 1956: A History of the Hungarian Revolution* (London: Allen and Unwin, 1971), 245.

146. Molnár, *Budapest 1956*, 245.

147. Khrushchev, *Memoirs*, 3:670.

148. Sebestyen, *Twelve Days*, 232. See also Béla Király, interview, *The Cold War*, "Episode 7: After Stalin," CNN, aired March 29, 1998; transcript, "Interview with Dr Bela Kiraly," available on the National Security Archive website, http://nsarchive.gwu.edu/coldwar/interviews/episode-7/kiraly2.html.

149. As Király explained, "The Hungarian government came to the conclusion that if it don't [sic] do anything, we are a member of the Warsaw Pact, an ally of the Soviet Union, the world . . . look it, alright [sic], that is a family quarrel, we don't interfere with Warsaw Pact internal affairs. But if we are independent, neutral country, probably the world would say, that we don't permit [sic]." Király, interview.

150. Sebestyen, *Twelve Days*, 232; Méray, *Thirteen Days*, 215.

151. Király, interview.

152. Molnár, *Budapest 1956*, 197–98.

153. Király, interview.

154. Király, interview.

155. Béla K. Király and Paul Jonas, *The Hungarian Revolution of 1956 in Retrospect* (Boulder, Colo.: Columbia University Press, 1978), 29–30.

156. Király and Jonas, 29–30.

157. Király interview.

158. Méray, *Thirteen Days*, 252.

159. Sebestyen notes that by this point Tito had also made a speech harshly critical of Nagy, causing Nagy to question how much longer the Yugoslav leader would continue sheltering him. Sebestyen, *Twelve Days*, 284. See also Méray, *Thirteen Days*, 251.

160. Granville, *First Domino*, 207.

161. Khrushchev used this term in a presidium discussion on November 3. Békés, Byrne, and Rainer, *1956 Hungarian Revolution*, 360.

162. Granville, *First Domino*, 23. Nagy was also appointed agricultural minister in the Moscow-organized Hungarian communist government after World War II. Granville, "Imre Nagy, aka 'Volodya,'" 34.

163. S. Khrushchev, *Nikita Khrushchev*, 185.

164. Békés, Byrne, and Rainer, *1956 Hungarian Revolution*, 307–8.

165. Kramer, "Malin Notes," 390.

166. See, for example, Kramer, "New Evidence," 369; Granville, *First Domino*, 72; Békés, Byrne, and Rainer, *1956 Hungarian Revolution*, 210; and Gati, *Failed Illusions*, 153. Fazal takes a similar view, writing that "the Poles received a 'green light' for reform," but Nagy pursued extensive change despite having been "given an explicitly limited set of conditions" for it to occur. Tanisha M. Fazal, *State Death: The Politics and Geography of Conquest, Occupation, and Annexation* (Princeton, N.J.: Princeton University Press, 2007), 191.

167. Jakub Zielinski, "Transitions from Authoritarian Rule and the Problem of Violence," *Journal of Conflict Resolution* 43 (1999): 213–28.

168. Heltai reports that the Soviet emissaries "made no commitment on Hungarian neutrality, implying that Hungary would in one form or another remain a member of the remodeled pact." Király and Paul Jonas, *The Hungarian Revolution of 1956 in Retrospect*, 53.

169. Karen Dawisha, *The Kremlin and the Prague Spring* (Berkeley: University of California Press, 1984), 140.

170. Dawisha, 149.

Chapter 6

1. "President Bush's 2003 State of the Union Address," *Washington Post*, January 28, 2003, http://www.washingtonpost.com/wp-srv/onpolitics/transcripts/bushtext_012803.html.

2. Robert Litwak, *Regime Change: U.S. Strategy Through the Prism of 9/11* (Washington, D.C.: Woodrow Wilson Center Press, 2007), 189; Ronald Bruce St. John, *Libya: From Colony to Revolution* (Oxford: Oneworld Publications, 2012), 201; and Bruce W. Jentleson and Christopher A. Whytock, "Who 'Won' Libya? The Force-Diplomacy Debate and Its Implications for Theory and Policy," *International Security* 30 (2005): 58.

3. Jentleson and Whytock, "Who 'Won' Libya?," 56; Brian L. Davis, *Qaddafi, Terrorism, and the Origins of the U.S. Attack on Libya* (New York: Praeger, 1990), 48.

4. Officials in the Bush administration argued that the invasion of Iraq would serve a humanitarian aim by liberating Iraqis from Saddam's rule, but many insider accounts stress either regional ambitions or security concerns as the primary motivations for war. See, for example, Douglas J. Feith, *War and Decision: Inside the Pentagon at the Dawn of the War on Terrorism* (New York: HarperCollins Publishers, 2008); Richard N. Haass, *War of Necessity, War of Choice: A Memoir of Two Iraq Wars* (New York: Simon and Schuster, 2010). Scholars also disagree as to whether the decision to pursue regime change in Libya was truly intended to solve the humanitarian crisis. See, for example, Alan J. Kuperman, "A Model Humanitarian Intervention? Reassessing NATO's Libya Campaign," *International Security* 38, no. 1 (2013): 105–36; Hugh Roberts, "Who Said Gaddafi Had to Go?," *London Review of Books*, November 17, 2011.

5. Although Qaddafi promulgated his own unique political philosophy, which was ostensibly a system of direct democracy, in practice the so-called Libyan Jamahiriya was similar to Saddam Hussein's Iraq—a one-party system dominated by an authoritarian leader who depended on a small coalition of supporters from his tribe, hometown, and extended family to maintain power. On personalist leaders, see Barbara Geddes, Joseph Wright, and Erica Frantz, "Autocratic Breakdown and Regime Transitions: A New Data Set," *Perspectives on Politics* 12, no. 2 (2014): 313–31.

6. Ethan Chorin, *Exit the Colonel: The Hidden History of the Libyan Revolution* (New York: PublicAffairs, 2012), chap. 6.

7. Jonathan B. Tucker, "The Rollback of Libya's Chemical Weapons Program," *Nonproliferation Review*, 16 (2009): 363, 366; Maalfrid Braut-Hegghammer, "Libya's Nuclear Turnaround," *Middle East Journal* 62 (2008): 69; and Jentleson and Whytock, "Who 'Won' Libya?," 57–58

8. In Iraq, the United States was in the process of withdrawing, which it completed in December 2011.

9. Until recently, these were housed at the Conflict Records Research Center at the National Defense University in Washington, D.C. Several have been published in Kevin M. Woods, David D. Palkki, and Mark Stout, eds., *The Saddam Tapes: The Inner Workings of a Tyrant's Regime, 1978–2001* (New York: Cambridge University Press, 2011).

10. Charles Duelfer, *Comprehensive Report of the Special Advisor to the Director of Central Intelligence on Iraq's WMD* [Duelfer Report], September 30, 2004, Washington, D.C.: Central Intelligence Agency, https://www.cia.gov/library/reports/general-reports-1/iraq_wmd_2004/

11. Duelfer, *Comprehensive Report*; Joyce Battle, ed., "Saddam Hussein Talks to the FBI," National Security Archive electronic briefing book no. 279, July 1, 2009, 6, http://www .gwu.edu/~nsarchiv/NSAEBB/NSAEBB279/index.htm.

12. These include, Hillary Rodham Clinton, *Hard Choices* (New York: Simon and Schuster, 2014); and Robert Michael Gates, *Duty: Memoirs of a Secretary at War* (New York: Knopf, 2014). Interviews are reported in Michael Hastings, "Inside Obama's War Room," *Rolling Stone*, October 13, 2011, http://www.rollingstone.com/politics/news/inside-obamas-war -room-20111013; Jo Becker and Scott Shane, "Hillary Clinton, 'Smart Power' and a Dictator's Fall," The Libya Gamble (article series), Part 1, *New York Times*, February 27, 2016, http:// www.nytimes.com/2016/02/28/us/politics/hillary-clinton-libya.html?_r=0; Jo Becker and Scott Shane, "In Their Own Words: The Libya Tragedy," The Libya Gamble (article series), *New York Times*, February 27, 2016, http://www.nytimes.com/interactive/2016/02/28/us/poli tics/libya-quotes.html; David E. Sanger, *Confront and Conceal: Obama's Secret Wars and Surprising Use of American Power* (New York: Crown Publishers, 2012); Joby Warrick, "Hillary's War: How Conviction Replaced Skepticism in Libya Intervention," *Washington Post*, October 28, 2011, https://www.washingtonpost.com/world/national-security/hillarys-war-how-con viction-replaced-skepticism-in-libya-intervention/2011/10/28/gIQAhGS 7WM_story.html.

13. "United Nations Resolution 686, Iraq-Kuwait (2 Mar)," United Nations, Security Council Resolutions—1991, http://www.un.org/Docs/scres/1991/scres91.htm.

14. Lawrence Freedman and Efraim Karsh, *The Gulf Conflict, 1990–1991: Diplomacy and War in the New World Order* (Princeton, N.J.: Princeton University Press, 1993), 416.

15. Freedman and Karsh, 421–25.

16. France was initially supportive of the more hardline approach advocated by the United States and United Kingdom but became increasingly critical of it. Sarah Graham-Brown, *Sanctioning Saddam: The Politics of Intervention in Iraq* (London: I.B. Tauris, 1999), 59.

17. Graham-Brown, 20. The UN secretary-general, Javier Perez de Cuellar, openly contested the US aim, arguing, "As Secretary-General, I cannot agree with measures that are aimed at overthrowing the government of a country which is a member of the United Nations. . . . If the objective of pursuing sanctions it to topple the Iraqi regime, then I do not agree. I cannot agree." Quoted in Freedman and Karsh, *Gulf Conflict*, 416.

18. Freedman and Karsh, *Gulf Conflict*, 415.

19. Charles Duelfer, *Hide and Seek: The Search for Truth in Iraq* (New York: PublicAffairs, 2009), 86; Freedman and Karsh, *Gulf Conflict*, 415–17.

20. Bob Woodward, *Plan of Attack* (New York: Simon and Schuster, 2004), 70.

21. For example, President Clinton's outgoing Defense Secretary, William Cohen, anticipated the incoming George W. Bush administration would end up reconciling with Saddam. Woodward, 11–12.

22. Thomas E. Ricks, *Fiasco: The American Military Adventure in Iraq* (New York: Penguin Press, 2006), 28; F. Gregory Gause, *The International Relations of the Persian Gulf* (Cambridge: Cambridge University Press, 2010), 189; and Peter Baker, *Days of Fire: Bush and Cheney in the White House* (New York: Doubleday, 2013), 91. As Gause notes, the Bush administration's efforts to revamp sanctions cast doubt on claims that it came to office determined to overthrow Saddam Hussein. For alternative interpretations, see Ron Suskind, *The Price of Loyalty: George W. Bush, the White House, and the Education of Paul O'Neill* (New York: Simon and Schuster, 2004), 85; Michael MacDonald, *Overreach: Delusions of Regime Change in Iraq* (Cambridge, Mass.: Harvard University Press, 2014), 15–16, 35–37.

23. Iraqi records captured after the war show that during the 1980s Saddam sought to use his growing WMD arsenal, not only to deter Israel but also as a shield from behind which Iraq could launch conventional attacks. Hal Brands and David D. Palkki, "Saddam, Israel, and the Bomb: Nuclear Alarmism Justified?," *International Security* 36, no. 1 (2011): 133–66.

24. Duelfer, *Comprehensive Report*, sec. Regime Strategic Intent, https://www.cia.gov/library/reports/general-reports-1/iraq_wmd_2004/chap1.html.

25. Duelfer, *Comprehensive Report*, sec. Transmittal Message, https://www.cia.gov/library/reports/general-reports-1/iraq_wmd_2004/transmittal.html.

26. Kevin M. Woods, Michael R. Pease, and Mark E. Stout, *The Iraqi Perspectives Report: Saddam's Senior Leadership on Operation Iraqi Freedom from the Official U.S. Joint Forces Command Report* (Annapolis, Md.: First Naval Institute Press, 2006), 92.

27. Duelfer, *Hide and Seek*, 407.

28. Woods, Pease, and Stout, *Iraqi Perspectives Report*, 25–26; Amatzia Baram, *Building Toward Crisis* (Washington, D.C.: Washington Institute for Near East Policy, 1998), 37–52.

29. Lawrence G. Potter and Gary Sick, *Iran, Iraq, and the Legacies of War* (New York: Palgrave Macmillan, 2004), 20.

30. Woods, Pease, and Stout, *Iraqi Perspectives Report*, 26.

31. Freedman and Karsh, *Gulf Conflict*, 411. According to Dilip Hiro, Iranian fighters crossed into Iraq to assist the Shi'a in the south. Iran, however, did not directly intervene in the rebellions. Dilip Hiro, *Neighbours, Not Friends: Iraq and Iran after the Gulf Wars* (London: Routledge, 2001), 35–36; Graham-Brown, *Sanctioning Saddam*, 19.

32. Woods, Pease, and Stout, *Iraqi Perspectives Report*, 26.

33. Dilip Hiro, *The Longest War: The Iran-Iraq Military Conflict* (New York: Routledge, 1991), 256; Potter and Sick, *Iran, Iraq*, 156–58.

34. Duelfer, *Comprehensive Report*, sec. Regime Strategic Intent.

35. In the north, Saddam made a clear threat to use chemical weapons again, by reminding Kurds of the regime's devastating 1988 attack. Duelfer, *Comprehensive Report*, sec. Regime Strategic Intent; Freedman and Karsh, *Gulf Conflict*, 420.

36. Duelfer, *Comprehensive Report*, sec. Regime Strategic Intent.

37. Saddam voiced his suspicion of the United States in his debriefing, saying that before Iraq's invasion of Kuwait, the "US was planning to destroy Iraq, an intention pushed by Zionism and the effect of Zionism on elections in the US." Battle, "Saddam Hussein Talks to the FBI." He later recalled to his advisors, "We expected America to behave unwisely when it seizes [*sic*] power and our expectations came true." Saddam continued, saying that everyone knew the US goal was to seek "domination over oil to make its economy distinguished from others." CRRC no. SH-SHTP-A-000-562, "Meeting Between Saddam and Iraqi Military

Notes to Pages 182–184

Commanders to Discuss Preparations to Defend against Attacks by Coalition Forces After the Gulf War," Conflict Records Research Center, National Defense University, Washington, D.C., early 1990s. On Saddam's views of the United States, see Hal Brands and David Palkki, "'Conspiring Bastards': Saddam Hussein's Strategic View of the United States," *Diplomatic History* 36 (2012): 625–59.

38. On allegations of US spying, see Richard Butler, *The Greatest Threat: Iraq, Weapons of Mass Destruction, and the Crisis of Global Security* (New York: PublicAffairs, 2000), 179–83; Duelfer, *Hide and Seek*, 147, 407. See also, Scott Ritter, *Iraq Confidential: The Untold Story of the Intelligence Conspiracy to Undermine the UN and Overthrow Saddam Hussein* (New York: Nation Books, 2005).

39. Duelfer, *Comprehensive Report*, sec. Regime Strategic Intent. Saddam claimed to have hoped for a security guarantee from the United States, but his attempts to negotiate were denied. Battle, "Saddam Hussein Talks to the FBI"; Duelfer, *Comprehensive Report*, sec. Transmittal Message.

40. Duelfer, *Comprehensive Report*, sec. Transmittal Message.

41. Duelfer, *Hide and Seek*, 81, 95–96.

42. Woods, Pease, and Stout, *Iraqi Perspectives Report*, 14.

43. Baram, *Building Toward Crisis*, 76–78.

44. Duelfer, *Hide and Seek*, 163.

45. In a meeting with the Revolutionary Command Council, Saddam advised that, "with France, we must seek to use all the correct reasons so that we can have it moving in the same direction as the Russians, because we need a united front among the three, France, China, and Russia." CRRC no. SH-SHTP-A-000–734, "Saddam Hussein Meeting with the Revolutionary Council," Conflict Records Research Center, National Defense University, Washington, D.C., November 26, 1994, 16. See also CRRC no. SH-SHTP-A-000–873, "Saddam and His Cabinet Contemplate the Results of Their Efforts Concerning the Lifting of Sanctions and Resolution 715," Conflict Records Research Center, National Defense University, Washington, D.C., date unknown.

46. Butler, *Greatest Threat*, 106. See also, Duelfer, *Hide and Seek*, 105, 120–21; Woods, Pease, and Stout, *Iraqi Perspectives Report*, 28, 91; and Graham-Brown, *Sanctioning Saddam*, 61.

47. According to Tariq Aziz, Iraq's former deputy prime minister, Saddam offered France and Russia, "millions of dollars' worth of trade and service contracts, with the implied understanding that their political posture . . . would be pro-Iraqi." Cited in Woods, Pease, and Stout, *Iraqi Perspectives Report*, 28.

48. Duelfer, *Hide and Seek*, 120–22.

49. Saddam manipulated the oil-for-food program by using "middlemen" to sell Iraqi oil. The vouchers allowed the holder to buy Iraqi oil far below its market value and then reap a profit by selling it at market price. Roughly 30 percent of these vouchers went to Russian officials and oil companies. French individuals and companies, including a former French foreign minister and the oil company Total, received about 15 percent of the vouchers, while Chinese entities received roughly 10 percent. American individuals and oil companies received 2 to 3 percent. Saddam also used kickbacks, surcharges, and illegal smuggling to profit from the oil-for-food program. Sharon Otterman, "Iraq: Oil for Food Scandal," *Council on Foreign Relations*, October 28, 2005, http://www.cfr.org/iraq/iraq-oil-food-scandal/p7631#.

50. Duelfer, *Hide and Seek*, 120–22.

51. Otterman, "Iraq: Oil for Food Scandal." Syria, for example, transported two hundred thousand barrels of Iraqi oil to its refineries daily and sold them at a discount. Anthony H. Cordesman, *Energy Developments in the Middle East* (Westport, Conn.: Praeger, 2004), 181.

52. Duelfer, *Comprehensive Report*, sec. Transmittal Message.

53. Graham-Brown, *Sanctioning Saddam*, chap. 8.

54. For example, one prewar study estimates that mortality rates for children younger than 5 years in southern and central Iraq rose from 56 to 131 per 1,000 live births during the sanctions period. Mohamed M. Ali and Iqbal H. Shah, "Sanctions and Childhood Mortality in Iraq," *Lancet* 355 (2000): 1851. On the postwar studies, see Michael Spagat, "Truth and Death in Iraq Under Sanctions," *Significance* 7 (2010): 120. See also Tim Dyson, "New Evidence on Child Mortality in Iraq," *Economic and Political Weekly* 44 (2009): 56–59.

55. David Rieff, "Were Sanctions Right?," *New York Times*, July 27, 2003, http://www.ny times.com/2003/07/27/magazine/were-sanctions-right.h tml.

56. "UN Sanctions Rebel Resigns," BBC News, February 14, 2000, http://news.bbc.co.uk/ 2/hi/middle_east/642189.stm.

57. The UN Security Council adopted Resolution 986 on April 14, 1995. Baram, *Building Toward Crisis*, 71–73; Litwak, *Regime Change*, 152; Duelfer, *Hide and Seek*, 228.

58. Duelfer, *Comprehensive Report*, sec. Regime Finance and Procurement.

59. Eckart Woertz, *Oil for Food: The Global Food Crisis and the Middle East* (Oxford: Oxford University Press, 2013), 137.

60. Marc Lynch, *Voices of the New Arab Public: Iraq, Al-Jazeera, and Middle East Politics Today* (New York: Columbia University Press, 2006), 102–23.

61. Kenneth M. Pollack, *The Threatening Storm: The Case for Invading Iraq* (New York: Random House, 2002), 202–3.

62. Ricks, *Fiasco*, 18.

63. Jeffrey M. Jones, "Public Support for Iraq Invasion Inches Upward," Gallup, March 17, 2003, accessed November 4, 2016, http://www.gallup.com/poll/7990/Public-Support-Iraq -Invasion-Inches-Upward.aspx. By February 2001, that number was down to 52 percent, but still a majority.

64. Clinton told a reporter, "I always tell everybody, 'I'm a Baptist. I believe in deathbed conversions.' If [Saddam] wants a different relationship with the United States and the United Nations, all he has to do is change his behavior." Gwen Ifill, "Gore Rules Out Regular Links with Iraq Chief," *New York Times*, January 18, 1993, http://www.nytimes.com/1993/01/18/ world/gore-rules-out-regular-links-with-iraq-chief.html.

65. Duelfer, *Hide and Seek*, 150; Duelfer, *Comprehensive Report*, sec. Transmittal Message.

66. Future Bush administration officials included Deputy Defense Secretary Paul Wolfowitz, Defense Secretary Donald Rumsfeld, Deputy Secretary of State Richard Armitage, and future UN ambassador John Bolton. See "Letter to President Clinton on Iraq," Project for a New American Century, January 26, 1998, accessed February 11, 2016, http://www.new americancentury.org/iraqclintonletter.htm.

67. Alfred B. Prados, "Iraq: Former and Recent Military Confrontations with the United States," *Issue Brief for Congress*, Congressional Research Service, October 16, 2002, 8, accessed December 15, 2015, http://fas.org/man/crs/IB94049.pdf.

68. Ricks cites Michael Knights, a defense analyst at the Washington Institute for Near East Policy, who notes that thirty-four thousand flight missions would be equivalent to flying the first Gulf War every three years. Ricks, *Fiasco*, 43.

69. Duelfer, *Hide and Seek*, 96.

70. Prados, "Iraq: Former and Recent Military Confrontations," 8–9.

71. Prados, 5–6.

72. Former Iraqi foreign minister Aziz told investigators that it would have taken Iraq roughly two years once sanctions had been lifted to reacquire WMD capability. The Duelfer Report also observed that "as resources became available and the constraints of sanctions decayed, there was a direct expansion of activity that would have the effect of supporting future WMD reconstitution." The Iraqi minister of military industrialization, 'Abd-al-Tawab Al Mullah Huwaysh, estimated a five-year time frame for Iraq to reconstitute its WMD programs. Duelfer, *Comprehensive Report*, secs. Transmittal Message, Regime Strategic Intent.

73. Duelfer, *Hide and Seek*, 143.

74. Ricks, *Fiasco*, 15; Linda J. Bilmes and Joseph E. Stiglitz, *The Three Trillion Dollar War* (New York: W. W. Norton and Company, 2008).

75. Ricks, *Fiasco*, 17–18.

76. In their 1998 book, Bush and his former national security advisor, Brent Scowcroft, cited the potential pitfalls of "mission creep," the difficulty of capturing Saddam, and the likely fracture in the alliance as reasons for their decision to limit their objective. Had the United States invaded Baghdad, they wrote, it "could conceivably still be an occupying power in a bitterly hostile land." George H. W. Bush and Brent Scowcroft, *A World Transformed* (New York: Knopf, 1998), 489.

77. Freedman and Karsh, *Gulf Conflict*, 415; Ann Devroy and Molly Moore, "Winning the War and Struggling With Peace," *Washington Post*, April 14, 1991, sec. A; Graham-Brown, *Sanctioning Saddam*, 19.

78. James Addison Baker and Thomas M. DeFrank, *The Politics of Diplomacy* (New York: G.P. Putnam's Sons, 1995), 441–42.

79. Woodward, *Plan of Attack*, 70; Graham-Brown, *Sanctioning Saddam*, 64; Clifford Krauss, "After the War," *New York Times*, April 4, 1991, http://www.nytimes.com/1991/04/04/world/after-the-war-baker-aide-talks-with-iraqi-dissidents-in-us.html.

80. Graham-Brown, *Sanctioning Saddam*, 64.

81. Freedman and Karsh, *Gulf Conflict*, 413–17.

82. In late 1992, for example, the assistant secretary of state for the region declared in a statement before Congress that the United States should support "the emergence of an Iraqi Government representative of Iraq's pluralistic society including the Shiites, Sunnis and Kurds." Graham-Brown, *Sanctioning Saddam*, 64.

83. Graham-Brown, 117. Although American officials claimed the administration had never agreed to support the INC coup attempt, reports indicate that doubts about its feasibility led the administration to withdraw its support at the last minute.

84. Woodward, *Plan of Attack*, 70.

85. This was done in January 1999, after Operation Desert Fox. Graham-Brown, *Sanctioning Saddam*, 65.

86. Charles Tripp, *A History of Iraq*, 3rd ed. (Cambridge: Cambridge University Press, 2007), 266–67.

87. David E. Sanger, "The Struggle for Iraq: The Exile; a Seat of Honor Lost to Open Political Warfare," *New York Times*, May 21, 2004, http://www.nytimes.com/2004/05/21/world/the-struggle-for-iraq-the-exile-a-seat-of-honor-lost-to-open-political-warfare.html.

88. Ricks, *Fiasco*, 17, 28. Nicholas Lemann, "How It Came to War: When Did Bush Decide He Had to Fight Saddam?," *New Yorker*, March 31, 2003, http://www.newyorker.com/archive/2003/03/31/030331fa_fact.

89. See, for example, Office of the Press Secretary, "President Bush Outlines Iraqi Threat," White House, October 7, 2002, http://georgewbush-whitehouse.archives.gov/news/releases/2002/10/20021007-8.html. See also Feith, *War and Decision*, 116–17.

90. Office of the Press Secretary, "President Bush Discusses Iraq with Congressional Leaders," White House, September 26, 2002, http://georgewbush-whitehouse.archives.gov/news/releases/2002/09/20020926-7.html.

91. Dina Badie, "Groupthink, Iraq, and the War on Terror: Explaining US Policy Shift Toward Iraq," *Foreign Policy Analysis* 6 (2010): 290.

92. "Washington Post Poll: Saddam Hussein and the Sept. 11 Attacks," *Washington Post*, September 6, 2003, http://www.washingtonpost.com/wp-srv/politics/polls/vault/stories/data082303.htm.

93. Frank Newport, "Seventy-Two Percent of Americans Support War against Iraq," *Gallup News Service*, March 24, 2003, accessed April 9, 2018, http://news.gallup.com/poll/8038/seventytwo-percent-americans-support-war-against-iraq.aspx.

94. Ivo H. Daalder and James M. Lindsay, *America Unbound: The Bush Revolution in Foreign Policy* (Washington, D.C.: Brookings Institution Press, 2003), 138; Feith, *War and Decision*, 48–52; Gause, *International Relations of the Persian Gulf*, 185.

95. Ron Suskind, *The One Percent Doctrine: Deep Inside America's Pursuit of Its Enemies Since 9/11* (New York: Simon and Schuster, 2007), 62.

96. Feith, *War and Decision*, 201–2; chap. 7.

97. Feith, 202. The CIA's chief of Iraq operations had also concluded that Saddam's regime was virtually coup-proof and that the Iraqi dictator could only be removed through a military invasion. Woodward, *Plan of Attack*, 71–73. This did not mean, however, that US policymakers were any less interested in convincing Saddam's supporters to defect. Indeed, US officials adopted a "no uprisings" policy during the invasion, urging Iraqi Kurds and Shi'a to stay home so as not to prevent Sunni elite and officials from defecting. Ḥāmid Bayātī, *From Dictatorship to Democracy: An Insider's Account of the Iraqi Opposition to Saddam* (Philadelphia: University of Pennsylvania Press, 2011), 180.

98. Feith, *War and Decision*, 202.

99. Feith, 202.

100. Woodward, *Plan of Attack*, 316. Feith, *War and Decision*, 202–3.

101. Condoleezza Rice, *No Higher Honor: A Memoir of My Years in Washington* (New York: Broadway Paperbacks, 2012), 193. Feith and other Pentagon officials reportedly pushed for handing power to Ahmad Chalabi and the INC. However, shortly before the war, the president was briefed on a plan that excluded only the top 1 percent of Baathists from power, retained a reduced Iraqi military, and established an interim Iraqi government. Ultimately, Bush chose to cast exile leaders, such as Chalabi, into a supporting role. Tripp, *History of Iraq*, 267–68; George Packer, *The Assassins' Gate: America in Iraq* (New York: Farrar, Straus and Giroux, 2005), 128–29.

102. Lemann, "How It Came to War."

103. See "Matthew Rycroft, Private Secretary to the Prime Minister, Cabinet Minutes of Discussion, S 195/02," July 23, 2002. Cited in John Prados and Christopher Ames, eds., "The Iraq War—Part II: Was There Even a Decision? U.S. and British Documents Give No Indication Alternatives Were Seriously Considered," National Security Archive electronic briefing book no. 328, October 1, 2010, http://www.gwu.edu/~nsarchiv/NSAEBB/NSAEBB328/index .htm.

104. Haass, *War of Necessity*, 5–6. By comparison, the State Department's postwar planning group held most of its meetings *after* July 2002. The CIA report, which also warned of potentially high costs, was not released until August 2002. Indeed, it was not until that month that Secretary of State Colin Powell met privately with Bush and Rice to warn of the consequences of invading Iraq. Woodward, *Plan of Attack*, 150.

105. Michael Elliott and James Carney, "First Stop, Iraq," CNN, March 24, 2003, http:// www.cnn.com/2003/ALLPOLITICS/03/24/timep.saddam.tm/. In his memoirs, Bush insists that he did not make the decision to invade Iraq until January 2002 and that the buildup of forces in the Gulf was meant to convince Saddam of the credibility of US threats. George W. Bush, *Decision Points* (New York: Crown Publishers, 2010), 250–55.

106. Russell A. Burgos, "Origins of Regime Change: 'Ideapolitik' on the Long Road to Baghdad, 1993–2000," *Security Studies* 17 (2008): 242.

107. Allawi later claimed to have used his contacts shortly before the 2003 war to negotiate with Iraqi military commanders in Ramadi and west of Baghdad to surrender. David Ignatius, "A Big Man to Watch in Baghdad," *Washington Post*, February 1, 2004, http://www .washingtonpost.com/wp-dyn/articles/A23–2004Jan30_2.html.

108. Bayātī, *From Dictatorship to Democracy*, 149.

109. Woodward, *Plan of Attack*, 6, 96–98; Len Scott and R. Gerald Hughes, *Intelligence, Crises and Security: Prospects and Retrospects* (New York: Routledge, 2013), 252; Donald H. Rumsfeld, "Beyond 'Nation-Building,'" *Washington Post*, September 25, 2003, https://www .washingtonpost.com/archive/opinions/2003/09/25/beyond-nation-building/dc884ed9-f1e4–4 ef8-b2e2–9812ae80e4ef/?utm_term=.bdf91800a88f.

110. Packer, *Assassins' Gate*, 114, 118, 132–33.

111. Gause, *International Relations of the Persian Gulf*, 217; Peter Slevin and Dana Priest, "Wolfowitz Concedes Iraq Errors," *Washington Post*, July 24, 2003, http://www.washington post.com/wp-dyn/articles/A37468–2003Jul23.html.

112. Packer, *Assassins' Gate*, 147.

113. Kevin M. Woods, James Lacey, and Williamson Murray, "Saddam's Delusions: The View from the Inside," *Foreign Affairs* 85 (2006): 2–26.

114. Duelfer, *Comprehensive Report*, sec. Regime Strategic Intent: Saddam the Dynasty Founder.

115. North Korea, in contrast, did not face UN sanctions until after it tested a nuclear weapon in 2006.

116. Woods, Pease, and Stout, *Iraqi Perspectives Report*, 92–93.

117. Woods, Pease, and Stout, 29.

118. A former Iraqi Republican Guard commander cited in Woods, Pease, and Stout, 93.

119. According to regime insiders, Saddam and senior leaders believed that, at most, the United States would launch an air attack and occupy southern Iraq. Woods, Pease, and Stout, 30–31. See also Woods, Lacey, and Murray, "Saddam's Delusions," 3.

120. Woods, Pease, and Stout, *Iraqi Perspectives Report*, 29.

121. "Transcript of Blix's Remarks," CNN, January 27, 2003, http://www.cnn.com/2003/US/01/27/sprj.irq.transcript.blix/.

122. "Hans Blix's Briefing to the Security Council," *Guardian*, February 14, 2003, http://www.theguardian.com/world/2003/feb/14/iraq.unitednations1; Duelfer, *Comprehensive Report*, sec. Renewing UN Inspections.

123. Blix also noted that, although Iraq had suggested individuals who could be interviewed to attest to the destruction of weapons material, inspectors were planning to ask for the interviews to be conducted outside Iraq to be sure that the interviewees were not being pressured by the regime. "Transcript of Blix's U.N. Presentation," CNN, March 7, 2003, http://www.cnn.com/2003/US/03/07/sprj.irq.un.transcript.blix/. See also "Blix's Briefing."

124. Mohamed ElBaradei, "The Status of Nuclear Inspections in Iraq," International Atomic Energy Agency, January 27, 2003, https://www.iaea.org/newscenter/statements/status-nuclear-inspections-iraq. See also Mohamed ElBaradei, "The Status of Nuclear Inspections in Iraq: An Update," International Atomic Energy Agency, March 7, 2003, https://www.iaea.org/newscenter/statements/status-nuclear-inspections-iraq-update.

125. Woodward, *Plan of Attack*, 314.

126. Bush reiterated in a meeting with congressional leaders the same day, "If Saddam Hussein leaves, we'll go in anyway." Later that month, Bush also discussed reports of Saddam's interests in exile with the Spanish prime minister but again insisted that Saddam would receive no guarantees of immunity. Woodward, *Plan of Attack*, 314, 369; Mark Danner, "'The Moment Has Come to Get Rid of Saddam,'" *New York Review of Books*, November 8, 2007, http://www.nybooks.com/articles/archives/2007/nov/08/the-moment-has-come-to-get-rid-of-saddam/.

127. George W. Bush cited the alleged assassination attempt in a September 2002 speech. John King, "Bush Calls Saddam 'The Guy Who Tried to Kill My Dad,'" CNN, September 27, 2002, http://edition.cnn.com/2002/ALLPOLITICS/09/27/bush.war.talk/. The most prominent work suggesting administration officials were predisposed to regime change is by former treasury secretary Paul O'Neill. Suskind, *Price of Loyalty*, 83–86. Other accounts indicate that psychological bias led decisionmakers to discount the costs of war or inflate the Iraqi threat. See, for example, David Lake, "Two Cheers for Bargaining Theory: Assessing Rationalist Explanations of the Iraq War," *International Security* 35, no. 3 (November 2010): 7–52; Badie, "Groupthink, Iraq, and the War on Terror." Another argument holds that humans are prone to favor hawkish policies due to psychological bias. See Daniel Kahneman and Jonathan Renshon, "Why Hawks Win," *Foreign Policy*, 158 (2007): 34–38.

128. Bruce W. Jentleson, *With Friends Like These: Reagan, Bush, and Saddam, 1982–1990* (New York: Norton, 1994), chap. 3.

129. Although some administration officials were arguing in favor of forcibly removing Saddam prior to 9/11, their preferences did not translate into policy. Gause, *International Relations of the Persian Gulf*, 189–90.

130. Paul 't Hart, *Groupthink in Government: A Study of Small Groups and Policy Failure* (Baltimore: Johns Hopkins University Press, 1994), 124. See also Badie, "Groupthink."

131. Packer, *Assassins' Gate*, 116–17; Badie, "Groupthink," 288. Packer notes that soon after the president's economic adviser, Lawrence Lindsay, projected the war would cost roughly $200 billion, he was reprimanded and dismissed. General Eric Shinseki had already

announced his retirement by the time he told Congress that stabilizing postwar Iraq would possibly require several hundred thousand troops, many more than the Bush administration claimed. However, after Paul Wolfowitz publically questioned Shinseki's estimate, Shinseki was marginalized. Ricks, *Fiasco*, 98–100; Thom Shanker, "New Strategy Vindicates Ex-Army Chief Shinseki," *New York Times*, January 12, 2007, http://www.nytimes.com/2007/01/12/washington/12shinseki.html.

132. See for example, Andrew Flibbert, "The Road to Baghdad: Ideas and Intellectuals in Explanations of the Iraq War," *Security Studies* 15, no. 2 (2006): 310–52; Ronald R. Krebs and Jennifer K. Lobasz, "Fixing the Meaning of 9/11: Hegemony, Coercion, and the Road to War in Iraq," *Security Studies* 16, no. 3 (2007): 409–51; and Brian C. Schmidt and Michael C. Williams, "The Bush Doctrine and the Iraq War: Neoconservatives Versus Realists," *Security Studies* 17, no. 2 (2008): 191–220.

133. Packer, *Assassins' Gate*, 147. Other scholars contend that the ideological views and leadership styles of individual policymakers explain their actions better than their bureaucratic incentives. Vaughn P. Shannon and Jonathan W. Keller, "Leadership Style and International Norm Violation: The Case of the Iraq War," *Foreign Policy Analysis* 3 (2007): 79–104; Roberta Haar, "Explaining George W. Bush's Adoption of the Neoconservative Agenda after 9/11," *Politics and Policy* 38, no. 5 (October 1, 2010): 965–90.

134. John J. Mearsheimer and Stephen M. Walt, *The Israel Lobby and U.S. Foreign Policy* (New York: Farrar, Straus and Giroux, 2008).

135. Otterman, "Iraq: Oil for Food Scandal." In fact, due to the oil-for-food program, the United States dominated Iraq's oil market before the war. In 2001, it imported 59 percent of Iraq's oil; this figure steadily declined after 2003. Iraqi oil, meanwhile, made up roughly 7 to 8 percent of US crude-oil imports from 1999 to 2001 but dropped to between 4.5 and 6.3 percent after the war. Data come from the Observatory of Economic Complexity, managed by the Massachusetts Institute of Technology Media Lab Macro Connections group, which draws its data from the University of California's Center for International Data and the United Nations' Comtrade database. See Observatory of Economic Complexity, "Where Does Iraq Export Crude Petroleum To? (1997)," accessed April 7, 2018, http://atlas.media.mit.edu/en/visualize/tree_map/sitc/export/irq/show/3330/1997/. See also US Energy Information Administration, "U.S. Imports from Iraq of Crude Oil," accessed January 31, 2018, https://www.eia.gov/dnav/pet/hist/LeafHandler.ashx?n=PET&s=MCRIMIZ2&f=A.

136. Woods, Pease, and Stout, *Iraqi Perspectives Report*, 30.

137. Saddam's domestic enemies were fundamental to the US decision to pursue regime change because they could be used to construct a replacement regime. His regional rivals, in contrast, could offer little more than military assistance, and some refused to do even that.

138. See, for example, Meghan L. O'Sullivan, *Shrewd Sanctions: Statecraft and State Sponsors of Terrorism* (Washington, D.C.: Brookings Institution Press, 2003), 202, 204; Litwak, *Regime Change*, 170; and Jentleson and Whytock, "Who 'Won' Libya?," 67.

139. Litwak, *Regime Change*, 170; O'Sullivan, *Shrewd Sanctions*, 204; and Jentleson and Whytock, "Who 'Won' Libya?," 67.

140. Jentleson and Whytock focus on three similar time periods but argue that US demands *decreased* over time. They contend that the United States went from demanding regime change during the Reagan administration to policy change under subsequent administrations. In contrast, I argue that the Reagan administration's primary objective was coercing

a change in Qaddafi's behavior, not regime change. Although the administration authorized covert operations to unseat Qaddafi, it did not abandon the possibility of a settlement with him. A primary goal of the 1986 US bombing raid was to "provide [Qaddafi] with incentives and reasons to alter his criminal behavior." Consistent with my definition of FIRC, I classify the Reagan administration's approach as one focused primarily on policy change. This policy change initially focused on ending Qaddafi's support for terrorism but would later expand to include compensation for the families of the Pan Am bombing victims and the surrender of Libya's WMD. See Jentleson and Whytock, "Who 'Won' Libya?,"; Bernard Weinraub, "U.S. Jets Hit 'Terrorist Centers' in Libya; Reagan Warns of New Attacks If Needed," *New York Times*, April 15, 1986, http://www.nytimes.com/1986/04/15/politics/15REAG.html.

141. Jentleson and Whytock, "Who 'Won' Libya?," 56.

142. Jentleson and Whytock, 56.

143. Davis, *Qaddafi, Terrorism*, 11, 18–19.

144. Inspections after the 2003 deal later revealed Libya's chemical weapons stockpiles were smaller and less advanced than initially believed. Libya's biological weapons program had failed to advance much beyond the planning stage, while its nuclear weapons program depended primarily on the import of parts from the black market run by Pakistani scientist, Abdul Qadeer Khan. Tucker, "The Rollback of Libya's Chemical Weapons Program," 363, 366; Braut-Hegghammer, "Libya's Nuclear Turnaround"; and Jentleson and Whytock, "Who 'Won' Libya?," 57–58.

145. When Sadat was assassinated in 1981, Israeli intelligence indicated a direct link to Libya. Davis, *Qaddafi, Terrorism*, 15, 48.

146. Jentleson and Whytock, "Who 'Won' Libya?," 59; Ronald Bruce St. John, " 'Libya Is Not Iraq': Preemptive Strikes, WMD and Diplomacy," *Middle East Journal* 58, no. 3 (2004): 387.

147. Sanctions fell short of a complete embargo, which countries reliant on Libyan oil opposed. Tim Niblock, *"Pariah States" and Sanctions in the Middle East: Iraq, Libya, Sudan* (Boulder, Colo.: Lynne Reinner, 2001), 41; O'Sullivan, *Shrewd Sanctions*, 181.

148. These demands were part of the original set of demands made by the United States and United Kingdom when the two countries formally indicted Libya in 1991. George [H. W.] Bush, "Statement Announcing Joint Declarations on the Libyan Indictments, November 27, 1991," Gerhard Peters and John T. Woolley, American Presidency Project, accessed April 7, 2018, http://www.presidency.ucsb.edu/ws/?pid=20281.

149. Martin S. Indyk, "The Iraq War Did Not Force Gadaffi's Hand," *Financial Times*, March 9, 2004, http://www.brookings.edu/opinions/2004/0309middleeast_indyk.aspx.

150. Jentleson and Whytock, "Who 'Won' Libya?," 74.

151. On Qaddafi's efforts to assert himself in the Arab world and in Africa, see Alison Pargeter, *Libya: The Rise and Fall of Qaddafi* (New Haven, Conn.: Yale University Press, 2012), chap. 5.

152. Pargeter, 105.

153. As I will explain more fully, US pressure increased only gradually throughout the 1970s. The Reagan administration significantly expanded US pressure, but concerns over the costs of some of these measures restrained it from using significant military force until 1986. Wyn Q. Bowen, *Libya and Nuclear Proliferation* (Abingdon, UK: Routledge for the International Institute for Strategic Studies, 2006), 14; Jentleson and Whytock, "Who 'Won' Libya?,"

57; O'Sullivan, *Shrewd Sanctions*, 176; and Edward Schumacher, "The United States and Libya," *Foreign Affairs* 65, no. 2 (1986): 334.

154. From 1975 to 1979, the Libyan economy grew more than 10 percent a year, a direct result of a precipitous rise in oil prices. Jentleson and Whytock, "Who 'Won' Libya?," 57. By 1981, the price of Libyan oil had increased by 208 percent over what it was in 1975. O'Sullivan, *Shrewd Sanctions*, 196.

155. O'Sullivan, *Shrewd Sanctions*, 189. In the 1970s the United States had imported large amounts of Libyan oil. But by the time the Reagan administration initiated sanctions in 1981, the United States was relying mainly on exports from the North Sea and Mexico. American business accounted for only 7 percent of the Libyan oil market. Gideon Rose, "Libya," in *Economic Sanctions and American Diplomacy*, ed. Richard N. Haass (New York: Council on Foreign Relations, 1998), 131. See also Pargeter, *Libya*, 139.

156. Davis, *Qaddafi, Terrorism*, 125–27; David C. Wills, *The First War on Terrorism: Counter-Terrorism Policy During the Reagan Administration* (Lanham, Md.: Rowman and Littlefield Publishers, 2004), 170.

157. Up to 1983, Libya purchased approximately $20 billion in military hardware from Soviet and Eastern bloc countries. Libya shipped these excess arms to the revolutionary movements it was backing worldwide. Reports also circulated that the Soviets were constructing their own bases in Libya as well. Davis, *Qaddafi, Terrorism*, 15, 43.

158. Bowen, *Libya and Nuclear Proliferation*, 55; Pargeter, *Libya*, 108–9.

159. Bowen, *Libya and Nuclear Proliferation*, 55; St. John, *Libya*, 195.

160. Bowen, *Libya and Nuclear Proliferation*, 146.

161. The April 1986 bombing raid was known as Operation El Dorado Canyon. Nicholas Laham, *The American Bombing of Libya: A Study of the Force of Miscalculation in Reagan Foreign Policy* (Jefferson, N.C.: McFarland and Co., 2008), 154; Joseph T. Stanik, *El Dorado Canyon* (Annapolis, Md.: Naval Institute Press, 2003), 211.

162. There had always been tension in the Libyan-Soviet relationship, but it increased as Libyan debts mounted in the mid-1980s. Davis, *Qaddafi, Terrorism*, 77–78.

163. The reforms were mainly economic, while the political reforms were limited to the replacement of the revolutionary courts and the criticism of overzealous ideologues, as well as other largely symbolic gestures, such as the release of nearly four hundred prisoners at Tripoli's Furnash prison. Pargeter, *Libya*, 148–49; St. John, *Libya*, 197–98.

164. This was after the United States provided $32 million to the Chadian army, in addition to antiaircraft missiles, to make the war more costly for Qaddafi. Yehudit Ronen, *Qaddafi's Libya in World Politics* (Boulder, Colo.: Lynne Rienner, 2008), 34.

165. Litwak, *Regime Change*, 176.

166. O'Sullivan, *Shrewd Sanctions*, 181; Rose, "Libya," 135; and Dirk Vandewalle, "Qadhafi's 'Perestroika': Economic and Political Liberalization in Libya," *Middle East Journal* 45, no. 2 (1991): 216–31.

167. Mary-Jane Deeb, "Qadhafi's Changed Policy: Causes and Consequences," *Middle East Policy* 7 (2000): 149; Niblock, *"Pariah States" and Sanctions*, 75, 78; and O'Sullivan, *Shrewd Sanctions*, 213.

168. Mary-Jane Deeb, "Political and Economic Developments in Libya in the 1990s," in *North Africa in Transition: State, Society and Economic Transformation in the 1990s*, ed. Yahia H. Zoubir (Gainesville: University of Florida Press, 1999), 80.

169. Pargeter, *Libya*, 158–61.

170. Pargeter, 166.

171. Deeb, "Qadhafi's Changed Policy," 146; Jentleson and Whytock, "Who 'Won' Libya?," 66.

206172. Deeb, "Political and Economic Developments," 148; Niblock, *"Pariah States" and Sanctions*, 85–86.

173. On the revolutionary committees, see Pargeter, *Libya*, 118.

174. Ronen, *Qaddafi's Libya*, 54.

175. Chorin, *Exit the Colonel*, 67; Pargeter, *Libya*, 155.

176. Quoted in Pargeter, *Libya*, 146.

177. Jentleson and Whytock, "Who 'Won' Libya?," 70.

178. Deeb, "Qadhafi's Changed Policy"; Pargeter, *Libya*, 170; and Ian Black, "The Libyan Islamic Fighting Group—from Al-Qaida to the Arab Spring," *Guardian*, September 5, 2011, http://www.theguardian.com/world/2011/sep/05/libyan-islamic-fighting-group-leaders.

179. Niblock, *"Pariah States" and Sanctions*, 44; Pargeter, *Libya*, 177.

180. O'Sullivan, *Shrewd Sanctions*, 184.

181. He also asked former South African president Nelson Mandela to address Libya's General People's Congress to ensure domestic public support. Jentleson and Whytock, "Who 'Won' Libya?"; Niblock, *"Pariah States" and Sanctions*, 50, 58; Chorin, *Exit the Colonel*, 67; and Pargeter, *Libya*, 179.

182. O'Sullivan, *Shrewd Sanctions*, 202.

183. Jentleson and Whytock, "Who 'Won' Libya?," 77–78.

184. The termination of UN sanctions in April 1999 partially explains the Libyan economy's turnaround, but the resurgence of the oil market was more important. O'Sullivan, *Shrewd Sanctions*, 202.

185. Flynt Leverett, "Why Libya Gave Up on the Bomb," *New York Times*, January 23, 2004.

186. Indyk, "The Iraq War."

187. Stephen Fidler, Roula Khalaf, and Mark Huband, "Return to the Fold: How Gadaffi Was Persuaded to Give up His Nuclear Goals," *Financial Times London*, January 27, 2004.

188. Braut-Hegghammer, "Libya's Nuclear Turnaround," 67.

189. David D. Palkki and Shane Smith, "Contrasting Causal Mechanisms: Iraq and Libya," in *Sanctions, Statecraft, and Nuclear Proliferation*, ed. Etel Solingen (Cambridge: Cambridge University Press, 2012), 269; Robin Wright, "Ship Incident May Have Swayed Libya," *Washington Post*, January 1, 2004, https://www.washingtonpost.com/archive/politics/2004/01/01/ship-incident-may-have-swayed-libya/69244c5f-c895-4ec5-87bc-e17d34bffbe8/.

190. Pargeter, *Libya*, 181; Diederik Vandewalle, "The Origins and Parameters of Libya's Recent Actions," *Arab Reform Bulletin* 2 (2004): 3–5.

191. Ronen, *Qaddafi's Libya*, 63.

192. Quoted in Fidler, Khalaf, and Huband, "Return to the Fold." On shifting attitudes toward WMD within the Libyan regime, see Braut-Hegghammer, "Libya's Nuclear Turnaround."

193. "Gadhafi: Iraq War May Have Influenced WMD Decision," CNN, December 22, 2003, http://www.cnn.com/2003/WORLD/africa/12/22/gadhafi.interview/.

194. Judith Miller, "How Gadhafi Lost His Groove: The Complex Surrender of Libya's WMD," *Wall Street Journal*, May 16, 2006, A14.

195. Robert Litwak, *Outlier States: American Strategies to Change, Contain, or Engage Regimes* (Washington, D.C.: Johns Hopkins University Press, 2012), 115.

196. In 1973, for example, the Nixon administration imposed restrictions on arms sales and recalled its ambassador. It was not until 1979 that the United States initiated a full arms embargo and closed its embassy in Tripoli.

197. Cited in Wills, *First War on Terrorism*, 171. See also Litwak, *Regime Change*, 173.

198. Davis, *Qaddafi, Terrorism*, 84.

199. St. John, *Libya*, 133; Davis, *Qaddafi, Terrorism*, 87.

200. Wills, *First War on Terrorism*, 170.

201. Whether this pressure would have been sufficient to modify Qaddafi's behavior is unclear because high oil prices and Soviet support still insulated Qaddafi against foreign pressure.

202. In 1982, such a rift occurred over the construction of a Siberian natural gas pipeline, which the European subsidiaries of American companies had helped build. Davis, *Qaddafi, Terrorism*, 87; Rose, "Libya," 132.

203. Laham, *American Bombing of Libya*, 67; Davis, *Qaddafi, Terrorism*, 123.

204. The raid also may have energized Qaddafi's efforts to seek a nuclear weapon. Braut-Hegghammer, "Libya's Nuclear Turnaround," 58, 64.

205. Stanik, *El Dorado Canyon*, 145.

206. The American public, in contrast, was largely supportive. Adam Clymer, "Tension in Libya: Polling the American Public; a Poll Finds 77% in U.S. Approve Raid on Libya," *New York Times*, April 17, 1986, http://www.nytimes.com/1986/04/17/world/tension-libya-polling-american-public-poll-finds-77-us-approve-raid-libya.html.

207. Although Libya's growth rate was only 0.8 percent a year during this period, sanctions did not decrease Libya's oil production. In fact, Libya's oil sales increased from 940,000 barrels in 1989 to 1.13 million barrels in 1995. O'Sullivan, *Shrewd Sanctions*, 195; Pargeter, *Libya*, 157; and Niblock, *"Pariah States" and Sanctions*, 64–65. O'Sullivan notes that Libya was able to withdraw assets before the United States imposed an asset freeze. Sanctions, however, had indirect effects on the Libyan economy, such as discouraging foreign investment. O'Sullivan, *Shrewd Sanctions*, 198–99.

208. Chorin, *Exit the Colonel*, 55–56, 62; Geoff L. Simons, *Libya and the West: From Independence to Lockerbie* (New York: Palgrave Macmillan, 2003), 134.

209. The Iran and Libya Sanctions Act imposed penalties on foreign companies investing more than $40 million in the Libyan energy sector. Chorin, *Exit the Colonel*, 62; Jentleson and Whytock, "Who 'Won Libya?," 65; O'Sullivan, *Shrewd Sanctions*, 216; and Dirk J. Vandewalle, *Libya Since Independence: Oil and State-Building* (Ithaca, N.Y.: Cornell University Press, 1998), 146.

210. Niblock, *"Pariah States" and Sanctions*, 47, 51.

211. Quoted in Jentleson and Whytock, "Who 'Won' Libya?," 69.

212. O'Sullivan, *Shrewd Sanctions*, 184.

213. These small-scale efforts focused primarily on funding exile opposition groups. Litwak, *Regime Change*, 174.

214. Bob Woodward, "CIA Backs Anti-Qaddafi Plan," *Washington Post*, November 3, 1985.

215. Even CIA director William Casey had opposed the plan, which called on working with Libya's neighbors to undermine Qaddafi, because no US allies supported it. Woodward, "CIA Backs Anti-Qaddafi Plan."

216. Wills, *First War on Terrorism*, 173–74.

217. As Air Force Major General David Forgan explained, "If we caught Qaddafi in bed, that would be a bonus, but that was not the goal." Wills, 210.

218. Davis, *Qaddafi, Terrorism*, 122. For similar opinions, see also Stanik, *El Dorado Canyon*, 150; Laham, *American Bombing of Libya*.

219. Although there were reports of internal struggles following the bombing, the attack itself failed to inspire an uprising. Qaddafi had conducted purges after previous coup attempts and carefully rotated military commanders to ensure no one could gather sufficient strength to challenge him. He also had moved the military's headquarters to a remote desert village three hundred miles from Tripoli. The April bombardment thus failed to incite Libya's already weakened military to take action against its supreme leader. Schumacher, "United States and Libya," 336–38. See also Pargeter, *Libya*, 158–61; Rose, "Libya," 133.

220. St. John, *Libya*, 254.

221. "Attacks Draw Mixed Response in Mideast," CNN, September 12, 2001, http://www.cnn.com/2001/WORLD/europe/09/12/mideast.reaction/.

222. In addition to the Pan Am flight bombing, Libya was linked to a number of other terrorist attacks during this period. As one author notes, "[Qaddafi] actually responded to the U.S. attack [in 1986] with a murderous campaign of terrorist attacks through the Abu Nidal Organization and the Japanese Red Army. Serving as proxy organizations for Libya, these groups attacked American and British targets in Pakistan, Italy, India, Sudan, and Indonesia." Yoram Schweitzer, cited in Jentleson and Whytock, "Who "Won" Libya?," 59.

223. Davis, *Qaddafi, Terrorism*, 89; St. John, *Libya*, 197.

224. Chorin, *Exit the Colonel*, 69. See also Jentleson and Whytock, "Who 'Won' Libya?," 73.

225. Michael Hirsh, "Botlon's British Problem," *Daily Beast*, 2005, accessed December 20, 2015, http://www.thedailybeast.com/newsweek/2005/05/01/bolton-s-british-problem.html; Chorin, *Exit the Colonel*, 69. See also Jentleson and Whytock, "Who 'Won' Libya?," 73.

226. "Gadhafi: Iraq War."

227. Barack Obama, "Remarks by the President in Address to the Nation on Libya," White House, March 28, 2011, https://www.whitehouse.gov/the-press-office/2011/03/28/remarks-president-address-nation-libya.

228. Obama.

229. Although Serbian leader Slobodan Milošević later lost power, regime change was not part of the settlement. Walter Rodgers, Matthew Chance, and John King, "Milosevic Accepts Peace Plan, Finnish Envoy Says," CNN, June 3, 1999, http://www.cnn.com/WORLD/europe/9906/03/kosovo.peace.04/.

230. Kuperman, "Model Humanitarian Intervention?," 117.

231. These deals were partly based on business interests but were also related to Qaddafi's ability to pressure the West with a flood of African migrants. Kelly M. Greenhill, *Weapons of Mass Migration: Forced Displacement, Coercion, and Foreign Policy* (Ithaca, N.Y.: Cornell University Press, 2016), 1–2, 310–11, 331.On the termination of the European Union embargo, see Council of the European Union, "Press Release, 2609th Council Meeting, General Affairs and External Relations, External Relations, Luxembourg, October 11, 2004," Stockholm International Peace Research Institute (SIPRI), http://www.sipri.org/databases/embargoes/eu_arms_embargoes/libya/libya-1986/EU_Presse_276. See also Chorin, *Exit the Colonel*, 133.

232. The Libyan government had accused the medics of infecting Benghazi children with the human immunodeficiency virus (HIV). Although the French government denied it, critics called the deal a quid pro quo. Saif al-Islam Qaddafi later alleged that Sarkozy had accepted a £42-million campaign contribution from Libya for his 2007 presidential campaign. Chorin, *Exit the Colonel*, 132, 135.

233. Chorin, 136.

234. "Italy to Pay Libya $5 Billion," *New York Times*, August 31, 2008, http://www.ny times.com/2008/08/31/world/europe/31iht-italy.4.15774385.html.

235. Al-Megrahi was said to be dying of cancer; however, Qaddafi's heir apparent, Saif, confirmed that the regime had all along intended to secure his release, stating that "in all commercial contracts for oil and gas with the United Kingdom, al-Megrahi was always on the negotiating table." David Rose, "The Lockerbie Deal," *Vanity Fair*, December 31, 2010, http://www.vanityfair.com/news/2011/01/libya-201101; Chorin, *Exit the Colonel*, 161. See also Elise Labott, "Britain Rejects Claim That Bomber Release Tied to UK Trade Deals," CNN, August 21, 2009, http://www.cnn.com/2009/WORLD/europe/08/21/britain.lockerbie.deal/.

236. Al-Libi had given the information while in Egyptian custody but later recanted. He was transferred to Libyan custody in 2005 and reportedly committed suicide in his cell there in 2009. Associated Press, "Libya: Fabricator of Iraq-Qaeda Link Dies, Newspaper Says," *New York Times*, May 12, 2009, http://www.nytimes.com/2009/05/13/world/middleeast/13briefs -Libyabrf.html; Rod Nordland, "Files Note Close C.I.A. Ties to Qaddafi Spy Unit," *New York Times*, September 2, 2011, http://www.nytimes.com/2011/09/03/world/africa/03libya.html.

237. CBS/AP, "Libyan Intel Docs Show Ties to CIA Renditions," CBS News, September 3, 2011, http://www.cbsnews.com/news/libyan-intel-docs-show-ties-to-cia-renditions/; Nordland, "Files Note Close C.I.A. Ties."

238. One reason for this was the revelation that Libya was behind a plot to assassinate Saudi Arabia's Crown Prince Abdullah. Patrick E. Tyler, "Two Said to Tell of Libyan Plot against Saudi," *New York Times*, June 10, 2004, https://www.nytimes.com/2004/06/10/world/ two-said-to-tell-of-libyan-plot-against-saudi.html.

239. Ronald Bruce St. John, "Libya and the United States: A Faustian Pact?," *Middle East Policy* 15, no. 1 (2008): 141–42.

240. Jill Dougherty, "Ambassador to Libya May Be Replaced over Leaked Cables, Official Says," CNN, January 6, 2011, http://www.cnn.com/2011/US/01/05/wikileaks.libya/.

241. Chorin, *Exit the Colonel*, 193; Frank Gardner, "'Libya Protests: Second City Benghazi Hit by Violence," BBC News, February 16, 2011, http://www.bbc.com/news/world-africa -12477275.

242. Chorin, *Exit the Colonel*, 193–95.

243. Kuperman, "Model Humanitarian Intervention?"; Roberts, "Who Said Gaddafi Had to Go?"

244. Human Rights Watch, "World Report 2011: Libya," 2011, https://www.hrw.org/ world-report/2011/country-chapters/libya.

245. Chorin, *Exit the Colonel*, 202. Kuperman argues that many of these reports were overstated. He notes that Qaddafi made clear that those who surrendered their weapons would not be targeted. Kuperman, "Model Humanitarian Intervention?"

246. "In Swift, Decisive Action, Security Council Imposes Tough Measures on Libyan Regime," United Nations, SC/10187/Rev.1, February 26, 2011, http://www.un.org/News/ Press/docs/2011/sc10187.doc.htm.

247. "Security Council Imposes Sanctions on Libyan Authorities in Bid to Stem Violent Repression," UN News, February 26, 2011, http://www.un.org/apps/news/story.asp?News ID = 37633#.USKiemcrF hJ.

248. "Security Council Approves 'No-Fly Zone' over Libya, Authorizing 'All Necessary Measures' to Protect Civilians, by Vote of 10 in Favour with 5 Abstentions," United Nations, SC/10200, March 17, 2011, http://www.un.org/press/en/2011/sc10200.doc.htm.

249. "Libya: Nicolas Sarkozy Calls for Col Gaddafi to Step Down," *Telegraph*, February 25, 2011, http://www.telegraph.co.uk/news/worldnews/africaandindianocean/libya/8348009/Libya-Nicolas-Sarkozy-calls-for-Col-Gaddafi-to-step-down.html.

250. "The President on Libya: 'The Violence Must Stop; Muammar Gaddafi Has Lost the Legitimacy to Lead and He Must Leave,' " White House, March 3, 2011, https://www.whitehouse.gov/blog/2011/03/03/president-libya-violence-must-stop-muammar-gaddafi-has-lost-legitimacy-lead-and-he-m.

251. "Security Council Approves 'No-Fly Zone' over Libya," United Nations, March 17, 2011.

252. Obama, "Remarks by the President in Address to the Nation on Libya."

253. Christopher S. Chivvis, *Toppling Qaddafi: Libya and the Limits of Liberal Intervention* (New York: Cambridge University Press, 2014), 26.

254. "Timeline—Libya's Uprising Against Muammar Gaddafi," Reuters UK, May 10, 2011, http://uk.reuters.com/article/2011/05/10/uk-libya-timeline-idUKTRE7492Q820110510.

255. Chivvis, *Toppling Qaddafi*, 159.

256. Jason Pack, ed., *The 2011 Libyan Uprisings and the Struggle for the Post-Qadhafi Future* (Basingstoke, UK: Palgrave Macmillan, 2013), xv, 113; Kuperman, "Model Humanitarian Intervention?," 117.

257. Chivvis, *Toppling Qaddafi*, 31.

258. Pack, *2011 Libyan Uprisings*, xvi.

259. "Libyan Army Calls for Benghazi to Surrender as Saif Gaddafi Says Town Will Fall Within 48 Hours," *Telegraph*, March 16, 2011, http://www.telegraph.co.uk/news/worldnews/africaandindianocean/libya/8385250/Libyan-army-calls-for-Benghazi-to-surrender-as-Saif-Gaddafi-says-town-will-fall-within-48-hours.html.

260. Qaddafi also assured that "anyone who throws away his weapon and stays at home peacefully will be pardoned no matter what he did in the past." Cited in Kuperman, "Model Humanitarian Intervention?," 113.

261. Chivvis, *Toppling Qaddafi*, 39.

262. Hastings, "Inside Obama's War Room."

263. Elisabeth Bumiller and David D. Kirkpatrick, "Allies Say Libya Cease-Fire Is Not Enough," *New York Times*, March 18, 2011, http://www.nytimes.com/2011/03/19/world/africa/19libya.html.

264. Chris McGreal, "Benghazi Celebrates No-Fly Zone, but Distrusts Gaddafi's Cease-fire," *Guardian*, March 18, 2011, http://www.theguardian.com/world/2011/mar/18/benghazi-celebrates-no-fly-zone.

265. As of 2018, 123 countries have ratified it. "The States Parties to the Rome Statute," International Criminal Court, accessed April 7, 2018, https://asp.icc-cpi.int/en_menus/asp/states%20parties/Pages/the%20states%20parties%20to%20the%20rome%20statute.aspx.

266. The United States pushed for Taylor's extradition from Nigeria and trial at the ICC in response to his continued meddling in Liberian politics. David Stout, "U.S. Vows to Help

Bring Liberian to Justice," *New York Times*, May 6, 2005, http://query.nytimes.com/gst/abstract.html?res = 950DEFDD1430F935A35756C0A9639C8B63.

267. All three later agreed to NATO's involvement in Libya, but Germany and Poland made clear they did not plan to participate. Chivvis, *Toppling Qaddafi*, 75.

268. The Turkish president accused France of a "hidden agenda." Warrick, "Hillary's War."

269. Pew Research Center, "Public Wary of Military Intervention in Libya: Broad Concern That U.S. Military Is Overcommitted," Pew Research Center: U.S. Politics and Policy, March 14, 2011, http://www.people-press.org/2011/03/14/public-wary-of-military-intervention-in-libya/.

270. Pack, *2011 Libyan Uprisings*, 135–36.

271. This was similar to the initial response of the George H. W. Bush administration to the 1991 Shi'a and Kurdish uprisings. When Saddam's crackdown generated international calls for action, the administration ultimately responded with Operation Provide Comfort, which led to the creation of the northern no-fly zone. On the US response to these events, see Freedman and Karsh, *Gulf Conflict*, 411–27.

272. The Responsibility to Protect norm was formally accepted by all member states at the 2005 UN World Summit. See "Resolution Adopted by the General Assembly on 16 September 2005: 60/1. 2005 World Summit Outcome," United Nations, October 24, 2005, http://www.un.org/en/ga/search/view_doc.asp?symbol = A/RES/60/1.

273. Gates, *Duty*, 511–12.

274. Gates, 511–13.

275. Gates, 512.

276. While stating, "America does not presume to know what is best for everyone," President Obama added, "I do have an unyielding belief that all people yearn for certain things: the ability to speak your mind and have a say in how you are governed; confidence in the rule of law and the equal administration of justice; government that is transparent and doesn't steal from the people; the freedom to live as you choose. Those are not just American ideas, they are human rights, and that is why we will support them everywhere." Todd Holzman, "Obama Seeks 'New Beginning' with Muslim World," National Public Radio, June 4, 2009, accessed November 29, 2015, http://www.npr.org/templates/story/story.php?storyId = 104891406.

277. Biden, in an interview with Jim Lehrer on the PBS News Hour. "Biden: Mubarak Is Not a Dictator, but People Have a Right to Protest," PBS News Hour, January 7, 2011, http://www.pbs.org/newshour/bb/politics-jan-june11-biden_01–27/.

278. Another sign of growing costs was the refusal of Egyptian youth groups to meet with Secretary of State Hillary Rodham Clinton due to Washington's initial support for Mubarak. Hastings, "Inside Obama's War Room."

279. Warrick, "Hillary's War."

280. Becker and Shane, "Hillary Clinton, 'Smart Power' and a Dictator's Fall."

281. Helene Cooper and Steven Lee Meyers, "Obama Takes Hard Line with Libya After Shift by Clinton," *New York Times*, March 18, 2011, http://www.nytimes.com/2011/03/19/world/africa/19policy.html?pagewanted = all.

282. Sanger, *Confront and Conceal*, 345.

283. Hastings, "Inside Obama's War Room."

284. Sanger cites a source who was present at the March 15 meeting. Sanger, *Confront and Conceal*, 346. For a similar account, see Chivvis, *Toppling Qaddafi*, 58–59.

285. Sanger, *Confront and Conceal*, 346.

286. Chorin, *Exit the Colonel*, 225.

287. Becker and Shane, "In Their Own Words: The Libya Tragedy."

288. Hastings, "Inside Obama's War Room."

289. Chorin, *Exit the Colonel*, 245.

290. Igor Kossov, "Libyan Revolt's Quiet Mastermind: Mustafa Abdel Jalil," *Daily Beast*, August 29, 2011, http://www.thedailybeast.com/articles/2011/08/29/libyan-revolt-s-quiet -mastermind-mustafa-abdul-jalil.html.

291. Chorin, *Exit the Colonel*, 158, 269; Pargeter, *Libya*, 189, 211.

292. Pack, *2011 Libyan Uprisings*, 20; St. John, *Libya*, 287; Chivvis, *Toppling Qaddafi*, 32.

293. Clinton, *Hard Choices*, 301–2.

294. Younis defected before the NATO intervention began; Kusa defected ten days later. "Libyan Officials Urged by UK to Follow Koussa and Quit," BBC News, March 31, 2011, http://www.bbc.com/news/uk-12915685.

295. John F. Burns, "Qaddafi and Zuma Meet but Reach No Agreement," *New York Times*, May 30, 2011, http://www.nytimes.com/2011/05/31/world/africa/31libya.html.

296. Younis, for example, was later assassinated by rivals.

297. For more on the role of Islamist groups in the rebellion, see Noman Benotman, Jason Pack, and James Brandon, "Islamists," in Pack, *2011 Libyan Uprisings*, 208–12.

298. Deeb, "Qadhafi's Changed Policy."

299. Pack, *2011 Libyan Uprisings*, 197.

300. Pack, 212–13; Kuperman, "Model Humanitarian Intervention?"

301. James Risen, Mark Mazzetti, and Michael S. Schmidt, "U.S.-Approved Weapons Transfer Ended Up with Libyan Jihadis," *New York Times*, December 5, 2012, http://www.ny times.com/2012/12/06/world/africa/weapons-sent-to-libyan-rebels-with-us-approval-fell -into-islamist-hands.html.

302. Hastings, "Inside Obama's War Room."

303. Chorin, *Exit the Colonel*, 243–44, 254; Dirk Vandewalle, *A History of Modern Libya* (Cambridge: Cambridge University Press, 2012), 205–8.

304. Helene Cooper and John F. Burns, "Plan Would Keep Qaddafi in Libya, but Out of Power," *New York Times*, July 27, 2011, http://www.nytimes.com/2011/07/28/world/africa/ 28libya.html.

305. Dougherty, "Ambassador to Libya May Be Replaced."

306. Gates, *Duty*, 519.

307. Robert Jervis, "Hypotheses on Misperception," *World Politics* 20, no. 3 (1968): 455–56.

308. Kuperman, "Model Humanitarian Intervention?"

309. One account of the Libya case finds mixed support for a bureaucratic politics explanation. Mikael Blomdahl, "Bureaucratic Roles and Positions: Explaining the United States Libya Decision," *Diplomacy & Statecraft*, 27 (2016): 142–61. Another stresses threat perception, but also highlights the role of domestic actors. Kevin Marsh, "'Leading from Behind': Neoclassical Realism and Operation Odyssey Dawn," *Defense & Security Analysis*, 30 (2014): 120–32.

310. Gates, *Duty*, 511.

311. Although Saddam indicated that he was interested in exile, there is little way of knowing whether his interest was sincere or what terms he would have accepted had the Bush administration seriously considered this option. His interest, for example, might have faded had the United States insisted he remain under house arrest in exile and be denied the opportunity to communicate with his supporters in Iraq.

Conclusion

1. G. R. Gleig, *Sale's Brigade in Afghanistan, with an Account of the Seisure and Defence of Jellalabad* (London: J. Murray, 1846), 181. British and Indian troops returned to Afghanistan after the massacre and inflicted reprisals, but a change of government in London led the United Kingdom to withdraw.

2. Jeffery J. Roberts, *The Origins of Conflict in Afghanistan* (Westport, Conn.: Praeger, 2003), 19; Brian Robson, *The Road to Kabul: The Second Afghan War 1878–1881* (London: Arms and Armour, 1986), 299.

3. Mark Landler, "The Afghan War and the Evolution of Obama," *New York Times*, January 1, 2017, https://www.nytimes.com/2017/01/01/world/asia/obama-afghanistan-war.html.

4. The only exceptions are Gerald Ford, who served less than three years in office, and Jimmy Carter. However, Carter, after assiduously adhering to a policy of nonintervention, attempted to facilitate the ouster of Nicaraguan dictator Anastasio Somoza toward the end of his administration. Rebels, however, refused Carter's offer and overthrew Somoza without US assistance. Robert A. Pastor, *Condemned to Repetition: The United States and Nicaragua* (Princeton, N.J.: Princeton University Press, 1987), 160–66; William Michael Schmidli, "'The Most Sophisticated Intervention We Have Seen': The Carter Administration and the Nicaraguan Crisis, 1978–1979," *Diplomacy and Statecraft* 23, no. 1 (March 2012): 82–83.

5. Though this new plan called for using all means short of direct military action, Kennedy also considered launching a second invasion. Aiyaz Husain, "Covert Action and US Cold War Strategy in Cuba, 1961–62," *Cold War History* 5 (2005): 23–53.

6. Robson, *Road to Kabul*, 46.

7. John J. Mearsheimer and Stephen M. Walt, "An Unnecessary War," *Foreign Policy* 134 (February 2003): 50–59.

8. Some Islamist rebels did apparently support the establishment of an elected government. Abdelhakim Belhaj, who headed the LIFG, ran in the July 7, 2012, elections as a candidate of the Al-Watan Party. "Profile: Libyan Rebel Commander Abdel Hakim Belhadj," BBC News, July 4, 2012, http://www.bbc.com/news/world-africa-14786753.

9. Stephen C. Schlesinger and Stephen Kinzer, *Bitter Fruit: The Untold Story of the American Coup in Guatemala* (Garden City, N.Y: Anchor Books, 1984).

10. I also prove this point formally in Appendix 2.

11. See, for example, Bruce W. Jentleson and Christopher A. Whytock, "Who 'Won' Libya? The Force-Diplomacy Debate and Its Implications for Theory and Policy," *International Security* 30 (2005): 47–86.

12. The debate over the effectiveness of coercion has spawned an enormous literature. Art and Cronin conclude that coercive diplomacy succeeds roughly thirty-two percent of the time. Robert J. Art and Patrick M. Cronin, *The United States and Coercive Diplomacy* (Washington, D.C.: United States Institute of Peace Press, 2003), 405. Hufbauer and his coauthors

estimate a similar success rate for sanctions of roughly 34 percent. Gary Clyde Hufbauer et al., *Economic Sanctions Reconsidered* (Washington, D.C.: Peterson Institute for International Economics, 2009), 93. Deterrence, however, is often viewed as more effective. Huth and Russet, for example, conclude in their study that deterrence succeeded in 34 of 58 cases, or roughly 60 percent of the time. Paul Huth and Bruce Russett, "Deterrence Failure and Crisis Escalation," *International Studies Quarterly* 32 (1988): 29–46. Richard Ned Lebow and Janet Gross Stein critique Huth and Russett's coding, and not only identify fewer cases of deterrence, but also fewer successes. See Richard Ned Lebow and Janice Gross Stein, "Deterrence: The Elusive Dependent Variable," *World Politics* 42 (1990): 336–69. See also, Paul Huth and Bruce Russett, "Testing Deterrence Theory: Rigor Makes a Difference," *World Politics* 42 (1990): 466–501; James D. Fearon, "Signaling versus the Balance of Power and Interests: An Empirical Test of a Crisis Bargaining Model," *Journal of Conflict Resolution* 38 (1994): 236–69; and James D. Fearon, "Selection Effects and Deterrence," *International Interactions* 28 (2002): 5–29. Other studies that stress the limits of coercion include Robert A. Pape, "Why Economic Sanctions Do Not Work," *International Security* 22 (1997): 90–136; Clifton Morgan and Valerie L. Schwebach, "Fools Suffer Gladly: The Use of Economic Sanctions in International Crises," *International Studies Quarterly* 41 (1997): 27–50; Daniel Byman and Matthew C. Waxman, *The Dynamics of Coercion: American Foreign Policy and the Limits of Military Might* (Cambridge: Cambridge University Press, 2002); and Alexander L. George, William E. Simons, and David Kent Hall, *The Limits of Coercive Diplomacy*, 2nd ed. (Boulder, Colo.: Westview Press, 1994. For more recent work on coercion, see Kelly M. Greenhill and Peter Krause, *Coercion: The Power to Hurt in International Politics* (New York, NY: Oxford University Press, 2018).

13. For work focused on the success and failure of regime-change operations, see Alexander Downes and Jonathan Monten, "Forced to Be Free: Why Foreign-Imposed Regime Change Rarely Leads to Democratization," *International Security* 37 (2013): 90–131; Goran Peic and Dan Reiter, "Foreign Imposed Regime Change, State Power, and Civil War Onset, 1920–2004," *British Journal of Political Science* 41 (2011): 453–75; and David Edelstein, *Occupational Hazards: Success and Failure in Military Occupation* (Ithaca, N.Y.: Cornell University Press, 2008).

14. See Charles Duelfer, *Hide and Seek: The Search for Truth in Iraq* (New York: PublicAffairs, 2009), 170.

15. Piero Gleijeses, *Shattered Hope: The Guatemalan Revolution and the United States, 1944–1954* (Princeton, N.J.: Princeton University Press, 1991), 363.

16. Alan J. Kuperman, "A Model Humanitarian Intervention? Reassessing NATO's Libya Campaign," *International Security* 38, no. 1 (2013): 109.

17. Makoto Iokibe, "American Policy Towards Japan's 'Unconditional Surrender,'" *Japanese Journal of American Studies* 1 (1981): 32.

18. James D. Fearon, "Rationalist Explanations for War," *International Organization* 49 (1995): 383.

19. Giacomo Chiozza and H. E. Goemans, "International Conflict and the Tenure of Leaders: Is War Still Ex Post Inefficient?," *American Journal of Political Science* 48 (2004): 604–19; Branislav L. Slantchev, *Military Threats: The Costs of Coercion and the Price of Peace* (Cambridge: Cambridge University Press, 2011); Robert Powell, *In the Shadow of Power: States and Strategies in International Politics* (Princeton, N.J.: Princeton University Press, 1999);

Robert Powell, "War as a Commitment Problem," *International Organization* 60 (2006): 169–203; and Andrew Coe, "Costly Peace: A New Rationalist Explanation for War" (working paper, School of International Relations, University of Southern California, Los Angeles, 2011).

Appendix 2

1. I build on Slantchev's model, which shows that a state may have to mobilize more troops to threaten war than it does to prefer going to war. Branislav L. Slantchev, *Military Threats: The Costs of Coercion and the Price of Peace* (Cambridge: Cambridge University Press, 2011), 84–95.

2. In principal, m could reflect the cost of any signal that S_1 uses to demonstrate its intent to fight. These signals could include the formation of a wartime coalition, the passing of a UN Security Council resolution, the application of limited force, or the acquisition of additional weaponry. I focus on troop levels because an incremental increase in troops is directly transferable to an incremental increase in cost, whereas the additional expense of acquiring more allies, weapons, or Security Council votes is not.

3. Slantchev, *Military Threats*, 82.

4. Since S_3 always attacks when S_2 accepts, I do not include it in the game as a strategic player with a decision node.

INDEX

Mexico, 67–68
Mićunović, Veljko, 164–65
Mikoyan, Anastas, 142, 156–58, 162–63, 171–72
militarized interstate disputes (MIDs), 77, 81, 94
military force: costs of using, 40, 49, 61–62; in Hungary 163, in Iraq, 186–88; in Libya, 225; in Poland 150–51
military governments, 82, 95, 237
military of imposing states: capabilities of, 2, 81; measurement of, 82. *See also* mobilization for war, by foreign powers
military of target states: anticipation of enhanced capabilities of, 62–64, 236; in Bolivia, 124, 134; capabilities of, 2, 81, 94, 280n69; in Guatemala, 109–10, 115–19; incapacity of, 38; internal weakening of, 37; in Libya, 203, 221, 311n219; opposition groups' use of, 38; role of, in coups, 57
Milošević, Slobodan, 66
MNR. *See* Movimiento Nacionalista Revolucionario
mobilization for war, by foreign powers, 31–32. *See also* military of imposing states
Molotov, Vyacheslav, 170
Molotov-Ribbentrop Pact, 144
Mongolia, 12
monitoring, of compliance, 4, 34, 63; in Iraq, 180
Monten, Jonathan, 98, 101
Mosaddeq, Mohammad, 16, 37, 59
Movimiento Nacionalista Revolucionario (MNR), 103–4, 124–38
Mubarak, Hosni, 193, 209, 220
Münnich, Ferenc, 165–66, 171
Muslim Brotherhood, 204, 222

Nagy, Imre, 22, 140, 142, 150, 155–74, 237–38, 240, 242, 246
Napoleon III, 67
National Front for the Salvation of Libya, 203
nationalization, 125–26, 128
National Transitional Council (NTC) (Libya), 221–23, 234
nation-building, 230
NATO. *See* North Atlantic Treaty Organization

Nazi Germany: domestic opposition groups as aids to, 36; regime change imposed on, 63–64, 245, 273n33; and settlement with Vichy France, 34
neorealism, 10, 262n12
Netherlands, 17
Nicaragua, 12, 15, 36, 38, 117–18, 316n4
Nicaraguan Contras, 15
9/11 terrorist attacks, 177, 188, 189, 195–96, 210–11, 227, 233–34
The 1956 Hungarian Revolution (Békés, Byrne, and Rainer, eds.), 142
Nixon, Richard, 57, 76
no-fly zones, 180, 182, 186–87, 214, 217–20
nonstate actors, 17
Noriega, Manuel, 28, 32, 40–41, 53, 59, 60, 69, 91
North Atlantic Treaty Organization (NATO): and Afghanistan, 68; and Hungary, 160, 164; and Kosovo, 32, 66, 220; and Libyan regime change, 1, 15, 65, 175–77, 213–14, 218, 220–23, 225; Serbian bombing campaign by, 66
North Korea, 17, 33–34, 42, 76, 192
nuclear weapons, 10, 42, 62. *See also* weapons of mass destruction (WMD)
Nyerere, Julius, 37, 66

Obama, Barack, 1, 22, 178, 213–14, 216, 218–26, 230, 232–33, 238, 244, 247
occupation, of foreign countries, 34
Ochab, Edward, 144–45, 147, 173
one percent doctrine, 190
Operation Desert Fox, 183
Operation Desert Storm, 180
Operation El Dorado Canyon, 207, 209
Organization of African Unity, 208
Organization of American States (OAS), 115–18
Owen, John, 98, 101

Pahlavi, Mohammad Reza Shah, 16, 26, 38, 59
Pahlavi, Reza Shah, 25, 31
Palmerston, Lord, 67
Panama, 12, 28, 32, 40–41, 53, 59, 60, 65, 69, 91, 243
Pan Am flight 103 bombing, 199–201, 203–5, 207–8, 210, 212–14, 242

ACKNOWLEDGMENTS

Many of the ideas in this book arose from seminar discussions and conversations with mentors and colleagues with whom I have been fortunate enough to cross paths. One of those to whom I owe the greatest debt is Arthur Stein. He read my work more times than I can count, helped me stay on track when I might have wandered, and encouraged me to keep swinging for the fences, though it meant I kept coming back to him for more advice. His thought-provoking questions and incisive comments continually forced me to reconsider my argument, grapple with its flaws, and find better answers. Marc Trachtenberg was also an ever-steady source of advice, encouragement, and insight. I am particularly indebted to him for his tutelage in historical research methods. Ken Schultz, Hein Goemans, Dick Rosecrance, Barry O'Neill, Jeff Lewis, and Deborah Larson also offered invaluable feedback and guidance throughout the project.

At the Belfer Center for Science and International Affairs, I was fortunate to find another community of scholars who pushed me to sharpen my argument and consider its practical implications. I am especially grateful to Steve E. Miller and Stephen Walt for their advice and support. Kelly Greenhill also offered helpful feedback and organized a working group that benefited me and many others. Friends and colleagues at the Belfer Center helped me keep my sanity by giving counsel and lending a sympathetic ear. Though there are many more people to thank than I can list here, deserving of special mention are Anoop Sarbahi, Ahsan Butt, Josh Shrifinson, Andrea Strimling Yodsampa, Maalfrid Braut-Hegghammer, Michal Ben-Josef, Aisha Ahmad, Jennifer Dixon, and Peter Krause, each of whom either read or listened to multiple iterations of the argument. Susan Lynch was also a constant source of support. Larry Rubin, David Palkki, Dane Swango, Phil Potter, and, especially, Koji Kagotani lent moral support, read drafts, helped me pin down my ideas, and encouraged me early in the process. I am also grateful to Amy Davis, whose keen eye helped sharpen my prose.

At the University of Vermont, I have again found myself surrounded by supportive colleagues and helpful mentors. Their collegiality has made working here a joy. Greg Gause, Michele Commercio, Caroline Beer, Alec Ewald, Martha Thomas, and Ellen Andersen read drafts and offered advice to help me finalize the book. Garrison Nelson, Bob Taylor, Bob Bartlett, Lisa Holmes, and Abby McGowan have also mentored me. Peter Henne arrived just in time to help me as I finished the manuscript. Maggie Love provided helpful research assistance. I am also grateful to Amy Yuen, Dan Reiter, Michael Poznansky, Michael McKoy, and Charles-Philippe David, who read versions of the argument along the way, and to participants in seminars and workshops at Dartmouth's Dickey Center for International Understanding, the University of Quebec at Montreal, Middlebury College, and the Belfer Center. The anonymous reviewers also offered enormously useful feedback. I gratefully acknowledge the financial support of the Louis Rakin Foundation, the Belfer Center for Science and International Affairs, and the Institute on Global Conflict and Cooperation.

Finally, and most especially, I thank my family. My parents have been my most ardent supporters. My mother painstakingly read every word of my manuscript in all of its iterations, helping me to comb out errors. My husband, Doug Foster, has sustained me throughout this journey. He listened patiently to my ideas, managed our home so I could work, and kept me laughing along the way. After more than fifteen years, I am still in awe of his patience, warmth, and good humor. My children have cheered me on as well. My daughter Amelia was born when I began the project; my son, Evan, was born shortly before I came to UVM; and my daughter Maggie arrived just as I was finishing the book. I can only aspire to bring the joy to their lives that they bring to mine. It is to them that I dedicate this book.